FRANCES MOLONEY

CO-FOUNDER OF THE
MISSIONARY SISTERS OF SAINT COLUMBAN

Frances Moloney

CO-FOUNDER
OF THE
MISSIONARY SISTERS
OF SAINT COLUMBAN

Sheila Lucey ssc

DOMINICAN PUBLICATIONS

First published (1999) by
Dominican Publications
42 Parnell Square
Dublin 1
Ireland

ISBN 1-871552-69-9

Cover design: David Cooke

The cover shows Frances Moloney
as a young widow in Dublin.

The background is an
eighteenth or nineteenth century
Chinese painting on silk
reproduced by kind permission of the
Trustees of the Chester Beatty Library.

Printed in Ireland by ColourBooks Ltd

Contents

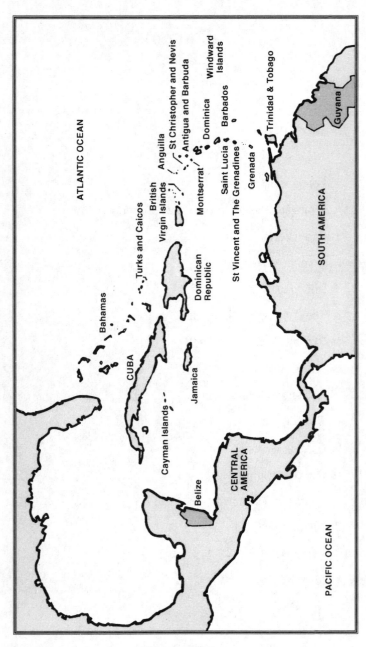

The Caribbean

China, showing the Columba missions

Illustrations

between pages 142 and 143

1. Frances Owen Lewis on her presentation at Court in 1892 (*The Gentlewoman*, by permission of the British Library).
2. Frances's wedding photograph, 1897.
3. A welcoming party for Sir Alfred and Lady Moloney on their arrival in Grenada.
4. A riding party, Grenada. Frances Moloney second from the left; Sir Alfred sixth.
5. Government House, Grenada. Frances Moloney third from the left, second row; Sir Alfred Moloney third from the left, third row.
6. Frances Moloney on her favourite mount. Taken soon after arriving in Grenada.
7. The Corbally girls, Rathbeale Hall, Frances's friends. Mary is in the centre and Angela on the left.
8. Sir Alfred and Lady Moloney in San Girolamo, Fiesole, 1913.
9. Frances Moloney during the Motor Mission in Wales, 1914.
10. Freddie Chevers, Frances's only sister.
11. John Chevers, with his daughters Aylish and Frances.
12. St Brigid's, Cahiracon, cradle of the congregation.
13. Chinese Mission Convent, Cahiracon.
14. The first novices, 1922: Sisters Mary Patrick Moloney (second row L), Mary Joseph McKey, Teresa Brannigan, Emmanuel Dalton, Finbarr Collins, Margaret Mary Scanlan, Brigid McSwiney, Francis Xavier Mapleback, Brendan Walsh.
15. Novices and postulants in 1923, with the Irish Sisters of Charity who trained them: Sister Mary Alphonsus Harnett, Mother Mary Camillus Dalton and Sister Mary Bartholomew McHugh.
16. The first departure for China, 13 September 1926. (L to R): Father John Blowick with Sisters Mary Theophane Fortune, Agnes Griffin, Patrick Moloney, Mother Mary Finbarr Collins,

Sisters Mary Philomena Woods and Lelia Creedon. Six Columban Fathers who travelled with them were (L to R): Fathers Alphonsus Ferguson, Michael Fallon, James Linehan, Charles Donnelly, Joseph Hogan, John Loftus.

17. First Columban Sisters' community, Hanyang. First Row: Mother Mary Theophane with Chinese friends. Second Row: Sisters Mary Lelia, Agnes, Patrick and Philomena.

18. The Hanyang community in 1930, with Bishop Edward Galvin.

19. Sisters visiting flood victims, Hanyang, 1931.

20. Sister Mary Patrick ministering to one of the flood victims.

21. Mother Mary Patrick before leaving on her first visitation as Superior General (1937).

22. Mother Mary Patrick with Mrs Seán T. O'Kelly (wife of the President) who opened the Sisters' Christmas Sale on 29 November, 1945. (Photo: *Irish Press*)

23. Aylish Fane-Saunders, her husband Bernard, sons Kevin and Terence, and nephew Seán Smith, visiting 'Aunt Frances' in Cahiracon.

24. Mother Mary Patrick, Sister Mary Brendan and Sister Joan Sawyer with Father Michael McHugh, the chaplain.

25. Mother Mary Patrick in 1954. (Photo: Adele Godetz)

26. Mother Mary Patrick at the General Chapter of 1958.

27. St Columban's Convent, Magheramore, Wicklow.

Acknowledgements

First of all, I wish to thank Sister Marie Galvin who while she was Superior General asked me to write the life of Mother Mary Patrick, giving me every encouragement and support. Her successor, Sister Mary Nolan, and her council also facilitated the project in every possible way, giving me time and space to pursue the necessary research, and to write.

A book like this would have been practically impossible to write if I had not been able to avail of some highly significant sources. Therefore, I would like to thank those who were responsible for preserving the records of Mother Mary Patrick's life and of the role she played in helping to found the Missionary Sisters of St Columban. Over the years people had suggested that she put her life story in writing. Finally she agreed, on the urging of Sister Mary Vianney Shackleton, her successor as Superior General: 'Now in my eighty-first year, before it is too late, it seems right to record some experiences which may prove useful later on, to those who come after.' These valuable memoirs, written in simple school notebooks, cover her life from childhood up to the years immediately preceding the foundation of the congregation.

The account of the foundation had been recorded many years earlier: while recuperating in hospital in 1925, Sister Mary Patrick, still a novice, began to write about the beginnings of the 'Chinese Mission Sisters', as they were popularly known at the time. In doing so she was responding to a request by Mother Mary Camillus Dalton of the Irish Sisters of Charity, Superior and Novice Mistress of the first Sisters. I would like to pay tribute to Mother Camillus for her foresight and to Father John Blowick who co-operated whole-heartedly, offering to fill in any gaps in the story. This account of the beginnings of the congregation was my second most important source.

I would also like to thank the many people who shared with me their recollections of Mother Mary Patrick: first of all, members of the Columban congregation, and secondly her few surviving friends and relatives among whom I would like to mention with particular gratitude her only remaining niece, Mrs Aylish Fane-Saunders, and her grandnephew Max Chevers, who not only supported the project all through, but supplied valuable information about the Owen Lewis and Chevers families. I also wish to thank Patrick J.T. Stephenson for sharing family recollections relating to his step-grandmother Mother Mary Patrick.

Various archivists, librarians and others extended help courteously as the need arose. Those on whom I made most demands were Sister Rita Dooney, archivist of the Columban Sisters and Father Patrick Crowley, archivist of the Columban Fathers. Others should also be mentioned: Sister Marie Bernadette (archivist of the Religious Sisters of Charity); David Sheehy (Dublin diocesan archivist); Father Fergus O'Donoghue SJ (Irish Province archivist); Father Thomas McCoog SJ (English Province archivist); Father William Halliden (at the time Columban Procurator, Rome) and his contacts: Monsignor Charlie Burns (archivist of the Archivio Segreto Vaticano, Rome) and Father Charles O'Neill SJ (Institutum Historicum Societatis Iesu, Rome); Father Bernard T. Smyth (Society of St Columban); Father Leo Clarke (Society of St Columban); Sister Redempta Twomey SSC; Sister Mary Coke RSCJ (archivist, the Society of the Sacred Heart, English Province) and Sister Marie Thérèse Carre RSCJ (archivist of the French Province); Sister Francis McAndrew SJC (Sisters of St Joseph of Cluny, Dublin) and Sister Columba Carthy SJC (Sisters of St Joseph of Cluny, West Indies); Sister Mary Anastasia Taggart MMM (archivist, Medical Missionaries of Mary); Sister Carmel Kidd LCM (Province archivist, Little Company of Mary); Sister Mary Michael LCM and Sister Margaret LCM (Fiesole); Sister Chantal de Seyssel (archivist, Helpers of the Holy Souls, Paris); Sister Margaret Stack SMG (Poor Servants of the Mother of God, London); Father Thomas Davitt CM (Vincentian archivist); Sister Una Agnew SSL and Sister Mary de Lourdes SSL; Theo McMahon (Clogher Historical Society); Maureen O'Kelly (Gurtrae, Portumna); Lord Petre (Ingatestone Hall, Essex); Susanne Groom (assistant to the Curator, Hampton Court Palace); T.A. Heathcote (Curator, The Royal Military Academy, Sandhurst); Dr Clare Pollard (Curator of the East Asian Collection, Chester Beatty Library); John Haugh.

Among the librarians who facilitated my research were those in the National Library of Ireland; Trinity College Library; the Gilbert Library; the Central Catholic Library, Dublin; the Central Library, Ilac Centre; Registry of Deeds, King's Inns; the British Library; Colindale Newspaper Library; the Public Record Office, London; Rhodes House Library, Oxford; Kew Gardens Library; the Imperial War Museum Library; the Commonwealth Institute Library.

I am also grateful to those who helped to provide photographs and illustrations, and to Sister Maureen Grant SSC for sharing her expertise in this regard. Moreover, I wish to thank Sister Mary Nolan SSC, Congregational Leader, for reading the manuscript and writing the Foreword, and Sister Ita Hannaway SSC, who also read the manuscript.

There is one person in particular to whom I owe a deep and abiding debt of gratitude: Sister Angela Bolster RSM, who kindly read each chapter as it was written, making invaluable comments and suggestions. Above all, she helped by her constant affirmation and encouragement.

For much-appreciated and time-consuming technical help I am indebted to Sister Ursula Scullane SSC. Sister Angela Suh SSC and Sister Maria Choi SSC helped with computer difficulties. I am also grateful to Sister Isabelle Smyth MMM for putting me in touch with Father Michael Browne SPS who solved a problem of incompatible disks.

I would also like to acknowledge my gratitude to Father Austin Flannery OP, and Father Bernard Treacy OP, Dominican Publications, for undertaking the publication of this book.

I also wish to thank all those whose interest and encouragement helped me along the way: Columban and other friends, and my family – especially Betty and Cyril Warde, my sister and brother-in-law, and Conn and Darina Lucey, my brother and sister-in-law.

Finally, this book is dedicated to the memory of Mother Mary Patrick, as a tribute to her and to all those involved with her in founding the congregation of the Missionary Sisters of St Columban. I present it with hope and gratitude to all my Columban Sisters past and present who have been inspired and who continue to be inspired by the spirit and faith of this heroic woman.

Foreword

Over the years those of us who never met Mother Mary Patrick have caught glimpses of her through the memories, written and unwritten, of those who travelled the missionary journey with her. Now in 1999, as we celebrate the seventy-fifth anniversary of the foundation of the Missionary Sisters of St Columban, we are able to get in touch with the whole story of her life. It is a story that spans the passing of the British colonial era, touches on the place of the Anglo-Irish in history, and traces the life of a family that was immersed in that changing world. The members of the Owen Lewis family were privileged in many ways, and yet were sensitive and alert to human suffering. The story of the family is one of courage, conviction and single-mindedness. These gifts were nurtured in Frances Owen Lewis while at home, and later through her experiences as the wife of Sir Alfred Moloney. Frances's single-mindedness eventually led to her leaving all, in order to help bring about the foundation of a congregation whose members would be servants of the Gospel among the people of China and beyond.

In the earlier part of this work, we are introduced to the people and places that set the tone for Frances's approach to life. Not many of us today can resonate with the lifestyle of the 'ascendancy' class of the late 1800s. Trips to France, to Italy, and first-class schooling were not the norm for the young women of Ireland at that time. The family chaplain also provided a 'Catholic' experience that was foreign to the ordinary Catholic families of the time. But, whatever the experience, Frances went beyond it to reach deep personal relationships with people and with God. These would be her strength in the many trials that lay ahead of her.

Though she had numerous friends, one notices a certain aloneness along much of Frances's journey. Setting off to the Caribbean as the young wife of Sir Alfred Moloney; dealing with illnesses; accompanying her husband as a colonial authority in changing

times; his failing health and his death; all these and more, led her
to be a woman of great human resilience and deep faith. These gifts
served her well when she was called to endure enormous setbacks
on her later journey.

When Frances became a widow at the age of forty, the love of
God seemed to impel her to reach out to the poor and the suffering
of Europe. There was to be no rest. And then came the 'dream' of
China: could it become a reality that a group of women would be
involved in the 'Maynooth Mission to China'? With other like-
minded women, with Father Blowick and other Columban Fathers,
with spiritual directors, and with much prayer, Frances searched
for the way forward. And true to form she was willing to give it no
less than her all. In 'light' and 'darkness' she searched for the way.
She watched in wonder or in pain as her companions in the search
came to crossroads and made other choices. Frances was no
stranger to adversity, yet she suffered through the many setbacks.
Eventually it became clear that the way forward was to be through
the founding of a new religious congregation whose specific
mission would be to the people of China. With this conviction came
new energy to collaborate in the project of founding the 'Missionary Sisters of St Columban'.

Frances Moloney's entrance into religious life led her to a whole
new period of suffering, mingled with joy. With her younger
companions she endured the rigours of life in the rural Ireland of
the 1920s. The constraints of the religious lifestyle were many; yet
she seemed to relate well with the Irish Sisters of Charity who were
entrusted with the formation of our fledgling congregation. She fell
into ill-health, and so her time of first profession was delayed.
However, it would seem that her personal freedom in discerning
the way forward left her in no doubt about her call.

Sister Mary Patrick, the new name given to Frances Moloney,
was eventually to arrive in China, the country that had been
attracting her for many years. She loved the Chinese people and
was particularly attentive to the needs of the sick. Her ten short
years among them came to an abrupt end when she was recalled to
Ireland to take up the office of Superior General of the congrega-

tion. During her term in office, she paved the way towards making the congregation one of pontifical right.

Mother Mary Patrick is an example to us of docility in the hands of God. She seemed to have had a perception that whatever happened was an expression of God's choicest plan. Being faithful in the flow of events, however, was not an easy option, as she seemed to be tossed about in troubles and disappointments. She carried many human frailties, and part of her greatness lay in being able to live with them. We give God thanks that, in the words of Father Blowick, she was 'the lady who began the work'.

Mary Nolan SSC
Congregational Leader

An Anglo-Irish Background

Frances Owen Lewis – subsequently Lady Moloney and later again Mother Mary Patrick of the Columban Sisters – was born on 17 April 1873 at 19 Seymour Street, London, the residence of her parents Henry Owen Lewis and Frances Elsegood. Notwithstanding her birth in London and the fact that she did not visit Ireland until 1885, she insisted on an Irish rather than an English ancestry. In her old age, when she wrote her memoirs, she looked back on her first visit to Ireland, saying: 'We felt we were going to our real home and country at last.' [1]

The Lewis family owned extensive property – upwards of 3,000 acres – in Co. Monaghan. According to family tradition the first Lewis to settle in Ireland around the middle of the seventeenth century was of Welsh origin. Consequently, Henry Owen Lewis liked to claim as ancestor Father David Lewis who was martyred for the Catholic faith at Usk in Monmouthshire on 27 August 1679. [2] A document in the Genealogical Office in Dublin would seem to validate the family claim to a Welsh origin: it confirms the granting of arms, on 10 June 1857, to Henry Owen Lewis's father, Lt Col Arthur Gambell Lewis of Seatown, Co. Dublin and Clanamully, Co. Monaghan. Significantly, the motto under the coat of arms is in Old Welsh: *Bidd llu hebb llydd,* of which the most favoured translation is 'Let many [literally, a host] be without hindrance.'

In 1820 Arthur Gambell Lewis, who was estate agent to Lord Rossmore of Rossmore Park, Co. Monaghan, married Hester Westenra, a cousin of his employer. By her he had three daughters and a son, Maurice Peppard Warren Lewis. After Hester died in 1837 he married Henrietta, widow of the Honourable Richard Westenra, second son of Lord Rossmore. Henrietta was the only daughter and heiress of Henry Owen Scott of Scotstown, Co. Monaghan. The only issue of this marriage was Henry Owen Lewis, whose three half-sisters and half-brother, Maurice Peppard

Warren Lewis, have no further relevance to this study. What is relevant, however, is that Arthur Gambell Lewis, who would have acquired a measure of wealth during his years as agent on the Rossmore estate, was also regarded by Lord Rossmore as a friend, until he married his daughter-in-law.

When no longer agent to Lord Rossmore, Arthur Gambell Lewis managed to retain his extensive land-holdings and was affluent enough to purchase a house at 10 Fitzwilliam Square West, where the two half-brothers, Maurice Peppard Warren Lewis and Henry Owen Lewis, resided during their years at Trinity College. Both were listed in the College's *Alumni Dublinenses* as Senior Commoners, which indicated that their parents paid more than average fees and that they were thus eligible for certain privileges. In 1858, the year in which Henry Owen Lewis enrolled in Trinity College, he became a Governor of the Royal Hospital for Incurables in Donnybrook, Dublin. He remained a Life Governor from the date of his enrollment until his death in 1913. He took his responsibility seriously and in later years came over regularly from London to attend meetings of the Board.

On 6 August 1866, he married Frances Sophia Elsegood in the Parish Church, Monkstown, Co. Dublin, 'according to the Rites and Ceremonies of the United Church of England and Ireland.'[3] The officiating clergyman was William Lake Onslow, Sandringham Rectory. Henry's residence at the time of the marriage was listed on the marriage certificate as Monkstown, while Frances's address was 6 Baker Street, London. Monkstown Parish Church, with its dramatic skyline and Moorish Gothic echoes, is one of the most attractive churches in South Co. Dublin. The poet John Betjeman wrote of 'the blank that would be created if Monkstown Church were to disappear / A blank in the environment/ A blank in the hearts of individuals'.[4] The architecture of the roof, reminiscent of some gigantic chessmen, was an apt symbol of the Owen Lewis couple's future life together, when knights and bishops would enter their story, and circumstances would cause them to make tactical moves from place to place.

As one of the weddings of the season it merited an entry in the fashionable English journal *The Gentleman's Magazine,* while *The Irish Times* of 10 August 1866 in its column 'Fashionable Intelligence' listed among the latest arrivals at the Breslin Hotel, Bray, 'Mr & Mrs Lewis and Suite'. Breslin's Royal Marine Hotel was one of the luxury hotels built in Bray after William Dargan extended the railway there. It would seem that after their honeymoon Henry Owen Lewis and his wife travelled northwards to Co. Monaghan. By this time both Arthur Gambell Lewis and his wife Henrietta had died, as had also two of Henry's half-sisters and his half-brother, Maurice. Consequently he was the sole heir to extensive property. John Bateman's, *The Great Landowners of Gt. Britain and Ireland* lists Henry Owen Lewis as holding 3,773 acres, bringing him an annual income of £2,863.[5] In *The Landowners of Ireland,* U.H. Hussey de Burgh breaks down the acreage as follows: 617 in Co. Cork, 590 acres in Co. Dublin; 522 in Co. Longford; 173 in Co. Meath and 2,488 in Co. Monaghan.[6]

Enniskeen is given as the only family address in Co. Monaghan for these and subsequent years. But the Owen Lewises also had two houses in Dublin: 43 Fitzwilliam Square and Trimleston House, Merrion.[7] Sometime after 1870 they gave up Trimleston House and, like many of the Irish landed class, moved to England where they took up residence at 19 Seymour Street, London. (In 1890 they added 30 Oriental Place, Brighton, former home of Mrs Owen Lewis's parents, to their other addresses.) It was in Trimleston House that the first tragedy of their marriage occurred: their first child, Henry Owen, called after his father, died there on 17 September 1867, just six days old.

Meanwhile, in 1868 Henry Owen Lewis became a Catholic. He was received into the Catholic Church by the famous Father P. Gallwey SJ, an Irishman and at the time Rector of the Jesuit community at Farm Street in London. According to those who knew him, he had an extraordinary gift for drawing people to the Catholic Church. Shortly after her husband's reception into the Catholic faith, Frances Owen Lewis was herself received into the Catholic Church by Cardinal Cullen of Dublin. There is no direct reference to the event in Cardinal Cullen's papers in the Dublin

Diocesan archives. However, in Henry Owen Lewis's letters to the Cardinal, among the Cullen papers, we find him thanking Cardinal Cullen for the 'many marks of kindness' he had received from him (26 June 1871); he invariably conveyed Mrs Owen Lewis's greetings and in a letter of 30 January 1874 he invited the Cardinal, on his wife's behalf, to stay at their home on his next visit to London. It would seem that Mrs Owen Lewis as well as her husband owed some personal debt of gratitude to the Cardinal.

There was also a political angle. Henry Owen Lewis's first letter to Cardinal Cullen, written from 19 Seymour Street London on 26 June 1871, had to do with Irish politics:

> I see by a telegram in the *Times* of this morning that Colonel Leslie, MP for County Monaghan died yesterday. If possible I should wish to get in, in his place, and if your Eminence would kindly write to the Bishop of Clogher on my behalf, asking him to use his influence for me, I think I should have a good chance. If you will do so I shall feel more than ever indebted to your Eminence from whom I have already received so many marks of kindness. If returned, I should give an independent support to the Government, and try to obtain a religious system of Education for Ireland, which I believe to be the real panacea for its wants.[8]

Evidently Cardinal Cullen did write to the Bishop of Clogher, James Donnelly, because early in July Henry Owen Lewis announced that he was contesting the seat as a Liberal. His platform included the secret ballot, denominational education, and the defence of the Pope's temporal interest. Bishop Donnelly would have supported Owen Lewis if he believed that he had a good chance. However, when Isaac Butt entered the contest any Catholic and Liberal support that Owen Lewis had won moved over to Butt, whose platform was Home Rule and Tenant Rights.[9] Owen Lewis withdrew. Eventually it was the orthodox Conservative, John Leslie, son of the deceased MP, who got the seat. However, Butt had shown his strength. Emmet Larkin, in *The Roman Catholic Church and the Home Rule Movement in Ireland,* says, 'What the

Monaghan election clearly proved was that the Catholic electors in that county, at least, preferred Home Rule to the Gladstonian alliance as represented by Cullen's protégé, H. Owen Lewis.'[10]

Despite his failure to secure a seat for Co. Monaghan in 1871, Henry Owen Lewis retained his interest in Irish politics and in 1874 was elected MP for Co.Carlow. This was largely due to the support of Father James Maher, uncle and godfather of Cardinal Cullen, at the time parish priest of Carlow-Graigue. A student and admirer of Bishop James W. Doyle of Kildare and Leighlin (the legendary JKL), like him he played a prominent part in the politics of the day, especially when they impinged on religion or the rights of the poor. Among his people he was revered as a saint.

Peadar Mac Suibhne, in *Paul Cullen and his Contemporaries*, says that Father Maher's last political triumph was that he helped to have Henry Owen Lewis, Cardinal Cullen's protégé, elected as MP for Carlow. It was significant that, in spite of all his episcopal patronage, in order to secure election Owen Lewis had to endorse the cause of Home Rule, a topic which was anathema to the majority of the Bishops. Yet Father Maher, who would have adhered to Cardinal Cullen's policies, gave him his whole-hearted support. He was close to death at the time and had received the Last Sacraments.

> He rallied a little however and when towards the end of the following January Owen Lewis came to contest the borough Father Maher could not refuse his services and feeble though he was he drove about with the candidate and was received with the greatest enthusiasm. Father Maher's biographer, Cardinal Moran, adds significantly that the venerable old priest was greatly consoled by the reflection that though in his long career he had occasionally been deceived by political adventurers, God had sent to Carlow before he died a member of such honour and integrity as Owen Lewis.[11]

The general election of 1874, in which Henry Owen Lewis became a Member of Parliament for Carlow, was the first to be determined by secret voting in accordance with the Ballot Act of

1872. One of the issues high on the agenda of the newly elected government was Home Rule: Isaac Butt's Home Rule movement had captured more than half of the Irish seats. However, Butt was soon to be supplanted as leader of the Home Rule party by the newly elected Charles Stewart Parnell. Furthermore, Michael Davitt had arrived on the Irish political scene and he too cast his lot with Parnell. He had been released from prison in England having served seven of the fifteen years of penal servitude imposed on him for his Fenian activities. Davitt and Parnell, despite their different backgrounds, recognised and valued each other's leadership qualities, which were soon to be put to the test. An economic crisis hit the rural population of Ireland in the winter of 1878-79. Severe weather, crop failures and falling prices meant that many small farmers were facing disaster. Davitt threw in his lot with the tenant farmers and founded the Irish National Land League to fight their cause. He succeeded in persuading Parnell to become its president.

In 1880, in the midst of the Land War agitation (1879-82), another general election took place which brought Gladstone back to power. This time Henry Owen Lewis did not secure a seat. A contributory cause may have been that his patron, Cardinal Cullen, died in 1878. More significant was the power now held by the Land League, which was unlikely to support a landlord candidate. By this time the movement had become so powerful that it was almost an alternative government, with its own courts and its own sanctions. The government retaliated by enforcing special coercive powers aimed at putting an end to agrarian unrest. Many of the Home Rule parliamentarians took exception to the indiscriminate way these powers were exercised, and there were several protests. One of Henry Owen Lewis's last political acts as MP for Carlow was to register his objection.

No more weighty protest was uttered than that of Mr H. Owen Lewis, a deputy-lieutenant for the County Monaghan, Home Rule member for Carlow Borough. He was forced, of course, out of Irish politics by the Davitt-Parnell Jacobinism. Now he gave the weight of his position and high character to an emphatic declaration that the coercion system in Ireland was contrary to the Constitution, and productive of disorder rather then peace. "You are making of Ireland," said Mr Owen Lewis, "another France before the Revolution. Kilmainham Jail is your bastille. Lord-Lieutenant's warrants are your *lettres de cachet*." [12]

During his years in Parliament Henry Owen Lewis was only too well aware of the situation building up in Ireland. He could see Parnell and Davitt consolidating their power, and he realised that the future was bleak for the landed gentry of Ireland. He witnessed the anger of the people when the old patriot, John Mitchell, who won a seat in Tipperary unopposed, was disqualified 'as a felon' from sitting in Parliament. On that occasion tempers flared high and within the space of two weeks Disraeli's government introduced a Coercion Renewal Bill for Ireland. This at a time when the British Government had recognised the Republic in France.

Even before he entered Parliament, Henry Owen Lewis as an Irish Catholic could see how his fellow-countrymen were being treated unfairly, and he was hopeful that as a member of Parliament he might help to alleviate some of their wrongs. However, within months of his election he was stung into writing impulsively to Gladstone, countering the charge of being ultramontanist in his views of the Catholic Church and the papacy.

Sir,

As the only Irishman in the House of Commons, who born and bred a Protestant has embraced the Catholic religion, I trust you will excuse my asking you to answer the following question. Do you wish it to go forth to the people of Ireland – by whom you were kept in office for years, with power and influence such as no British minister has for a generation enjoyed – as your deliberate opinion that no one can join their Church without forfeiting his moral and mental freedom, and placing his civil loyalty and duty at the mercy of another?

I am, Sir,

Your obedient Servant,

H. Owen Lewis, M.P. Carlow[13]

His faith evidently meant much to him, because two years later, in July 1876, he again entered into correspondence with Gladstone about a French apostate priest, Père Hyacinthe Loyson, who was giving a course of lectures in London. Not only did Gladstone attend; he also presided at the first of these lectures. The correspondence, which survives among Gladstone's papers, was submitted by Owen Lewis to *The Guardian* and published in the issue of 26 July 1876.[14] Père Loyson had made a strong case against the practice of clerical celibacy, which he maintained had been systematically violated down the centuries, and he cited many instances of corruption in the Catholic Church. 'The opinion of M. Loyson matters little to Catholics,' Owen Lewis wrote to Gladstone, 'for we know that some are apt to measure the morality of others by their own fidelity to their vows; but it becomes a different matter when an illustrious English statesman appears to endorse it even by his silence.'[15]

As already noted, Henry Owen Lewis was one of several Irish landlords who lost their seats in 1880 to Land League candidates. However, he always retained his deep interest in Irish affairs and continued to lobby on behalf of Irish Catholics through his contacts in political and clerical life and through his writing.

It was into this setting that his young daughter, Frances, was born in 1873, the year the Home Rule League was founded. For the first impressionable years of her life she breathed in Irish politics and Irish affairs. No wonder she could say about her first visit to Ireland in 1885, that she and her sister Freddie felt that they 'were going to our real home and country at last'.[16] Undoubtedly there were many who regarded them more Anglo-Irish than Irish. Some years later Stephen Gwynn spoke for them and many of their class when he wrote, 'I was brought up to think myself Irish without question or qualification, but the new nationalism prefers to describe me and the like of me as Anglo-Irish.'[17]

ONE

Early Years

Even though Frances Owen Lewis liked to think of herself as Irish and not Anglo-Irish, it is a fact that she was born in London at 19 Seymour Street, off Portman Square, on 17 April 1873. As the first daughter after four sons, the eldest of whom had died soon after birth, she was particularly welcome. She had three brothers to fuss over her and protect her: Arthur, five years older, Frank three years of age and Cyril two.

Evidently it was a difficult birth, which almost cost the child's mother her life. Eighty-one years later Frances remembered hearing that there was such concern for her mother that after she was born she herself was tossed onto the lap of the family's German nursemaid, Becker.[1] The much-loved Becker was to stay with the family well into her old age.

On 19 April 1873, two days after her birth, Frances was baptised and given the names of Frances Isabel Sophia Mary. The baptism took place in the former Spanish Place church, which has since been rebuilt. Eight years beforehand someone who was to be an admired friend in her later life was baptised in the same font. This was Raphael Cardinal Merry del Val, born a stone's throw away from the Owen Lewis family home.

Soon after her birth Frances became critically ill. In later life she wondered if this was due to the state of her mother's health at the time. Her father carried her in his arms to Paris to lay her on the tomb of Père Olivaint, one of the martyrs of the Commune of 1871.[2] It was a daring and trusting gesture: to carry a sick infant-in-arms by train from London to Dover, then onto the ferry to Calais, and again by train to Paris. This father's faith was rewarded: the child recovered. Frances's parents attributed her recovery to the intercession of Père Olivaint and in later life her father enjoined on her that she visit his shrine whenever she should pass through Paris. This she did, often at great personal cost to herself. It became more difficult when an anticlerical French government closed the churches of religious orders. However, 'a Louis-d'or to the guardian acted as an open sesame.'[3]

But that is looking ahead. Back in 1873, once the new baby had recovered her health, life proceeded happily for the Owen Lewis family. In later years Frances recalled her old home with affection. One thing in particular remained in her memory: the almost life-size statue of the Sacred Heart on the hall landing, surrounded by potted plants and at its feet a red lamp always lighting. Visitors on their way upstairs to the drawing room could not but notice it and one of them attributed her conversion to Catholicism to its devotional appeal. This image of the Sacred Heart imprinted itself on Frances's childhood memory and became one of her earliest and most enduring devotions, the beginnings of a spirituality which subsequently characterised her entire life. She, who was so much influenced by her father, would have seen him pray before this statue which he had brought home after a visit to Paris. He would have told her about his pilgrimage to Paray-le-Monial in the summer of 1874. It was there, in the late seventeenth century, that St Margaret Mary had received her visions of the Sacred Heart of Jesus. Henry Owen Lewis was so deeply impressed by this visit that the following October, writing from Paris to his friend Cardinal Cullen of Dublin, he said, 'It is a great pity there is not an Irish pilgrimage organised there. I am sure it would succeed and the expense would not be very great.'[4]

In that same letter of 6 October 1874, Henry Owen Lewis asked Cardinal Cullen to pray for Frances. She would have been a year and a half at the time. 'Our little girl has been delicate for some time, I am sorry to say. I trust that Your Eminence will kindly remember her at the altar.'[5] He had already, some months earlier, asked Cardinal Cullen to get permission for him from the Holy Father to have a private chapel in the family home at 19 Seymour Street.

The clergy have advised me to ask you to obtain direct from the Holy Father a general permission to have a Chapel & Mass in it wherever I may be. If you can obtain this for us, it will be much easier, as The Archbishop of Westminster cannot then raise any objections, but if I were to go direct to him he might refuse permission ... We are desirous of having a domestic Chapel for our children, and also on account of the constant sickness we have had all the time we were in Seymour St. which having Mass in the house may prevent a recurrence of.[6]

Henry Owen Lewis repeated his request the following October, adding that the family sometimes had priests staying with them who could celebrate Mass daily. Whether or not Cardinal Cullen pursued his friend's request, it is clear that there was no private chapel at 19 Seymour Street while Frances was a child.

On 10 April 1877, after being the baby of the family for four years, Frances acquired a little sister. In later life she remembered how Mrs Grant, the children's nurse, tried to make her jealous of the baby and said something to the effect that it might be a good idea to drown her in the baptismal font. Not understanding what was implied, Frances nodded her assent.

This earned for me the reputation of a green-eyed monster. To make matters worse, in an honest endeavour to amuse the little one, I put a basket on my head to make her laugh. The poor child cried instead, and I was severely punished. My sister was dear to me from the beginning, and throughout her life remained my closest friend.[7]

A minor crisis occurred over the baptism of the new baby. King George V of Hanover,[8] a friend of the child's mother and of her maternal grandmother, wired his congratulations and offered to act as godfather, *in absentia*. Cardinal Manning had to be consulted, because the King was not a Catholic. The Cardinal advised the parents to accept the honour, but also to request a priest to be present in the same capacity. They invited Canon McKenna, their parish priest in Monaghan, who was happy to accede to the request. He brought gifts from Ireland for his godchild, including a beautiful set of Beleek china.

George V of Hanover sent a gift of a large gold goblet and asked that the child be called after his daughter, Princess Friederike. Henry Owen Lewis and his wife complied with his wish and the new baby was christened Frederica, the English equivalent of the German name, although among her family and friends she was always known as Freddie. Her second name, Sophia, had also been one of Frances's baptismal names, the reason being that their grandmother, Mrs Owen Lewis's mother, claimed descent from a Hapsburg Princess Sophia (1777-1845).

If all had gone according to plan, it should have been Frances, not Freddie who became the Hanoverian George V's godchild. Among Cardinal Cullen's papers are eight letters written by Henry Owen Lewis to the Cardinal between 1871 and 1874, two of which have already been referred to. On the whole they concern political matters but a letter of 22 January 1873 written three months before Frances's birth asks Cardinal Cullen's advice about having George V of Hanover as a sponsor for the expected baby:

> Mrs Owen Lewis is expecting to be confined in April and we should feel greatly obliged if your Eminence would tell us whether the King of Hanover, in the event of His Majesty proposing it, could be a sponsor, or not. His Majesty has been very kind to us, and we would like if possible to have him as godfather.[9]

A follow-up letter from Henry Owen Lewis suggests that perhaps the King of Hanover could be godfather by proxy: he, the child's father, could represent him at the font. However, for whatever reason, George V of Hanover did not become godfather to Frances, but to Freddie four years later. And, from the time of Freddie's birth until he himself died in 1878, George V often visited the Owen Lewis home, accompanied by his daughter Friederike.

On 24 April 1880, three years after Freddie's birth, her namesake Princess Friederike married Baron von Pawel-Rammingen of Hanover in the private chapel of Windsor Castle. They were given a suite of rooms in Hampton Court Palace, which had ceased to be the residence of the reigning sovereign in the time of George III.

During his reign, the whole building, except the state rooms, was gradually divided into suites of apartments, allotted by the 'grace and favour' of the reigning monarch to certain individuals, usually as a reward for some service done. It was only in relatively recent times that this practice was discontinued.

Shortly after the Princess and her husband moved into their apartment in Hampton Court Palace, the Owen Lewis family came to live nearby. Princess Friederike who was expecting her first child was glad to have the comfort and support of Mrs Owen Lewis. She and her husband visited the Owen Lewis family occasionally and liked to listen to the children reciting for them in French.

Hampton Court Palace was a gloomy old place in those days, and rumours abounded that it was haunted by the ghosts of the wives of Henry VIII. The Princess and her husband had their own eerie experience. In the process of knocking down an inner wall to provide a nursery for the expected baby, they made a gruesome discovery: the wall concealed a small room in which was found the skeleton of a woman seated at a spinning-wheel. The remains were said to be those of Lady Jane Grey's nurse, who had been walled up alive for trying to help her mistress escape. Now, more than three hundred years later, she was at last given Christian burial. The spinning-wheel went to a museum.

Princess Friederike's baby was eventually born at Hampton Court Palace on 7 March 1881, and given the name Victoria. But all was not well. Every night the nurse's sleep was disturbed by the appearance of an old lady dressed in the costume of bygone days. The child's mother asked the Owen Lewises if anything could be done to bring peace to the restless spirit. Mr Owen Lewis suggested bringing a priest from London to bless the apartment, but the child's parents declined, afraid that if the matter were known in Court circles they might lose their privilege of a 'grace and favour' apartment. Things continued as they were, and the baby died after three weeks. The distraught parents left Hampton Court Palace and went to live in Biarritz. They had no further children. Occasionally they returned to England for short visits. Frances remembered Baron von Pawel-Rammingen coming to visit her sister Freddie, whom he addressed as 'le petit George', because of her illustrious godfather.

The Owen Lewis family continued to live in the vicinity of Hampton Court Palace for some months after the departure of the von Pawel-Rammingens. Also living in the same neighbourhood were their friends the Balfe family from Co. Roscommon, who later would live near them in Fitzwilliam Square, Dublin. They were Catholics, as were some of the widows of high-ranking British Army officers, who had suites in Hampton Court Palace.

During their stay at Hampton Court Freddie nearly died of croup. In later years Frances remembered the hushed house, the visit of a specialist from London who held out little hope, and her father's grief: 'The tears were running down his face, but his holy prayers saved the precious child.'[10] Freddie remained delicate as a child and her older sister did all she could to help her, not always successfully.

> Once she was toddling along the garden-path with uncertain balance. Rushing to her assistance, just as I reached her, she fell, scratching her poor little face. Screams brought our nurse who accused me of pushing my sister down, and I was severely punished. On another occasion I came upon her trying to open the garden door. Clumsily placing my hand over hers I tried to open it for her. She cried aloud and I was carried off and beaten. The injustice and humiliation of this undeserved chastisement affected me for days. Too young to understand the value of suffering and sacrifice these misunderstandings caused a withdrawal into self with resultant shyness. It may have been God's way of building up one's character.[11]

Another way in which God worked in Frances's life at that time was through a new governess, Mademoiselle Clementine Mayer from Alsace. Looking back many years later, Frances could say that they were truly blessed in having had for their early education a woman of such remarkable character. Mademoiselle Mayer had hoped to enter religious life but when her father was killed in the Franco-Prussian War she had to change her plans in order to support her mother. She taught the older boys, Arthur and Frank, until they went to the Jesuit-run Beaumont College at the ages of nine and eight years respectively. She then took on the three younger children. From her they learned to speak French fluently.

Cyril and Frances were under her care during school hours, each following a different programme of study. Freddie was still in the nursery where Mrs Grant was in charge, assisted by a nursemaid, Teresa Barnes. Teresa's brother, Brother Barnes SJ, belonged to the Beaumont Jesuit community, where one of his ministries was to administer the punishment meted out to naughty little boys. Consequently, Teresa was looked up to with respect and the children pleaded with her to ask her brother not to whack Arthur and Frank too hard. Not daring to presume too much on Teresa's good graces, the boys always brought back with them after the holidays a supply of tolley paste, popular with schoolboys of the period because of its reputation for soothing sore palms.

Frank made history in his early days at Beaumont when Queen Victoria came on a formal visit and he was deputed to present her with a bouquet. With as much dignity as he could muster, nine-year-old Frank approached the carriage, carefully holding the large bouquet. One of the Princesses put her hand out the carriage window to take it, but the little boy told her indignantly that it was not for her but for her Mamma.

It was during these years at Hampton Court that Frances first awoke to the beauty of nature. It was a love which was to stay with her throughout her life and which, in later years, was expressed in her painting and in her writing. 'The walk to Hampton Wick with my governess, on a path carpeted with falling May blossoms, the lively contrast of laburnum and lilac bowing gracefully overhead, has remained a joyous memory.'[12]

In 1882 the family left Hampton Court and moved back to London, this time to Lancaster Gate, where they rented a large airy house overlooking Kensington Gardens. For the first time in her young life Frances had a room to herself. 'It was desperately lonely at first, but after a while I found consolation in the large crucifix over my bed. Jesus looked lonely, and how cold he must be, naked on the cross.'[13] She found some cotton wool in the nursery and covered the figure on the crucifix. Despite the fact that it was removed by the nursemaid every morning, every night she repeated the procedure. Frances was never a person to give up easily, nor did she ever lose this early devotion to the crucified Jesus. It was a devotion that was to grow with the years until it became one of the outstanding features of her spiritual life.

Soon after the family returned to London, Frances's father began bringing her to the Jesuit church at Farm Street to attend catechism classes given by Father Leslie SJ, who called her 'the little girl in blue'. From birth, both Frances and Freddie were dedicated to Our Lady. Frances wore blue in her honour until she was eleven years old, and Freddie until she was seven. Symbols are powerful, especially where small children are concerned, and this symbol of her dedication to Our Lady undoubtedly laid the foundation for Frances's strong devotion to Mary throughout her life.

Her father was the biggest influence in Frances's early years. In spite of his involvement in political and religious issues relating to both England and Ireland, he gave much time and care to his children. Not only did he share his early morning walk with them, and initiate them into archery and rowing, but he often gave them an hour before bedtime, 'cultivating their tastes, while opening their minds to the beauty of the Faith as depicted by Catholic artists'.[14] His chief concern was the spiritual development of his children, but this early introduction to the masterpieces of religious art also influenced Frances by helping her develop a critical appreciation of good art. It also laid the foundation for her future skill in painting. But this is to anticipate. What she was meant to be learning now was how a good little girl should behave: 'He would not allow any spiritual weeds to grow up in the garden of our souls. I remember how seriously he warned me of my outbursts of temper, so displeasing to God. Owing to this firm but gentle guidance, I made real efforts to overcome myself.'[15]

Frances's mother, on the other hand, was more concerned with developing the children's social gifts. Highly gifted herself, she tried to obtain for them some of the advantages she had enjoyed as a child. Twice a week they had lessons in drawing and painting. However, music was Mrs Owen Lewis's chief delight. Her less musically gifted children found their music lessons an ordeal, though they did enjoy the elocution classes and dramatic productions organised by their teacher. They were given minor parts in some Shakespearean plays, one of which, *A Midsummer Night's Dream*, was staged in honour of Mr Gladstone, then Prime Minister, who reputedly enjoyed the production. Freddie was Puck, while Frances had to be content with being Cobweb.

Henry Owen Lewis was not enamoured of these worldly entertainments for his children. In this he differed from his wife, who threw herself fully into the social life of the London of her day. For him it was more important to get his children enrolled in the Holy Childhood Association, and to help them understand what this organisation was doing for destitute orphans in China. Every week he encouraged his children to give a penny of their pocket-money to help abandoned Chinese orphans. In this way they were made aware of the needs of China at a very early age. This may well have been how the seed of her future missionary vocation was implanted in Frances's impressionable mind.

Not only did her father bring her to catechism classes in Farm Street but he also brought her along occasionally to High Mass on Sunday. Sometimes a famous preacher would address the congregation. On one such occasion Frances was sitting in one of the front seats between her father and his friend, George E. Ranken, then editor of *The Tablet*. She recounted what happened:

> The cultured voice of the preacher had an unfortunately somnolent effect – the two gentlemen slept audibly. To my confusion the preacher looked rather reproachfully in our direction, as if expecting me to take action. Then, taking each of their missals, the little girl quietly dropped them on the feet of the sleepers.[16]

Their response was not recorded.

All kinds of people frequented the Owen Lewis home at Lancaster Gate. Among them was Lady Georgiana Fullerton, noted for her

charitable projects, who sometimes enlisted Mrs Owen Lewis to
help her organise fund-raising concerts. Mrs Owen Lewis also put
on her own musical entertainments. One such occasion was to
welcome Don Carlos, Pretender to the Spanish throne, when the
house was filled with marguerites in honour of his wife, Dona
Margarita. Priests sometimes came to stay. Among them were the
Abbé of San Denis from Paris and Father Porter SJ, the first English
Jesuit to go to Bombay as its new archbishop. Dora, the sister of
John Redmond who at that time was trying to organise the Irish
Parliamentary Party, sometimes stayed when she needed Mrs
Owen Lewis to chaperone her to dances. Years later Frances met
her daughter, Dame Teresa Howard, in Kylemore Abbey. It was
Teresa's uncle, John Redmond, who had brought the Benedictine
nuns of Kylemore to Ireland, after they had been shelled out of
Ypres in 1916.

On Saturdays the young Owen Lewis children played with the
children of their parents' friends. Among these were Daniel
O'Connell's grandchildren, the children of his son, who was also
called Daniel. However, the Owen Lewis children found these
young friends a poor substitute for their father who often had to
make business trips to Ireland. He still owned widespread properties
in Co. Monaghan and elsewhere though, because of the land
agitation, they were gradually becoming less remunerative. When
in Ireland he usually stayed with his cousin Derry, Lord Rossmore,
at Rossmore Park in Co. Monaghan, or at Glaslough as guest of the
Leslie family. Derry, the fifth Lord Rossmore, was regarded as
'one of the brighter sparks of the Prince of Wales's set' and in his
time Rossmore Park was a lively place.[17] Derry's memoirs, called
This I Can Tell, give a glimpse of the kind of life enjoyed by the
ascendancy in Ireland in the second half of the nineteenth century.[18]
Racy and anecdotal, they were undoubtedly considered daring
when first published, not the kind of reading that Derry's more
reflective cousin Henry Owen Lewis would favour.

Disappointed that their father would not bring them with him to
this land they had heard so much about, Freddie had the bright idea
of sending their dolls instead. She and Frances hid them in their

father's luggage before they themselves left for Brighton to spend their uneventful summer holidays with their maternal grandmother Mrs Elsegood, evidently a strait-laced lady. In later life Frances remembered one occasion when she was in Brighton on her own, visiting her grandmother. Paddling happily in the water, oblivious of her knees being bare, she pretended not to hear the young maid who, following the grandmother's command, was calling her to come out. Not only was she sent home in disgrace but she was also punished by her parents. More than seventy years later she remembered how she had been miserable for days.

Back in London after her ignominious banishment from Brighton, Frances, helped by her very sympathetic governess, began in 1882 to prepare for her First Holy Communion. Looking back many years later she recalled:

> From the depths of her beautiful soul she found words to dispose her young pupil to receive the Bread of Life worthily, and to understand the greatness of the act. She excited a hunger for Holy Communion, that longing for God which is at the foundation of all religion.[19]

A longing for God seems to have been a facet of Frances's personality even at this early age. It grew stronger with the years and a Sister recalls how in her old age she reacted with warmth and enthusiasm to the words a young Sister chose to have engraved on her Profession ring: St Augustine's famous cry: 'You have made us for Yourself, O Lord'. The words seemed to echo her own longing throughout a long life.

What was to become perhaps the dominant devotion in Frances's life now began to take shape as she prepared for her First Communion. 'My crucifix, always my chief devotion, grew dearer,' she remembered. A significant remark. Many years later, when the first Columban Sisters were given their religious names, each Sister was allowed to add to her name a mystery or devotion which attracted and influenced her. Frances chose to be called Sister Mary Patrick of the Holy Cross. At five years of age Frances used to cover the body on the crucifix over her bed with cotton wool against the cold. Now four years later, she knelt on her bed at night to kiss the five wounds of the crucified Christ, spending some time in prayer in spite of the winter's cold.

From her bedroom overlooking Kensington Gardens she could enjoy the night sky. 'In the frosty weather of December 1882, the firmament of deep azure blue shone with a galaxy of stars. One large planet shone right into the room. Night after night I gazed at it, imagining to myself it was the same star that led the Magi, and was beckoning me on to receive Our Lord.'[20]

Father Leslie, whose catechism classes Frances had attended in Farm Street from the time she was five years old, believed that she was ready to make her First Communion. Her mother felt that she was too young but eventually Father Leslie had his way. A date was fixed, 23 January 1883, feast of the Espousals of Our Lady and St Joseph, a feast dear to her father who was as happy as she was about this important event in her life. Frances always retained a great devotion to this feast, and a beautiful painting based on the theme, which she brought with her to Cahiracon, hung for many years in the motherhouse.

After making her confession to Father Leslie on the eve of the feast, Frances went looking for her mother to apologise for any trouble she had caused her because of her faults. Her mother, busily checking some new tableware, did not understand at first what the little girl was trying to say. When she did, she hugged her warmly, assuring her that she had never caused her any problems.

Early in the morning of 23 January 1883 the whole family, accompanied by Mlle Mayer and Mrs Grant, the children's old nurse, set out for Farm Street church. There Father Leslie celebrated Mass for them at the altar of St Joseph, and Frances received her First Holy Communion. 'It was a moment of ineffable joy, and I made rather a prolonged thanksgiving.' Recalling the occasion many years later, she added: 'It is well to teach children how to welcome their hidden God. It is only in later years one learns to listen to him.'[21]

Frequent Communion was not common in those days, but her father, understanding her longing to receive Our Lord, brought her with him either to Farm Street or to some other London church every First Friday. Her happiness seemed complete. Then, suddenly, some months after receiving her First Communion, she was plunged into a period of darkness and doubt about the real presence of Christ in the Eucharist. This became almost unbearable, and she felt like running away from the altar in case she might commit a sacrilege. Even her spiritual director, Father Leslie, did not seem to understand, and she was ashamed to talk to her father or to Mademoiselle. She still longed to receive Communion and, in spite of everything, she continued to prepare herself carefully.

It was only at the last moment, when the priest was about to put the Sacred Host on my tongue, Satan renewed the attack on my faith. Feeling like a traitor and a criminal, it appeared a mortal sin to have received our Divine Lord under such conditions. My poor little soul was plunged in darkness.[22]

This painful situation continued for some months and then vanished suddenly, never to return. She attributed the victory to St Michael and to her Guardian Angel. Mademoiselle had taught her to be devoted to both and, even when she was much younger, she had experienced the care of her Guardian Angel.

I remember as a small child standing at the top of a steep flight of stairs in nervous fear of the semi-darkness. A few seconds later I found myself standing at the bottom of the staircase without any volition on my part or apparent outside assistance. It seemed quite natural at the time, for is it not the business of Angels to look after little ones.[23]

The summer after Frances made her First Communion the whole family went to Boulogne for their holidays. This was not their first visit: Boulogne had several family associations. Frances's mother had been to school there, as well as in Hanover and England, and her father often stayed with a close friend who lived in the neighbourhood.

More than half a century later, Frances remembered this particular holiday of 1883. On the feast of the Assumption, dressed in her

First Communion clothes, she took part with several other little girls in a procession in honour of Our Lady. 'No princess could have felt prouder or happier than I did that day!'

But there was another side to Frances too. She was a lively girl and loved fun and games. Having grown up with three older brothers, she had been initiated into their games early on and always wanted to be out playing with them and their friends.

> On one occasion with a number of other youths, we had a picnic at Pont-de-Briques, a little country place not far from the town. Romping with them in tomboyish fashion I rolled down a steep incline and without warning found myself on a railway line with an approaching train. My brothers were far ahead, and no one seemed to know of my plight. One thoughtful boy looked round, saw what was happening, and rushing down dragged the foolish little girl up the embankment.[24]

Things went differently when Mademoiselle was around. They then went for ladylike walks along the town ramparts, or sat with their governess in the nearby cornfields. 'I can still see her sitting among the poppies and marguerites while we listened spellbound to the marvellous history of the Curé of Ars whose cause had been introduced for Beatification.'[25]

Frances was just twelve when her much-loved governess finally achieved her desire to enter religious life. For many years she had wanted to enter Carmel but was unable to pursue her vocation because her aged mother needed her support. After her mother died, her spiritual director encouraged her to join a teaching order. Consequently, she entered a Dominican convent at Sèvres, but she soon discovered that this was not her vocation. Eventually, with the help of Frances's parents, she was able to enter a Carmelite community in Hainault, Belgium, where she lived happily for the remainder of her life. Some of her later years were spent in a French Carmel when persecution drove the Carmelites of Hainault to France. Throughout her long life she remained in close contact with the Owen Lewis family, who continued to be her friends and benefactors.

Mademoiselle Mayer's departure caused Frances great sorrow. Perhaps it was to help them to cope with this loss and, in her own words, to 'cheer the drooping spirits', that she and Freddie were at last sent on a holiday to Ireland.

We felt we were going to our real home and country at last. Up before dawn, we gloried in the beautiful approach to Dun Laoghaire. My father pointed out the Dublin Mountains, Howth and Ireland's Eye. In the soft morning haze everything looked wonderful and mysterious. The spiritual atmosphere, of which we were subconsciously aware, comforted me, and the greeting of old friends cheered the drooping spirits.[26]

On this and subsequent occasions the Owen Lewises stayed at 'an old fashioned family hotel' at the corner of Nassau Street and Kildare Street called, at the time, the Nassau Hotel. After a happy though too short visit to Ireland, the children returned to London. There they found a new governess installed. The first inkling they had was when they saw some strange luggage in the schoolroom. Frances remembered how 'Freddie relieved her feelings with a good kick to the trunk! ... Our hearts were still sore from the parting with the one who had been like a second mother to us, and even an angel coming after her would have been unwelcome.'[27]

Fräulein Flouan could hardly have been different from Mademoiselle Mayer. She was a tall, gaunt, shortsighted and unfashionably dressed German. 'Her unprepossessing appearance was accentuated by a double pair of spectacles, one blue and the other white. During our lessons she usually adjusted a third pair which fitted on to the end of a long pointed nose.'[28] From the beginning, the new governess found fault with the children and to say that they found her uncongenial is an understatement. She constantly complained about them to their mother who, because of her German connection and sympathies, tried to be understanding and kind. The girls' older brothers, home on holidays from Beaumont, sided with their sisters and devised many pranks to annoy the Fräulein. In her memoirs, Frances recalled that although the boys were behind most of the mischief she was the one blamed.

Nor was she altogether blameless. One evening she found Freddie kneeling with the governess before the altar in the night nursery, candles lighting, making a novena for her conversion. This was more than she could take. Making for her sister, she gave her a good punch, which effectively put an end to that night's prayers. But, realising that Freddie was merely obeying instructions, they were soon reconciled.

After a few months of this, Fräulein Flouan decided that the children were more than she could handle. The Owen Lewis parents paid her fare back to Germany and peace returned to the household.

It was possibly this episode which was the deciding factor in the two Owen Lewis girls being sent away to boarding school. At first, there was question of the Sacred Heart Convent at Roehampton, because the Superior there was Mother Digby whose mother had been Freddie's godmother. However, the final decision was in favour of the Sacred Heart Convent at Hove near Brighton. This was considered a healthier place for growing children. From the first, Frances fitted in, though in the early days she was often overcome by feelings of loneliness for home. At such times she sought refuge in the convent chapel where she found comfort in a huge picture of the Sacred Heart, which reminded her of the life-sized statue on the landing at home. The Society of the Sacred Heart withdrew from Brighton in 1966, after being there since 1877, and the school is now Newman School, one of the larger of the Catholic schools in the south of England. However, the convent chapel is still as it was in Frances's time, with its dark wooden choir stalls and well-scuffed benches where the boarders would have knelt.

Frances and Freddie were given cubicles facing one another and between them, to their joy, was a window looking out over the sea, which was also visible from their desks side by side in the study hall.

Many a glance was stolen from my lesson books as I dreamed of future adventures across the sea. These thoughts were stimulated largely by a book being read in the refectory by Lady

Burney. The authoress had travelled the world over in her yacht, and knew how to describe all that she had seen. When later, at our mid-day meal, the Life of Ven. Mother Duchesne became the food of our minds, my thoughts took a different turn. The same longing for adventure remained, but the scene and purpose reached out to missionary labours. The Lord has His own designs, and He waits patiently for a wayward soul – even unto the eleventh hour.[29]

On 23 April 1887, when the two Owen Lewis girls arrived at the Sacred Heart Convent in Brighton, Frances had turned fourteen but Freddie was only ten years of age. Always the family pet, she found boarding school hard. She had been allowed to bring her favourite doll with her to school, and fell asleep at night cuddling it to herself. To keep her little sister happy, Frances used to smuggle up food for the doll's supper, and the two sisters often got into trouble for talking together in the dormitory. Freddie, in desperation, decided to write to her godmother, Mrs Digby, hoping that she might use her influence with her daughter, Rev. Mother Digby of Roehampton. 'I do not dislike school as much as I thought I would,' she wrote, but the letter was handed back to be re-written: it was not what a little girl should write to the mother of Rev. Mother Digby. One wonders if Freddie had got a little help from her older sister.

On 9 June 1887, less than two months after starting school in Brighton, Freddie made her First Communion, by all accounts looking like an angel. The occasion reminded Frances of her own First Communion day; soon she would be allowed to receive Communion three or four times a week, a privilege in those years.

By this time the two girls had made many friends, some of whom they were to keep in touch with throughout their lives. One of these was Margaret Petre who in 1897 would be one of Frances's bridesmaids. In 1934 Margaret Petre, then Mrs Clutton, wrote her reminiscences of her eight years at school in Brighton for the school magazine. Her account gives a lively picture of what a boarder's life was like when Frances and Freddie were at school there. They played rounders in winter, cricket in summer. Their

approach to cricket, admits the writer, would make the present
school smile, though Father Scannell, the chaplain, did try to instil
the rules and procedures of the game. 'But, dear present generation,
we made runs, we howled joyously, we were thrilled to the marrow,
our umpires were quixotically fair, so even if our Cricket was
'weird', may we not be said to have played the game.'[30]

There were other games too, such as 'Holy Sepulchre' based on
the Crusades, a game of chase and capture and tremendous high
spirits. 'It would begin with the autumn, continue through winter,
and might conceivably, like some of the real crusades, never finish
at all.'[31]

It was a tough regime by today's standards. Afternoon tea was
reserved for feast-days and holidays, and thus became 'an ambrosial
feast'. Otherwise there was 'unlimited dry bread, placed on the
playground in biscuit tins, followed by mugs of water as we passed
indoors to four o'clock study.'[32] However, they always had a snack
during afternoon recreation, bread and jam on Mondays, buns on
Tuesdays, Saturdays and Sundays.

Frances's best friend during her time in Brighton was Mercedes
de Laski, who was a boarder there from 1883 to 1890. From the
beginning, Frances felt drawn to her and enjoyed her high spirits.
They shared the same sense of fun, which often got them into
trouble. But they always stood by one another. 'But, Mother,
Mercedes is a saint!' Frances would plead, while Mercedes would
say the same about her. Their friends nicknamed them, 'The Two
Saints'.

However, there was someone who saw beneath the bravado and
the schoolgirlish escapades and for a short time became a strong
influence in Frances's life: Mother Gertrude Newdigate seems to
have taken over where Mademoiselle Mayer left off. Frances could
say about her, 'Through some enchantment she discovered some
inclination for virtue in me and fostered its feeble growth.' Because
of this gentle influence, Frances became more docile. Then,
unexpectedly, Mother Newdigate died on 31 May 1888, at the age
of twenty-six. Looking back over a span of nearly seventy years,
Frances remembered the exact day and time when she realised that

her friend was gravely ill. It was on the feast of Corpus Christi 1888, and she and Freddie were running to the parlour to meet Canon Lalor, an old friend with whom the family had sometimes stayed in Petworth, Sussex. On the way, they saw Mother Newdigate struggling to open a door, and Frances stopped to ask her if she was sick. The only reply she got was a faint smile. That evening the Mistress General came to the study hall to ask the children to pray for Mother Newdigate who was very ill. She died that night.

The following day the Mistress General of the school, Mother Alice Woodward, sent for Frances. 'It was to give me,' she said, 'a precious remembrance of my soul's friend, for such she had been to me.' The day before she died, Mother Newdigate had copied out for Frances a prayer she had promised her on love and sacrifice. 'It was finished, all but a few lines, in her own small and well-formed writing. It was one of my most cherished treasures for more than half a lifetime.'

Mother Woodward seized the opportunity to talk to Frances about her friendship with Madeleine de Laski, suggesting that instead of encouraging one another in mischievous pranks they try to help one another to be better. 'I tried,' Frances recalled in her memoirs, 'but Mercedes thought I was preaching – and our friendship cooled off.'

On 10 June 1888, just ten days after Mother Newdigate's sudden death, Frances, Freddie and some other children received the sacrament of Confirmation. Frances remembered how carefully they were prepared.

My soul was filled with sweetness and unction ... I was convinced that I would always remain on the road to sanctity, that the exercises of patience, humility and obedience in which we were being drilled, would become easy, but alas, the law of self-control and all that it implied remained as difficult as ever![33]

After the ceremony Frances and Freddie were called to the parlour to meet Bishop Butt of Brighton and Arundel, who had confirmed them. They had met previously when the children were staying with their friend, Canon Lalor. Throughout their schooldays and for long afterwards, Bishop Butt retained a fatherly interest in them.

That summer the family enjoyed a long holiday in Scotland where they stayed with the Duff-Gordons. Frances, in her memoirs, described some escapades that she and her school-friend, Lina Duff-Gordon, got into as they roamed through the countryside. During this holiday, they became close friends and exchanged many confidences. From their positive experience of nuns, especially the Sacred Heart nuns at Brighton, they decided that they too were destined to become religious. However, nobody took them too seriously. Frances's family travelled widely through Scotland, visiting places of historical or literary importance, and ending up with a pilgrimage to Abbotsford in honour of Mr Owen Lewis's 'favourite author and distant kinsman' Sir Walter Scott.

By the end of September 1888 Frances and Freddie were back at school. Frances had returned with a heavy cold and seemed to have lost all her energy. But so many of the children had colds that she played down her own illness and turned a deaf ear to her friends' advice that she should see the Infirmarian. Finally, at Benediction on the feast of All Saints, she collapsed in the chapel and woke to find herself in the school infirmary. The doctor diagnosed a severe case of pneumonia, but soon other more disturbing symptoms presented themselves. Frances's parents were sent for. When they arrived hurriedly from London she could hardly recognise them. Her mother stayed on in Brighton, visiting her every day.

Other doctors were brought in for consultation and their verdict was that Frances would not live more than three weeks. The Superior, Rev. Mother Moloney, sent to London for Father Leslie who years earlier had prepared Frances for her First Holy Communion and who had been such a good friend. She had made her First Confession to him; now she made what could well be her last. Mother Moloney began to prepare her for death, though Frances kept insisting that she was not dying. She received the Last Anointing from Father Scannell, the young Irish priest, who as well as being the convent chaplain, was also unofficial cricket coach to a crowd of unruly schoolgirls. He told her nervously that it was his first time to administer that sacrament, and she replied, 'I hope, Father, that you enjoyed it as much as I did!'

Another unexpected joy was the fulfilment of an unexpressed wish when she was consecrated a Child of Mary on her deathbed. 'It was a touching little ceremony, at which all my companions, bearing lighted candles, were present, and tears were shed!' A novena was begun in honour of Ven. Mother Barat for her recovery, her mother brought Lourdes water and her brothers came from distant parts to say goodbye.

At the insistence of Frances's parents, a famous specialist was now called in. He advised a new surgical procedure not yet in general use, which involved draining fluid from the lungs. It was a painful experience but in Frances's case it worked. Afterwards, every day for six weeks the draining tube had to be removed, cleaned and reinserted. This caused intense pain each time. The doctors advised fresh air. Consequently, every day of early January 1889, Frances was wheeled out into the convent garden, wrapped in blankets and surrounded by hot water jars, against the severe cold. It was the only way she could meet her school-friends, who always gathered around to cheer her up.

Finally on 10 January 1889, her mother came to take her home to her grandmother's house in Oriental Place, Brighton. The house now belonged to Mrs Owen Lewis, who had inherited it on her mother's death. Frances was sad to say goodbye to Rev. Mother Moloney and the nuns who had meant so much to her. She would have been more upset if she had known that her schooldays in Brighton were over for good. Throughout her life she retained the warmest affection and reverence for the Sacred Heart nuns she had known, and for their spirit. Looking back years later, she could say:

> The kindly way of the Sacred Heart Nuns in giving correction always had the effect of making me sorry and ashamed. They never spoke hastily or showed any irritation with the offender. By example, as well as precept, they put a high ideal before their pupils, and by their natural manner one unconsciously learnt and

valued humility, simplicity, and a strong sense of duty.[34]

Freddie stayed on in Brighton for another four years. Her experience of convent school life was less positive than her sister's. The school register, in the column headed 'Observations', notes after her name that her parents were finally asked not to send her back after the holidays. Freddie's best friend also left under a cloud the following year. After her name the school register has a note: 'Was sent away as she helped a child to carry on a forbidden correspondence.' Standards were different in those days and Freddie, at least, does seem to have made amends. She attended the Golden Jubilee reunion of Old Girls in 1927. A few programmes of the occasion survive, autographed by some of those who attended. Freddie has signed herself, 'Frederica S. Chevers, E. de M'. So the privilege of receiving her Child of Mary medal, of which she was deprived as a schoolgirl, was bestowed on her in later years.

TWO

Coming of Age

Throughout the early weeks of 1889 Frances continued her convalescence at Oriental Place, Brighton, under the care of a member of
a French nursing order. When sufficiently recovered to be able to
travel, her parents brought her to Boulogne. Her nurse accompanied them and stayed until Frances could manage on her own. To
thank Our Lady, to whom she attributed her daughter's cure, her
mother then brought her to Lourdes. It was the month of February
and snow was still on the ground, yet they went to early Mass at the
Grotto each morning. On the feast of Our Lady of Lourdes, 11
February, they were amazed at the length of the torchlight procession; people had come from all over for the occasion. It deepened
their own faith to witness such devotion. Later, when they visited
St Bernadette's home, Frances 'gazed longingly' at the simple
wooden bed where the saint had been born, and the Saint's brother,
the only surviving member of the Soubirous family, took out his
pen-knife and chopped off a splinter to give her as a relic. It became
one of her most treasured possessions.[1]

In Lourdes, Frances's mother hired out a horse-drawn carriage,
the driver of which took pleasure in showing the two foreign ladies
the magnificent scenery in the neighbouring countryside. They
went as far as possible into the heart of the mountains, and nothing
would do Frances but to attempt a climb.

> With new blood coursing in my veins the frosty air acted as an
> intoxicant. I sprang from rock to rock ever higher, like a young
> goat, regardless of the calls of my poor mother, puffing behind.
> Yet another instance of incurable wilfulness! It was perhaps also
> a little ungrateful, considering all the unselfish devotion be-
> stowed on me during the recent illness.[2]

Encouraged by the guide, who tried to help Mrs Owen Lewis
along, they continued their climb to a halting site halfway up the
peak, where they hoped to recoup their energies. Unfortunately for

them, they arrived only to find the resthouse closed. That meant that they were forced to retrace their steps down the icy path. They arrived back at their hotel footsore and hungry.

Some days later they left for Pau, a fashionable resort where Mrs Owen Lewis had some acquaintances. Twenty-three years earlier she and her husband had spent part of their honeymoon there, and the hotel proprietor still remembered them. Consequently, he gave Mrs Owen Lewis and her daughter his best rooms at a nominal price. Meanwhile, the Owen Lewis family, possibly with Frances's health in mind, had decided to spend the rest of the year in Boulogne where they had been able to rent, quite inexpensively, a pleasant house called Villa Notre Dame. Frances and her mother now prepared to return there. On the way, they spent a night in Paris with their hospitable friends, the d'Hericault family, who had invited some of their own acquaintances to meet them. Not accustomed to grown-up parties, Frances found this particular one somewhat embarrassing.

> Thinking to do justice to the occasion – though neither fish nor fowl – only an overgrown schoolgirl – I donned a silk frock with open neck and elbow sleeves. Apparently this was quite against French etiquette, as my dear friend Marie-Josephe [d'Hericault] delicately informed me. Also her father pointed out, in a paternal way, a young lady never offers her hand to a gentleman! I further put my foot in it by addressing a polite remark to a young man sitting next to me, who merely put on a look of well-bred surprise.[3]

Fortunately the evening ended happily for her, and her embarrassment was forgotten when she and her friend Marie-Josephe were able to slip away together to chat and exchange confidences.

Eventually Frances and her mother reached Boulogne. Once again Mrs Owen Lewis set about cultivating her daughter's talents, as she had when she was a child. She discovered an excellent teacher who could continue her voice training, and who could help her to build up a popular repertoire of French and operatic songs. She also engaged a portrait painter to give her lessons. But

Frances's first effort, an attempt to paint her brother Cyril, caused such merriment in the family that after a month she decided that portrait painting was not her forte. She then took up landscape painting, where she was more successful. She was expected to measure up to a high standard of excellence: her mother, a skilled artist, had been a pupil of W.P. Frith RA, one of the most eminent, if not the most eminent of the mid-Victorian realists. So popular was he that on five occasions when he was exhibiting paintings at the Royal Academy they had to be protected by barriers from over-enthusiastic admirers.[4]

However, Boulogne meant more to Frances than either her singing or her art classes. It was here that, for the first time, she got involved in direct work for the poor. Marie Dunne, a young Irish girl, introduced her to Sister Joseph of the Daughters of Charity with whom she had been visiting the poor. Frances was immediately drawn to do likewise. Despite its magnificent cathedral, pleasant boulevards and fashionable shops, Boulogne also had a less salubrious area which tourists never saw – narrow alleyways with steep stone steps and noisome open sewers. Here Sister Joseph introduced Frances to her friends, the sick poor of the neighbourhood. Soon Frances was also their friend, the recipient of their noisy welcome, when she accompanied Sister Joseph each day, carrying the food which had been collected and which was now augmented by items from the Owen Lewis table. She also helped Sister Joseph when she attended the sick and dressed their sores. 'Up and down those steps we trudged on our daily rounds. It was a valuable apprenticeship to be of use in later years.'[5]

Then came the summer holidays and Freddie arrived home from school. Other young friends came later. Frances succeeded in getting them involved in helping the poor and between them they were able to provide clothes for a number of First Communicants. She also persuaded her mother to take on as maids two young women Sister Joseph was trying to help. Practical-minded even then, Frances banked most of their wages for them so that when they later decided to return home they had accumulated quite an amount to bring back to their families.

A sudden cholera scare meant that the Owen Lewis family had to leave Boulogne sooner than they had intended. Fortunately the holidays were nearly over so Mrs Owen Lewis brought Freddie back to England and school. Mr Owen Lewis took the rest of the family to Paris, the city that he loved of all others. There they stayed in an inexpensive hotel near the holy places he wanted to visit, among them the shrine of Père Olivaint, to whom he attributed Frances's remarkable cure as an infant, and the basilica of Montmartre, then in process of being built. There he subscribed to have the names of all the family members inscribed on so many bricks. They also visited the Sacred Heart Convent in rue de Varennes, to meet Frances's friend Lina Duff-Gordon, who was finishing her education there; her mother, who had shown the Owen Lewis family such hospitality on their visit to Scotland the previous summer, had died suddenly. Later Lina was put under the guardianship of a Protestant aunt. She then gave up the practice of her religion. Over the years Frances made many attempts to contact her friend, but her letters were never answered.

From Paris they visited Sèvres to see the famous porcelain factory, but chiefly to meet Mademoiselle Mayer their former governess who was now a novice in a teaching order. They found her unhappy, still yearning to be a Carmelite. They visited her again before they left Paris and were able to arrange for her to withdraw from the novitiate. A few years later, with the help of the Owen Lewis family, she achieved her heart's desire and entered Carmel where she lived happily for the rest of her life.

By autumn the whole family were together again in London. For reasons of economy they had moved from their house at the corner of Lancaster Gate to a more modest one nearby, almost as spacious but without the attractive view of Kensington Gardens. Mr Owen Lewis had to sell part of his library, including some rare first editions, to pay school fees.

Life would have been bleak enough for Frances at this stage if Molly Milbanke, who had just finished her education at Roehampton, had not come to stay. Her mother had died some years previously, after leaving her husband. Molly's father, a great-grandson of the poet Byron, left with many unhappy memories, had no time for his daughter and most of her early life was spent in boarding schools. Her stepmother now asked Mrs Owen Lewis to introduce her to London society. Although Molly was two years older than Frances they had much in common. Both were Sacred Heart girls and they liked to pray together the devotions they had learned at school. Every week they walked over to Farm Street for confession. They attended various lectures and concerts and read the classics with Mr Owen Lewis. Sometimes they visited the art galleries, accompanied by Father Leslie SJ, still Frances's spiritual director and a family friend. 'He developed my artistic tastes by frequent visits to the National Gallery where he explained to us the beautiful masterpieces, and how to distinguish the various schools of art.'[6]

It was around this time that Father Leslie said to Frances that she had a great capacity for holiness. 'I have a great capacity for worldliness!' she replied. 'The two generally go together,' he retorted. Her 'worldliness', as she called it, was borne in on her when her mother brought Molly Milbanke to evening parties which she herself was considered too young to attend. Consequently she was forced to devise her own entertainment. This took the form of reading romantic novels, for which she developed a taste, which she later realised could have weakened her spiritually. There are echoes here of the young Ignatius Loyola. Like him she gradually began to take note of what she considered instances of worldly vanity in herself. Turning away from them, she renewed her good resolutions. God's grace, she recalled later, had kept her from any serious lapse.

Her faith now stronger than ever, she was able to encourage others to remain faithful. This was to happen in the case of her friend, Molly Milbanke. After living with the Owen Lewis family for almost a year, Molly was taken up by her grandfather, the Earl of Lovelace, who did not approve of how his son had treated his only child. Cinderella, Frances remarked, now became the Princess. But she had a problem: in her first letter she told Frances that her grandfather would not allow her to attend Sunday Mass. Frances wrote by return of post.

I wrote back immediately strongly urging her to make a stand for her faith. If her grandfather refused to send a carriage with her, she should start walking to the church, no matter how distant. This plan worked! Molly trudging along the country roads on a Sunday morning heard the galloping of horses behind her. The aged Earl had sent his carriage to convey his granddaughter to Mass.[7]

After Molly Milbanke left London, the Owen Lewis family decided to let their house at Lancaster Gate and live for a time in Brighton in the house Mrs Owen Lewis had inherited from her mother. Perhaps a consideration was Mrs Owen Lewis's poor health at the time. This may have been connected with anxiety about the state of the family finances when no rents were forthcoming from their Irish estates. Frances tried to ease the situation by relieving her mother of the task of supervising the housekeeping. She had been attending cookery classes at the South Kensington Institute, where she had learned how to produce inexpensive meals. Irish stew, herrings and margarine now became part of the family cuisine. Not accustomed to such food, some members of the family registered objections. Anyway, Frances's small economies did little to improve the financial situation, which was really due to the Land War in Ireland.

As a result of the Land League, founded by Michael Davitt in 1879, and the subsequent Land War, many tenants had stopped paying rent. Even some of the larger tenant farmers who had identified themselves with the peasant class were also withholding rent. Absentee landlords such as Henry Owen Lewis, who was only one of many, were particularly badly affected. Before long their families were obliged to economise in unanticipated ways. In a letter written to her sister Freddie many years later, Frances reminisced: 'We were terribly hard up in those days and when you wanted a new frock the Mater and I pooled our very limited knowledge of dressmaking to manufacture it for you ... I myself was attired in a riding suit made from an old habit of the Mater's which had been adjusted to the prevailing fashions! However, we kept the faith and got many a joke out of life.'[8] When matters got worse and the family found themselves heavily in debt, a sudden decision was made to go abroad again until things should improve. At least the cost of living would be less, and educational opportunities good.

This time they decided to go to Germany. Five of them travelled together: Mr and Mrs Owen Lewis, Frank, Frances and Freddie, who had to leave school. Their first stop was Cologne. Frances never forgot how enraptured they were with that city which she, Frank and Freddie were seeing for the first time. It was early morning and 'the lace-like towers of the Cathedral shone like fairy sentinels, and the beautiful old bells were calling people to Mass.'[9] From there they travelled by riverboat on the Rhine as far as Wiesbaden, enjoying the magnificent scenery on either side. A small branch railway brought them from Wiesbaden to Bad Schwalbach, a small spa famous for its baths. Here Mrs Owen Lewis got some relief for her rheumatism, and Frances and Freddie spent their time socialising in the Pump Room, walking along the promenades, or listening to the band, as if they were reliving a novel by Jane Austen. They took up riding, because it did not cost much to rent out a horse. In later years riding became one of Frances's favourite forms of sport, and it stood her in good stead when she accompanied her husband on his travels into remote areas of the Windward Islands and Trinidad.

When Mrs Owen Lewis had finished her course of baths she returned to England to try once more to sort out the family finances. Meanwhile her husband brought the rest of the family to Heidelberg. The idea was that Frank would study at the university while Freddie would attend the Ursuline Convent school. They stayed at a guest house which Frances disliked because it was frequented by a number of male students who showed such interest in the two English girls that, as she recalled later, she dared not lift her eyes off her plate. When she and Freddie tried to escape their attentions by going for a walk it was almost as bad. 'Every street was full of these unfinished gentlemen who gallantly ranged themselves on either side of the path for us to pass down the centre of them.'[10]

Often the two sisters escaped down some convenient lane to avoid
the unwelcome attention.

While Freddie was at school during the day Frances again took
up her painting. She did an oil painting of the ruins of Heidelberg
Castle and was pleasantly surprised when it turned out well. It was
later accepted for an exhibition of oil paintings in London.

During the Christmas holidays they moved again, this time to
Frankfurt where they were able to get spacious accommodation
within easy reach of the cathedral. Freddie continued her education
as a day-pupil in a local convent school while Frances spent her
mornings at an art studio, encouraged by the fact that she was
making good progress. In the evenings they went skating and
sometimes they were lucky enough to get to the opera. Frances
recalled that it was an education in itself to hear Wagner as
produced in Germany. Like the rest of the audience, they brought
sandwiches with them to the longer productions.

Summer came and Mrs Owen Lewis was still in London, still
involved in tedious legal business relating to the family's finances.
Her husband, who suffered from digestive problems, was advised
to try the waters at Neuenahr, a health resort on the Ahr, one of the
tributaries of the Rhine. The family decided to move there for the
summer. Frequented for the most part by invalids and hypochon-
driacs, it was not a place for lively young women like Frances and
Freddie. They were happy when the time came to return to
Frankfurt. There Frances resumed her painting and, obviously on
instructions from her mother, again took up singing classes. 'The
maestro was intent on obtaining full use of his pupil's vocal cords
– the mouth to be opened in the shape of an O. As the lesson
proceeded he peeped down my throat to observe whether the larynx
was properly expanded. Not appreciating the proximity of his
grisly head, I stepped back a pace and kept stepping back till my
back was against the wall, when the lesson ended.'[11]

Early in 1891 Mrs Owen Lewis was able to rejoin the rest of the
family. Evidently her efforts to improve the family finances had
been successful. They would never be as well off as they had once
been and they would need to economise, but at least they would be

able to live again in England. A fitting ending for their 'grand tour', she felt, would be a visit to Switzerland. Years earlier she and her husband had shown hospitality to Mr Karl Benziger, of the well-known publishing firm, on his first visit to England. He was now living in Einsiedeln in Switzerland and had sent a pressing invitation to the family to visit him there. They left Frankfurt, travelling by boat and train via Strasbourg and Basel. It was springtime and the scenery was magnificent. During their few days in Zürich they visited the famous mountain shrine of Our Lady of the Hermits, sometimes called the Lourdes of Switzerland. From there they went to Lucerne, where they did some mountain climbing and enjoyed the magnificent vista of snow-capped peaks on all sides. Back then to Berne, where Frances lost a cuff with gold links while throwing buns to the bears in the bear garden.

Again it was Mrs Owen Lewis who decided that the best way to end their time abroad would be a pilgrimage to Paray le Monial. She shared her husband's great devotion to the Sacred Heart, and it would not be their first time to visit the holy place where St Margaret Mary had been granted apparitions of the Sacred Heart. In fact, seventeen years previously Henry Owen Lewis had been in correspondence with his friend Cardinal Cullen of Dublin, urging him to arrange for pilgrimages from Ireland to Paray le Monial.[12]

After some days in Paray le Monial, the Owen Lewis family left for London. Frances felt sad that this European interlude had come to an end. Back in London her mother was determined to give her what she considered the worldly advantages of a season in town. Frances did not look forward to this social merry-go-round, especially when she knew that her mother would be hard pressed to cope with the expenses involved. However, once Mrs Owen Lewis had set her heart on something, it happened. She immediately set to, making all the preparations necessary for Frances's presentation at Court. Long sessions with dressmakers and lessons in the art of curtsey and Court etiquette took up the greater part of each day. It made it slightly easier for Frances that her friend, Raphael Fortescue, was making her debut at Buckingham Palace at the same time, also chaperoned by Mrs Owen Lewis. In later years Frances remembered the occasion with a measure of amusement:

> Hyde Park was full of carriages containing ladies in court
> dresses with large white bouquets. Our trains, measuring four
> yards, were held over the left arm while we waited a couple of
> hours in one of the long drawing rooms of the palace. Our names
> were called out, the trains spread out by attendants as we entered
> the Throne Room. Queen Victoria sat in state with the princesses
> and ladies-in-waiting. We curtseyed, without mishap, were
> saluted by the Queen, the Princesses smiled, and out we went by
> the further door where our trains were hastily bundled over our
> arms.[13]

That afternoon a reception was held for family and friends in the
Owen Lewis home in Cranley Gardens, a much smaller house than
the one they had enjoyed in Lancaster Gate. Its one redeeming
feature, according to Frances, was its nearness to Brompton Oratory which meant that she and her father were able to attend daily
Mass. When the reception ended, Frances slipped around to the
Oratory to lay her presentation bouquet of white lilies and roses at
Our Lady's altar. Photographs of Frances and some of her fellow-
debutantes were published, as was usual, in the fashionable ladies'
journals of the time. *The Lady* carried a pleasing photograph of
Frances as a happy self-confident young woman, alert to what was
happening around her, wearing her debutante's gown with poise
and, on her head, behind the massed curls, the three obligatory
Prince of Wales ostrich feathers.

Afterwards, there was the usual round of parties. Frances's first
official adult party was a reception in honour of Cardinal Vaughan
at the home of Sir Charles and Lady Clifford. The Duke of Norfolk
was present, together with many members of the old Catholic
families of England. Frances was happy to be introduced to the
younger members of these families. When she accepted invitations
to other than Catholic functions she was likely to be embarrassed
because, knowing so few people, she could be a wallflower for the
whole evening. A dance she remembered with pleasure was one
given by the Duchess of Newcastle, who had been at school with

her mother in the days when both of them were Protestants. More than sixty years later she remembered the dress she wore on that occasion.

> My mother had spangled a beautiful bertha of Limerick lace for me, to adorn the bodice of a pale blue moire ball dress, the material having lain by for nearly half a century in a trunk of my grandmother's. The whole confection had cost less than a pound – I thought it prettier than any other frock at the party, especially as it was Our Lady's own colour.[14]

Raphael Fortescue, who had made her debut with Frances, was also at this party. She and her sister Clare had organised a group of young women to help the factory girls of East London. They invited Frances to join the group, which she did. This work came to mean much to her and she never missed a meeting. Each time, some of the factory girls met her at the nearest underground station and accompanied her there again at the end of each visit. The place, made notorious by Jack the Ripper, had scared others away but Frances was never a person to give way to fear.

An Irish friend, May Langan, came over to enjoy what remained of the London season. She was too late for the first parties of the season and, at this stage, 'Invitations to dances were few and far between, in fact not to be expected when we could not afford to give a ball in return. One lesson I learned during that time in London was not to count on the friendship of fair-weather friends.'[15]

Mrs Owen Lewis, disappointed that the season in London had not been as successful as she had hoped and that no marriage proposals had been forthcoming for her daughter, now came up with another plan. 'It would be better for us as an Irish family to return to our own country, she decided, where we would take our place among the county families to which we were entitled by descent'.[16]

It was a wise decision which worked out well for all the family, who were welcomed back warmly by their friends and relatives and had no problem inserting themselves into Irish society. For some years their house in Co. Monaghan had been leased, so they stayed in Dublin, first in St Stephen's Green and later in Upper Merrion Street.

Frances's brothers Arthur and Frank later joined the family in Dublin, where Arthur contributed to the social life of the city by producing plays in which Frances sometimes acted. There was now no shortage of invitations to dances, nor was she ever again to be a wallflower. 'I enjoyed the absence of formality, so different from England, and positively let myself go to the frivolities of a worldly life.'[17] Then, in the spring of 1892 she attended a retreat in University Church, given by a Father Russell SJ. Once again she began to wonder if God was calling her to enter religious life. Her father had always hoped that she might be given the grace of a religious vocation, and had once remarked how well she would look in the coif of a Sacred Heart nun, to which she responded with an emphatic 'No!' Now her brother Frank, to whom she was very close, guessed what was preoccupying her thoughts and said, 'Surely you are not thinking of shutting yourself up in a convent away from us all? We would never see you again except through a grille, and Freddie will be rolling by in her carriage and pair. You are not made to be a nun.'[18] She agreed and assured him that she would never be boxed up in a convent, that she could do good in the world without becoming a religious. But in her heart there was a little niggling doubt, so she had a talk with her retreat director. He assured her that she did not have a vocation to the religious life, and the matter ended there. 'Much water flowed under the bridges till I heard the call again – and then it was unmistakeable.'[19]

If she did not have a religious vocation, she decided, then the only way to live life to the full was by being a dedicated laywoman. Most mornings she took a short cut across St Stephen's Green to attend early Mass at University Church, and she was faithful in attending the Children of Mary meetings in the Sacred Heart Convent in Leeson Street. She got to know Mary and Josephine Plunkett, daughters of her father's friend, Horace Plunkett. Mary and Josephine were involved in all sorts of good works in Dublin, and soon Frances was accompanying Josephine every week to the Royal Hospital for Incurables, as it was then called, in Donnybrook. Then she started going along on her own to sing for the patients. This led to some teasing at home, her brothers claiming that the number of vacancies for patients had increased as a result of her singing. Frances would have been aware of the fact that her father was a Life Governor of the hospital, one of its few Catholic governors.

The Royal Hospital has changed radically since the days when Henry Owen Lewis and Frances visited there. Founded in 1743, its original charter defined its purpose: 'To diet, lodge, clothe and maintain poor persons who are afflicted with disorders, declared by qualified medical authority to be incurable, and to supply them with medical and surgical assistance, medicines, and all manner of necessaries, without fee or reward.'[20] Nowadays the Royal Hospital has a much wider focus and caters for a totally different clientele.

Possibly one reason why Frances felt confident enough to sing for the patients in the Royal Hospital was that after coming to Dublin she had resumed her singing classes, this time under a Signor Negroni, a well-known Dublin maestro. Believing that her voice had been developed too early, he limited her singing to the mezzo-soprano range. However, this injunction did not prevent her from using the full register when asked by her friends to sing at parties.

Balls tended to be held in private homes in those days, and Frances attended several. Her social life seems to have been pleasantly full. One event in which she participated was a bazaar in aid of Jervis Street Hospital, held at the Royal Dublin Society. The bazaar, called Araby, consisted of stalls representing different Eastern countries and the stall attendants were dressed in corresponding native attire. It was the social event of the season and many prominent Catholic women had stalls. Frances was invited to help Mrs James Power of Leopardstown Park who was in charge of the Japanese stall. Sixty years later she was reminded of the occasion when, on a wall in Jervis Street Hospital, she saw a photo of herself 'with a babyish face', dressed as a Japanese.

Frances and her mother also visited the Royal Dublin Society

grounds in Ballsbridge for the Spring Show. The chief attraction
for Mrs Owen Lewis was the display at the Irish Industries
Association stall, especially the lace, because she herself had
helped to initiate a small lace industry in Co. Monaghan to help the
Owen Lewis tenants.

Life became quite hectic when Cyril and Freddie joined the
family in Dublin in early 1893. Even though Freddie was only
sixteen, too young to be a debutante, she revelled in parties and
could never have enough of them. The spacious house in Upper
Merrion Street, to which the family had moved from St Stephen's
Green, meant that they could entertain on a large scale. They held
a number of Saturday-night 'Cinderellas', so called because the
dances were supposed to end at midnight. Frances's father was
insistent that they should end on the stroke of twelve, if not earlier,
so that nobody would have an excuse for being late for Sunday
Mass.

Every morning Frances and Freddie attended Mass in the chapel
at the south side of Merrion Square. In his old age, the priest who
had been chaplain at the time, shared with Frances his memory of
seeing two young women tearing down Merrion Square almost as
fast as his own bicycle. In those years the chapel belonged to the
Daughters of the Heart of Mary, who had come to Dublin from
France in 1872. With Cardinal Cullen's approval, they had established Perpetual Exposition of the Blessed Sacrament, being the
first group to organise Perpetual Adoration in Ireland. In 1905 the
Sisters of Marie Reparatrice took over the Merrion Square convent
and chapel of the Daughters of the Heart of Mary, continuing their
apostolate of Perpetual Adoration.

One of Frances's best friends at this time was Angela Corbally,
who often stayed overnight with the Owen Lewis girls. In return,
Frances and Freddie sometimes stayed with her in the Corbally
home, Rathbeale Hall, Swords. There they had opportunities to
attend some big race meetings because Angela's father, who
owned prize-winning racehorses, brought the girls along. It was at
such a race meeting at the Curragh that Freddie first met and lost
her heart to John Chevers of Killyan, Co. Galway. He came from

a well-known family of landed gentry in Co. Galway and as heir to the family property was considered a highly desirable match. Freddie's parents were stunned when he asked for her hand: she was only sixteen years. Her father objected, urging that she first finish school, but her mother, knowing Freddie's personality and popularity, felt that an early marriage might be the best thing for her.

The wedding took place in the Brompton Oratory, London, on 23 January 1894, feast of the Espousals of Our Lady and St Joseph, the feast on which Frances had received her First Holy Communion eleven years earlier. Bishop Butt of Southwark officiated. In 1888 when he was Auxiliary Bishop of Brighton and Arundel he had confirmed both Freddie and Frances. The Bishops of Elphin and Emmaus were also present. The guests, several of whom were titled, could have comprised a select Who's Who of British and Irish society of the 1890s. As was customary, the fashionable ladies' journals of the time carried detailed accounts: what the bride and her bridesmaids wore, the bouquets carried, the bridegroom's gifts to the bride and her attendants, the bride's going-away outfit when she and her husband left for their honeymoon on the Riviera. These wedding accounts also referred to Freddie's connection with King George V of Hanover, noting that among her lavish wedding gifts was a set of gold and silver spoons from HRH the Princess Friederike of Hanover.

Freddie's marriage made a big change in Frances's life. John Chevers, realising his young wife's inexperience, and very likely prompted by her, had asked Frances to accompany them on their homecoming to Killyan. They travelled by train to Ballinasloe, where a carriage and pair awaited the arrival of the master and the new mistress. Along the ten mile route to Killyan they were cheered on by groups in the different villages. Then, near Castle ffrench a large gathering of John Chevers's tenants had assembled. They expressed their welcome by unharnessing the carriage and pulling it themselves.

When they reached the house the old steward, Pat Kelly, read an address of welcome which included a long account of the history of the Chevers family. The Killyan branch owed their origin to a Sir William Chevre, an Anglo-Norman who had come to Ireland with Strongbow and settled in Wexford at a place called Killiane. The headquarters of the family was Monkstown Castle, Co. Dublin, given to them by Strongbow. Because of the Rebellion of 1641 they lost their lands in Wexford, Meath and Louth. Finally, on 16 December 1653, Walter Chevers of Monkstown Castle, together with his family and servants, was ordered to proceed to Connaught. The Cromwellian Settlement of Ireland gives the reason: 'He was a Catholic, and an Irishman and was, moreover, guilty of another crime: he had a fine house and estate.'[21] He and his servants built Killyan House, Co. Galway, originally a thatched dwelling, also a small chapel nearby. Over the years the thatched house had been replaced by a more substantial building, and in 1872 Michael Chevers, John's father, had added a modern facade with cut stone steps and pillars on either side of the front door.

From her brief experience of managing the household in Brighton, Frances was now able to help her sister in her new role of châtelaine, so that she would not lose too much face with the Chevers's elderly housekeeper. She also accompanied the newly married couple to many parties in their honour hosted by the neighbouring county families, the ffrenches, D'Arcys, Grattan-Bellews and others. After three months her mother recalled her to Dublin. A plan was afoot. Mrs Owen Lewis was so pleased with Freddie's marriage that she was arranging what she considered an equally suitable match for her elder daughter. While Frances had been busy enjoying herself in Co. Galway, her mother had been working hand in glove with the mother of a certain eligible Catholic man, heir to a large estate. 'I was quite in love with the mother,' Frances remarked, 'but indifferent to the son, whose attentions I had hitherto managed to avoid'.[22] Dismayed at the turn of events she appealed to her father who took her side and assured her that he would never give his consent to a marriage she did not want.

To prevent embarrassment to the young man and his family, Frances then went abroad again, advised by her doctor to take the waters at Bad Schwalbach in Germany. She was accompanied by her former governess, Mademoiselle Mayer, who had left the teaching order and was preparing to enter Carmel. They went on many long walks together and one day came across a small poorly-decorated Catholic chapel. Frances immediately decided to remedy the situation by painting an 'Ecce Homo', which she presented to the chapel. While Mademoiselle Mayer approved of the painting she looked less favourably on the fact that Frances was going riding with two German officers, though Frances assured her that 'the attraction was equine and not masculine.' Yet, well into old age Frances remembered both men's names.

On her return to Ireland nothing more was said about marriage, but the social merry-go-round continued. Catholic society in Ireland at this time, the late nineteenth century, was an elite world all its own, consisting of families like the Lambert-Butlers, Fitzgerald-Kennys, Corballys, Barneses, McDermots, Martins, Deases and ffrenches. Frances could hardly keep up with all the invitations she received that winter season in Dublin. 'It was a worldly existence which effaced to a certain extent the spiritual life which had appealed so sweetly during my years at the Sacred Heart Convent. Decidedly, I persuaded myself, I am meant to remain in the world.'[23]

After Freddie's first child Frieda was born in May 1896, Frances went down to Killyan again to join her mother who had been there for the baby's birth. At her sister's request she stayed on for some weeks. Her brother-in-law John Chevers also welcomed her company on his walks around the property. She helped him exercise his thoroughbreds and enjoyed galloping through the parkland and over the stone walls of Co. Galway. For all this, John Chevers rewarded her with a mount. Family tradition has it that on occasion she acted as Joint Master of the hunt with her brother-in-law.

Soon after her return to Dublin in the early autumn of 1896 Frances, in her own words, met her destiny. This is how it happened. Mrs Corbally of Rathbeale Hall, Swords, her friend Angela's mother, had organised a house party for the Horse Show. Frances, who by this time was a friend to all the family, was invited. It seems to have been a lively occasion. Besides dances every

evening in the large hall or the long dining room, there were many
less formal events: pillow fights and sponge fights, and all sorts of
practical jokes played on the unwary. Frances was part of it all. But
there was one guest considerably older than the others who preferred to look on with amusement, though he did show his enjoy-
ment by his hearty laughter. During the first few days of her visit
Frances saw little of him, though she heard from her friend Angela
that he was Sir Alfred Moloney, Governor of British Honduras, a
widower. He had been invited because one of the Corbally boys
was his aide-de-camp. But Frances soon saw that there was another
unspoken reason for the invitation: Mrs Corbally was hoping to
arrange a marriage between Sir Alfred and her eldest daughter,
May. However, one evening Mrs Corbally sent Frances in to dinner
with Sir Alfred and she found him a fascinating dinner partner.
Unlike her usual partners who expected her to share their interests
in horses and dogs Sir Alfred was a man who could talk on any
topic.

On the last morning of the house party Mrs Corbally asked
Frances why she was ignoring Sir Alfred Moloney. Amazed, and
hoping that she had not seemed impolite, Frances replied that she
thought he was practically engaged to May. Mrs Corbally then told
her that it was she, not May, to whom Sir Alfred was attracted.
Somewhat startled by this unexpected turn of events, Frances said
her goodbyes and left to rejoin her parents, who had returned to live
in London.

When her father heard about Sir Alfred Moloney, he showed his
strong disapproval of her marrying someone who was twenty-five
years her senior. But Frances insisted that this made Sir Alfred all
the more attractive: 'at last I had met one to whom I could look up
for his qualities of intellect and heart, and as an outstanding
Catholic.'[24] One Saturday morning after her return to London, Sir
Alfred Moloney called to visit Frances, and eventually caught up
with her praying in the Lady Chapel of the Jesuit church on Farm
Street. There, before Our Lady's altar, they became engaged. That
afternoon he asked her parents' consent. Frances's father relented
when he saw how happy she was, and her mother was immediately

captivated by Sir Alfred's courtesy and attractive personality.

May Corbally's disappointment did not last long because she was soon betrothed to an Irish peer, Lord ffrench, a much more distinguished match in the eyes of Irish society. She and Frances remained lifelong friends, although Frances was closer to May's sister, Angela, whom she invited to be one of her bridesmaids.

However, there was no word yet of the wedding. Sir Alfred had suggested postponing it until he should be posted to a healthier location; he did not want to expose Frances to the unhealthy climate of British Honduras, where his first wife Constance Knight had died of yellow fever two weeks after her arrival in the country. Consequently he decided to return alone to British Honduras, but before leaving he brought Frances to visit his only child, Gladys, a boarder in the Sacred Heart Convent, Roehampton. Just six years old when her mother died, at nine years of age she went away to boarding school. In the meantime she had been living in England, cared for by her mother's family and her father's two sisters, Kathleen and Eileen Moloney. Now, at the age of eleven, she was to acquire a new mother. Much to Frances's joy, Gladys took to her at once and even told her Aunt Kathleen that her father was a very lucky man. He was aware of that too, and tried to bridge the miles between himself and his future bride by his frequent letters. 'Spontaneously written, they showed a depth of character, a sincerity of purpose, a pure and warm affection which served but to deepen the bonds between us.'[25]

Mrs Owen Lewis was in her element as she prepared for her daughter's wedding. Frances herself was pulled in two directions: she was deeply in love, yet she felt totally unfit for the position she would be assuming as a colonial governor's lady. Her mother, she remarked wryly, would have shone in such a position, for which she now tried to prepare her daughter. Encouraged by her mother, Frances agreed to take up some courses at the university, though she got more satisfaction from the classes she had resumed for the factory girls of East London. There she taught French and dancing, as well as what she vaguely called 'more worldly pursuits'. 'The long months of waiting,' she said, 'were sweetened by the daily

round of Holy Mass and a little pilgrimage to Our Lady's shrines
at the Oratory.'[26]

Finally, in January 1897, the long-awaited news came: Frances's
fiancé had been appointed Governor of the Windward Islands in the
West Indies. This was promotion. It also meant that he could now
bring his future bride to live in a healthier climate than that of
British Honduras. He wrote to tell her that he would soon come
home on short leave, asking if it would be possible to have the
marriage then because he would have to take up his new appointment after Easter. Frances and her family understood Sir Alfred's
situation and were happy to agree on an early date for the wedding:
2 March 1897. Invitations went out and each day Frances prayed
that Jesus and Mary would be at her wedding. Her old friend and
spiritual director, Father Leslie SJ who had prepared her for her
First Communion, now prepared her for the sacrament of matri-
mony. Her mother, as would be expected, added 'some wise
counsels'.

The morning of 2 March 1897 dawned sunny but cold. Frances
and Alfred met at the altar rail of Brompton Oratory where both of
them received Communion. It was then back home where the
faithful Becker fussed over Frances as she helped her into her bridal
attire. At least four of the fashionable women's journals of the day,
The Gentlewoman, *The Lady*, *Lady's Pictorial* and *The Queen*
reported this society wedding in great detail, listing all the illustrious guests as well as those who officiated. Bishop Butt of Southwark who had married Freddie again performed the ceremony,
assisted by four priest friends of the family, including Father Leslie
who preached. If Freddie's guest list sounded like a society Who's
Who, Frances's was even more so. Among those present were the
Dowager Duchess of Newcastle, her mother's friend, and the
Dowager Lady Rossmore, a relative of her father's, together with
over twenty other titled couples. The Anglican Bishop of Honduras
and his wife Mrs Ormsby were among the guests. However, at a
fashionable wedding it is the bride and her bridesmaids who are the
focus of attention. *The Lady* described how they looked on 2 March
1897:

The bride, who was given away by her father, was dressed in rich ivory duchesse satin, the front of the skirt being embroidered in pearls, and edged with a cascade of Carrickmacross lace, made in the schools on Mr Owen Lewis's estate in Monaghan; her bodice was finished with revers, embroidered in pearls, and edged with the same lace, with vest and long sleeves of gathered chiffon, ornamented with bunches of orange-blossoms; her long Court train of white brocade was lined with silk, and turned back at the left corner with bunches of orange-blossoms and bows of chiffon; she wore a wreath of orange-blossoms and long tulle veil, and carried a magnificent bouquet of orchids, white lilac, and orange-blossoms.[27]

The five bridesmaids were Angela Corbally, Margaret Petre, Clare Fortescue, Isabella Jimenez and Eileen Moloney, Alfred's sister. They were dressed in white Irish poplin trimmed with Carrickmacross lace, with sashes of St Patrick's-blue. All wore gold brooches set with pearls in a design of roses and shamrocks, a gift from the bridegroom, and they carried bouquets of pink tulips and lily-of-the-valley also provided by him. The best man was Sir Joseph Turner Hutchinson and the groomsmen were Frances's three brothers and Alfred's two aides-de-camp. Recalling the occasion in her old age, Frances's memories were still vivid:

> To the strains of the Wedding March I came down the church with Alfred who looked remarkably handsome in full uniform and decorations. Many friendly hands stretched out to greet us. The dear factory girls from East London had turned out in force to congratulate us. The second largest tier of the wedding cake was specially reserved for their delectation.[28]

Frances and Alfred honeymooned on the Riviera, where Mrs Harvey Lewis, a cousin of Frances's father, owned a villa at Monaco, between Nice and Menton. Recalling the occasion many years later, Frances could say, 'The beautiful sunshine over land and sea was emblematic of the happiness given us by God.'

Two weeks before Easter they were back in London, preparing for their departure. Alfred had bought a handsome carriage for which John Chevers provided 'two fine Galway-bred horses'. This meant that Frances had the joy of bringing her mother for many drives during their last days together, a rare treat for someone who for financial reasons could seldom enjoy such luxury. Frances recalled many years later how her heart ached to think that she could enjoy all this while her mother 'was reduced to bus rides and to doing without other comforts to which she had long been accustomed.'[29] Fittingly, their last day together was Good Friday. At the ceremonies in Farm Street both of them broke down and had to leave the church.

THREE

Life in the West Indies

'At last I had met one to whom I could look up for his qualities of intellect and heart.' This was how Frances Owen Lewis many years later recalled her first impression of Alfred Moloney, an impression that was reinforced and enhanced throughout the sixteen years of their married life together.

What kind of a person was this forty-eight-year-old widower who captured the heart of twenty-three-year-old Frances Owen Lewis? At first sight she would have seen a handsome well-built man of military bearing, with keen eyes and heavy dark moustaches. His physical appearance and presence would have conveyed the assurance of someone who had reached the peak of an eventful career, begun in the army and culminating in the British Colonial Service. When Frances first met him he was Governor of British Honduras, in line for further promotion, and with the expectation of eventually acquiring the Governorship of Hong Kong, regarded at the time as one of the more prestigious postings in the Colonial Service. He had been knighted in 1889: he was now Sir Alfred Moloney. This would have been an added attraction, if not to Frances, then certainly to her mother.

Cornelius Alfred Moloney, to give him his full name, was born into an army family in 1848. His father, Patrick Moloney from Croom, Co. Limerick, had enlisted in the 67th Regiment (Foot) in 1840, and had served in North America, England and Ireland before his marriage in 1847. His regiment was stationed in Cork at the time, and he was one of a company detached to Skibbereen. He had arrived in Ireland in December 1844, a matter of some months before the potato blight, then sweeping across Europe, had struck Ireland. Skibbereen was one of the places worst affected. *The Illustrated London News* carried weekly reports of the dire famine conditions there and in Schull. In the winter of 1846 and in early 1847 it noted that government relief supplies in West Cork were administered by the army.[1] That may explain the presence of a company of the 67th Regiment (Foot) in Skibbereen in 1847.

Patrick Moloney's marriage in 1847 very likely took place in Skibbereen, or elsewhere in Ireland where he had served during the preceding three years. Much research into army and parish records has failed to produce evidence as to where precisely he was married and to whom. The headquarters of his regiment in Winchester does retain documentation on officers of the period, but not on enlisted men. However, family tradition maintains that Patrick Moloney's wife was also Molony (spelled without the 'e'). Moreover, she may have been connected with the well-known Molony landed gentry of Kiltanon, Co. Clare, because in later life her eldest son used the coat of arms of the Kiltanon Molonys, and 'Kiltanon' was the name of a favourite horse.

Five months after his marriage, Patrick Moloney set sail with his regiment for Gibraltar where he served for the next three years. At the time his wife was four months pregnant with her first child Cornelius Alfred Moloney who, in later life, consistently claimed Ennis as his birthplace. This would seem to indicate that Patrick Moloney's wife did not accompany her husband abroad on this particular posting. Many army wives did, but the more common practice was to stay at home in accommodation provided by the army.

On 1 June 1853, when he was serving with his regiment in the West Indies, Patrick Moloney transferred to the 1st West India Regiment, which had its headquarters in Barbados. Very likely the prospect of promotion was the motive behind this. In 1858, at Nassau in the Bahamas, he was promoted regimental sergeant major and shortly afterwards he was given a commission and the office of quartermaster. After nineteen years in the army he was now Captain Moloney.

As a commissioned officer he was able to get his eldest son Cornelius Alfred into Sandhurst, the British academy for training army officers. He could also benefit from the reduced scale of fees available for the sons of military officers. Consequently, Gentleman Cadet Cornelius Alfred Moloney enrolled in Sandhurst on 1

February 1866, and left to join the 1st West India Regiment exactly one year later. Young Moloney's Sandhurst records show that he received two decorations of merit in his first term and three in the second. His conduct was noted as 'Exemplary' and his progress in study 'Very good'.

Evidently he had a good academic foundation before entering Sandhurst. In Walford's *County Families of Great Britain and Ireland* it is stated that Cornelius A. Moloney was educated at 'Ennis College, Co. Clare.'[2] There was a well-known classical school in Ennis at the time, run by two laymen, and the Irish Christian Brothers also had a flourishing school, established in the lifetime of their founder.[3]

During Cornelius Alfred Moloney's time at Sandhurst his father was stationed in the West Indies. Consequently, the young man's end of term reports were sent to his guardian, a certain C. Moloney Esq. It was C. Moloney who was notified by Sandhurst on 12 December 1866 that Gentleman Cadet C.A. Moloney had satisfactorily completed his two terms in Sandhurst and that he now qualified for a commission in the army, though not 'without purchase'. This meant that if his family could not purchase a commission for him he had the option of returning for a third term to compete again for a commission 'without purchase'.

Purchasing commissions was a feature of British army practice up to 1871. It seems to have existed as far back as the reign of Edward VI. An officer had to purchase his original commission, and he paid for every step of subsequent promotion. Often a rich man might command a regiment before the age of thirty, while his seasoned captains and subalterns would grow grey in the lower ranks. It was a system which led to many abuses and to an ever-widening gap between the men in the ranks and the officers, who treated their regiments as 'a lounge they had taken on lease'.[4] Small wonder that all sorts of ruses were resorted to in order to raise money to purchase a commission. There was a recognised auction room for purchasing commissions in Charles Street, London, where competition was often keen. It is alleged that close to the time when Cornelius Alfred Moloney was hoping for a commission, a cavalry lieutenant-colonelcy was purchased there for as much as £18,000.[5]

Even at a much lower price, Captain Patrick Moloney, who by now had four other children, could not afford to buy his son a commission. Back in London from the West Indies, and preparing to rejoin his regiment then serving in West Africa, he wrote in early January 1867 to the Adjutant General of the Horse Guards, Lord Poulet, making a strong case for his son to be given a 'commission without purchase' in Patrick's own regiment, the 1st West India or, failing that, in any other of the West India Regiments. He, Patrick Moloney, would be able to get him his outfit and his son could then accompany him on his return to the regiment. 'It would be a great benefit for me in not sending him back to Sandhurst for the third term for which he is eligible, having to provide a home in England for four young children during my term of service in the Western Coast of Africa.'[6]

His request was acceded to and on 16 January 1867 Cornelius Alfred Moloney was granted an 'ensigncy without purchase' in the 1st West India Regiment.

In March 1867, Cornelius Alfred Moloney set sail with his father for the West Coast of Africa, both of them wearing the colourful uniform of officers of the 1st West India Regiment.[7] The greater part of the next three years was spent in Sierra Leone and the Gambia. Soon after they arrived in Sierra Leone, Cornelius A. Moloney was made acting civil commandant. Evidently the army authorities even at this early stage recognised his gift for administration. In 1870 the entire regiment crossed the Atlantic and until 1874 served in Jamaica, Nassau and Honduras.

In 1874 he set sail from Kingston, Jamaica, with the expeditionary force that invaded Ashanti territory (Gold Coast), and managed to dictate terms of peace. After the Ashanti campaign he became private secretary to the Governor of the Gold Coast. He held various administrative offices in the Gold Coast: Acting Auditor, Acting Inspector-General of Constabulary, Colonial Secretary. After he moved into full-time colonial administration he ceased to be a member of the army. Very likely he sold his commission, because he is not mentioned in later years among those on army pensions.

On 28 December 1881 he married Constance Thomson Knight, daughter of William Clifford Knight, Russian Consul at the Cape of Good Hope, at the Roman Catholic chapel in Richmond, Surrey. At the time, the bridegroom was thirty-three years of age and the bride twenty-one. On the marriage certificate the bridegroom listed as his profession, 'Late Army Captain'. Moreover, he signed himself 'Alfred' Moloney, dropping 'Cornelius'. It was by this name that he was to be known henceforth.

Shortly after the marriage, Alfred Moloney and his bride set sail for Lagos where Alfred had been Acting Governor since 1879. From 1884 to 1886 he was Administrator of the Gambia. In 1887 he became Governor of Lagos and he held that post until he was appointed Governor of British Honduras in 1891.

During his years in West Africa Alfred Moloney got involved in what was to become for him a lifelong interest: the detailed study of the botanical and agricultural resources of the different colonies in which he served. This was with a view to helping the local people build up their economy, and ultimately for the benefit of the British government. Even if there were no people to be helped, or no British government to benefit from his exertions, it would seem likely that a person of his calibre would still immerse himself in this work which expressed a vast curiosity about God's world, as well as an optimistic cast of mind which could find potential riches in all living things. No wonder this man could fascinate a woman like Frances Owen Lewis.

He wrote various articles and papers on natural history. His *magnum opus*, modestly called *Sketch of the Forestry of West Africa*, in reality far more wide-reaching than its title suggests, was published in London in 1887 to commemorate the jubilee of Queen Victoria.[8] This bulky volume of 533 pages is a huge compilation of useful information about the different plants and products grown in the British colonies of West Africa. Alfred Moloney's dedication of the book to his wife, Constance, is of interest because of the light it throws on both of them and on their relationship.

This work, which monopolised much of its Author's spare time that should otherwise have been devoted to her society, is gratefully dedicated to one of the best of women and the most devoted of wives, who, during its preparation, generously supported him by her consideration and self-sacrifice, and shared conjointly the hope that it would prove of some advantage, in the direction of the enlightenment and progress, to the people of West Africa for whom chiefly it has been put together.[9]

One of the most interesting chapters is that on coffee. In it we find how abhorrent the whole concept of slavery is to the author: he hopes that 'through the instrumentality of the bean of Liberia' former slaves and children of slaves will be welcomed home to their rightful inheritance, no longer in the power of others but as free labourers.

In this book, Alfred Moloney refers several times to botanical specimens he has sent home to Kew Gardens over a period of many years, and to the establishment of botanic stations in key centres of the West African colonies. A series of letters in the Kew library archives bears witness to the fact that he had a highly satisfactory ongoing relationship with successive directors of Kew Gardens. In a typical letter he refers to samples he has sent home of locally made cigars, rum made from mango, and chocolate together with the beans used. He encloses drawings of orchids – those drawing classes in Sandhurst were not wasted – and refers to some thirty or more specimens of orchid he had already sent to Kew. Another letter recommends that one of his staff be sent to Cairo to study methods of growing cotton, which could then be implemented in the West African colonies. He was also interested in a proposed scientific expedition to Kilimanjaro, and wrote to Kew recommending a young doctor who had worked with him on the Gold Coast, on some botanical projects.'He indulges in photography,' he wrote, 'and carries about with him the necessary appliances – no small factor in estimating his worth on an expedition as is contemplated.'[10]

The last of the series of Moloney letters in Kew library was written on 23 September 1892 from British Honduras, on black-bordered mourning paper headed with the family crest and motto of the Kiltanon Molonys: *In Domino et non in arcu meo sperabo* (I will put my hope in the Lord and not in my bow). Alfred Moloney was still mourning his wife Constance who had died of cholera within a year of his posting to British Honduras in 1891. With this letter he sent some dried leaves of an Australian tree for identification and classification.

An official printed report in the Kew archives from the same year, 1892, paid tribute to Alfred Moloney's botanical work:

It is satisfactory to find that Sir Alfred Moloney is adopting similar steps in British Honduras to those he inaugurated at Lagos with regard to developing the botanical resources of the Colony. Whilst Governor of Lagos, Sir Alfred Moloney took considerable interest in the subject, and was the author of several works giving detailed information regarding the agricultural resources of the Colony, and I hear that an important work bearing upon the botanical and agricultural resources of British Honduras may before long be available for those who are interested in the progress and development of the Colony.[11]

Alfred Moloney was obviously a man who had earned a place among the most distinguished in the field of botany and horticulture. So well known had he become that many years later he was given an entry in Ray Desmond's *Dictionary of British and Irish Botanists and Horticulturists*.[12] The biographical entry lists his publications, and also refers to his founding of the botanic station in Lagos, and to the fact that Kew Gardens contains plants and economic products which he contributed.

The tribute paid him in the Kew Gardens Report of 1892 referred to a forthcoming book on British Honduras. However, no book on the scale of his tome on West Africa, came out of that experience. Perhaps one reason was that his wife Constance was no longer at his side to encourage him. Some years later, however, when he was Governor of Trinidad, he did publish a short pamphlet called

Reminiscences of My Work and Wanderings in British Honduras.[13]
This short account expresses a warm affection for the people of
British Honduras which Alfred Moloney did not experience to the
same degree in subsequent postings. He found British Honduras

> ... a Colony of intense interest and considerable promise, one
> for which I shall always have a very soft corner in my heart, for
> I owed and owe much to its kind, generous and loyal people, as
> well as to the sympathetic attention and generous support it was
> my good fortune and privilege to enjoy from all classes during
> my administration of its affairs, the fortunes and further progress
> of which I shall always follow with the deepest interest, having
> been so intimately and so long directly associated with its
> history.[14]

Throughout his years in the colonial service, music was another
of Alfred Moloney's interests, in particular the tribal music which
was so much part of life in the West African colonies. And, being
Alfred Moloney, he liked to share his enthusiasms. Consequently,
on 15 November 1889 we find him reading a paper to the members
of the Manchester Geographical Society, with the title, 'On the
Melodies of the Volup, Mandingo, Ewe, Yoruba, and Houssa
People of West Africa'. Rhodes House Library has a copy of this
paper which was later printed in the Manchester Geographical
Society's journal.[15] This is just one of many papers on African
tribal music which Alfred Moloney read to interested groups in
England.

This particular paper on the melodies of the people of West
Africa has several interesting features. It reveals the writer's keen
appreciation of music as well as his meticulous research. Interestingly, Alfred Moloney had a violinist at hand to play the airs as he
referred to them, because only the violin or the cello could produce
the 'peculiar intervals' of tribal music, such as diminished or
increased flats or sharps. As in his other writings, Alfred Moloney
shows his familiarity with Shakespeare and has some apt quota-
tions. He ends his well-researched paper with the music notation of
the muezzin call to prayer.

For many a person in Alfred Moloney's position the temptation would have been to sit back and enjoy the privileges of high office, perhaps with the help of the 'fire-water' he sometimes castigated. But with his many interests and abilities he lived life to the full, his endlessly enquiring and keen mind enriching not only himself but his own and future generations. In some senses he could be called a later-day Renaissance man, with his military training, his experience of colonial administration, his meticulous and practical interest in botany and horticulture, his economic projections for the benefit of the British Empire and its dependents, his interest in archeology and geology, in tribal customs and tribal music, even in a scientific expedition to Kilimanjaro. At home in the classics, the Latin terminology of flora and fauna posed no problem to him, and he had Shakespeare at his fingertips. His compassion for the underprivileged was a consistent theme in his writing, also his abhorrence of slavery and of what could diminish people, his efforts to guide those under his jurisdiction towards economic self-sufficiency and, finally, the respect with which he treated them. Frances Owen Lewis judged wisely and well when she said, 'At last I had met one to whom I could look up for his qualities of intellect and heart.' Now, with this man at her side, she sailed into the unknown.

On their long voyage across the Atlantic Alfred Moloney would no doubt have talked to his young bride about his previous life and his many postings. His favourite of these had been British Honduras (now called Belize). He carried with him many memories, both happy and sad of this place where he had enjoyed such rapport with the people and had experienced their loyalty and support, but where, on the other hand, his wife Constance had died so tragically.

British Honduras was the westernmost British possession in the Caribbean. Located on the eastern coast of Central America, it is bounded by Mexico to the north and west, and by Guatemala to the south and the remainder of the west. Its eastern frontier is the Gulf of Honduras. A British colony from the year 1862, it achieved full independence as recently as 1981, and now ranks as a sovereign state within the British Commonwealth. Once called, 'Little England in Central America', it was one of those colonies which never developed its potential as fully as had been hoped; steady economic decline had set in since the days when it carried on a lucrative trade in mahogany with Victorian England. Alfred Moloney noted that in his day the Cunard liners plying between Liverpool and New York were all panelled with Honduras mahogany, also the dining room of the Savoy Hotel, 'that attractive and dazzling centre for giddy London society'.[16] He was full of hope for the future of this British possession, which he believed showed considerable promise, but these hopes were not to be realised.

His future now lay in the Windward Islands towards which he and his young wife were sailing closer each day. This was Frances's first time to cross the Atlantic, with which her husband was so familiar. As a young lieutenant in the British army he had served in the Bahamas, from 1871 to 1873. And as Governor of British Honduras he would have travelled back and forth to London on official business and for occasional furloughs.

Frances has left no record of her first voyage across the Atlantic, but for someone with her great love of nature it must have been a fascinating experience, especially when they came in sight of the Windward Islands. This chain of islands runs along the eastern rim of the Caribbean Sea, rising spectacularly from the ocean. In Alfred Moloney's time the Windward Islands comprised St Lucia, St Vincent, Grenada and the Grenadines, a chain of about six hundred small islands, not all of them occupied or cultivated, stretching between St Vincent and Grenada. (In the 1970s St Lucia, St Vincent and Grenada became independent republics within the British Commonwealth, and the Windward Islands ceased to be a collective political entity.)

Grenada, the southernmost of the Windward Islands, was the seat of government and journey's end for Alfred Moloney and his new bride. As the steamer sailed into port at St George, the chief town on the island, he would have shown her, high up on the hill overlooking the harbour, a large white house with verandas. This was Government House, the Governor's residence where Frances would make a home for Alfred and herself, entertain on his behalf, and preside in her own right over the many functions it would be the lot of the Governor's lady to become involved in. She would not have been human if she had not felt some apprehension in the face of the daunting task ahead of her symbolised by the large house on the hill. She was barely twenty-four years of age, a total stranger to the complexities and politics that are part of colonial life, beginning married life with a man twenty-five years her senior, a widower, and with the expanse of the Atlantic between her and her family and friends.

As the steamer drew into dock the extraordinary strangeness of her surroundings must have swept in on her: the crowds and the noise and an unusual pungent aroma, which she later discovered was nutmeg. It was nutmeg that gave Grenada the name, 'Isle of Spice'. It had become the chief crop of the island after slavery was abolished and the sugar plantations in Grenada, as elsewhere, had begun to decline. To give the newly-emancipated slaves a crop, which they could grow easily on their small plots of land, a local doctor had introduced nutmeg from the Portuguese East Indies. Today nutmeg and mace (the outer covering of the nut) are the island's chief exports. So important to the economy is nutmeg that it is featured on the national flag, replacing the Union Jack that would have flown from all the important buildings in St George to greet Governor Moloney and his wife.

A salvo of guns announced their arrival, and there on the quayside was a welcoming party of government officials and a guard of honour which Alfred was called on to inspect. All the while Frances was being inspected by the officials' wives and the curious Grenadians, who had never before seen a Governor's wife looking so youthful or so stylishly dressed. A parade of carriages escorted them to Government House. Sixty years later Frances remembered her first delighted impressions:

A hill at the back of the house was ablaze with colour: purple bougainvilleas, the vivid red of the bois immortelle and golden oleander. It was all so thrilling and enchanting, I felt in fairyland. In the garden hummingbirds buzzed like bees, parrots and brilliant hued butterflies alighted in and out among the flowers. Everything was delightful, and I thanked God for so much beauty and happiness.[17]

The artist in Frances would have revelled in all this wealth of beauty and colour. It is not surprising to hear that while in the Windward Islands she designed a stamp for the colony. Her step-grandson Paddy Stephenson remembers seeing it, but all he can remember is that it was blue in colour and large. Perhaps it featured one of those aspects of natural beauty that enchanted her so much when she first arrived at Government House.

But the stamp came later. Her immediate concern was learning how to cope with her official duties as Lady Moloney, consort of the new Governor. Some elderly wives of members of the Governor's Council were all set to advise and instruct her. However, Alfred insisted on her taking her rightful place as the Governor's wife. There she sat nervously at the head of a table acutely conscious of all the older and more experienced women in the group. Listening with courtesy to their opinions she shared hers tentatively, though she deferred a final judgement until she had visited the place under discussion – a poorhouse for indigent Creoles – and seen for herself the facts of the case. She found it 'in a deplorable condition of repair and cleanliness'. With Alfred's consent she decided to produce a pageant to raise funds for the necessary improvements. Her timing was good. Rehearsals had begun on the pageant, based on the life of Columbus, when her brother Frank arrived in Grenada to be Alfred's aide-de-camp. (One wonders if the reason for this appointment was to provide some family companionship for Frances.) Some years earlier Frank had discovered that he had a unique gift for directing amateur dramatics. He now put the finishing touches to his sister's production, which ran for several nights and brought in more than the amount needed to make the poorhouse liveable.

Within a few months of their arrival in Grenada Frances accompanied her husband on a horseback tour of the island. Even though Grenada could not be called large in terms of land area, being a mere 133 square miles in extent, still this journey was a physically demanding venture. It meant several tiring days on horseback, negotiating difficult, often mountainous terrain, sleeping rough at times on camp-beds in some remote police station, meeting strangers, dealing with business that awaited the new Governor at their many stopping places. Many a Governor's wife would have taken the easy option of staying at home and leaving all this to her husband. But not Frances. An experienced horsewoman, she could cope with physical discomfort and impromptu meals for the sake of being with Alfred and in the hope of getting to know the place and the people under his jurisdiction. To her delight she found that the rest of the island of Grenada was even more beautiful than what she could see from Government House.

This first official visit was important. It put the relationship between the Governor and the people on a good footing. According to Frances, 'Alfred's charming personality and genuine interest in the people won all hearts.' He had a special concern for the poor, and to help them he saw to it that taxation on many of the smaller native houses was abolished. He also introduced legislation to improve the quality of housing and to provide a proper water supply. There was a certain amount of opposition to all this, especially from the powerful descendants of the early colonists, but eventually he overcame their prejudices and fears.

The next official visit was to the neighbouring island of St Vincent. This time they travelled in comfort on a warship which had been put at the Governor's disposal. They sailed by the Grenadines, that chain of small islands some of which almost touch one another, and put in for an hour at Cariacou, the largest. There they were given a liturgical welcome by the local priest, who had never before met a Catholic government official, much less a Catholic governor.

Unlike most of the other islands in the Caribbean, St Vincent's had not been colonised by either Spain or France. It was a British possession developed by English colonists. Because of this, it differed from most of the West Indian islands in being almost entirely Protestant. People were surprised to see the new Governor and his wife visiting the small wooden Catholic chapel. The Church of England and other Protestant groups had more imposing places of worship. When Frances and Alfred attended Sunday Mass in the little Catholic chapel in Georgetown, much to their embarrassment, the priest drew attention to their presence, speaking of the good example given by the new Governor.

One afternoon Alfred and Frances set off with some local officials to look at the fortifications overlooking the harbour. On the way they stopped at the government leprosarium, part of Alfred's responsibility. Soon after they arrived, it began to rain. A suggestion was made that Frances should stay there under shelter, while the men continued their climb up to the fortifications. Frances was dismayed. She would far rather have braved the tropical rain than waited in what she called, 'the foetid atmosphere of that charnel house'.[18] The lepers crowded around her, touching her with their disfigured hands. Some of the faces were almost eaten away. She made an attempt to comfort them, but inwardly she was terrified. Eventually, after about an hour, the official party returned. As a result of the visit, the government built more hygienic quarters for the patients and organised better care. Frances never forgot that visit, or her subsequent reaction.

> The horror of this my first sight of leprosy was so great that on arriving home I burnt every stitch of my clothing, even to a smart Parisian hat, all part of my trousseau, and took a bath of disinfectant. Years to come brought with them more grace and more courage.[19]

Many years later she comforted a young Sister, who confessed to a similar revulsion when she first encountered leprosy, by sharing with her her own impulsive reaction.

Apart from her experience with the lepers, the rest of the time in St Vincent was one triumphal journey. Arches of palm leaves and flowers were set up all along the route. Planters and local people presented addresses of welcome and also petitions to which they hoped the new Governor would be willing to accede.

During this visit to St Vincent Frances almost lost her life, and in a second incident both she and Alfred were in real physical danger. When they were crossing a swollen river on horseback, Frances's horse lost its footing and was being carried downstream with Frances clinging to its mane. Frantic with anxiety, Alfred could only look on helplessly. Fortunately, horse and rider were swept against a tree or a rock which blocked the turbulent flow of the river and they were able to scramble up the river bank.

It was when they were visiting the mountain called Soufrière, with its active volcano, that the second incident happened. Alfred and Frances had decided to climb the peak on mules, guided by a muleteer. However, instead of going by the safer, longer route, they chose a shorter way which, after an easy beginning, turned into a narrow pass and soon into a mere ledge of slippery rock. They were unable to turn back because the trail by now was too narrow. On one side was straight rock and on the other a 2,000 foot precipice. One turn led to the next; the mules were struggling and slipping and then finding their footing again. Alfred kept calling out to know if Frances was all right and she, though scared, kept assuring him that she was. 'One could but trust blindly to God's Providence; the Father's Hand was leading us.'[20] Finally the mules staggered to the top ledge. 'Thankfully the thought of God's mercy was borne in on us. His power and protection have been evident in a similar way all through the varied events of life.'[21]

Nothing was growing in the vicinity of the huge crater. The place looked dead and desolate. And then out of nowhere a golden macaw flew past, filling the barren place with beauty. Her heart 'in hiding stirred for a bird', and nothing would do her but to get one of those rare and most beautiful of birds to take home on their first furlough. In 1902, when Alfred was Governor of Trinidad and St Vincent was no longer under his jurisdiction, Soufrière erupted, devastating a third of the island and killing two thousand people. Frances must have recalled the crater that she almost did not live to see, and she may have shuddered when she realised the violence of that sleeping beast. She may have wondered too if the species of the golden macaw had been extinguished by the violence of the eruption – if its bright light was quenched.

After leaving St Vincent, Alfred and Frances spent a night at Barbados with some friends. During their short visit they met many people with Irish names, descended from those sent there from Ireland in Penal times. Barbados, the most easterly of the Caribbean islands, was discovered by Columbus in 1502 and had been a British colony from 1627 onwards. Alfred and Frances Moloney found Barbados less interesting and less picturesque than St Lucia, their next stop.

'The weather was ideal, and the scene beautiful beyond description as we steamed into the splendid harbour of Castries, the capital of St Lucia.'[22] Frances and Alfred noticed several ships in the harbour, so they were not too surprised to find on arrival at Government House that a large party had come to welcome them. The Administrator, Sir Charles King-Harmon of Rockingham, Co. Roscommon, had put on a reception in honour of the Governor and the Governor's lady. Frances found this reception something of an ordeal: she was not yet at home in her new role. When she entered the long reception room dressed in her wedding gown, and faced the welcoming line of officials and other important people, she felt like disappearing through the floor. But Alfred whispered in her ear that she should not look like a frightened fawn. She then pulled herself sufficiently together to face the guests with equanimity.

Next morning Alfred and Frances visited the local convent of the St Joseph of Cluny Sisters to find out the time for Mass.[23] The Sisters were delighted to discover that the new Governor and his wife were Catholics. Their visit was recorded in the five-year report submitted to the motherhouse in Paris.

Sir Alfred Moloney visited with his wife; they were Catholics and as this was the first time a Governor had been seen in a Catholic Church, they were given a great public 'HURRA' after Mass. This was during the summer holidays, so he promised to come when school re-opened. He [later] visited first St Mary's College [a training school for Catholic teachers], then the Primary School and last the Convent. He was conducted in to 'Rule Britannia' on the piano in duet form.[24]

This was not the first time for Frances and Alfred to meet the Sisters of St Joseph of Cluny. Alfred had met Sisters of the same congregation during his years in the Gambia, and he and Frances were glad to meet them again in Grenada. Sometimes after Sunday Mass in St George, Alfred and Frances visited the Sisters and enjoyed a cup of tea in the convent. They were impressed by the quality of education in the Sisters' schools, and they appreciated the admirable work they were doing in Alfred's jurisdiction, both in Grenada and St Lucia. Their provincial at the time was an Irishwoman, Mother Milburge Walton from Tipperary. She resided in Trinidad but would have met the Moloneys on her regular visits to the Grenada community.

While Sir Alfred and Lady Moloney were chatting to the Sisters in Castries, Archbishop Flood OP arrived. The Irish prelate and the Irish Governor would have much in common, but, as this was an official visit for both of them, they agreed that His Grace should visit one side of the island while the Governor toured around the opposite side. 'Between the two dignitaries,' Frances Moloney commented, 'every turkey and chicken must have died in St Lucia that week!' Archbishop Flood was the fifth Archbishop of Port of Spain (Trinidad). His jurisdiction covered a vast area, including the Windward Islands. Like Mother Milburge he too would have met the Moloneys whenever he visited Grenada. Later, when Sir Alfred became Governor of Trinidad and Tobago they were in more frequent contact.

But on this occasion the Archbishop headed off on horseback in one direction, and the Moloneys also on horseback took a different route. After finishing their tour of St Lucia, Frances and Alfred returned to Grenada for the winter. Then the social round began. A number of visitors arrived, personal friends, and others carrying letters of introduction from the Colonial Office. The recently appointed Governor of Trinidad and his wife, Sir Hubert and Lady Jerningham, stopped off on their way to Port of Spain. And the Hon. Rupert Guinness spent a while with them, recuperating after a serious illness. They lent him one of their Irish horses.

The house was full of visitors when Frances experienced her

first earthquake. Not realising the danger, she was one of the last to leave the house and join her guests assembled in the garden. What they were experiencing was a massive earthquake, whose epicentre was Venezuela to the west of the Caribbean Sea. It destroyed much of Caracas and left thousands homeless. Consequently, in his first months as Governor, Alfred Moloney was called on to launch a rescue operation to help the afflicted people of a neighbouring country. Soon another natural calamity was to hit his own territory: in September 1898 a hurricane practically devastated the Windward Island of St Vincent. Many houses were thrown into the sea, hundreds of people were killed and forty thousand left homeless. Many years later Frances recalled the experience:

> Alfred, as Commander-in-Chief, sent for a man-of-war, and organised immediate relief. Shiploads of food were brought to the starving people whose crops had been completely destroyed. By cruiser we travelled to St Vincent … Scarcely a house had escaped; the churches, with the exception of the Catholic church, were all down. The Catholic church became a hospital, and any other building available was used for the wounded. Lady Thompson [the Administrator's wife] had already initiated relief work and I gladly seconded her efforts. Together we set out every morning after breakfast and worked the whole day, with a few sandwiches for our midday meal.[25]

Appeals sent to English newspapers were responded to generously. Frances's brother Frank who had come out to be Alfred's ADC was put in charge of reconstructing a large area of the island which had been almost totally devastated. 'Sheltering in a log cabin of his own construction, he depended for nourishment on whatever supplies we could send him, and dealt out food and materials to the survivors of this gigantic disaster.'[26] Alfred was given due recognition for his heroic work for the survivors of this disaster. And he, in turn, rewarded Lady Thompson, the Administrator's wife, by having a royal honour bestowed on her. This was something that Frances refused to accept. She felt strongly that it would not be right for her to receive worldly honour for performing a corporal work of mercy. Years later she said that many of her experiences in the West Indies were a preparation for her future life on the missions. When she first experienced calamities such as major earthquakes and devastating hurricanes, she was still a young woman in her twenties, yet she showed the same heroism then as she was to show many years later in China. It cannot have been easy, and it left an indelible impact:

> The heat was intense, an undefinable odour of death and disease pervaded the island. Corpses were discovered hidden under the fallen trees. In one place a man's head severed from his body had been carried a mile distant by the whirlwind. We were all run-down and suffered from boils as a result of the poisoned atmosphere.[27]

When some degree of order and normality returned to the inhabitants of St Vincent, Frances and Alfred sailed back to Grenada. Alfred now applied for a six months furlough. They were busy preparing to leave when they were called upon to entertain an unexpected visitor: Erskine Childers had just arrived in the West Indies, having travelled by slow cargo boat from Liverpool to the Caribbean. At the time he was Clerk of the Commons, living in London with his sisters. Much of his early life had been spent with his Barton relatives in Co. Wicklow, where his love of Ireland had been nurtured. After this visit to the West Indies he fought in the Boer War, which seems to have transformed him from being an entrenched Tory into a Liberal. Later he became active in the cause of Home Rule for Ireland and in July 1914 he and his wife were involved in the Howth gun-running. Still he fought again for Britain in World War I. On demobilisation in 1919, he and his family came to live in Ireland where he immersed himself in the republican cause. In March 1921 he became Dáil Éireann's director of publicity and in October he was appointed chief secretary to the Treaty delegation. Afterwards he opposed the Treaty and fought with the republicans in the ensuing civil war. Captured by Free State troops on 10 November 1922, he was court-martialled. He was executed on 24 November 1922.

Exactly twenty-four years earlier, on that same date, 24 November, he wrote home to his sisters from Government House, Grenada, describing his travels in the Caribbean in 'one of the little negro-manned sailing vessels which ply a humble and precarious trade between the islands'. As a skilled sailor himself he found the experience entertaining. It was like 'a party of children out for a frolic, without any question of a serious commercial venture.' He described the warm hospitality he was experiencing, though he admitted that he found the formality of Government House under Sir Alfred Moloney somewhat off-putting: 'It is too grand and respectable and you have to wear stick-up collars which in the tropics are absurd.'[28]

Years later Frances recalled the visit of Erskine Childers and remembered that while in Grenada he was writing a book. He may well have been working on *The Riddle of the Sands*, for which the inspiration had come to him while sailing in the Baltic the previous year. He was a young man of twenty-eight years when he stayed with the Moloneys in Grenada. Many years later Frances met him again in Glendalough, Co. Wicklow, not long before his tragic death.

All the pressures on Frances during those months in St Vincent, caring for the hurricane victims, had taken their toll, and she was depleted both physically and emotionally. A diary kept by the Sisters of St Joseph of Cluny in Grenada has the following entry for 1899: 'Departure of Sir Alfred and Lady Moloney to Europe for a change, the latter being in ill health.' They left from Barbados. The first few days, full of happy anticipation, were most enjoyable. Then suddenly they were in the midst of a raging cyclone. It was a terrifying experience for the passengers. Alfred, in his concern for Frances, had her chair tied to a pillar in the saloon, and there she remained holding on, rosary in hand. The captain realising that they were in grave danger – no ship could weather such a storm – wisely changed course. Frances's distraught parents were waiting at Southampton, not knowing what had happened, when the ship eventually arrived some days overdue.

As soon as they had gone through the usual formalities, Frances and Alfred crossed over to Ireland where Frances's parents had rented a large house in Bray for the summer. Called Galtrim, it overlooked the sea. This large mid-nineteenth-century house, with its seven bays and two stories over a basement, was large enough to house not only the Owen Lewis family, but also the Chevers, Freddie's family. The extensive grounds with two tennis-courts gave the children plenty of room to play. Alfred's little girl Gladys was home on holidays from her school in England; Arthur too was in Ireland on leave and Frank, who had been Alfred's ADC, was able to spend some time with his young son and daughter. It was a joyful family reunion, the last time that the whole group would be together. Before they met again as a family, Frank had died in action in South Africa and Frances's mother had passed away suddenly and unexpectedly. It was good that they had this happy time together to look back on.

There was much good-humoured fun and chaffing, a lot of it caused by Frances's brother, Arthur. He sometimes composed funny verses to amuse the children. One day his father challenged him to find a word to rhyme with Roehampton and, to tease Gladys, he at once came up with the following:

> There once was a girl at Roehampton
> Whose feet were so large they got stamped on.
> For such a small body, said good Mother Oddie,
> I never saw such feet at Roehampton!
> When she walked in the grounds at Roehampton
> Which an army of troops might have camped on
> There was no room for the others
> So the Sisters and Mothers
> Had to send her away from Roehampton.

He was referring to the fact that Gladys had survived only two years in the Sacred Heart Sisters' school in Roehampton. Boarding school was evidently a traumatic experience for this motherless nine-year-old little girl. After leaving Roehampton she studied in another convent school and fared little better. Later her father would bring her out to stay with them in the West Indies, but this

time, after her long happy holiday in Galtrim with the family, she
returned to school in England. The rest of the party dispersed and
Frances and Albert returned to the Windward Islands.

On Good Friday of the following year, 1900, Frances and Albert
were on the island of St Lucia, when suddenly Frances felt
overwhelmed by feelings of sadness. A few hours later she was
handed a telegram. She knew instinctively that her mother had
died. Alfred accompanied her to the church and together they made
the Way of the Cross. Evidently Mrs Owen Lewis's death was
unexpected, the result of influenza. When Frances and her husband
got back to Grenada letters awaited them from Frances's father,
giving the sad details. Freddie also wrote. At the time she was
expecting her third child. Overcome with grief she begged Frances
to come home and stay with her until her delivery. Alfred was
reluctant to let Frances travel on her own, but realising Freddie's
precarious condition he eventually gave in. Frances stayed with her
sister until she had recovered from the birth of the new baby.
Afterwards there was time for a short holiday with her father at
Boulogne-sur-mer before she embarked again for the West Indies.

FOUR

The Land of the Green Bay Tree

In December 1900 Alfred Moloney became Governor of Trinidad and Tobago, and he and Frances moved southwards from Grenada the Island of Spices, to Trinidad the Land of the Humming Bird. In 1889 Trinidad and its adjoining islands, together with the much smaller island of Tobago, were united as one administrative unit, though physically, historically and culturally they are completely different entities. Trinidad geographically is an extension of Venezuela which is only eleven miles distant, and the mountain range which crosses the island is a continuation of the Andes. Tobago, situated between Grenada and Trinidad, is geologically closer to Grenada and the other islands of the Windward group than to Trinidad.

Their histories too are different. Trinidad was discovered by Columbus in 1498 and remained Spanish until seized by Britain in 1797. An earlier attempt had been made by Sir Walter Raleigh in 1595 when he burned down the then capital San Jose de Oruna, and reputedly caulked his boats with tar from the Pitch Lake near La Brea. The Dutch raided the island in the early eighteenth century, and the French later in the same century. In the latter years of the eighteenth century the Spanish began to encourage foreign settlers, and many French arrived from Haiti and elsewhere as a result of the French Revolution.

When the English seized the island in 1797 they imposed an English Governor on a country with Spanish laws, more or less run by French people. There were many people too of African origin, brought in as slaves, though slavery existed for a relatively short time in Trinidad, not much more than half a century. After it was abolished in 1834 Indian contract workers came in as agricultural labourers and many of them settled permanently. Because of the racial variety, Archbishop Desmond Tutu in our time could call Trinidad 'The Rainbow Country'.

In contrast to the relative stability of Trinidad, the island of Tobago changed hands thirty-one times between the Dutch, French, Spanish and English, before it was joined to Trinidad at the end of the nineteenth century. Up to then it was hard to determine who, if anyone, had a valid claim to ownership. English, Dutch and French periodically raided the island, wrecking each other's fortifications, and the island was a welcome haven for pirates. There are those who claim that Daniel Defoe had Tobago in mind when he wrote *Robinson Crusoe*. Over the years it became a typical sugar-and-slave colony. It was recaptured by the British from the French in 1793, and remained in British hands until independence in 1962. By the end of the eighteenth century the population had grown to 15,000, of whom 94 per cent were slaves. The abolition of slavery put the whole sugar industry into crisis. This came to a head in 1884 when the London company, representing over half of Tobago's sugar estates, collapsed. In 1889 the British Colonial Office made a decision which was unpopular in both Tobago and Trinidad: to combine the two islands into one state.

Obviously, it was no easy task that faced Alfred Moloney when he took on his new appointment as Governor of Trinidad and Tobago. It was promotion, of course, and he and Frances were pleased about that. As one of the higher ranking appointments in the colonial service it carried a salary of £6,000 a year. (The equivalent in today's terms would be approximately £420,000.) Other emoluments were also attached to the office. But Frances has said that if the salary were three times as much, Alfred in his boundless generosity would have spent it all: he was hospitable to a fault. Ships of various nationalities put in at Port of Spain and the officers could always count on a warm welcome at Government House. Local society too had to be entertained: British officials and their families, and old established colonists, together with immigrants who had made good in their respective spheres. Frances found the official receptions and the viceregal pomp trying, especially the fortnightly at-homes. 'One's arm ached after shaking hands with a thousand people and again on the departure of our visitors.'[1] Nor did she enjoy sitting in state in the Governor's landau, being drawn by four horses with outriders through the fashionable Queen's Park savannah. She preferred to rise early, before dawn, and go on horseback to some distant village in time for early Mass.

She liked to go on expeditions with Alfred into the interior. 'I think we penetrated further into the jungle than any other officials had attempted. Alfred, having served many years in Africa, had the instincts and techniques of an explorer and I was young enough and keen enough for any kind of adventure.'[2] She and Alfred undertook a long trek through virgin forest to find the place where some early Spanish missionaries had been captured and killed. They also visited the famous Pitch Lake at La Brea, associated with Sir Walter Raleigh, from which asphalt has been exported to the United States and to several European capitals. The lake is 148 acres in extent, the world's largest natural asphalt lake. Frances and Albert would have also seen some early drilling for oil. Oil would later become the mainstay of the country's economy, putting into second place what in their day were the principal cash crops: sugar cane, citrus fruits, cocoa and coffee.

Frances took up Spanish, so as to be better able to communicate with the evergrowing number of non-English-speaking Venezuelan immigrants, as well as with the rank and file of Trinidadian citizens. A fluent French speaker, she had no problem in communicating with the descendents of former French colonists. She enjoyed the scenery and the fabulous wild life in both Trinidad and Tobago and found Tobago especially enchanting, more exotic than Trinidad. 'Flights of parrots passed over our heads and the funniest little monkeys swung on the trees. Birds and butterflies of brilliant hue darted through the air, while a musical hum of insects filled our ears.'[3] It is recorded that there are four hundred species of birds in Trinidad and Tobago, and six hundred species of butterfly. The tiny and beautiful humming-bird which features on the country's coat of arms was a particular delight, as was the rare scarlet ibis.

It was an idyllic setting, and Frances and Alfred might have enjoyed it for many years if they had not come up against bigotry and misunderstanding soon after their arrival. Their predecessors

had not survived long either. Alfred was a Catholic and an Irishman, representing a Protestant sovereign in a British colony. That
did not endear him to a certain section of Trinidadian government
officials. It was also unfortunate that soon after their arrival Alfred
and Frances were put into a situation which served to deepen these
people's distrust. In January 1901 Queen Victoria died. The
shutters were drawn in Government House and Albert and Frances,
dressed in mourning, received those who came to tender their
official condolences. The Protestant Bishop announced a memorial service to be held in the Protestant Cathedral. Alfred consulted
Archbishop Flood about attending this service in his official
capacity, but the Archbishop refused to give a dispensation. Consequently, while the bells of the Protestant Cathedral were inviting
people to the official service, Alfred and Frances drove to the
Catholic church to pray for the Queen.

Next day the local papers had blaring headlines denouncing the
Governor and calling him as well as Archbishop Flood 'disloyal
Irishmen'. Each day more and more abusive letters appeared in the
papers. But the Anglican Bishop of Trinidad, Bishop Hayes, soon
put a stop to that: he wrote to the papers saying that Sir Alfred
Moloney as a Catholic could no more take part in a Protestant
religious service than he, Bishop Hayes, could attend a Catholic
service. To some extent the tumult died down. But already signa-
tures had been collected and a complaint had been forwarded to the
Colonial Office in London. Alfred was asked to furnish an explanation, which he did, saying that as a Catholic he had gone to the
Catholic church, but that he had been represented by the Colonial
Secretary and by his ADC at the memorial service. This explanation satisfied the authorities but some lingering prejudice remained.

A few months later Frances went to Barbados to meet her young
cousin, Katie Lewis, who had been invited out to Trinidad to be her
companion. As soon as they met aboard the steamer Katie informed
her that she thought that one of her fellow passengers, Captain
Willis, was going to propose to her, and she introduced him to
Frances. Thinking that this might be no more than a shipboard

flirtation, Frances made light of it until she saw that the young man was in earnest. She agreed that he might visit Katie in Trinidad in a month's time, which he did. He and Katie became engaged and planned an early marriage in Trinidad. Both of Katie's parents were dead, so she asked Frances as the only relative at hand to give her away. However, Katie was a Protestant. Once again it meant approaching Archbishop Flood. This time he was more accommodating. He gave his permission, provided that Frances would not take part in the service. She just walked up the aisle with the bride on her arm.

She now had to turn elsewhere to find the companion she needed. She said of herself: 'I had never completely overcome my feeling of shyness in dealing with a crowd of strangers. This must have been trying to my husband, who was more social minded, so after Katie's departure on her honeymoon, we decided to invite another girl friend who would help me to do the honours.'[4] They thought of Angela Corbally, a close friend of Frances for many years and one of her bridesmaids. It was at the Corbally home, Rathbeale Hall near Swords in Co. Dublin, that she had initially met Alfred. Matthew Corbally, Angela's brother, had been Alfred's ADC in Honduras.

Angela Corbally was delighted at the prospect of spending the winter in Trinidad, and she arrived out in due course. Soon Frances had another romance on her hands. Angela was a very attractive young woman and before long there was a dramatic increase in the number of naval officers visiting Government House. Two months after she arrived a letter came to Frances from the young Commander of the Fleet, Reginald Tyrwhitt, asking her to bring Miss Corbally to tea on his ship, together with the daughter of the Governor of Barbados who happened to be visiting Trinidad at the time. As soon as tea was over he took Frances aside, telling her that he was in love with Angela and asking her help. She pointed out that Angela was a Catholic and that her family might well object on that score. He assured her that he would never interfere with Angela's practice of religion.

Returning on the launch that evening, Angela would hardly

speak to Frances, annoyed with her for monopolising 'the nicest man on board'. However, when she discovered the reason, she was embarrassed because even though she liked Commander Tyrwhitt she was not sure if she wanted to marry him. Frances helped her to make up her mind by giving a dance to the fleet due to sail a few days later. Shortly afterwards Angela and Reginald Tyrwhitt became engaged, subject to the consent of Angela's parents. This was given. The marriage was a very happy one, and Frances became godmother to their only son with whom she corresponded throughout her long life. Angela's husband eventually became Admiral of the Fleet.

Early in May of that year, 1901, the volcanoes of Soufrière in St Vincent and Mont Pele in neighbouring Martinique began to erupt. The rumblings could be heard even in Port-of-Spain, and volcanic ash fell from the skies. A warship steamed into the harbour to see if they were safe; a rumour had gone out that Trinidad had been destroyed in an earthquake. The ship's commander told them of the total destruction of the town of St Pierre in Martinique, a town of forty thousand inhabitants. Alfred left on the warship with some officials, priests and emergency supplies, leaving Frances to organise accommodation for the survivors.

She got busy and saw to having all the spare rooms in Government House prepared, as well as a vacant chalet in the grounds. She also organised a collection of clothing and food for the refugees. When these arrived they had sad stories to tell. Some had lost family members; all had lost their homes. Frances was glad that she had so much clothing ready. 'Every article of clothing had to be supplied to these poor refugees whose garments were burnt into holes. As I combed out the girls' beautiful long hair, whole tresses came away, having been singed at the roots.'[5] The refugees stayed in Trinidad for some months until accommodation could be prepared for them in Martinique. As well as caring for their physical and psychological needs, Frances characteristically did all she could to help them spiritually. 'We were able to get every one of them back to the sacraments,' she recalled.

Things returned to normal after the refugees left. Those first

months in Trinidad had certainly been a baptism of fire for both
Frances and Alfred. Now they had time for more congenial pursuits. They visited St Joseph's Convent in Port-of-Spain. The
school records took note of the occasion: 'We have a new Governor, a Catholic and an excellent Christian. On June 4th, 1901, the
Governor assisted at the School Prizegiving ceremony. The Lady
Governor sent six lovely prizes – five of them worth about 30 francs
each.'[6] The new Governor was also invited to the convent school
in Arima.

> The Governor assisted at the school Prizegiving and was accom-
> panied by Lady Moloney. Lady Moloney received the ladies of
> Arima in our house while the Governor received the men in the
> town. Afterwards he came to the convent with his entourage. He
> complimented the children and the Sisters – spoke highly of our
> Sisters whom he knew in Africa and elsewhere and said they did
> great work. He congratulated the people of Arima on having
> Sisters of St Joseph of Cluny and said it was a real blessing for
> them.[7]

Frances was glad to be able to give some time to Alfred's
daughter Gladys who arrived in Trinidad around this time. As was
noted in a previous chapter, she was finding school life difficult.
Consequently, her father decided that the best thing would be to
bring her out to Trinidad where she could continue her studies
under the care of a governess. She was a high-spirited girl, not yet
sixteen, and she threw herself whole-heartedly into the social life
of Government House. This was not exactly what Alfred had in
mind. Frances said that he tried to 'moderate the young girl's
buoyant spirits'. Inevitably there were clashes, because both were
strong-willed people. Frances found herself often acting as peace-
maker. She was fond of Gladys, whom she regarded as her own
child, and was sorry when in the early spring of 1902 Gladys
returned to England with her governess. It was a consolation to
know that she and Alfred would join her before long. They were
unable to travel with her because of the forthcoming celebrations
in honour of the coronation of King Edward VII which were

scheduled for 26 June 1902, more than a year after the King's accession.

To honour the occasion, Frances asked Archbishop Flood to preside over a solemn High Mass in the Catholic Cathedral, which the Governor and his entourage would attend in state. (This time nobody would have any criticism to make about the Governor's loyalty or co-operation.) Frances, who in earlier years had taken part in many theatricals, helped to organise a pageant representing scenes from the lives of the seven English kings who bore the name Edward. The festivities had already started on 24 June with a huge garden party and gymkhana in the grounds of Government House when a telegram came saying that the coronation had been postponed until 9 August because the King was gravely ill.

Because everything was in place for the celebrations, and in good hands, Alfred applied for leave and he and Frances arrived in England in time for the coronation. After the ceremony in Westminster Abbey, while Frances waited for her carriage she found herself shivering in her light evening dress. She and Alfred crossed over to Ireland that night and by the time they reached Killyan she had a high fever. The Chevers's family doctor Dr French of Ballygar diagnosed malaria, a common tropical illness usually accompanied by an intermittent fever. Alfred Moloney himself had a serious bout of malaria while he was Governor of British Honduras but, as far as is known, this was Frances's first experience of what can be a highly debilitating illness. She would not have been totally recovered when she and Alfred returned to London.

On their arrival she was dismayed to see how much her father had aged since his wife's death. He was living alone with a few faithful servants; none of his family were close at hand. The articles and reviews he was writing for *The Tablet* and other Catholic papers were not enough to fill the huge gap left by his bereavement. Once again Frances found herself planning a marriage. She remembered her mother's old friend, Louise von Robendorff; she knew that her father liked Louise and that they had many interests in common. So she invited her to visit. Before long she saw the friendship between her father and Louise blossom into love, and she was not surprised when one day her father asked her what she thought about his remarrying. She assured him that all his children would like to see him happy, enjoying the congenial companionship he needed. Before she left to return to Trinidad it was arranged that the wedding would take place quietly the following spring.

On 27 February 1903 Henry Owen Lewis married Louise von Robendorff in a quiet ceremony in the Servite church on Fulham Road, London.[8] He was sixty years old and Louise was forty-seven. Some weeks after the wedding Frances's father wrote to her telling her how happy he was: 'God has indeed been most merciful to me. He has rolled away the load of sorrow which like a heavy stone lay upon my heart, and has given me the love and devotion of a sweet and holy woman, who is indeed a helpmate for me, and of whom I am not worthy ... May this marriage, which He himself arranged, bring us both nearer to Him, in time and eternity.'[9] Frances must have smiled, knowing her own part in the arranging.

What kind of a person did Frances choose for a stepmother? She could only choose someone whom she liked and admired, a deeply religious person like her father. From early childhood Louise von Robendorff had been brought up in different convents of the Society of the Sacred Heart: in Paris, in Blumenthal (Holland), and in Roehampton (London). The Roehampton school records have the usual entry confirming her date of entrance as a boarding-pupil, the date she left, and anything of note regarding her school-days. It records the fact that she was a boarder in the Paris Convent of the Sacred Heart at the age of four, and that she had been 'adopted' by the foundress, Mother Madeleine Sophie Barat. In that delightful book called *Happy Memories of a Saint*, Pauline Perdrau RSCJ talks about two children brought to the Sacred Heart Convent in Paris when they were mere infants.[10] One of them was Louise von Robendorff.

According to the Roehampton records Louise's guardian, who paid her school fees, was Charles Duke of Schleswig-Holstein-Sonderburg-Glucksburg. Both he and Louise were related to Queen Alexandra of England. When Louise married Henry Owen Lewis, the Queen sent her a beautiful diamond pendant as a wedding gift.

But this is to anticipate. As a little tot in the Paris Convent of the Sacred Heart, Louise was one of Mother Barat's favourite children and, while she was a pupil in the junior school, she was one of the privileged few invited on Ascension Thursday 1865 to a final meeting with her a few weeks before her death. She stayed on in the Paris Convent of the Sacred Heart until November 1869, when she left for the Sisters' boarding-school at Marienthal in Germany. In 1873 a decree of expulsion was announced and the community were given six months to leave. Consequently, Louise went to another Sacred Heart school, Blumenthal in Holland, and finally to Roehampton in London. She was now nineteen years of age and had already completed her secondary education and some years of finishing school. She was a gifted pianist, so it is likely that as well as helping to improve her English her two years in Roehampton would have made it possible to further her education in music. The well-known Mother Henrietta Kerr was headmistress at the time. She and Louise became lifelong friends. It was Mother Kerr's brother, Father William Kerr SJ, who officiated at Louise's wedding twenty-eight years after she had left Roehampton.

After setting the wheels in motion for her father's marriage Frances was now free to introduce her stepdaughter Gladys to London society. To prepare her, she brought her along to make a retreat being given by Father Bernard Vaughan SJ. However, Gladys made no attempt to keep the silence required and the much-sought-after retreat director sent her home. Frances left with her, hoping to shield her from her father's displeasure. In this she was not altogether successful. Not unduly upset, Gladys set about enjoying the social life of London. She loved parties, and went along happily with her parents when they were invited to a banquet and ball at Windsor Castle. Frances took her responsibility for Gladys seriously, and the young woman seems to have accepted this, realising how deep was her stepmother's affection. One day, to Frances's surprise, she said, 'I love you, Mother, because you do not always let me have my own way!'

Entrusting Gladys's social life to her Moloney aunts, Frances and Alfred left again for the West Indies and by early autumn of 1902 they were back in Trinidad. A new Colonial Secretary arrived, Sir Hugh Clifford, who was to be a good support and a loyal friend to Alfred in the ensuing months. As Governor, Alfred was faced with some major problems. The first was in connection with the newly discovered oilfields, which were to become the source of Trinidad's later prosperity. The government saw the need to put extensive financial resources into their development. That meant that there was less money to cope with the more immediate problem of the organisation and administration of a proper water supply for Port of Spain.

There was a reasonably good water supply already, but it was unequally distributed. The rich enjoyed it in abundance; some even had swimming pools in their homes. The poor had to fetch their own water, often from a distance or from a communal pump. In an attempt to control wastage, the government imposed a tax based on the amount of water used. The wealthy citizens of Port of Spain banded together in opposition. Many of them were members of the Rate-Payers Association (RPA), which had been formed in 1901 by influential businessmen to safeguard the rights of Port-of-Spain rate-payers who had no elected representation since Joseph Chamberlain, Secretary of State for the Colonies, had abolished the borough council in 1898. The leaders of the RPA resented the abolition of the borough council. Moreover, they were agitating to have elected members in the legislative council. Only 185 rate-payers were members of the RPA but they were able to mobilise support from the working class.[11]

One of the leaders of the RPA, a shrewd and influential businessman, saw a way of making money out of the situation. He offered to sell, at an exorbitant price, some land he owned beside a natural reservoir outside the city. Governor Moloney declined the offer; there was equally suitable public land that the government could use. This led to some animosity. The frustrated businessman and his colleagues launched a campaign of lies and innuendoes which was taken up by the local press. Undoubtedly, it was all part of the growing opposition to Crown Colony government and in particular to the policies of Joseph Chamberlain. A public protest was organised for 23 March, the day on which the legislature was to debate the second reading of the Water Works Ordinance, adjourned from 16 March.

Looking back fifty years later, Frances said that 23 March 1903 had remained engraved on her memory as one of the darkest days of her long life. Assuring her that there was no need to worry, Alfred left that morning for Government Building with his ADC. What happened after his arrival is well documented.[12] Some years later Frances wrote her own account.[13] The report of the commission appointed by the Colonial Office to conduct a public enquiry also survives. Frances's account, shorter than the official report, conveys the atmosphere of that day: the apprehension of violence, the tension, the fear and anxiety that she and those with her in Government House felt for Alfred and the officials accompanying him. Frances's own personal courage on that occasion was outstanding. The first she knew of what was happening was when a terrified coachman galloped up the drive of Government House with the carriage horses, without the Governor's carriage. Rioting had started, he told her, and a mob had seized the carriage, had ripped out the lining, then had dragged it down to the beach and thrown it into the sea. The coachman had saved the horses and had only barely managed to escape. Immediately, Frances called for her horse, to go to her husband's help, but was forestalled by a message from him telling her to stay in Government House.

Archbishop Flood rode over to see if she was all right, and the Anglican Bishop Hayes phoned. Events quickly moved totally out of control and things looked ominous for Frances and her friends in Government House.

Bent on destruction, the unruly mob surged towards Government House shouting and screaming. 'Bring out the white woman. We will strip and scourge her.' Clutching my Child of Mary medal I prayed for help. There was a delay; the rioters stopped to set fire to a schoolhouse near our gate. At that moment the Marines marched up from a ship which had touched

port, accidentally. They fired among the crowd, but a few shots
– a few were wounded unfortunately and the remainder were
quickly scattered. That evening, after dark, Alfred arrived with
Captain Dutton, both dusty and dishevelled, and my poor
husband with blood on his face.[14]

The rioting lasted only one day. The following morning Bishop
Hayes 'who always remained our friend' called and suggested that
Frances should visit the injured in hospital with him. She decided
to go alone, bringing food for the patients. She asked one woman
why people had behaved like that to the Governor. The woman
replied that the Governor was a bad man because he wanted to
measure the water and not permit the poor to have any. 'It was the
other way,' Frances explained, 'he wanted the poor to have all they
wanted, for nothing!'

Two days after the rioting, 25 March the feast of the Annuncia-
tion, Alfred and Frances walked to Mass unaccompanied: Alfred
refused to have a bodyguard. A number of prominent businessmen
called to say how sorry they were that they had been influenced by
the organiser of the rioting. But already exaggerated reports had
been sent to the Colonial Office. A Commission was appointed to
set up a formal enquiry, and 295 witnesses were examined. The
investigation was completed by mid-October and a detailed report
was sent to the Colonial Office.

The sequence of events as given in the official report went like
this: On the morning of 23 March sixty-four police were marched
over from their barracks to Government Building, popularly known
as the Red House. The previous day the building had been secured,
leaving only two entrances, one for the Governor and his officials,
the other for those members of the public who had tickets. Some
belligerent members of the Rate-Payers' Association demanded
entry without tickets. When the police repelled them, they withdrew and held a meeting some distance away, inciting the people
to violence. While the draft Water Works Ordinance was being
read to the Legislative Council, a crowd gathered around the
building, singing and shouting so as to disrupt the proceedings. The

national anthem was sung, and 'Rule, Britannia'. The beating of tin pans and empty oil cans added to the commotion. Once again the people tried to storm the entrance, and again they were repelled. Then stones began to fly. By this time the crowd consisted of five or six thousand people. Bricks, stones and bottles were hurled 'with great rapidity, accuracy and violence.'[15] Everyone in the Council Chamber had to dive for shelter. The Governor was prevailed upon to seek shelter in the Education Office, where he would be safe from the attack; other officials joined him. It appears that they locked themselves in.

Early that afternoon Government Building was set on fire. The fire spread rapidly and soon reached the Council Chamber. The situation was desperate. Because it was impossible to communicate with the Governor, still in the Education Office, the Inspector General applied to the Colonial Secretary to authorise the reading of the Riot Act so that the crowd could be dispersed by gunfire if necessary. The necessary authority was given and the Riot Act was read from both balconies. But it had little effect on the stone throwers. Finally the police were ordered to fire on the crowd. The police seem to have got totally out of hand and, as a result, there were many fatalities.

The government claimed that sixty people were injured, of whom sixteen died. But the report of the commission of enquiry, set up by the Colonial Office, said that this was hardly credible in view of the fact that 471 rounds of ammunition had been fired that day. Besides those who died from gunshot wounds, the report alleged that four or five people met their death by bayonets, among them two women. On the other hand, official reports from the Governor, the Attorney General and the Solicitor General denied this. The commission of enquiry, whose members were biased against the Port-of-Spain government, for their part claimed medical evidence for the numbers of those killed and injured.[16]

Later accounts show that the commission's report was greatly exaggerated. Moreover, in focussing on the water problem only, the commission was in opposition to the Governor who believed that what was really at stake was the demand for representative government. Back in London, the Colonial Secretary Joseph Chamberlain accepted Moloney's point of view, and instructed him to see to the restoration of the borough council as a partly elected body.[17]

The chairman of the commission of enquiry claimed that if Governor Moloney had postponed discussion on the Water Bill until a full explanation had been made, and if he had acted more promptly in reading the Riot Act, he would have put an end to the trouble. It is easy to be wise by hindsight. In the actual situation many possibilities must have crossed Alfred Moloney's mind. The last time he was in a similar situation, during labour riots in British Honduras in 1894, he had been criticised by the Colonial Office because the administration had not confronted the workers' delegation. At that time he had written to the Secretary of State explaining the action taken:

> The presence of an armed force at the moment when the answer to their lawful petition was again read would either have so exasperated the crowd of labourers and others that bloodshed would have ensued – a result which it was obviously the duty of the government to endeavour to avoid, even at the risk of some display of turbulence – or else the armed force being on the spot would have pacified the crowd for the time being. But the result would have been dearly bought by evil effects more far-reaching and permanent than those which, it will be seen, have ensued. The crowd could very naturally have argued that the government was taking the part of the employers against the employes.[18]

The British Honduras rioting had fizzled out with no loss of life; a few shops were burnt and some ringleaders arrested. Alfred Moloney possibly hoped that something similar would happen in Trinidad. He did not gauge the gravity of the situation, or how it might develop. Reluctant to use force, he left the action to others, and again he had to carry the blame. Certainly he acted out of character in agreeing to lock himself into the security of the Education Office; on the other hand, he had implicit trust in the

Inspector General of Police, Lieutenant Colonel Brake. Unfortunately, Brake was also a member of the Legislative Council and in that capacity he was inside Government House attending the meeting. By the time the rioting started he was inside the Council Chamber where he could not personally supervise the details of police operations. In view of what happened, and in the light of the strong feelings that were being roused beforehand by the media, it would look as if the Inspector General should have been better prepared.

But it was Alfred Moloney who was blamed. The commission was clearly biased against him. A member of the commission had been to school with the chief instigator of the riot, and he had accepted his friend's interpretation of events. Frances, out of loyalty to Alfred, issued no invitation to the members of the commission until the chairman made it known that they would like to visit Government House, 'where they were solemnly entertained to dinner'. Frances's reaction was understandable and honest, but it may not have helped the situation. Both she and Alfred saw where the sympathy of the commission lay, and they were not surprised when the report more or less exonerated the Inspector General and put all the blame on Alfred.

One thing that the report made much of was Alfred's taking shelter in the Education Office:

It was the Governor's duty as the head of the Executive and Commander in Chief to remain at his post, and give the necessary orders to his subordinates despite the inducements of his friends to seek shelter and abandon his post, which although possibly one of danger, was also one of honour. Of the large number of persons who remained in the Council Room none were seriously injured, and this seems to show that the danger from which His Excellency was induced to seek the welcome shelter of the Education Office was more imagined than real.

Alfred was also blamed because the government was so slow in taking action afterwards against those who had led the rioting. Even though the Inspector General of Police took upon himself the responsibility for not proceeding against them, the commission ruled that the responsibility did not lie with him but with the executive government.

One of the recommendations that emerged from the enquiry was that Alfred Moloney should retire. 'He took the humiliation in his own great noble way,' Frances recalled, 'Not a word of discontent or disparagement escaped his lips.' The Colonial Office suggested that he leave at the end of January, but Alfred asked that the date of departure be postponed to the beginning of April or the end of March. Anything else, he felt, would play into the hands of the government's opponents. A further reason was that two British fleets were due in Trinidad in January, and the Governor could not entertain the admirals if he himself was in process of leaving. The Colonial Office granted the extension: 'We have already told him that it is desired to avoid any course which would enable the ungodly to rejoice.'[19] It was also made clear that, according to protocol, he should entertain the admirals, if he was still in the colony.

Alfred referred to the reason given for his retirement in a confidential dispatch to the Colonial Office on 2 December:

I note that while stating, for which I thank you, that you are satisfied that I have always discharged the duties entrusted to me with complete loyalty and to the best of my ability, you add that you are compelled to arrive at the conclusion that my action in the emergency which I was called upon to face was not characterised by those qualities of promptitude in decision and judgement which were to have been expected from a governor of my standing and experience. You add that you recognise that I have had exceptional difficulties with which to contend, and that I have been subjected to violent and unscrupulous attacks on my conduct for which there is no justification.[20]

He went on to say that the problems he had to cope with in Trinidad had been inherited; he had not created them. He had ample grounds for saying this. His predecessor had also found the situation intolerable and had taken early retirement. One difficulty

inherent in the situation was the colour question. 'This question,'
he wrote, 'enters into and poisons every phase of the life of this
Colony … the manifestations of feeling are in many respects very
subtle, very insidious, very deceptive, and misleading.'

On the part of the white population colour prejudice is very
strong – more especially among the members of the old Creole
families – but coloured men are not excluded from the clubs,
white men sit at table, transact business, play games of skill and
chance with them, and generally speaking meet them upon equal
terms. But here the line is drawn with great sharpness.The
association between the white and coloured people of good
standing in the community begins and ends with the intercourse
which subsists between the men of both races. All social
amenities between white and coloured women are forbidden.[21]

Alfred Moloney blamed prejudice against the coloured people
as the chief cause of all the problems in Trinidad, including the
rioting. The Water Bill only provided the occasion for turbulent
feelings to erupt. Perhaps it was his experience in Africa which
made Alfred so sensitive to the plight of coloured people everywhere. In that respect he must have been one of the more enlightened of Britain's colonial administrators. It was not enough for him
that white men and coloured could interact freely. He wanted a
similar situation to exist among the womenfolk of both races. Very
likely Frances helped to make her husband aware of the disparity
of treatment accorded to coloured women in Trinidad.

As Governor of British Honduras he had also come up against
racial discrimination, though in a less obvious form than in Trinidad. In a letter to the Secretary of State at that time he had written:
'I cannot but feel thankful that in every action of the Government
all distinction between colour and class has been studiously
avoided.'[22] More than ten years later, in the dispatch of 2 December
already referred to, Alfred Moloney could say:

As my own past record of service shows, I think, conclusively,
I have always felt the deepest sympathy with the coloured
populations whose affairs I have been called upon to administer,

and since my arrival in Trinidad, I have spared no pains to bridge over, as far as in me lay, the gulf which severs the coloured race from the white.

It is significant that the fifty-six-page report of the commission of enquiry makes no reference to the colour problem, but limits itself to the single incident of the rioting without analysing the underlying racial problem. In more ways than one it was an incomplete and biased report. When Alfred and Frances Moloney had heard who would constitute the commission they guessed rightly that their days in Trinidad were numbered. Although it was a full year before they were to leave, there was a sense of finality about those last months. Official functions and public receptions continued as formerly. It was not a happy time. Frances confessed that she found it hard not to show resentment towards those who had damaged her husband's reputation. 'When the wife of his chief enemy came to one of our public receptions I received her coldly, which was a mistake.'[23]

It was at this time that they got an invitation from the British Representative in Venezuela to visit that country. Alfred could not accept, but he urged Frances to go. It was a welcome respite after all she had gone through in the previous weeks. The remaining months in Trinidad passed quickly. Frances urged her husband to economise because of the possibly lean years ahead, but that would have been totally against his nature.

He nobly conceived the principle that the salary he was receiving was intended to maintain the position of a Colonial Governor and disapproved of the policy of others in the same position who considered a certain amount of nest-feathering justifiable. He was the most unselfish of men.[24]

Among the guests who enjoyed the hospitality of Government House at that time were Sir Hugh Clifford, with his wife Minna and children, who had taken up more or less permanent residence. Sir Hugh Clifford was indignant about the way Alfred had been treated, and he said that when his own term in Trinidad would end, he would write a book he would call *The Land of the Green Bay*

Tree. He was referring to the Book of Common Prayer version of Psalm 37:35: 'I myself have seen the ungodly in great power, and flourishing like a green bay tree.'

Those who from the beginning had shown opposition to a Catholic governor were now rejoicing at his humiliation. In these last months there were fewer invitations. Frances often found herself visiting the leper asylum and the Dominican Sisters' orphanage, also the enclosed Dominican convent, and 'the dear Sisters of St Joseph of Cluny'. It was in these places that she felt most welcome and at home. She was deeply impressed by the dedication of the Dominican Sisters who looked after the leper asylum and she often spoke in later years of their self-sacrificing charity. She was gradually being freed from her horror of leprosy. The revulsion she had experienced on her first arrival in the West Indies was a thing of the past. Her next encounter with lepers would be some decades later in China. Then the memory of the Dominican Sisters in Trinidad would help her to express her own deep compassion for these disfigured, suffering people, in the practical ways of love.

It was with mixed feelings that Frances and Alfred Moloney finally bade farewell to the 'land of the green bay tree'. Because of the painful experience of the previous year they were reconciled to leaving. At the same time they were sorry to part from the many good friends they had made during their three and a half years in the colony. As their ship steamed slowly away from Trinidad, they may have looked back at what was called The Dragon's Mouth, the strait beyond which lay the open sea and as they saw the green hills receding into the far distance they must have sensed some relief that they had escaped this particular dragon's mouth.

FIVE

'Bobbie, find me a home!'

As their ship steamed slowly away from Trinidad, Frances and Alfred Moloney would have realised that they were facing into the unknown. Alfred was still coping with the trauma of feeling abandoned by the British government, in the service of which he had unstintedly spent the best years of his life. He carried with him a sense of injustice and betrayal, having been prematurely deprived of what had given his life meaning for so many years: his status as a high-ranking colonial administrator. No longer was he in control of his own destiny, not to mention that of others. Frances, an optimist by nature, would have tried to raise his spirits, but she was dealing with a man whose spirit was more or less broken. This journey was not an easy one for her either, as she stood by her husband's side aware of his deep hurt and sense of futility, and of her own helplessness to do anything about it.

They docked at Southampton and went first to Ireland where they stayed some weeks with Frances's sister and her brother-in-law in Co. Galway. Freddie and John Chevers hoped that they might decide to settle down near them, and John even went so far as to find a house that might be suitable on his cousin's land at nearby Castle ffrench. This they could have at a nominal rent. But the idea did not appeal to Alfred. So they crossed over to England. There Frances began to pull strings on his behalf. She went to see the new Colonial Secretary, A. Lyttelton, who had shown sympathy and a measure of understanding for her husband. She pointed out that in two years time Alfred Moloney would have been eligible for promotion to Hong Kong. As a result of her visit, Alfred was allowed an annual pension of £1,000. (Today's equivalent would be approximately £70,000.) Interestingly, it was Alfred Moloney's services in West Africa, in particular his botanical researches, which earned him this pension. During his years in the Gambia he had discovered rubber which had become a rich source of revenue

for the British government. It was a substantial pension and would
have been adequate for most people, but not for someone like
Alfred Moloney.

They were invited to visit the homes of some of the old English
Catholic gentry whose family members had enjoyed their hospitality in Trinidad. Others who had also stayed with them there chose
to ignore them. Frances came to realise that altered fortunes meant
fewer friends. At a house party in the stately home of the Fitzherbert
family, Gladys got a marriage proposal. Frances had encouraged
other romances but found herself reluctant to do so this time. She
understood Alfred's opposition to the marriage. Tommy Fitzherbert
as the fourth in line for the family title had little to offer his
daughter, and Gladys herself had only a small fortune inherited
from her mother. (Eventually Tommy did inherit the title, becoming Lord Stafford. But they were not to know that then.) Three years
later Gladys married Hubert Manley with her parents' blessing.

The trauma of the previous year was beginning to take its toll on
Alfred's health, which up to then had never caused any serious
problem. He found it too painful to talk about what had happened,
and Frances found it hard to see him suffering in silence, grieving
for the loss of what had been such a successful career. They had
finished the round of invitations. 'We literally had nothing to do,'
she said, 'and nowhere to go.' Then one day Alfred, tired of being
dependent on others' hospitality, turned to her and said sadly,
'Bobbie [his pet name for her], take me somewhere. Find me a
home.'[1]

After much searching, Frances discovered that an apartment in
Ingatestone Hall in Essex, where she had stayed as a girl, could be
leased on reasonable terms. The lovely old red brick building
dating back to 1540 had belonged to the Petre family since Tudor
times. It had been partly modernised in the eighteenth century after
the family moved to neighbouring Thorndon Hall. Later it was
subdivided into separate apartments, some of them occupied by the
estate staff, and some by outside tenants such as the bestselling
author Mary Braddon whose most popular book, *Lady Audley's
Secret*, had Ingatestone Hall as its setting.[2] The resident chaplain

had his own quarters near the chapel, which served the local Catholic community as their parish church. Chapel and chaplain were major attractions for the Moloneys, also the fact that the house had stayed in Catholic hands down through the centuries, even in Penal times. There were extensive grounds, in keeping with the spaciousness of the old house. Altogether it seemed ideal and early in 1904 they leased one of the vacant apartments.

Since 1992 Ingatestone Hall has been open to the public during the summer months, so it is possible to retrace the Moloney's stay there. Externally the house and gardens are as they were in their time, but after the Petre family moved back to Ingatestone in 1919 they set about restoring the house to its original Tudor appearance and layout. The rooms used by the Moloneys have now been absorbed into the larger plan, but it is still possible to reconstruct the kind of gracious living that went with such a house, and the Catholic atmosphere that pervaded it.

Two priests' hiding places may still be seen, one of which was uncovered as late as 1937, long after the Moloneys stayed there. The entrance to the other was off Alfred's dressing room, so he and Frances had inescapable reminders of the faith that meant everything to both of them. Usually the fugitive priests posed as members of the household. Consequently, the hiding places were used more often to conceal Mass requisites than priests.

Estate papers relating to the Moloney's stay in Ingatestone Hall still survive. These consist of copies of letters sent to them by Lord Petre's agent, Francis Coverdale, and refer mostly to concrete facts that new tenants needed to know: shooting arrangements and the payment of the gamekeeper, the fencing off of the garden, and access to the Lime Walk, a sore point with Alfred Moloney. It is a matter of interest that most of these letters were addressed to Lady Moloney, not to Sir Alfred. Evidently, at this time, it was Frances who looked after the business side of things. Towards the end of their first year at Ingatestone a letter from the agent shows that she had complained about the high rent and had begun to make tentative moves to transfer the lease. With that in mind, she consulted the agent about certain repairs necessary and suggested

combining their apartment with the adjoining one. He did not
concur at the time, but her suggestion was acted on later. One of her
main concerns was the safety of the water, both for drinking
purposes and in the freshwater fish-pond which carried the quaint
name of the Stew Pond.

Because of Alfred's health they decided that he should winter
abroad. Frances's cousin in Monaco, Mrs Harvey Lewis, in whose
villa she and Alfred had spent their honeymoon, had left her a small
legacy. It was just enough to cover the cost of a Mediterranean tour
for Alfred, a costly luxury in those days. Trying to economise,
Frances did not accompany him, though she said afterwards that
she might as well have done so because of all the expensive
souvenirs he brought home. While he was away she had the
companionship of his sister Kathleen who had joined them when
they went to live in Ingatestone Hall. Frances and Kathleen were
always good friends. Frances admired her sister-in-law's devotion
to others: to Alfred's daughter Gladys after her mother died, to
Alfred's mother, and later to his brother Captain George Moloney
who had been wounded in Africa.

Alfred returned from his tour in better health and better spirits,
able now to take an interest in the house and property. He and
Frances appreciated being under the same roof as the Blessed
Sacrament, and the whole Catholic atmosphere of the place. Their
landlords, Lord and Lady Petre, showed great friendliness and
introduced them to other county families. It looked as if they were
settled for life in this pleasant place. But it was not to be. The agent,
living in the adjoining wing, was not willing to make certain
concessions that Alfred asked for, and a time came when he found
the situation intolerable. At the end of one year he gave notice of
leaving, and was adamant, even though Lord Petre rode over from
Thorndon Hall to ask him to reconsider his decision.

Once again Frances and Kathleen did the round of the house
agents. One of these showed them pictures of a beautiful old house
in Monmouthshire, called Cefntilla Court, and they knew immediately that this was what they were looking for. The lovely ivy-
covered stone house belonged to Lord Raglan, grandson of the first

Lord Raglan, Wellington's secretary and later commander of the forces in the Crimea. The house had been presented to his heirs by a grateful nation. The present Lord Raglan had been appointed Lieutenant Governor of the Isle of Man and was looking for suitable tenants for his country seat. For a house of its kind, with extensive grounds, the rent asked was nominal, £100 a year. (The present equivalent would be approximately £7,000.)

There was only one flaw. The nearest Catholic church was three miles away at Usk. Having enjoyed the nearness of the Blessed Sacrament and frequent Mass at Ingatestone Hall, Frances and Alfred hoped that before long they could have their own private chapel at Cefntilla. Happily for them, soon after they arrived their neighbours the Vaughans of Courtfield invited them to lunch to meet their local bishop, Bishop Hedley of Newport. They seized the opportunity to put before the bishop their request for a private chapel, and he was happy to accede. Immediately they got busy and fixed up a suitable room. One of their workmen, a skilled carpenter, made an altar, and 'tall silver candlesticks and vases to match, which had served many a festive occasion in the West Indies, were now put to a better purpose.'[3] Bishop Hedley arrived and was delighted with what he saw. He said Mass and left instructions for the parish priest of Usk to come once a fortnight to celebrate Mass. All the servants were Catholic, and Frances arranged their work schedules so that each one could spend a half hour daily before the Blessed Sacrament. In the intervals the family kept up adoration.

There were social occasions too. Many of the county families of the area called to welcome them, inviting them to visit: the Herberts of Llanarth, the Raglan Somersets, the McDonnells of Usk, and others. But their closest friends were the Rookes of Bigsweir House, who later became Catholics, and for whom Frances and Alfred acted as sponsors. Visitors came and went. Frances's father and stepmother were frequent guests. The Chevers arrived from Galway, and Frances's brother Arthur from Dublin. Frances's spiritual director of many years ago, Father Leslie SJ from Farm Street, now an old man, wanted to meet Freddie and herself. The only way they could get permission for him to visit was to arrange a retreat, which they did. In the autumn, Frances's favourite brother Cyril arrived from South Africa. The former Attorney-General of Trinidad was visiting with his wife at the same time. They had arrived with heavy colds which developed into influenza. Cyril picked up the infection but making light of it went on to London. Three weeks later Frances got a telegram to say that he was critically ill. Immediately she caught a train for London and was at her brother's side when he died. Frances had always been close to Cyril, to whom she came next in the family. His death at the early age of thirty-four was an immense sorrow.

Later that year Alfred and Frances visited Sir Hubert and Lady Jerningham, their predecessors in Government House, Trinidad, who were now living in Berwick-on-Tweed. Lady Jerningham was seriously ill, suffering from heart trouble, but there was good hope that she would recover. After saying goodbye to her, the Moloneys went on to London where Frances had to go into a nursing home for minor surgery. A few nights after her operation she had a strange psychic experience. She clearly saw her friend, Sissie Jerningham, standing between the bed and the fireplace. 'Her appearance was ethereal, her face of unearthly delicacy with an expression of peace.'[4] Frances asked her if she was happy. She replied that she was near her happiness and she asked Frances to pray for her. Then she disappeared. Frances spent the night praying the rosary for her until she fell asleep. The following morning when she received Holy Communion she knew instinctively that her friend was in heaven.

Back in Cefntilla after her operation, Frances, with Kathleen Moloney, began to visit the many poor people in the neighbour-hood and those ending their days in the nearby workhouse. Among them were several lapsed Catholics whom they followed up and invited whenever there was a Sunday Mass at Cefntilla. Soon they had gathered a regular little congregation. They provided breakfast for those who came from a distance.

It is not surprising that before long Frances realised that they could not continue showing hospitality and paying the wages of so many servants on Alfred's pension alone. Her father suggested that she take up journalism as a means of supplementing their income. A fashionable and luxuriously produced weekly women's journal called *The Throne* was at the planning stage, and Frances was lucky in being asked to provide the Social and Personal section. This usually ran into three or four folio pages, so it covered a vast amount of material. Its title was 'The Whispering Gallery', and the subtitle was a quotation, 'Society is a vast Whispering Gallery'. In those days a by-line was not usual for a column of this nature, but it is not difficult to detect Frances's hand. There are characteristic references to old English Catholic families; to 'the Catholic marriage of the year'; to Father Bernard Vaughan's sermons; to her friend, Sir Hubert Jerningham; to the eccentric Lord Lovelace, father of her friend Molly Milbanke. There are also detailed reviews of art exhibitions, familiarity with colonial affairs, and a special interest in Irish society.

Frances also contributed 'Notes and News' to another ladies' journal called *The Planet*. This was a less expensive production and Frances was paid correspondingly less. While she earned two guineas for a thousand words in *The Throne* the paying rate of *The Planet* was £1 for the equivalent length. Many years later in a letter to her niece Frieda, Frances, now an old lady of eighty-five years, told her that when she and Alfred 'were rather hard up', her writing had earned them up to fourteen guineas a week, a substantial amount in those years.[5] In the same letter she advised her niece how to go about getting her own work published, offering to send her a Fleet Street manual with addresses and fees offered, and assuring her that if she could get at least one short story placed she could use it as a means to gain entry to various other magazines and journals.

There is no problem in detecting Frances's hand in *The Planet*, even though again her column is unsigned. Here the individual items are longer than in *The Throne*, and the reader senses that Frances has more scope to say all she wants. In the issue or 29 June 1907 she described 'a charming musical At Home' given by her stepmother, Mrs Owen Lewis, without revealing her own connection: 'This accomplished lady, who is herself a musician of no mean repute, always collects around her some of the best amateur

talent of London.' In the 14 September issue of the same year
Frances wrote in some detail of 'A Forthcoming Marriage of
Interest', which was in fact that of her stepdaughter, Gladys.

> Among the many engagements which are just announced is that
> of Gladys, only child of Sir Alfred Moloney, K.C.M.G.,J.P. late
> Governor of Trinidad, with Mr. Hubert Manley, of Spofforth
> Hall, Yorks. The future bridegroom, who is a rising young man,
> represents Lloyds, Reuter's, and many other important concerns
> in Egypt. The Manley family is among the oldest in England,
> and is mentioned on the roll of Battle Abbey. Spofforth Hall,
> which has been the seat of one branch of the family for many
> generations, was left to Mr. Hubert Manley by his father. The
> prospective bride is an exceedingly pretty girl with dark eyes
> and lovely complexion; she is a clever amateur actress, brilliant
> musician, and good at games. The wedding will shortly take
> place at Cefntilla Court, Monmouthshire, the residence of her
> father.[6]

Frances used the occasion to talk about her husband's family:

> Sir Alfred Moloney is a member of the family of Moloney of
> Kiltanon, who are descended from the old Irish chieftains of
> Clare, and were possessed of large tracts of country at the time
> of Henry II. One of his ancestors was the famous Archbishop
> Moloney, who founded the Irish College in Paris at the time of
> Louis XIV.

In another issue of the same journal Frances described a garden
fête held at Troy House, Monmouth, in aid of the Good Shepherd
Sisters, and again referred to her husband: 'Sir Alfred Moloney,
who is tenant of Lord Raglan's beautiful seat in the neighbourhood,
made a short speech, calling upon Father Bernard Vaughan to open
the bazaar.'[7] Frances obviously had her sister and brother-in-law in
mind in her paragraph, 'Dancing on a Volcano', where she touched
on the land war in Ireland. At this stage of her life Frances would
have associated herself with the landlord class. In later years, when
her sympathies were with the republican cause, she would not have

written the following:

> Unfortunate landlords of ancient lineage, who have always been the fathers of their people, and who have lived on their estates for centuries, spending their rents among the peasantry from whom they received them, encouraging the industries and promoting the welfare of the people, are now treated as pariahs and lepers. We have one house in our mind as we write, from which no poor person has ever been sent away unrelieved, where no case of distress has ever remained unassisted, and where the beautiful chatelaine and her little children are now insulted and ill-treated in the grossest manner. Every man and boy who found employment on the estate has been called away, orders have been issued to every shopkeeper for miles around to refuse to supply food, the most hideous howlings and yells and the beat of Land League drum, like those which greeted the last appearance of the victims of the Terror on the scaffold, are heard incessantly around the demesne, with sinister effect, both night and day.[8]

These sobering remarks were sandwiched in between a paragraph on what was worn by fashionable society at Leopardstown, and another on a colourful floral display at the Horticultural Show in the grounds of Holland House, London. Items like those were more typical of Frances's 'Notes and News'. It is unlikely that she would have referred to such a serious political topic as the land war in Ireland, and in such strong terms, were it not for her close family tie with the Chevers. She was much more likely to inform her readers that, 'The Queen, as usual, was dressed in the most faultless taste, wearing a delicate shade of pale grey with bunches of white flowers adorning the front of her dress. Lady Aberdeen had on this occasion selected a soft shade of heliotrope, and Lady Grenfell looked very dainty in pale pink with roses in her hat of a deeper shade.' She described balls and house parties, Ascot Week, speech days and stately homes, but, being Frances Moloney, she also drew her readers' attention to forthcoming charitable events.

How she was able to accumulate so much society gossip is a

mystery. Cefntilla was a long train journey from London, one not often undertaken. She said that her father helped her with material, but there must have been others too who supplied her regularly with society news. She admitted some years later that writing a Social and Personal column would not have been her favourite form of writing, adding that what she wrote had no literary value, though it did keep the pot boiling. Perhaps she down-played herself. Even at a distance of almost ninety years and as descriptions of a vanished world her writing is still eminently readable. Nor is it without a certain sense of style: she had a happy facility for language as well as the keen eye of a skilled artist. Instinctively aware of the importance of a telling detail, she knew how to entertain her readers with the occasional unusual or amusing anecdote.

She had more scope for her writing talent in two long descriptive articles published in the early issues of *The Throne* in August and October of 1906. The first of these carried the title, 'A Trip to the Grenadines in a Man-of-War by Lady Moloney', and the other, with a similar attribution, was called, 'Eight Days in South America'. This time the articles were signed with her distinctive strong signature, 'Frances Moloney'. The first article ran to 2,500 words and the second to 3,300. These were more than pot-boilers; they were vivid and well-written accounts of places and people, aptly illustrated. In the issue of *The Throne*, which has the first of these articles, the major contributors are given a page with their pictures and proposed topics. In Frances's case this was: 'My Official Life, and Adventures in the West Indies'. The picture that she submitted was a head-and-shoulders version of one showing her on horseback, taken in Grenada or Trinidad. It is an attractive picture. Frances, in her white, wide-brimmed panama hat, looks girlish and rather self-conscious. Because it is a head-and-shoulders version, the reader cannot see the well-cut riding habit which accentuates her eighteen-inch waist.

Frances took her writing seriously. Consequently, she found it helpful when Alfred decided that they should take a house in Brighton for the winter of 1906: from there it would be easier for her to make personal contact with her editors, and easier too to gather material. 'Visits to friends, attendance at social functions and occasional tea on the terrace at Westminster, enabled me to glean material for the social and personal columns. By avoiding sensationalism, a decent standard was maintained, and my father's guiding hand was never far away.'[9]

Besides writing for popular society journals, Frances had many visitors to entertain. Archbishop Flood, whom they had not seen since they left Trinidad, came over from Ireland on a visit. Bishop Hedley was visiting at the same time. Frances would have preferred if their visits had not coincided. 'The two Bishops, both great churchmen, were of entirely different temperaments, with divergence of tastes … Rather reticent by nature, the dry humour of Bishop Hedley was no match to the Celtic enthusiasm and joyous outbursts from His Grace of Trinidad.'[10] Archbishop Flood seemed to be in good health when he visited Cefntilla, but not long afterwards the Moloneys were saddened by news of his death in June 1907 in Port-of-Spain.

Frances also kept in touch through letters with her other friends in Trinidad. Early in 1907 she heard the sad news that her friend Minna Clifford had died, after being thrown by her horse. It added to Frances's sorrow that the horse involved was her own high-spirited mount that she had left behind in Trinidad. There was an unfortunate sequel to the tragedy. Minna's husband, who had succeeded Alfred Moloney as Governor, decided to have his wife buried in the grounds of Government House. The last time the burial ground had been used was when there was an epidemic of yellow fever some decades earlier, and the opening up of the ground brought a further outbreak of the fatal disease. Within a few days of Minna Clifford's funeral, the Governor's ADC and two others who had been present at the funeral died of yellow fever.

True to her caring nature Frances invited the three Clifford children, who had arrived back in England, to come to Cefntilla for an extended visit. The lonely little children came with their grandmother and spent some time with the Moloneys. After they left, Frances gave a dance in honour of Gladys's coming out, and invited

many of Gladys's young friends in the county. Among them were
some of the young Vaughan men who were later to leave their mark
on the Catholic Church in England. The youngest of them, who
danced longer and more exuberantly than any of the others, left
early the following morning for Valladolid to enter religious life.

Not long afterwards Frances and Alfred celebrated Gladys's
engagement. The announcement in *The Planet* (already quoted)
leads us to believe that this time Gladys's parents were happy about
her choice. The marriage took place on 23 September 1907. For
whatever reason, Frances did not describe Gladys's wedding in her
memoirs. Nor was it written up in the society pages of *The Planet*
or *The Throne*. But the two journals that had described her own
wedding, *The Lady* and *The Gentlewoman*, gave space too to
Gladys.

In *The Lady* Gladys's wedding is noted in the column, 'The
Lady in Dublin', which refers to the fact that there were several
celebrations in honour of the occasion at Cefntilla Court. The style
is reminiscent of Frances, who may have provided the story,
directly or indirectly. *The Gentlewoman* gives a more detailed
account of the wedding, and features a full-length picture of the
bride, dressed in the elaborate gown she wore at her presentation at
court. A separate picture shows the groom in fashionably casual
motoring attire. The columnist reports that the officiating clergyman was Bishop Hedley. In marked contrast to Frances's own
wedding, her stepdaughter's was a modest affair: 'The ceremony,
according to the wish of both bride and bridegroom, was a very
quiet one, only the immediate relations on both sides being invited
… There were no bridesmaids or pages … The bride and bridegroom left immediately after the ceremony in their motor car for
their honeymoon.'[11]

When the excitement of Gladys's wedding had died down,
Alfred accepted an invitation to travel to Genoa on a cargo boat of
the Tatem Line. The owner, Sir William Tatem, was a friend who
reserved comfortable cabins on his ships for acquaintances who
might like to avail of them. The Moloneys sometimes did. This
time Alfred's sister Kathleen accompanied Frances and Alfred. It

was Frances's first glimpse of Italy which would soon figure so prominently in her story, and she was captivated. Like so many other tourists arriving in Genoa, they visited the Campo Santo and the shrine of St Catherine of Genoa. They then paid a quick visit to Bologna and proceeded to Pisa. Many years later Frances recalled the beautiful paintings that she found so moving on that first visit.

Eventually they reached Rome, where their first visit was to St Peter's. A family connection, a Canon of St Peter's, showed them all the treasures of that great basilica. In the meantime they found a suitable apartment conveniently situated for the many places of interest in Rome. Frances's father had given them a letter of introduction to Cardinal Merry del Val; he had known him and his family for many years. When this was presented they were received immediately with the Cardinal's typical graciousness. Frances described the impression he made:

> Very tall and distinguished looking, his large black eyes mirrored a depth of soul through which shone a luminous mind. I felt rather in awe of this commanding figure and imposing personality, till he began to speak in affectionate terms of my father, which put me completely at my ease. To Alfred he spoke as man to man, asking about affairs in Trinidad.[12]

They also had a private audience with the Holy Father, Pope Pius X. All that Frances remembered of this occasion was the Pope's large dark eyes which seemed to read the secrets of a person's soul. One day a friend of Alfred's who sometimes visited them, brought along the young Bishop of Killaloe, Dr Michael Fogarty, who was making his first *ad limina* visit to the Holy Father. Frances found him 'strikingly handsome, a delightful conversationalist and raconteur'.[13] He was delighted to meet Alfred Moloney with his Clare name and Clare connections, and they had much in common. Little did Frances know that nineteen years later this same Bishop of Killaloe would receive her vows as a Columban Sister in the convent chapel at Cahiracon, Co. Clare.

During her first Roman winter Frances took up painting again, at the studio of a well-known Italian water-colourist. She made such progress that he encouraged her to enter some sketches at a forthcoming exhibition. However, a few weeks before the date of the exhibition Frances and Kathleen Moloney were invited to attend a retreat to be given by an American Jesuit in the Reparation Sisters' convent. Frances was in a quandary: if she attended the retreat she could not finish her painting in time. She knew that she was producing good work and she would have appreciated the affirmation of being placed high in the exhibition: 'I had never felt so ambitious for success on any previous occasion as far as I can remember.'[14] Monsignor Hugh Benson was lunching with Frances and Alfred the day she was trying to make up her mind. When she told him her predicament, he said gently, yet reproachfully: 'How can you hesitate?' Frances made the retreat, and she said that it was the turning point of her life.

Father Elder Mullan SJ, who directed the retreat that influenced Frances so profoundly, was a member of the Maryland-New York province of the Society of Jesus. He was on the Generalate staff from 1906 to 1915, as librarian and assistant to the Secretary of the Society of Jesus. Throughout her life Frances had several Jesuit spiritual directors. In childhood and adolescence, and occasionally afterwards, there was Father William Leslie SJ. After Father Mullan's retreat in early 1908, which she called the beginning of her conversion, she regarded him as her director. She was in frequent contact with him, especially when she and Alfred wintered in Rome and later when they moved there permanently. Some letters survive, written to her by Father Mullan between 1912 and 1919.[15] Whether because of ill-health or for other reasons no letters from him to Frances exist for the period after 1919. By that time she was living in Dublin and going to Father Michael Browne SJ for direction. In a letter to Father Browne, she told him that after she left Rome she missed 'the very searching and intimate direction' she had experienced for some years, but that it might not have been as necessary as at the beginning of her 'conversion'.[16] In the meantime she had learned to depend partly on prayer and on books. Her friend Father Mullan died in 1925, at the age of sixty. She kept his letters throughout her long life.

A month after the retreat that Frances believed had 'converted' her, the Moloneys returned to Cefntilla. The principal retreat resolution for both Frances and Kathleen Moloney had been daily Communion. That was easy in Rome, but quite a different matter in the heart of the Welsh countryside. The nearest church was three miles away in Usk. But Frances and Kathleen Moloney were undaunted. Every morning they set out fasting on their long walk. Sometimes, on the way home, they took a train from Usk to a village only two miles away from Cefntilla, and thus shortened their journey by a mile. Fortunately, after a few months the long morning walk was no longer necessary. They were able to provide a home for an elderly French Jesuit, Father Jean Berard, in exile and homeless because of his government's anticlerical laws. There was no longer any problem about daily Mass.

Up to the autumn of 1908 Frances submitted her usual society pages to *The Throne* and *The Planet*. Then an acute attack of neuritis brought it all to an abrupt end. But the experience was not wasted. Her few short years working for ladies' journals provided her with a demanding apprenticeship in the art of writing and gave her a lasting respect for the power of the media.

Late in 1908, when her doctor advised Frances to give up writing for the time being and to take a sea voyage, she and Alfred were again able to avail of the courtesy of their friend the owner of the Tatem Line. They decided to go to Egypt where Gladys and her husband were living. Kathleen stayed behind at Cefntilla to look after the place. Frances and Alfred came ashore at Alexandria, where they were met by Gladys and her husband Hubert Manley. They were delighted to see Gladys again, but they were disappointed to find Alexandria so modern, with little trace of its former Christian glory. After a week there they moved to Cairo. Gladys would have liked them to stay longer, but Frances remembered that her own mother had always told her that in-laws should not stay long with a young couple. Moreover, Alfred and his son-in-law seemed to hold quite a number of significantly divergent views.

In Cairo, Alfred and Frances visited the holy places associated with the Holy Family and the Flight into Egypt, and made excursions up the Nile, to Memphis and Karnak. They visited some Coptic and Maronite churches and were deeply impressed by the pyramids of Gizeh.

For some time they had been longing to visit the Holy Land. Realising that in Egypt they were relatively near, they crossed the eastern Mediterranean on a French steamer and landed at Jaffa. There they visited what was said to be Simon the Tanner's house, and a shrine in honour of Dorcas, whom St Peter had raised from the dead. But the real goal of their pilgrimage was Jerusalem. Of all the holy places they visited, what Frances found the most moving was the hill of Calvary. Her lifelong devotion to the Cross, evident from early childhood, was once again nurtured in that holy place.

> The walls and surroundings seemed to disappear and the mental picture of Christ hanging on the cross at this spot was almost more than one's overflowing heart could bear. We forgot the tawdry surroundings put up by the devotion of various nationalities. Our souls were satisfied by the invisible reality of all that had happened within these very precincts. Silently we came away with the truth of God's love for man filling our very beings.[17]

They found Bethany 'the most homely of all the places connected with Our Lord's life'. In their imagination they were able to reconstruct the village from the existing ruins. When they visited the place traditionally identified as the house of Martha and Mary, Frances sketched what was said to be the opening leading to the tomb of Lazarus. Another high point of their pilgrimage was their visit to Bethlehem and the Grotto of the Nativity, where they were directed down steps to the small chapel associated with the manger. Frances recalled: 'There was just room for a very small altar, the celebrant and server. I managed to squeeze myself in by the side of the latter, and together, Alfred and I received Christ Our Lord in even tinier shape than when he first came into the world. No words could describe the joy of that moment.'[18]

Before Frances and Alfred left Jerusalem they were received as probationer tertiaries of St Francis. Frances took the name, Magdalen 'who loved Christ so dearly' and Alfred, in memory of Frances's favourite brother who had died two years earlier, asked for the name Cyril. From now on they were committed to the daily recitation of the Little Office of the Blessed Virgin. A year later, on 1 June 1909, they were to make their profession in the Third Order of St Francis in the Portiuncula Chapel at Assisi, into the hands of the English Provincial of the Franciscans.

When their pilgrimage ended they left again for home, stopping off briefly in Egypt to visit Gladys. Back in Cefntilla, Frances resumed her writing, and did some entertaining. However, because of Alfred's health, they decided to return to Rome for the winter, happy to be able to rent the apartment they had lived in the previous year. Frances was glad to be able to avail again of Father Mullan's guidance, and Alfred, who up to then had never felt the need of a spiritual director, decided to take Father Herman Walmesley SJ as his spiritual guide. It is possible that Frances played a part in this decision. Like Father Mullan, Father Walmesley was also a member of the Generalate staff, counsellor of the English Assistancy.

They knew how hard they would find it not to get totally caught up in the social life of Rome. Their neighbours in Wales, the Vaughans, were in Rome for the winter, holding court at their hotel in the Piazza di Spagna. Other friends had also arrived. Frances and Alfred could not ignore all the invitations, yet they knew they had set their sights elsewhere. Though they attended some of the Christmas parties, they made sure that they were present at all the ceremonies in the Basilica of St Mary Major, wishing that they were back again in the cave of Bethlehem where a few months earlier they had received Holy Communion.

On 28 December 1908 word reached Rome that a severe earthquake had that morning devastated the cities of Messina and Reggio Calabria and much of the Calabrian countryside. The Christmas festivities in Rome came to an abrupt end. This was one of the most disastrous earthquakes on record. In Messina alone, 84,000 lives were lost, and the total number of those who died as a result of the earthquake would have been between 100,000 and

200,000. Thousands were homeless, many of them also seriously injured. A major relief operation was launched in Rome to bring help to the stricken area. Pope Pius X gave the lead, offering one of the Vatican palaces to house some of the survivors. Others followed suit. Special trains manned by the Red Cross carried food, medicines, blankets, as well as volunteer relief workers, soldiers, doctors and nurses. On the return journey they brought those in urgent need of major surgery or hospitalisation.

Among the first nurses to reach the disaster area were two Sisters of the Little Company of Mary, from their hospital in Rome. Altogether six Sisters of the order were sent by Mother Potter, the foundress, at the request of Queen Margherita the Queen Mother. Extra beds were hastily prepared in all the hospitals. Rome's society ladies gave up their usual Christmas parties to meet the trains that came in throughout the night, serving coffee and food to the exhausted victims and the helpers. Frances and some of her friends organised a sewing group to make clothes for the victims. The Poor Servants of the Mother of God in Via San Sebastianello gave them the use of one of their large parlours – the Moloney apartment in the Palazzo Gozzoli was too small to house all who wanted to help.

Every morning Frances accompanied a Sister belonging to the Helpers of the Holy Souls on her daily visit to the sick and injured. Victims kept coming in for more than three weeks after the earthquake. One in whom Frances took a special interest was a little boy, found three weeks after the earthquake under the dead body of his uncle. Gangrene had set in and his legs had to be amputated. But he recovered and was ready to return to Calabria with the other evacuees in the spring. Frances's sewing group had worked so hard that they were able to provide an outfit for all the victims before they left. It was Frances's job to distribute the clothes to the boys. Each of them got a coat and trousers. But when she came to little Carlo sitting in a wheelchair, Frances gave him a coat and a waistcoat. She was devastated when he asked her with tears for trousers to cover the little legs that were no longer there.

Soon after Easter the Moloneys returned to Cefntilla. Spring was at its most beautiful and Alfred was able to enjoy the weather and the sense of being home again. But after a few weeks Frances noticed that the old restlessness had returned. Happily they were able to sublet Cefntilla for the summer months to friends who were willing to keep on the servants and Father Berard was able to get a temporary chaplaincy elsewhere. With Alfred's sister Kathleen they again availed of the hospitality of the Tatem Line and at the end of May they travelled to Genoa.

This time their focus was a pilgrimage to scenes from the life of St Francis. Perugia, where St Francis had met Pope Innocent III, was their first stop. Frances would have liked to stay longer in 'the lovely old city astraddle a spur of the Appennines', but their time was limited. They moved on to Assisi. There they visited the basilica built over the tomb of St Francis, enriched by the art of Cimabue and Giotto. 'For some undefinable reason,' wrote Frances, 'we could not capture the spirit of the Little Poor Man so well in the grandiose mausoleum erected over his remains, as we did in the Church of Our Lady of the Angels at the bottom of the hill.' There they found the little Chapel of the Portiuncula, the cradle of the Franciscan Order, and the tiny cell where St Francis died.

They visited the tomb of St Clare and the Convent of San Damiano, and Frances and Kathleen practised Italian conversation with the kind superior of the Poor Clare nuns in Assisi, who helped them spiritually as she talked to them about St Francis and St Clare. Before leaving, Frances wished to make some financial contribution but the Sister declined. 'So, while in my first fervour as a Franciscan Tertiary,' recalled Frances, 'I presented her with the valuable lace I had inherited from my mother, also a handsome length of Carrickmacross lace which had adorned my wedding dress.'[19]

They next visited the hermitage where St Francis had received the stigmata. Several friars were living as hermits around the cell. Frances and Alfred assisted at Mass in the little chapel and later visited a bigger chapel where Frances noted the della Robbia ceramics, just as her eye had earlier caught the paintings by Giotto and Cimabue in Assisi. They felt close to St Francis on the lonely mountain-top where he loved to pray. Even the birds reminded them of his love for all living things, especially there at the place where tradition holds that he preached to his feathered friends.

After ending their pilgrimage in Umbria they moved to Florence where their first visit was to the Franciscan church of Santa Croce, to see Giotto's frescoes of the life of St Francis. They admired other frescoes by Giotto in the Dominican Church, also work by Ghirlandaio and Fra Filippo Lippi. And they visited the monastery of San Marco to see the frescoes of Fra Angelico, 'who painted not for fame,' Frances noted, 'but for the spiritual delight of his brethren in religion.' She was moved by the faith that animated these painters and was convinced that nothing so appealing or so devotional was produced in later centuries.

Because it was getting too hot for sightseeing in the city, they visited cooler places in the vicinity of Florence. They were refreshed by the cool shade of the trees at Vallambrosa and visited the former monastery which had become the headquarters of the forestry department. Alfred seemed to need constant change and movement; Frances attributed this to his poor health. He did have a keen mind and he enjoyed all their excursions and pilgrimages to places of religious or historic interest. 'On every spur of the Appennines within easy reach of Florence,' Frances said, 'may be found ancient, almost forgotten shrines or monastic buildings'. They discovered many of them. They joined every little group of pilgrims, often not knowing what saint they were honouring. On one of these local pilgrimages they found a little boy who had run away from home because his stepfather was ill-treating him. Moved with pity for him they decided to bring him back to Florence to their friend Father Strickland SJ, who had a house for homeless boys and found work for them. Even though the house was overflowing, he made room for Luigi who found himself at last among friends. Whenever he had a free afternoon he visited the Moloneys as long as they stayed in Florence.

One of the places that came to have a special meaning for them was Fiesole in the hills above Florence. They found it a place of beauty and historic interest. While there they visited San Girolamo where the Little Company of Mary had a convent and a nursing home. They were welcomed warmly and Alfred discovered that he had known Mother Edith, the superior, as a young girl. She was the niece of Bishop Bagshawe, who together with Mother Potter had founded the Little Company of Mary. Little did Frances and Alfred know that in the space of a few years they would return again to San Girolamo and that Alfred would spend his last days there.

What was uppermost in their minds now was that it was time to return to Cefntilla. The tenants to whom they had sublet the place were leaving in October. Would Alfred's health be able to withstand the cold, damp winter of south Wales after sunny Italy? They decided reluctantly that he should remain on in Florence, while Frances and Kathleen returned to Cefntilla. They had taken on the lovely old house thinking of Alfred's needs in his old age. Now, in a sense, it had become a burden. But it did bring blessings too. That winter saw a big increase in the number attending Sunday Mass in their chapel. And Frances had the joy of having her brother Frank's daughter to stay.

After Frank had been killed in action in South Africa his wife Joanna had withdrawn their son, young Frank, from Beaumont College and his sister Margaret from Roehampton. She made it practically impossible for them to practise their religion. Then, unexpectedly, Joanna allowed Margaret to visit Frances. Margaret's stay in Cefntilla brought great joy to all the family. Frances believed that for Margaret it was 'the happiest part of an otherwise sad life'. Joanna asked Frances to use her influence to get a position in the Colonial Service for young Frank. Frances brought him to Downing Street to meet the Under Secretary of State, who had held Alfred in high regard. As a result, Frank was offered a good position in Uganda. But his mother rejected the very idea, and was extremely angry with Frances for even considering the offer which would have sent her son to such an unhealthy climate. Their fragile rapprochement fell apart.

In the early spring of 1910 Alfred returned to Cefntilla, in much better health and spirits and glad to be home again. This time he was able to stay at Cefntilla for a whole year, and it was a happy time

for him and for Frances. They still had their French chaplain, Father
Berard, and that meant the blessing of daily Mass. Family and
friends came to visit, and Frances was again asked to chaperone a
young woman, Dolly Plowden, the only child of some English
friends of theirs in Rome. Her parents hoped that Frances would
help their daughter to make a good match. She introduced Dolly to
all the eligible young Catholic men in the neighbourhood, but the
young guest was not drawn to any of them. In desperation, Frances
appealed to her sister Freddie who invited Dolly over to a shooting
party at Killyan. There she lost her heart to a young cousin of John
Chevers, Willie Chevers Roche. Some months later they were
married in London.

At Christmas 1910 a group of family and friends gathered at
Cefntilla. Among them were Frances's father and stepmother who
came from London, and their neighbours Aileen and Douglas
Rooke with their two children, all four of whom had become
godchildren of Alfred and Frances when they became Catholics.
Alfred, noted for his hospitality, received them all 'with courtly
grace'. The French chaplain, Father Berard, who had been a
professor of music in a French seminary, found a kindred spirit in
Frances's stepmother Louise who was a gifted musician. According to Frances, she could make the piano sing.

This was to be the last house party that the Moloneys would host
at Cefntilla. It had become inescapably clear that Alfred's health
could no longer tolerate the unpredictable British climate. Consequently, when some friends indicated their readiness to take on the
remainder of the lease, Frances and Alfred decided to move
permanently to Italy. Frances found the parting hard. She loved the
old house and she knew she would miss it. She was sad too to bid
farewell to the small Catholic community that over the years had
joined them for Mass in their chapel. From now on, it would not be
so easy to visit her sister Freddie and the Chevers family in Ireland.
So, before leaving for Italy, Frances and Alfred visited Killyan.
They also spent a few days with Frances's brother Arthur in
Dundalk. They then left for Rome.

SIX

The Roman Years

Frances and Alfred Moloney had visited Rome for the first time in late 1907, and they spent the winter of 1908/09 there. In 1911 they came to stay. Their decision to live in Rome, rather than elsewhere with a similar pleasant climate, would seem to have sprung from their deep faith; moreover, in Rome they would be in contact with the spiritual guides of whom both felt the need at that time. Alfred may also have had an intuition that with his state of health he might not have many more years to live. Rome was where he and Frances chose to make their final home.

They stayed first at a private hotel in the Via del Babuino, and soon Frances was resuming her daily visits to the poor with Mother Ste Cécile of the Helpers of the Holy Souls. She had begun those visits at the time of the Messina earthquake.

A group of American schoolgirls from a fashionable New York school were staying in the same hotel, visiting historic and archeological places of interest in Rome. Frances, noticing that the focus of their daily excursions neglected places of Christian significance, decided to remedy that, and she offered to introduce them to Christian Rome, 'letting them see the Rome that really mattered'.[1] Before they left for home they thanked her with bouquets of luxurious hothouse flowers. She felt like crying, knowing how much the money spent on these flowers could have helped the poor people she visited daily with Mother Ste Cécile.

Looking back years later, she wrote: 'Life in Rome those days became an odd mixture of two social extremes. With Mother Ste Cécile of the Holy Souls, I tramped the working-class quarters of San Lorenzo where she attended the sick mothers and children and cooked the workman's dinner to be ready for his return at midday.'[2] It was around noon too that Frances would return home to Alfred, to spend the rest of the day with him or to prepare for one or other of the charitable or social functions to which she was often invited.

One morning she and Mother Ste Cécile helped a poor woman who was dying, and afterwards prayed with the family. Then Mother Ste Cécile sent the family out and showed Frances how to wash and lay out the body. It was a traumatic experience, but one which was to prove useful in later years. That day she and Alfred had been invited by friends to a luncheon party at the Hotel Excelsior. They had arranged to meet in the lobby. When Frances arrived at the hotel Alfred was waiting, and she discovered that the party had been delayed on her behalf. There was nothing for it but to proceed immediately to the dining room. Feeling nauseated after her morning's experience, she fiddled with her food and could eat very little. Her fellow guests attributed this to a certain abstemiousness. Frances knew better, but she could not inform them that she had just come from laying out a dead person in one of the poorer areas of Rome.

Father Elder Mullan SJ, Frances's spiritual director, asked her to find some charitable work for the three Dahlgren girls whose family were spending the winter in Rome. They were nieces of Mother Katharine Drexel who founded an American religious congregation, the Sisters of the Blessed Sacrament. Frances knew what it was to be young and idealistic and she found suitable work for the three girls.

Although they were comfortable in their hotel, Alfred once again longed for a private place of their own. After some searching, they found exactly what they needed in an apartment belonging to the Poor Servants of the Mother of God [3] in the Via San Sebastianello. Attached to the convent, it was comfortable and spacious. The only drawback was that it was on the upper floor. The Sisters allowed the Moloneys to use a tribune overlooking the chapel, so Alfred was not obliged to climb the stairs more than once a day, when he came down for Mass. In spite of his poor health, he liked to attend Mass daily. Once again the Moloneys had the consolation of living under the same roof as the Blessed Sacrament, as they had earlier on in Ingatestone Hall and more recently in Cefntilla. 'I loved the early morning hours,' Frances recalled, 'in the rather dark little church among the Italian frequenters. In the evenings also it was often possible to steal into the tribune unperceived by the nuns who were chanting their Office.'[4]

By this time the Moloneys were accepted not only by the expatriate British and Irish communities, but also by Roman society. Frances had an outgoing personality and made many friends; she had outgrown the shyness that marked her first experience of colonial society. Her work with the poor also continued to expand; she seemed unable to say no whenever they were involved. A member of an old Roman family, Donna Maria Salviati, got her help in supporting an orphanage she was maintaining in Montorio; with Donna Maria's other helpers she looked for donations in some of the big Roman hotels. Sometimes Father Mullan tried to restrain her. In May 1912 he wrote to her about an association she wanted to join: 'I do hope this is not an exclusive set of stylish people! If it is, please have nothing to do with it.' A month later he wrote to her: 'I don't much favour your joining that Temperance League. Sir Alfred wants you to drink wine sometimes, and there will be other obligations besides total abstinence obligations which you had better think about twice before undertaking.'[5]

There were two Roman women who were her special friends. One of them was the Princess di Cassano, who held a salon every fortnight where topics of intellectual interest were discussed. The real purpose of these meetings was to try to bring about a reconciliation between the followers of Victor Emmanuel and those of the Holy Father. Usually a leading ecclesiastic was invited to read an address. Many of these, not wishing to get involved in Roman politics, gave the Princess a wide berth, but the Dominicans, Frances recalled, were less nervous. On one occasion the Princess di Cassano invited Frances to accompany her to the Vatican to meet Cardinal Merry del Val, the Secretary of State, to inform him of political trends. The two women were received immediately, although many Church dignitaries were waiting in the antechamber. The Cardinal listened carefully to all that the Princess had to say, but when she spoke about a Catholic party in process of formation he responded emphatically, 'There is no Catholic party!'

'It may not be called so,' she replied, 'but the movement is growing.' Frances wondered how they gained admittance to the Cardinal's presence ahead of the waiting bishops, and was told that it was a privilege belonging to the old Roman aristocracy.

Her other friend was Donna Cristina Bandini, who had been asked by Pope Pius X to found the Catholic Women's League in Italy; branches were already flourishing in England, Belgium and France. Frances admired Donna Cristina for her 'intelligence, discernment and tact', qualities she needed in her dealings with the Masonic government of the time. She organised the Catholic women of Italy, and together with them succeeded in restoring religious education in the schools. They also brought about the repeal of a law forbidding Corpus Christi processions through the streets. Donna Cristina invited Frances to join the Italian Catholic Women's League and asked her to teach English at a working-girls' club. Her experience of teaching factory girls in East London, many years earlier, now gave her enough confidence to comply with the request. And just as she had won the hearts of the London factory girls, so now she was accepted whole-heartedly by these young Italian women. Her teaching seems to have been effective: after one term the girls were able to converse in simple English with the President of the Catholic Women's League and to recite some short poems. Donna Cristina also persuaded Frances to hold an English class for university students, prevailing over all her protests.

Pope Pius X urged the Catholic Women's League to do all they could to combat Freemasonry which, in those years before Communism, was regarded by the Catholic Church as its greatest menace. Donna Cristina organised a plan of campaign. She collected valuable information about the secret manoeuvres and anti-clerical plots of the Masonic organisation, not only from within Italy but from other parts of Europe. When her careful research was completed, she convened a large meeting in the historic Palazzo della Cancelleria, at which Frances was present. Donna Cristina spoke for hours and won over many by the logic of her presentation and her conviction.

The Poor Servants of the Mother of God, whose apartment Frances and Alfred were renting, also asked Frances's help. Mother Magdalen Aimée, niece of their founder Mother Magdalen Taylor, wanted to organise a club for English-speaking girls working in Rome, many of whom were Irish. More or less like the Filipino women there today, some were governesses, others maids, still others were working in shops and small businesses. Alfred approved fully of the project. A point in its favour, no doubt, was that the young women would meet in the convent parlour, so Frances would be near at hand. The Sisters lent their largest parlour and provided tea for all who came. It was they who contacted most of the girls. Frances organised a small committee from among her friends to supervise the club and to help with the running expenses.

Angela Boland, her old friend from Dublin, was one of Frances's most generous helpers, financially and otherwise. She brought along her uncle, Dr Nicholas Donnelly, Coadjutor to the Archbishop of Dublin, who was visiting Rome. He read Dante to the girls! They got more entertainment from a visit by Dr Michael Fogarty, the Bishop of Killaloe, who joined them for a cup of tea and showed a personal interest in each one.

A consistory was held in Rome on 27 November 1911, at which the Archbishops of Westminster, Paris, New York, Vienna and Boston were raised to the College of Cardinals. The Moloneys were invited to receptions in honour of the English-speaking prelates, and made friends with Cardinal O'Connell of Boston. This friendship stood Frances in good stead on more than one occasion in her life. One of these occurred while the Cardinal was still in Rome. Frances had been asked by the Christian Brothers to sell tickets for a programme in aid of their schools. She knew that the English-speaking residents in Rome were attending a course of sermons being given by Monsignor Hugh Benson, and she decided to seize the opportunity. She asked Monsignor Benson to mention the charity at the end of his sermon, and she waited at the door, tickets in hand. The sermon ended; the congregation streamed out; nobody stopped, and she was left holding her unsold tickets. The preacher had forgotten her request. Then Cardinal O'Connell appeared. He greeted her and she told him about her unsold tickets. 'Without a moment's hesitation this generous Churchman bought the whole lot. Years later I reminded Cardinal O'Connell of this incident when writing from China and received a reply far exceeding all our expectations.'[6]

The newly created Cardinal Farley of New York visited the Moloneys in their flat and told them stories of his student days in Rome. They saw a lot of Cardinal Bourne, who often visited the convent of the Poor Servants of the Mother of God – who were noted for their hospitality. Even though most of the Sisters were Irish, their convent was known as the 'English Convent', perhaps because of its English origins and the fact that it was attached to the Church of St George and the English Martyrs. Some prominent English Catholic laywomen living in Rome urged Cardinal Bourne to allow them to form a branch of the English Catholic Women's League, so that with the support given by such an organisation it would be easier to get involved in apostolic work. Because the President of the English C.W.L. approved, Cardinal Bourne gave his consent. Frances reluctantly agreed to become Secretary.

A few days later Cardinal Merry del Val sent for her, obviously displeased that a branch of an English Catholic organisation had been established in Rome without permission. 'I might as well start a branch of the Italian Women's League in London!' he said. With a spark of her native wit, Frances replied, 'That would be wonderful, your Eminence, for there are so many Italians in London who are not living up to their Faith.' He probably smiled. Certainly he gave this intrepid woman his blessing for herself and for the Catholic Women's League. One day, some weeks later, a rather autocratic American lady came to the Moloneys' apartment, to inform Frances that she had to join the Catholic Women's League, even though personally she did not totally approve. It transpired that Cardinal Merry del Val had sent her.

Next, Frances got a message that the Dutch Cardinal van Rossum wanted to see her. At the time he was Prefect of the Congregation for the Doctrine of the Faith. He told her that he was concerned about the number of American and British proselytisers, hostile to the Catholic Church, who were operating in Rome, even setting up schools to undermine the faith of children. Cardinal van Rossum put it to Frances that since all this was being done by English-speaking people, the people to counteract it should be English-speaking Catholics. He suggested that the English-speaking Catholic Women's League undertake this task, prudently and with discretion. This they did with a good measure of success. They were helped greatly by the Sisters of St Dorothy,[7] an Italian teaching order. Whenever the proselytisers set up a school, very soon the Sisters of St Dorothy opened another in the same street and the proselytisers were forced to close down.

Cardinal van Rossum entrusted another matter to Frances, a delicate situation referred to him by the wife of a German diplomat. Evidently a priest was involved, because there was danger of a scandal to the Church. Cardinal van Rossum advised Frances on how to deal with the case. The couple in question called on her, and she helped them to realise the consequences of their relationship. After talking to her, they agreed to separate if a livelihood could be found for the woman. The man entered a monastery. Frances was able to raise some money from among her friends to find work for the woman. Again she was summoned by Cardinal Merry del Val, who told her that a case like that had nothing to do with the Catholic Women's League and that she was interfering in the work of the Holy Office. 'Your Eminence', she replied, 'when it comes to saving a soul, is it not the duty of every Catholic?' At that the Cardinal relented, and speaking more gently he allowed her to continue as she was doing.

Early in 1912 Frances Moloney had to return to England alone, to complete some legal formalities in connection with the handing over of Cefntilla Court on which the Moloneys' seven-year lease had expired. For health reasons Alfred could not travel, but he authorised Frances to act on his behalf. It was a hard journey. Frances reached England in the midst of a general rail strike which lasted for several weeks and slowed things down for her considerably. At Cefntilla her sister-in-law Kathleen was waiting for her, and they went to see the agent together. To their dismay they were presented with a large bill for damages and repairs. Frances had to act on the power that Alfred had vested in her. The only way to raise the necessary money was to sell some of their furniture.

> I decided to sell some valuable furniture of black carved oak with which we had furnished the inner drawing room. Ordinarily it should have fetched some hundreds. The auction took place at Usk, the stoppage of trains prevented the attendance of buyers and our belongings were knocked down at a pitifully low figure.[8]

Frances gave the chapel furniture to Bishop Hedley for a newly-founded mission, and she and Kathleen worked hard to leave the place in as good a condition as possible. She paid a quick visit to Ireland, where she was always sure of a heart-warming welcome from her sister's family. It was a joy to meet them again. Killyan had always been her 'home of predilection', she once said. She then travelled straight back to Rome. 'It was good to see Alfred's dear face after the weeks of absence which he declared had been a lonely time for him, and better still to feel him at my side at daily Communion.'[9]

Frances's former governess, the Carmelite Marie de Sacrè Coeur, wrote asking her to get a relic of Pope Pius X for a sick member of her community. The Pope's reputation for sanctity was widespread even in his lifetime. Frances and Alfred decided to enlist the help of Cardinal Gotti, a Carmelite. The Cardinal received them kindly. He had been anxious to meet Alfred to discuss the situation of the Church in Trinidad. There had been a long delay in appointing a successor to Archbishop Flood, because it was hard to find someone acceptable to all the different nationalities in the colony. Alfred was able to explain the complex political situation. Within a day or two a letter was carried by hand to the Moloneys, signed by the Holy Father and sending his blessing to the sick Carmelite.

Other friends also wrote asking them to get the Holy Father's blessing. Rumours had spread afar of the miracles attributed to him, some of which happened during public audiences. The Holy Father

had a special care for sick children and many of them were restored
to health by his touch, although he himself always attributed such
happenings to the 'Power of the Keys'. It is not surprising that
Frances had no problem in getting the Holy Father's blessing for
her young niece who was about to receive her First Communion.
Shortly afterwards her friend Angela Boland wrote from Dublin,
asking her urgently to get the Pope's blessing for her brother John's
child, who was gravely ill. (At that time John Boland was Whip of
the Irish Party.) Frances was embarrassed to ask again so soon.
Cardinal Merry del Val assured her that he had been authorised by
the Holy Father to sign in his name, but she stood her ground
bravely, saying that nothing but the Holy Father's own signature
would satisfy Mr Boland. The Cardinal went straight to the Pope's
apartment and returned immediately with the signed blessing. The
child recovered.

Among the Moloneys' friends in Rome were Sir George and
Lady Greville. Sir George's family in Co. Westmeath were Protestant, but he had become a Catholic on his marriage to a French-
woman. Both were very devout and, like the Moloneys, had
become tertiaries of St Francis whose practice of poverty they
adopted literally, selling all their property and choosing instead to
live a nomad existence in hotels. Lady Greville, Frances soon saw,
had a talent for finding hidden and often unusual holiness. Occasionally she brought Frances with her on her spiritual pilgrimages.
In Rome they visited a religious with the stigmata, who told them
'things past, present and to come'.[16] They also travelled to Viterbo
to meet a saintly Cistercian nun. She spoke to Frances of a future
event, which startled her at the time, but which she had reason to
recall in later years.

This visit to Viterbo was unusual for Frances. She rarely left
Alfred's side except to engage in works of charity, most of them
connected with her membership of the Catholic Women's League.
As secretary she had to attend all the meetings. Alfred's health was
causing her some concern, but as he himself made little of it only
gradually did she realise how ill he was. Alfred's friend Abbot
Gasquet was among those who did notice it, and he asked Frances

not to leave her husband alone so much. Because of this Frances resigned as Secretary of the Catholic Women's League. It was not so easy to disengage herself from some of the other charities in which she had become involved. She was in process of doing so when Alfred's condition deteriorated further. In her memoirs, Frances recalled what must have caused her immense pain: 'Finally, my poor husband could not bear me out of his sight. His increasing ailments caused a degree of fretfulness which nothing could satisfy. His character seemed completely changed, his inborn courtesy deserted him, and I suffered intensely both with him and for him.'[10]

Years later Frances said she would have been spared much heartache if she had known at the time that Alfred's testiness and seeming lack of consideration for her, were symptoms of the obscure tropical disease he suffered from. But she did not know that in 1912, in Rome. The specialist who examined Alfred (the Holy Father's own doctor) was unable to diagnose anything organically wrong. He put Alfred on a diet, which the patient refused to follow. Bishop Hedley, in Rome for his *ad limina* visit, stayed with them for a few weeks. That was as much as Alfred was equal to. The only person he seemed pleased to see was his spiritual director, Father Walmesley SJ. Frances was at her husband's side constantly. She did not have to go out, because she could attend Mass in the Sisters' chapel. That was the high point of each day. 'The privilege of daily communion,' she said, 'upheld me during this period of anguish and anxiety.'

One sad situation caused Frances to break her resolution of not leaving her husband alone. She discovered that the elderly wife of a dying German, who had been a porter in one of the big hotels, needed help in nursing him. Because of a certain amount of anti-German feeling, she had been unable to get help anywhere. Frances tried some convents on her behalf, and was unsuccessful. She was amazed to find that in some cases religious were forbidden by their rule to nurse men. This exasperated her and left an abiding memory. Years later, when she talked with Father John Blowick about the spirit that should distinguish the Columban Sisters, she referred to this incident as an example of an attitude to be avoided.

In Rome in early 1913, when she could not get any religious to help the wife of this dying man, she decided that she would have to go herself. She chose a time when Alfred would be taking his siesta. Everything went well. She helped to change the dying man's clothes and bed linen, and to tidy him up, and was back home again before Alfred awoke. Another day she slipped out again on the same errand, but coming back, on the stairs outside the Moloneys' apartment she walked into Abbot Gasquez. 'At it again!' he said reproachfully. Frances remarked wryly that it was soon all over Rome that she was neglecting her husband.

Life would have been harder for her without Father Mullan's guidance and support. Realising how difficult it was for someone as outgoing as she was to be so confined, he suggested that she make the Ignatian Spiritual Exercises at home, according to the Nineteenth Annotation.[11] Sometimes this is called the Retreat in Daily Life, because it is a way of making the Spiritual Exercises while a person carries on with his or her normal occupations, ensuring a certain amount of time for prayer each day. There are regular, usually weekly, meetings with the retreat director, who gives the material for prayer for the following week. The content of what is known as The Thirty Days Retreat is stretched out to meet the needs of the individual.

Father Mullan's suggestion was exactly what Frances needed at this time. Early every Saturday morning she would go to the German College to meet her director and to get prayer material for the coming week. 'This retreat,' she said, 'was one of the great graces of my life and a wonderful preparation for the dark days ahead.' It helped that Alfred 'was fully in sympathy with the plan and seemed to appreciate any little spiritual bits which I could share with him.'

It is unlikely that Frances would have known at the time that her director was regarded as one of the outstanding experts on the Ignatian Spiritual Exercises. In 1909 he had translated the Exercises directly from the Spanish Autograph of St Ignatius. Seventy years later, when David Fleming SJ published his popular *The*

Spiritual Exercises of St Ignatius, A Literal Translation and a Contemporary Reading[12] the 'literal translation' he chose was Elder Mullan's version, which he placed in parallel pages with his own 'contemporary reading'. He also gave Elder Mullan's Preface in full. In his own Preface David Fleming explained why he chose the Mullan version: 'Father Mullan's translation has the merit not only of being quite accurate but also of capturing much of the flavour and characteristics of Ignatius' personal style. For example, the delicate balance between the grace of God and our own effort, which is reflected in his original Spanish, is maintained better by Mullan than by many more recent English translators.'[13] Frances was blessed in her director.

Her father was delighted to hear about her retreat. He wrote telling her that he was praying for her and for the retreat:

> You are really making a Herculean retreat. Poor sinners like myself and other worldly male beings have to be contented with four days and five nights at Manresa, where even novels and bezique [his favourite card game] are prohibited, to say nothing of bridge or billiards. You are called to 'Wuthering Heights' of spirituality.[14]

He went on to tell her that her sister Freddie was also beginning a retreat, in Mount Anville, and he ended his letter with a question: 'What is the matter with Alfred, and is there any real danger?'

At the time Frances could see little cause for alarm, even though Alfred was ignoring his doctor's advice about diet and had become more reclusive. He showed no inclination to go out or even to meet visitors. But he did get some comfort in reading. Frances too was a reader, and now she availed of this time alone with her husband to prepare for an examination in Christian Doctrine. All those teaching catechism in Rome were required by Pope Pius X to attend a course of lectures given by prominent theologians. Frances could not go out to attend these classes but she was tutored by one of the Canons of St Peter's, Monsignor Petit. She was well prepared and did remarkably well.

The examination was on 11 June. By the middle of the month,

to avoid the heat of the Roman summer, the Moloneys left for Florence. Alfred's health began to improve and he even took to walking along the Ponte Vecchio, watching the silversmiths at work. Then suddenly he became worse. A local doctor advised them to go to a health resort in the Apennines, Abetone. And like his Roman colleague he too stressed the importance of diet, telling Alfred to avoid red meat. Frances instructed the waiters accordingly, but if Alfred saw something that he liked on the menu he ignored the doctor's advice.

They travelled by easy stages up the mountain to the health resort on the summit. They were five thousand feet above sea level and they found the place unexpectedly cold. Alfred always found the cold hard to take, and the food that he was allowed was scarce and expensive in this remote resort. Frances recalled that 'chickens seemed to be worth their weight in gold!' Alfred began to grow weaker, and his wife suddenly realised the danger that he might die in that isolated place. In desperation she sent a telegram to the superior of the Blue Nuns in Fiesole: 'Sir Alfred very ill. Can you take us in?' The response was immediate and warm-hearted.

Their slow journey down the mountain by car took several hours. By now Alfred was too weak to eat, and Frances could only hope and pray that he would reach the journey's end alive. Finally, in the late afternoon, they reached the Villa San Girolamo. 'Mother Edith's motherly welcome was like coming home. A heavy weight slipped off my shoulders as she immediately began making arrangements for my poor husband's comfort.'[15]

Frances had asked for inexpensive accommodation, but Mother Edith gave them the best, on very reasonable terms. Alfred's health improved a little and he was able to sit out in the garden for some hours every day. In Florence away down in the valley the late summer sun had wilted the flowers, but the garden of Villa Girololamo was a mass of colour and fresh green. Alfred, with his love of nature, would have enjoyed those precious hours in the garden and the view across the valley to the hills beyond. 'In spite of his illness he was content and comfortable,' Frances said. 'His sunny disposition returned, and his sympathetic understanding.

We had some happy days together.'[16]

These special days helped to prepare her for what lay ahead. Alfred was not recovering, and Mother Edith suggested sending to Milan for a well-known specialist in internal medicine. He came and examined the patient. His diagnosis was that Alfred was suffering from an obscure tropical disease for which there was no cure, and he gave him another two or three months to live. More and more the sick man's thoughts became focussed on the next life. He asked to see his spiritual director and Frances wrote to convey this request. Father Walmesley replied that he could not leave Rome because of his obligations towards the Father General. But when Alfred's condition deteriorated further Frances wrote directly to the Jesuit Father General, explaining the situation and asking him to release Father Walmesley for a few days. The permission was granted. Father Walmesley arrived and stayed some days. He and Alfred spent many hours talking, and he got permission to say Mass in Alfred's room. When the time came to say goodbye to Frances, he told her that he had never seen such strong faith as her husband's. She replied that it was 'the Irish Faith'.

She had already contacted Alfred's daughter Gladys and his sisters, telling them how gravely ill he was. Gladys arrived with Alfred's sister Kathleen. The patient was so happy to see them that he began to rally.

> He talked so normally and naturally about his death one would have thought it was only an ordinary journey he was about to take. The atmosphere was that of a happy family gathering. When I look back on those days I realise what a wonderful grace it was from God. It was the first week of August and we talked of the best day for him to go. The Feast of the Assumption would be such a beautiful day.[17]

On that feast, forty-six years later, Frances herself went to God. Did she remember then that they had chosen that special day for Alfred, though he actually celebrated the feast in heaven? On 5 August, Mother Edith handed Frances a telegram that had come for her. She opened it and stood rooted to the ground in shock. The telegram read: 'Regret to inform you your father died suddenly last evening. Writing.' It had come from Father O'Donohue, the Rector of Manresa, Roehampton, London, where her father was on retreat. For the previous thirteen years he had made his annual retreat there. It was a novitiate house, not a retreat centre in the strict sense of the term, but the community accepted small groups of retreatants at a time.

Reluctant to upset Alfred, Frances did not tell him the sad news. But, possibly sensing something, he asked her if she had any news of her father and she had to tell him. 'What do you mean, Bobbie? He cannot be dead!' he exclaimed. When he realised that Frances's father had indeed died, he murmured to himself, 'How wonderful that God should take father and son together.'

He lingered for some days longer, some of the time lapsing into unconsciousness, with Frances constantly at his side. The Sisters brought in a wicker couch so that she could be beside her husband even while she rested. He was anointed and was able to join in the responses. As Frances knelt there she felt someone beside her, but on turning around saw nobody. She was convinced that it was her father. Late one night Mother Edith phoned the Vatican to ask the Pope's blessing for Alfred. Cardinal Merry del Val went straight to the Holy Father, who sent a final apostolic blessing to his 'dear son Alfredo.'

Up to his very last days, Alfred preferred to have Frances look after his bodily needs and he declined the help of the nursing sisters. But, in the end, this was necessary. Each day he grew weaker, and he begged God to take him. On the morning of 12 August, even though he was extremely weak, he asked to be shaved. When Frances demurred he insisted, saying that he was going to meet his Maker. He then asked to be dressed in his best shirt and she dressed him in 'a delicate shirt of fine linen' Always fastidious about his person and his clothes, he asked finally for his gold cuff links. He wondered if he would die that night, and Frances replied, 'I think Our Lord will come and fetch you in your sleep.' 'Will he come Himself?' he asked in awe, 'O Bobbie, I am not worthy!'

At his request, the Franciscan Third Order habit was brought from the Franciscan Friary in Fiesole. One of the friars had been most attentive to Alfred in his last illness and he now blessed him again *in articulo mortis*. Making a great effort, the dying man spoke: 'What a wonderful ... and a marvellous thing ... is the ... connecting link between ... the departing Christian soul ... and the next ... world.' Frances asked him if he was referring to the habit which had been laid on his bed. But he said clearly, and these were his last words, 'I mean ... the Catholic Church.'

It was a night that Frances would never forget. Midnight came and went. Alfred was unconscious and his breathing all the time was growing slower. She held the crucifix to his lips and he stopped breathing. Mother Edith, who was with her, told her to speak into his ear. Half a lifetime later she remembered it all as if it were yesterday. 'Climbing on the bed with my arms around my dearest one I spoke distinctly: "Alfred". A faint smile appeared, and the answer came back: "Bobbie". It was the end of his mortal life, in which he had achieved much for God and man. The period of trial and suffering was over and God would, I knew, grant him rest at last.'[18]

The Requiem Mass took place in the Sisters' chapel, and Frances, Kathleen and Gladys, together with the Sisters, watched by the remains throughout the day. At nightfall the Misericordia Brothers carried the coffin to the cemetery further up the hill. The members of this confraternity, founded in the fourteenth century, had as one of their purposes to bury the dead. Somberly dressed and hooded, with mere slits for their eyes, they prayed the rosary with lighted candles in their hands as they processed up the winding road to the cemetery. The memory of this strange funeral stayed with Frances to the end of her days, together with all her memories of her much loved husband. 'Though by God's grace I have been called to higher things,' she said, 'my years of intimacy with so noble a character can never be obliterated from my mind.'[19]

She had a memorial card printed. On it she noted that Alfred had been a Tertiary of St Francis and that he had died 'fortified by all the rites of Holy Church, and with the special blessing of His Holiness Pius X'. There are the usual aspirations one sees on such cards, but at the end comes a quotation from St John Berchmans which speaks more personally of the relationship between Frances and her husband: 'I die, but my love for you will not die. I will love you in heaven as I have loved you on earth.'

As soon as Frances's brother Arthur heard the news of his brother-in-law's death, he sent a telegram from Dublin to say that he would travel out to bring her home. But that was unnecessary: her sister-in-law Kathleen and her stepdaughter Gladys were travelling with her. Immediately after the funeral they left for Rome. Frances asked for an audience with the Holy Father. She wanted to thank him for sending Alfred his blessing as he lay dying. Her heart, she said, 'was overflowing with gratitude for the great consolation he had given my dear one.'

Pope Pius X welcomed Frances compassionately, and they talked together about her double bereavement. It was not easy to secure an audience with the Pope in that year, 1913. He had several serious illnesses throughout the year, and had delegated most of his audiences to Cardinal Merry del Val. It was also the sixteenth centenary of the Edict of Constantine, which had brought peace to the Church, and many pilgrimages had come to Rome from all over the world. In two months alone there were twenty-three groups, all wanting to get the Holy Father's blessing. It is significant that this saintly man made time to meet Frances. 'Poor little one!' he exclaimed, 'God will comfort you in His own way!' What else transpired at this meeting Frances regarded as too sacred to record. All that we know for certain is that it was to affect the whole future direction of her life. 'From that moment my vocation was decided,' she wrote to her sister, Freddie, several years later.[20] And in her memoirs, recalling that meeting with the saintly pope, she said: 'His holiness of vision seemed to look into the depth of my soul, and I came away with the inward conviction of God's designs for the future.'

God's designs for the future would not be apparent for some years to come. In the meantime she decided to return to Ireland. She passed through London where she spent a few days with her grieving stepmother Louise, who invited her to live with her.

Frances declined. She went on to Dublin where she visited her brother Arthur and his wife. They too pressed her to stay with them in their spacious home, Wilfield House, in Ballsbridge.[21] After a few days, she left for Killyan, her sister's home. There she was welcomed with open arms, and slowly, over several months, the love that surrounded her began to take the hard edge off the pain that would be hers for a long time to come.

Her sister Freddie, perhaps hoping to help both of them to come to terms with the loss of their father and to distract Frances from her double grief, suggested that they write a short account of their father's life. Frances decided that they should also include the notes of his last ten retreats, which he had sent to her faithfully each year. The relationship between Frances and her father was particularly close, and he had shared his inner life with her, almost as if she were a spiritual director.

Preparing *A Layman's Retreats* for publication would have been a labour of love for both Frances and Freddie. They chose as a frontispiece an attractive head and shoulders portrait of their father (the only portrait of Henry Owen Lewis that this writer has been able to find). It shows him in profile, probably in early middle age. His keen yet kindly expression, and the high cheekbones and deepset eyes all remind the viewer of his daughter Frances. His hairline has begun to recede, but the hair is still dark, though his well-trimmed moustache and goatee are sprinkled with grey. He wears the high collar of the period and a patterned tie and waistcoat.

The small octavo sized volume, maroon in colour, and hard-backed, was published by Burns & Oates, London, in April 1914. It was edited by Father Edmund Lester SJ, who had directed Henry Owen Lewis's unfinished last retreat. Bishop Hedley of Newport, Frances's friend from her Cefntilla days, wrote the preface. In it he described accurately the spirit and content of Henry Owen Lewis's retreat notes: 'The writer lets us see a soul in the process of purifying and elevating itself by the exercises. Simply and without pretence, he sets down, for his own soul's use, the matter and spirit of what he hears.'[22] Bishop Hedley speaks of Henry Owen Lewis's 'evidently genuine acceptance of practical Christianity – regular prayer, strictness and self-denial in food and recreation, carefulness in speech, considerateness to others, loyalty to the Church, and the courageous profession of Catholic life.'[23]

After Bishop Hedley's preface comes an introduction of thirty-one pages written by Frances and her sister. It is an eloquent tribute to their father as well as a short biography which serves to put his spiritual life in context. In publishing their father's retreat notes they say that they are carrying out what they believe was one of his last wishes. During his last retreat he had written: 'Resolution: to do something more now for the Glory of God; to help on Retreats; to get others to make them; to make them better known; to help to get working-men to make them, to pay for some.'

During the previous thirteen years, ever since his first wife died, Henry Owen Lewis had made his annual retreat at Manresa, 'and each succeeding one seemed to bring him nearer to God.' His daughters speak about his deepening spirit of prayer and his love of the Mass, his work for the St Vincent de Paul Society and the Converts' Aid Society. What comes through also is the warmth of the love between father and daughters. He was writing a letter to his daughter Frances when God called him in the middle of a sentence: 'This is the thirteenth retreat I have made in Manresa and I wonder why so many graces should have been given to me. What a ... '

Among Henry Owen Lewis's retreat notes is a beautiful prayer which he quotes so often that it could be seen as the theme song of his life. It was a prayer that he had shared with his daughter Frances and it was to have a profound influence on her life: 'Dearest Lord Jesus, if Thou wilt have me, by the help of Thy holy grace, I will have Thee, and do thou have me. Let us two be together, now and always.'

Frances and her sister decided that any profits from the book should go towards supporting retreat work. A book of this kind would have had a limited circulation and it is unlikely that it raised much money. But it would have been treasured by Henry Owen Lewis's family and friends. A copy exists in the British Library and another, Frances's own copy, in the Columban Sisters' archives.

Organising this tribute to her father helped to fill some of

Frances's lonely days in Killyan. Early each morning she slipped out of the house before anyone was awake, to walk two miles to Mass in Newbridge. But sometimes she was noticed stealing out, and then she could expect to hear her eleven-year-old nephew Michael galloping after her in the pony and trap. She was in touch by letter all this time with her spiritual director Father Elder Mullan SJ. A letter from him dated 15 November gives an idea of the direction her thoughts were taking:

> Please don't think of taking up any religious vocation at present. You are much too impressionable to jump at such a thing. Perhaps, when you settle down here, you can practise a little first. Detachment is indeed your lesson: learn it well. Very glad you gave up that ring ... Sorry about your paying that debt. Please [underlined thrice], hold on to all your money. No harm in learning all you can about the Brigettines. If you put me another query about penance, I'll withdraw the leave for what you were to do in Advent! My only wish in keeping you out of Rome is to have you come back fully fit for work.[24]

Elsewhere in the same letter he refers approvingly to ways in which she is being influenced by the life of the Little Flower, Soeur Thérèse of the Child Jesus.[25]

Frances stayed at Killyan until after Christmas and then, as she said herself, 'unable to stand too much idleness' she tore herself away from her beloved family and returned to Rome. She stopped off in London. Significantly she stayed at the Sisters of Mercy Convent in Cadogan Street, not with any member of her family. There she received another letter from Father Mullan, advising her not to return to Rome too soon. Believing that she was ready for anything, Frances continued on her journey.

It was a lonely homecoming to the flat she had shared with her husband. The place was loud with his absence. Everything re-minded her of him, and all she could hold on to was her determi-nation to give the rest of her life to God. Father Mullan had suggested that she 'practise' the religious life first before commit-ting herself for a lifetime. So now she drew up for herself a rule of life which she submitted to her director for approval. He made some modifications. Noticing that she had structured in no free time for herself, he inserted this. It was a demanding rule of life, and cannot have been easy to follow in a society that was used to seeing Frances Moloney present at all sorts of charitable and social functions. But having made up her mind to adhere to a rule of life, she did so with her accustomed thoroughness.

Her stepmother Louise arrived for a visit and stayed at a hotel near Frances's apartment. They met every day, and soon she was joining Frances on her visits to the poor. Freddie wrote from Killyan to know if Frances could take her daughter Frieda for the remaining months of the winter. Frieda arrived and, after she had seen and admired all that was to be enjoyed in Rome, Frances was able to arrange for her to attend the Sacred Heart School, the Trinità Dei Monti. There she was with young girls of her own age and in spite of her high spirits or perhaps because of them, she fitted in remarkably well. After a few months she was given the much-coveted Child of Mary medal which she had failed to achieve as a student at Mount Anville, her former school. Frances was overjoyed.

Together with her stepmother, Frances called on Cardinal Merry del Val who welcomed them like old friends. It was her first time to meet him since the deaths of her husband and her father, and his concern and sympathy moved her deeply. Frances and Louise also visited the two remaining sisters of Pope Pius X, Maria and Anna, who lived in an apartment near the Vatican. Their other sister, Rosa, who had kept house for her brother in earlier years, had died recently. The Pope himself was in very poor health – he was to die in a matter of months – and he was still grieving for his sister, so Louise was unable to have a papal audience. But she and Frances felt that they came close to Pius X in meeting his sisters. 'Very simple and very gentle they talked quite frankly about their exalted brother who always remained their dear Beppo.' Frances was moved by the simplicity of their lifestyle, which would not change even after their brother's death. They were the only ones mentioned in his will: 'I was born poor, I have lived in poverty and am sure to

die a poor man. I commend my sisters, who have always lived with
me, to the generosity of the Holy See, and beg that they be allowed
a small sum of money each month, to support them in their old
age.'[26]

Conscious of the fact that she was meant to be 'practising
religious life', Frances now began to model her practice of poverty
on that of the Pope's sisters. To save fourpence a day, she walked
instead of taking a bus. Without consulting her director, who might
not have approved, she worked out for herself various other ways
of practising poverty and a simpler lifestyle.

On the feast of the Purification 1914, when she was back in
Rome little more than a month, her director allowed her to make
private vows of poverty, chastity and obedience for a limited
period, until the following Easter. The ceremony took place in the
rooms of St Ignatius, adjoining the Gesù, kneeling at the altar
where St Ignatius had so often celebrated Mass. With great earnest-
ness she pronounced the following words:

> My Lord and Master, Jesus Christ, prostrate at Thy adorable
> feet, I, Frances Margaret Mary Moloney (in religion Magdalen)*,
> a most unworthy servant, not fit to aspire to be Thy spouse, do
> humbly beg to consecrate myself wholly and entirely to Thy
> love and service in the practice of Thy counsels of poverty,
> chastity and obedience, until the Feast of Easter 1914. Knowing
> my own miserable weakness and inconstancy, I implore of
> Thee, Jesus, my Lord and my God, to grant me Thine all-
> powerful grace, and with Thine assistance, I undertake for love
> of Thee, for the next year not to spend anything on myself
> beyond what is considered suitable or necessary to the condition
> of life in which thou, my dearest Lord, has placed thy poor
> servant. Moreover I purpose to use the material goods with
> which thou hast blessed me as if they were not my own. Thine
> they are and I consecrate them to Thy love and service, desiring
> only to use them as instruments for Thy honour and glory. Lord,

---

* Margaret was the name she took in Confirmation; Magdalen was her name as
a Franciscan Tertiary.

Thy servant, my husband is dead, and Thou knowest that Thy servant was one that feared God. I was not worthy of his goodness but grant me one day to be reunited to him in Thy heavenly kingdom. In my heart I hear Thee saying: 'I have espoused Thee to one husband that I may present thee as a chaste holocaust to God.' Grant me, O Lord, to spend the remainder of my days in purity and chastity. Thou hast told us that Thy meat is to do the will of Him who sent Thee. Give me, O Lord, to eat of this meat together with Thy Body and Blood, and make me like Thee, obedient unto death, even the death of the Cross. I undertake, therefore, always to obey all those who are placed in sacred authority over me, undertaking these three vows not to be binding in case of doubt on my part, and leaving their application in the hands of my confessor for the time being. Dearest Lord, without Thee I can but fail. Do Thou see to it that these three vows which I take in Thy presence and that of Thy Blessed Mother and the Heavenly Court be not to my undoing, but grant that they may be the feeble instruments to draw me nearer to Thee.[27]

When she came to the end of this long profession of vows according to the formula approved by her director, to his surprise she added a prayer of her own, the prayer so much loved by her father: 'If Thou wilt have me, by the help of Thy grace, I will have Thee, and do Thou have me. Let us two be together now and always.'

At first her spiritual director would allow Frances to make vows for a few months only. Afterwards she renewed these vows of poverty, chastity and obedience yearly, and each time she ended with the above prayer so that it became like a fourth vow, a vow of love. A prayer chosen to accompany the profession of private vows year by year tells us much about the personality of the person praying. It reveals what nurtured her spirit and gave life, as the sap does to the tree. It was the living out of this prayer that led her, step by step, along a path that only revealed itself finally to her when she met Father John Blowick in 1918.

But, in the spring of 1914 all that was clear was her great desire for the religious life, and her director's insistence that she first needed time to discern, and to 'practise' living the vows she had professed privately. With about forty other retreatants she made a six-day Ignatian retreat under Father Mullan in the Convent of Marie Reparatrice. Afterwards he enlisted her help in his campaign to encourage simplicity of lifestyle among his directees, several of whom were fashionable socialites. One day he sent for her to go to the Jesuit Generalate. She waited in one of the parlours, and he came in carrying as many 'glittering spangled ball dresses' as his arms could hold. He put them down on the rather austere functional chairs and hurried out for another batch. This time the tables were covered as well as the chairs. Frances wondered what the Father General would say if he walked in on this strange scene. She wondered too what she would be asked to do. Father Mullan soon enlightened her: he wanted her to dispose of all these beautiful gowns that had been given up by his directees. Two of them, like Frances, were interested in the religious life and like her were 'practising' for it.

In the meantime, she carried on her works of charity, going out each day with the Helpers of the Holy Souls to the poorest quarters of Rome. Once she had committed herself to this work she was consistently regular and punctual. Her day-to-day contact with these Sisters moved her to appreciate and admire their selfless dedication: 'the self-immolation practised by those holy nuns taught me the best way of assisting my beloved ones who had left this earth.' On 23 May 1914 she was received as an Associate Member of the Helpers of the Holy Souls. Soon afterwards she was invited to become a member of an association affiliated to the Society of the Sacred Heart. Father Mullan tended to discourage her from taking on any additional spiritual obligations, but she felt that she owed so much to the Sacred Heart nuns that she could not refuse. In addition to these extra prayer commitments, she was also faithful to the spiritual duties associated with being a Franciscan Tertiary.

At the last consistory to be called by Pope Pius X, in May 1914,

Abbot Gasquet was raised to the purple. Remembering his friend Alfred Moloney, he invited Frances and her stepmother to his reception of the cardinal's hat. Soon afterwards, Frances had the joy of accompanying her stepmother to the Vatican for a long-postponed audience with the Holy Father. There were other English-speaking pilgrims present, and the Pope asked Frances to act as his interpreter. When the audience came to an end, they knelt for the Holy Father's blessing. He blessed each one individually and gave each a souvenir. When he came to Frances, he smiled as he handed her a beautiful silver medal of the Holy Spirit, saying, 'For my dear interpreter'.

In June of that year, Frances sat the examination for the second year's course in Christian Doctrine, required of all religion teachers in Rome. One of the examination topics was an essay on the history, origin and meaning of devotion to the Sacred Heart. Guessing beforehand that she might have to write on this subject, she had prepared for it by getting help from her friends, the Sacred Heart nuns at the Trinità dei Monti. To their joy and hers, she acquitted herself surprisingly well.

She had already begun to teach catechism to little boys every Sunday afternoon, in the Carmelite Fathers' church. Teaching them in Italian she introduced them to the basic truths of their faith. She taught them how to pray and helped to instil in them devotion to Jesus in the Blessed Eucharist. It was a great joy to her to see them crowding together at the altar rails after the class was over, and soon she noticed that some of them were dropping in during the day for short visits. Older boys started coming along, and then Frances often had to enlist the help of a lay-brother to maintain order. Sometimes parents came along. Even if they were drawn by curiosity, Frances hoped that they might also learn a little and pass it on to their children.

The club for English-speaking girls, which Frances had helped to establish, continued to attract young women, especially those who were out of work or temporarily homeless. The Catholic Women's League realised that some kind of permanent accommodation was called for, and Frances thought of offering to share her roomy flat. But first of all permission would have to be obtained from the Cardinal Vicar of Rome. This was given and a subscription list opened. The Drexel Dahlgrens offered to lend their spacious apartment for a bazaar to raise funds for the proposed hostel. The bazaar drew a large crowd, including some eminent ecclesiastics, and it was successful beyond all expectations.

By now it was summertime and the heat was driving people out of Rome. Frances had been invited by some friends to join them in conducting a Motor Mission in Wales and, as nothing could be done about implementing the plans for the future hostel until after the summer, she prepared to leave. Little did she know that war was about to break out and that for her the Roman years were over. She would return for short visits, but never again to stay.

Frances Owen Lewis on her presentation at Court in 1892. (THE GENTLEWOMAN, by permission of the British Library.)

Frances's wedding photograph, 1897.

A welcoming party for Sir Alfred and Lady Moloney on their arrival in Grenada.

A riding party, Grenada. Frances Moloney second from the left, Sir Alfred sixth.

Government House, Grenada. Frances Moloney third from the left, second row; Sir Alfred Moloney third from the left, third row.

Frances Moloney on her favourite mount. Taken soon after arriving in Grenada.

The Corbally girls, Rathbeale Hall, Frances's friends.
Mary is in the centre and Angela on the left.

Sir Alfred and Lady Moloney in San Girolamo, Fiesole, 1913.

Above: Frances Moloney during the Motor Mission in Wales, 1914.

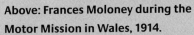

Left: Freddie Chevers, Frances's only sister.

Below: John Chevers, with his daughters Aylish and Frances.

St Brigid's, Cahiracon, cradle of the congregation.

Chinese Mission Convent, Cahiracon.

The first novices, 1922: Sisters Mary Patrick Moloney (second row L), Mary Joseph McKey, Teresa Brannigan, Emmanuel Dalton, Finbarr Collins, Margaret Mary Scanlan, Brigid McSwiney, Francis Xavier Mapleback, Brendan Walsh.

Novices and postulants in 1923, with the Irish Sisters of Charity who trained them: Sister Mary Alphonsus Harnett, Mother Mary Camillus Dalton and Sister Mary Bartholomew McHugh.

The first departure for China, 13 September 1926. (L to R): Father John Blowick with Sisters Mary Theophane Fortune, Agnes Griffin, Patrick Moloney, Mother Mary Finbarr Collins, Sisters Mary Philomena Woods and Lelia Creedon. Six Columban Fathers who travelled with them were (L to R): Fathers Alphonsus Ferguson, Michael Fallon, James Linehan, Charles Donnelly, Joseph Hogan, John Loftus

First Columban Sisters' community, Hanyang. First Row: Mother Mary Theophane with Chinese friends. Second Row: Sisters Mary Lelia, Agnes, Patrick andPhilomena.

The Hanyang community in 1930, with Bishop Edward Galvin.

Sisters visiting flood victims, Hanyang, 1931.

Sister Mary Patrick ministering to one of the flood victims.

Mother Mary Patrick before leaving on her first visitation as Superior General (1937).

Aylish Fane-Saunders, her husband Bernard, sons Kevin and Terence, and nephew Sean Smith, visiting 'Aunt Frances' in Cahiracon.

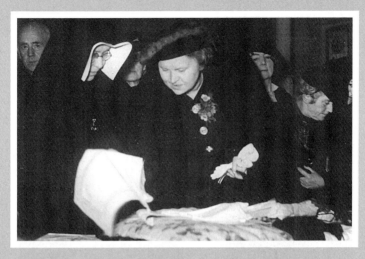

Mother Mary Patrick with Mrs Sean T. O'Kelly (wife of the President) who opened the Sisters' Christmas Sale on 29 November, 1945. (Photo: Irish Press)

Mother Mary Patrick, Sister Mary Brendan and Sister Joan Sawyer with Father Michael McHugh, the chaplain.

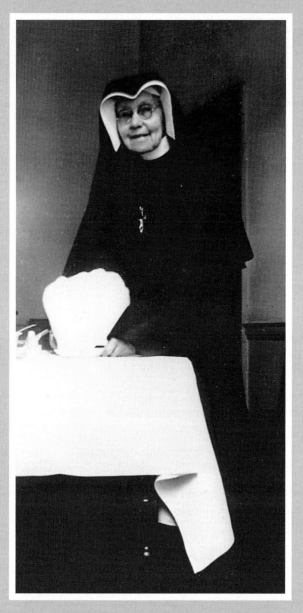

Mother Mary Patrick in 1954. (Photo: Adele Godetz)

Mother Mary Patrick at the General Chapter of 1958.

St Columban's Convent, Magheramore, Wicklow.

SEVEN

Call and Response

Frances Moloney arrived back in England in the early summer of 1914, and the following day she left for Wales with a small group of Catholic women to prepare for what was known as the Motor Mission. This was somewhat like an intensive parish mission, but it moved from place to place making use of a mobile chapel. A project of the Catholic Missionary Society, it was the inspiration of Father Herbert Vaughan SJ. When Frances and her companions arrived in Wales they arranged for accommodation in miners' cottages. They then began a house-to-house visitation along the Rhondda valley, explaining the mission and inviting people to attend. It was a mining community and among them Frances found many lapsed Irish Catholics. She gave them much of her time, and had the satisfaction of seeing most of them come along to the mission. A photograph exists of her handing out pamphlets to coal-dusty miners on their way home after their day's shift, she in deep mourning and they with faces as black as their clothes.

It was a short-lived venture, brought to a sudden end by the outbreak of World War I in August 1914. Frances returned to Ireland and there she got involved in work for Belgian refugees. On 14 September Augustine Birrell, Chief Secretary for Ireland, had written to Dr Walsh, Archbishop of Dublin, asking for hospitality for Belgian refugees:

> I am most anxious if possible to arrange that Ireland should receive and offer hospitality to some of those poor Belgian refugees, who, in the course of the next few days, will be reaching our shores in considerable numbers. I am writing to the Cardinal, whose general sympathy and support I would, of course, like to obtain, and also to the Lord Mayor of Dublin, but I shall be very glad if Your Grace can give me the benefit of your opinion and also any suggestions as to the best way of forming committees.[1]

The response was immediate and affirmative. A committee was set up by the Local Government Board to look after accommodation and support for the refugees. Frances, yielding to pressure, became a member. The Jesuit Provincial, Father T.V. Nolan, was in charge of the project and Frances was in correspondence with him about various local committees as well as the needs of the refugees.[2] At this period her address was her brother's house in Ballsbridge.

A long letter to Father Nolan written on 8 January 1915 would suggest that she had been asked to visit different refugee centres and to report on them. There was a problem in Greystones, she told him, because the local committee was irregularly formed and totally Protestant, only conceding to Catholic membership as a result of strong protest from the local parish priest, Father Flood. In Rathdrum, she had discovered a strange anomaly – all the refugees were men. She also wanted Father Nolan to know that the refugees in Gorey could not be moved because of an outbreak of scarlet fever. A refugee family in Dunshaughlin was starving, she wrote, because no allowance had been made for three extra boys. She also told Father Nolan that the contact person with the general committee in London, a certain Mrs Fowle, agreed with her that they should rent a house, so Frances suggested that she contact some house agents before the next committee meeting. Moreover, she added, the general committee would like Ireland to take one thousand refugees a week. Mrs Fowle evidently considered this impossible, but Frances, ever optimistic, and never one to let grass grow under her feet, believed that 'if we can only get the Bishops to take the matter up, that Ireland will take her share in offering hospitality. I have wired this morning to Father McArdle who is in Dundalk today, asking him to arrange if possible for me to see Cardinal Logue on Sunday.'

Frances's next letter to Father Nolan, a week later, was about the milk bill! A day later she wrote to ask about his health. 'The work is very heavy, but we are getting through all right, as Mr Fallon is simply splendid, and does the work of six ordinary people.'[3] She reported that she had sent a message to the Master of the Workhouse in Celbridge that a certain 'unsatisfactory person' would be removed in a week's time. Here she touched on a problem. Sometimes refugees who had been troublesome in England were sent to Ireland. Consequently it was decided that Frances would travel back and forth to England to assess suitable asylum-seekers. Assisted by a Belgian Jesuit chaplain, she was able to ensure that the refugees sent to Ireland were, on the whole, capable of adjusting. There were occasional exceptions, and Frances sometimes had to visit centres where problems had arisen.

She still found time for her family. In May 1915, her sister Freddie gave birth to her eighth child. Her husband John Chevers had rejoined the Connaught Rangers and, three weeks after she had given birth, Freddie got word that he was gravely ill abroad. She left immediately to be with him and Frances had to take charge of the family. Fortunately for her they were renting a house in Bray for the summer, so after she had found trustworthy helpers to look after the children and the housekeeping she was able to commute to Dublin each day to continue her work on the Refugee Committee. The older children helped to look after the younger. All went well until Norman and Michael returned from Stoneyhurst on holidays. As soon as he arrived, Norman hurried off to the local recruiting office and enlisted. Equally quickly Frances got the registration cancelled because Norman was under age, barely seventeen years. In September she had to get Michael ready for Clongowes. Soon after that, Freddie and her husband returned, and brought the family back to Galway.

Throughout these busy months, when she commuted each day from Bray to Dublin and looked after her sister's family as well as Belgian refugees, Frances was in touch by letter with her spiritual director in Rome. Early in the summer he wrote to her, suggesting that since she was still interested in the religious life she should consider a religious order whose members continue to live and work in the world, and who return to their convent at intervals for short visits. She replied that this 'divided kind of vocation' did not appeal to her: 'It must be one thing or another.'[4] He wrote in return:

This morning I said Mass for you, begging at the same time the grace of being able to say definitely what I think, so here it is:

1. I think you will do better to remain in the world, in Ireland, engaged in the work you have mentioned. The reasons are these: a) Your decision last year, approved by me at the time, was to work in the world; b) You have the advantage of your title, which is like a talent and should not be rendered useless; c) You are oldish for entering religion; d) You have been used to command; e) Your life has been, and, I think, must be, active.

2. The attraction to religious life is good and will help to keep you at the supernatural. Thank God for it – and do not yield to it. It is found in many who decide not to be Religious, and decide rightly.... I think you should give up the thought of Religion unless it becomes quite clear you should enter, the clearness being accepted as such by some spiritual-minded person.[5]

He suggested that she draw up a new plan of life and send it to him. This she did. She accepted his decision for the time being, but her longing for the total commitment of religious life stayed with her.

In the late autumn of 1915 she made arrangements to return to Italy: she needed to see to Alfred's grave and put up a proper memorial, and she had decided to give up her flat in Rome. It was a hazardous journey and a difficult one: Europe was in the throes of war and memories of the *Lusitania* were fresh in people's minds. Had she not been able to secure a diplomatic pass from the First Secretary of the British Foreign Office, Sir Maurice de Bunsen whose wife was her friend, she could not have made the journey.

On arrival in Rome her first concern was to meet the new Pope, Benedict XV. A monsignor whom she did not know was the new official in charge of papal audiences, and he seemed somewhat suspicious of this foreign lady who had arrived in Rome in the midst of war. She had to go to her friend Cardinal di Belmonte for a letter of introduction. This he couched in such flattering words that she presented it with some embarrassment. It worked, and an audience was arranged for the following day. Frances found herself in immediate rapport with the Holy Father, who seemed to enjoy her company and was reluctant to see her go. Through her he sent many blessings for Ireland, blessing in a special way the works she was involved in.

She then travelled north to Fiesole. To her disappointment, she found that the new cemetery where Alfred's remains would finally rest was not yet ready. She was asked to return in a year's time. She went back to Rome where she spent a few weeks, and was able to meet those friends who had stayed on in Rome despite the war. Some members of the girls' club had fallen on hard times and, to help them, she sold a valuable piece of Dresden china, part of Alfred's collection, still in the flat. Before leaving Rome she seems to have disposed of other personal belongings. The Poor Servants of the Mother of God, from whom she and Alfred had rented the flat, had for many years a beautiful carpet which used to be brought out for feast days, and which they called 'Lady Moloney's carpet'.

When she returned to Ireland Frances was able to give her full attention to the Belgian refugees, though the huge influx at the beginning of the war had died down and the work was less demanding. One wet and windy night in August 1916 she travelled over from Holyhead on the crowded mail-boat with a group of refugees. With some difficulty she found places for them, and was content to walk up and down the deck herself. Out of the darkness imposed by wartime restrictions she saw two figures emerge. They were old friends, her sister's in-laws, Jack and Fifi ffrench, who were returning from London after the execution of Sir Roger Casement.[6] As a young man Lord ffrench had visited Lourenço Marques in Portuguese East Africa when Casement was British Consul, and they had become lifelong friends. It was through Lord ffrench that Casement had made contact with the leaders of the Irish Party.[7]

The ffrenches invited Frances to share their cabin, but knowing that she had to be accessible to the refugees she declined. They then offered her Sir Roger Casement's overcoat that they had brought over from Pentonville Jail. This she accepted gladly, saying that she was proud to wear a garment belonging to a man who had sacrificed his life for his country. There was a further reason: Sir Roger Casement had been a close friend of her brother-in-law, Captain George Moloney, who was killed in action in Northern Nigeria.

One of the people Frances met daily in the office of the Belgian Refugee Committee was Thomas Fallon of the St Vincent de Paul Society, about whom she had written to Father Nolan with such praise the previous year. After some time, when the refugee work was running smoothly, Mr Fallon talked to her about the poor of Dublin and suggested that she consider their needs as well as those of the refugees. He introduced her to the slums on the north side of the city, where she saw and admired what the Society of St Vincent de Paul was doing to help the destitute. Very soon she was involved in that work, visiting poor families in the Pro-Cathedral parish and helping out at Ozanam House.

In the meantime, she had moved from her brother's house in Ballsbridge to the Marie Reparatrice convent at 53 Merrion Square. She said that she 'found great solace in the beautiful chapel', practically unchanged since the days when she and her sister, both in their teens, used to run there from Fitzwilliam Square for morning Mass. 'It was restful to soul and body to spend a Holy Hour of Adoration after a tiring day in the slums of North Dublin. Again and again the longing to devote myself entirely to God as a religious was uppermost in my thoughts and prayers.'[8]

But with her irregular schedule, as she got deeper into the work of the St Vincent de Paul Society, it became less convenient to continue boarding in the Reparation Convent. She looked out for alternative accommodation and was happy to find a suitable flat on the top floor of 119 St Stephen's Green. The lower three floors of this attractive Georgian house were given over to solicitors' offices. Frances's flat had its own private entrance and staircase and it was within easy reach of the Carmelite Church in Whitefriar Street. She had a pleasant view of St Stephen's Green from her front windows; from the back she had a vista of city rooftops and church spires, with the Dublin Mountains in the distance.

Frances was not long installed in her new flat when Thomas

Fallon saw needs in the Gloucester Street area of the Pro-Cathedral parish, with which he felt she could help. He introduced her to the parish priest, Father Turley, a man of great zeal and enthusiasm who had already done much to improve the situation in the parish. He now decided to invite the Redemptorists to preach a mission. Frances and her fellow members in the Guild of Our Lady of Lourdes, formed to work with the St Vincent de Paul Conference of the same name, undertook a house-to-house visitation. They were advised to omit one or two streets of ill repute, notorious for prostitution.

Father Frank Gleeson CC, Father Turley's assistant, had a special care for the youth of the parish and kindly and firmly he was able to influence them for good. He sometimes came along to the officers of the Guild of Our Lady of Lourdes, 'jingling a few shillings' and asking them to provide a picnic lunch for some boys he was bringing on an outing. That meant that they had to dip into their own pockets too and approach some friendly firms that might donate food. Mr Kennedy of Kennedy's Bread, a household word in Dublin for some generations, was always generous in supplying bread for sandwiches. Butter and meat came from other sources. Sometimes Father Gleeson was lucky in being offered a free meal for his young charges. Mother Joseph Conception, of the Irish Sisters of Charity, at that time superior of the Home for the Blind in Merrion, was his most generous benefactor. Later she was to play an important part in Frances's life as a religious, but they first met through their shared care for the poor of Dublin.

It was around this time that Frances took up her study of the Irish language. She seems to have been deeply moved by the heroism shown in 1916: it touched something in her own identity, which she had always considered to be Irish. It would seem that she regarded her birth in London as merely an accident of the Land War: she should have been born in Co. Monaghan. From her father she had inherited an interest in Irish politics and in the turbulent post-1916 years she made no secret of her republican sympathies. Her stepdaughter Gladys began to get alarmed, fearing that her step-mother was treading on dangerous ground.[9] But, as a colonial governor's wife, Frances Moloney had learned diplomacy: Gladys had no reason to fear.

Anyway, Frances was too busy to get actively involved in politics. While giving much of her time to the work of the St Vincent de Paul Society in the Pro-Cathedral parish she was still working for the Belgian refugees, helping with fund-raising benefits on their behalf. She also attended meetings of the Catholic Truth Society, the Catholic Business Girls' Club, the Catholic Girls' Protection Society, and she was faithful in going along to the Sacred Heart convent in Leeson Street for meetings of the Children of Mary. Entries in her diaries suggest that she played bridge occasionally and that she was a member of a study circle. All this on top of the demanding rule of life that she had worked out with her spiritual director.

Through it all she kept in touch with her friends. She always treasured her friendships and it was through a friend that God's will for her finally revealed itself. Early in 1918 her Jesuit confessor, Father Michael Browne , withdrew his opposition to her becoming a religious, 'unaccountably as far as human calculation could perceive'.[10] It now became a question of deciding which congregation she would apply to. She was attracted to the Daughters of Charity, whose love and care for the poor she had admired since she was a young girl. 'Then someone spoke of China and at Holy Communion on the Feast of the Finding of the Holy Cross, the Master's Will was made clear beyond all doubt.'[11] In her reverence for God's intimate dealings with the human soul, she has not revealed the manner in which God's Will was disclosed with such certainty on 3 May 1918.

The person who spoke of China was her friend from childhood, Anneence Fitzgerald-Kenny, of Clogher House, Ballyglass, Co. Mayo. She reminded Frances of a talk given in the Mansion House six months earlier on 11 October 1917 by Father John Blowick, about the newly-founded Maynooth Mission to China. Towards the end of his address he had spoken of the need for women to go to China to work in conjunction with the priests. Teaching religious would be needed, both nuns and brothers. There would be need too for missionary women with medical and nursing training; he envisioned 'a new congregation of nuns whose vow would be the medical care of the sick in pagan countries, whose members would be properly qualified in medicine, surgery and midwifery. Some of the members might be qualified as nurses or there might be a supplementary nursing order.'[12] Father Blowick also spoke about the foundation of a lay Irish medical missionary society for China, which would raise the funds necessary to cover the expenses of the hospitals and dispensaries to be staffed by this new medical congregation. The establishment of a medical missionary society, he said, had already been approved by Rome. The founding of an order of nun-doctors had been referred to the Congregation of Bishops and Regulars, and was being investigated.[13]

Frances Moloney and Anneence Fitzgerald-Kenny talked at length and wondered aloud how they could help to implement Father John Blowick's dream. Finally they decided to ask advice from the Bishop of Galway, Dr O'Dea. As well as being their mutual friend, he was associated with the beginnings of the Maynooth Mission to China and had welcomed the fledgling society into his diocese. The two friends went to Galway on 11 May 1918 and had three meetings with Bishop O'Dea: first of all in the confessional, then the following morning in the Mercy Convent, and later when the bishop invited them to dinner at his house. After questioning them at length and pointing out the difficulties they were likely to face, he advised them to talk to Father Blowick at Dalgan Park, Shrule, Co. Galway.[14]

After that, things began to move quickly. The day after they dined with Bishop O'Dea, the two friends went to Shrule to meet Father Blowick, but he had gone out for the day with the students: St Columban's College, Dalgan Park, had opened as a seminary for the Chinese Mission about three months earlier. On their return to Dublin Miss Fitzgerald-Kenny wrote to Father Blowick, whom she knew personally, telling him about their visit and the reason for it. On her part, Frances wrote to Dr O'Dea, asking him to recommend her for the Chinese Mission. She put in writing the history of her vocation during the previous five years, and gave Dr O'Dea

permission to share this with Father Blowick. This he did, and
Father Blowick wrote to her encouragingly, saying, 'The hand of
God seems to be in your work and I think that with His help we shall
be able to do something big and lasting to help the missions.'[15] He
enclosed a copy of a book by Dr Margaret Lamont, *Twenty Years
Medical Work in Mission Countries*, which he felt might give her
some ideas.

Dr Margaret Lamont, a Scotswoman, had qualified in medicine
at the London School of Medicine for Women in 1895. For almost
sixteen years she had worked as an Anglican missionary doctor in
India, New Zealand, Egypt and San Francisco. After becoming a
Catholic she worked in China, as a lone Catholic doctor in a vast
country where the whole medical profession seemed to be in the
hands of Protestants. She continually urged the need for Catholic
medical missions in China, and in particular for a congregation of
religious women who would be qualified in different branches of
medical and nursing care, including obstetrics and midwifery.
Chinese women, she pleaded, needed such, and even though Rome
at the time had forbidden religious to practise medicine and surgery
or to help at childbirth, she campaigned for a lifting of the
prohibition. In September 1917 she wrote from Shanghai to Archbishop Walsh of Dublin, trying to enlist his support for her plan to
get medical training for young Irishwomen willing to work on the
missions. She told him that some years previously, as a Protestant,
she had worked at the Rotunda Hospital in Dublin for three months,
and even there she had seen how acceptable women doctors were
to poor women at childbirth.[16]

Dr Lamont was not the first person to suggest a congregation of
qualified medical women for missionary work. The idea had
originated with another Scotswoman, Dr Agnes McLaren (1837-
1913). A Presbyterian for the greater part of her life, she became a
Catholic in 1898 and, in her retirement, offered hospitality in her
home in Antibes to missionaries needing a rest. That was how she
came to hear about plans for a hospital in Rawalpindi to look after
the needs of women, especially women in purdah. All her life she
had been working for women's issues, especially those relating to

healthcare. Now, at the age of sixty-seven, she took on this project, sought the support of bishops and organised a committee to finance the work and provide personnel.

Faced with the problem of finding a suitable medical director for the hospital, Dr McLaren became convinced that only missionary religious would have the necessary stability and dedication. She went to Rome in 1905 to urge a change in the law forbidding religious to engage in medical work. She was back again in 1909, and in 1910, 1911 and 1912. She was planning another visit to Rome in May 1913, when she died.[17] Frances Moloney met her in Rome on her last visit there in 1912, and she was deeply impressed by this indomitable Scotswoman.[18] Agnes McLaren did not live long enough to see her dream realised. It was not until 1936 that the door was open for religious to practise midwifery.

In the meantime, in the United States, her protégée and friend Anna Dengel was able to form the kind of medical missionary congregation that she had dreamt of. By taking private rather than public vows, Anna Dengel and her companions were exempt from Church law as applied to religious. In 1926, a year after the founding of the Medical Mission Sisters, Dr Lyons, one of the first group, left for Rawalpindi to take up again the work so dear to Dr McLaren. Others left in the following years, and as soon as Rome lifted the restriction on the practice of medicine and midwifery by religious the Medical Mission Sisters took public vows. They were formally approved by Rome as a religious congregation in 1941. Their long wait was at an end.

But all this was in the future. In June 1918, when Father Blowick sent Frances Moloney a copy of Dr Margaret Lamont's book about her medical work in mission countries, it was still a dream. There was no immediate hope of women religious being permitted to train or work in the mission field in any medical capacity, in spite of the efforts of people like Dr McLaren and Dr Lamont.

Frances read Dr Lamont's book with interest. It included a rule for the kind of religious congregation Dr Lamont had in mind. Rather undemocratic to modern eyes, it presumed a hierarchy of membership with doctors at the top, then medical students, nurses, paramedics and other helpers. On reading this rule for what was called a religious congregation, Frances saw immediately that there seemed to be no reference to the observance of the counsels, or to the spiritual training of the members. 'There were some provisions for spiritual duties, and an evidently sincere desire to assist the poor and the afflicted, but at that time, the compiler of the Rule was too recent a Catholic to understand the traditional spirit of the Church concerning Religious congregations.'[19]

Meanwhile she was trying to persuade her director that God could be calling her to work in China. Father Michael Browne SJ had replaced Father Mullan as her spiritual director: Rome was far away, especially in wartime. Father Browne was afraid that she was acting rashly and impulsively. He refused to discuss the matter further until after she had made her annual retreat. She wrote to Father Blowick telling him that in obedience to her director she could not make any decision in favour of China until after her retreat. When considering her vocation during her retreat, she told him, she would have to look at two options: that she enter the Sisters of Charity, if they accepted her, and wait until they made a foundation in China, or that she might co-operate with other women in forming a group to help the Maynooth Mission to China, 'somewhat on the lines suggested by Dr Lamont in her Rule, but possibly more like a religious order.' She was firm in her own mind about China, but she feared that because of her unworthiness, or other reasons, her services might not be accepted.

Understanding her dilemma, Father Blowick wrote reassuringly:

Somehow I have the feeling that you will ultimately be with us in forwarding the interests of the Master in China. It seems to me as if you were the person chosen by God to set on foot a new congregation or order. You will say you are unworthy and of course we all have to remember that we are unworthy of doing even the meanest thing for God, but it is His business that has to be done, and He will see to it that we do it all right if we give Him a chance in our own lives.[20]

Such a letter, Frances said, nearly carried her off her feet. She was hoping to work for God in some humble capacity and she found the responsibility suggested by Father Blowick 'positively terrifying'. But as she would not be free to make any decision until after her retreat she suggested that Father Blowick make enquiries about her from those who knew her, so that he would not accept 'one who might be a hindrance rather than a help'. For instance, the Archbishop of Dublin, she told him, had a poor opinion of her, and some of the public bodies she had worked with might regard her as 'rather aggressive'. What grounds she had for her remark about Archbishop Walsh is unknown, and her conclusion may well have been exaggerated. But it is a fact that in the Dublin diocesan archives there is a personal letter from her to the Archbishop, written in May 1915, asking for an interview. The Archbishop was meticulous about entering his day-to-day appointments in his diary. There is no record of any meeting with Frances Moloney. Nor is there any indication that her letter was even acknowledged. From time to time Archbishop Walsh seems to have suffered from poor health and he consequently tended to limit himself to essential diocesan business.

In her letter to Father Blowick, Frances also suggested that he make enquiries about her from her director Father Michael Browne SJ. It was Father Browne who directed the retreat she began two weeks later at the Ursuline Convent, Waterford. In a letter to Father Blowick the day after the retreat ended she summarised it in one sentence: 'I had consolation from Our Lord, but such great trials that I wondered whether you had all forgotten to help with your prayers!'

Elsewhere she described in more detail what seem to have been very painful days. Prudently, but with great kindness, Father Browne tried to dissuade her from throwing in her lot with the priests of the Maynooth Mission to China. Like her previous director, Father Mullan SJ, he feared that she might act rashly and forfeit the means of doing good that came from her social position and her means. But what concerned him most was that the young priests of the Maynooth Mission to China had no experience of religious life. He also felt that it was unrealistic of them to think of starting a congregation of women religious for China until they themselves had been allocated a definite mission area. With arguments such as these, others had been prevented from offering themselves for the China Mission. But Frances weighed them against her conviction that God was calling her to give herself for China. For three painful hours she wrestled in prayer, facing the options open to her, trying to discern where God was calling her. Along the corridor going to the refectory, there hung a picture of St Peter walking towards Christ on a stormy sea. Frances, with a storm in her own heart, stood in front of the picture, and Christ with his arms outstretched seemed to say directly to her, 'It is I, fear not.' She said that she cried out 'in fear and anguish: "If it is Thee, Lord, bid me to come unto Thee," and the determination was taken.'

But Father Browne still advised delay, though he did give permission to work 'in a quiet hidden way towards the object in view, without altering her ordinary way of life.' She wrote to Father Blowick suggesting that she and Miss Fanny O'Connor, her housekeeper and friend, take a course in midwifery at Holles Street Hospital as extern students for three days a week. 'Until you have made a start in China and are able to tell us from practical experience what you want, I am not allowed to undertake anything more than this.'[21] In this letter, she also tells Father Blowick how hard she finds it to be held back from doing all she would like to do; she feels that she is offering so little. 'On the other hand, should I go against obedience, my services could bring no blessing with them. I realise how presumptuous it was of me to think that God's work could be carried into effect so easily, and since the retreat I understand better how much He asks of those who long to serve Him.'

In view of Father Blowick's words, in his letter of some weeks earlier, that he believed that she was 'the person chosen by God to set on foot a new congregation or order', it is of interest that in this letter written immediately after her retreat Frances said: 'You know, whoever God thinks best will be sent to you, and if it is not me, I accept His decision with cheerfulness, and will gladly work with whoever He sends.'

While Frances was on retreat in Waterford, her friend Miss Fitzgerald-Kenny began hers at the Sacred Heart Convent, Roscrea, under another Jesuit, Father Downing. A few days after returning to Dublin Frances had a telegram from her friend, telling her to come at once to Roscrea to meet Father Downing. She complied with what was more or less an order, and 'entirely contrary to her usual practice of obedience', she talked to her friend's director about her call to the Chinese Mission. To her surprise, his attitude was totally different from that of Father Browne and both of them, she remarked, were skilled spiritual directors. Father Downing was certain that her call came straight from God and that she should allow nothing to divert her from following it. She spoke of her strength of will, fearing that it might prove an obstacle, but he told her that she would need all that strength of will for the work ahead when she would encounter much opposition, especially from good people, maybe even from bishops.

Much affirmed about her vocation, she went to pray in the convent chapel. There, in front of Our Lady's altar, 'God vouchsafed to lift for a few moments the veil of the future, and in an agony she saw the bitter chalice which He asked her to drink. In this way and no other could His work be done. Overwhelmed in her own weakness, she was given strength from above to utter the Master's "Fiat".'[22]

Every week she went to see her spiritual director Father Browne, each time laying before him what she felt was God's call. His opposition caused her pain and she prayed continually that one day he would understand. Very soon an occasion arose when she was torn between her love for her family and what she believed was God's call to China. Father Blowick had written to say that he would at last fulfil his promise of visiting her in her flat. That same day a telegram came from her brother-in-law, asking her to accompany her sister Freddie who was travelling to England to visit her son, who had been seriously wounded in France. At the time, Freddie was in poor health. Frances was now faced with a dilemma: she had not told her family about China, yet she felt that she could not afford to miss this opportunity of meeting Father Blowick for the first time: up to now all their communication had been in writing. Love for family was deep-rooted in her character, and now, 'unable to give any explanation for a refusal which cut her to the heart, the first sacrifice was consummated for Christ on the altar of family affection.'

Frances's first meeting with Father Blowick, the person who had changed the whole direction of her life, took place on 2 August 1918. Her first impression was his youthful appearance: 'He looked singularly boyish for one called upon by God to lead a big Crusade. But the fervour of a great soul, shining through the buoyancy of his manner, communicated enthusiasm and inspired veneration'.[23] Frances could identify with his 'ardent nature', and she had no problem in giving her allegiance as well as her confidence to this young priest, almost twenty years her junior. He reaffirmed what he had said earlier in a letter to her about his conviction that she had been sent by God to co-operate with him in founding an institute of Missionary Sisters. 'So with joy, mingled with awe, and fear of her own unworthiness, she accepted to become God's instrument in whatever way He should choose.'[24]

The next day she took the early boat to England, and joined her sister at the bedside of her nephew who was in hospital in Salisbury. From there she wrote to Father Blowick, suggesting that on her return journey she visit the Franciscan Missionaries of Mary in London, who might be able to help them: they had houses in China. She also thought it might be a good idea to visit Queen Charlotte's Lying-in Hospital to find out about training requirements. After visiting the Franciscan Missionaries of Mary, she wrote to Father Blowick giving what information she could about their institute. She informed him that they had twenty convents in China and had just taken over a hospital in Shanghai. One conclusion she drew from her visit was that it would seem wiser to get any medical or nursing training before beginning the novitiate. It occurred to her that she could easily do her midwifery course in London at Queen Charlotte's Lying-in Hospital without drawing too much attention to the fact; she had not yet told her family about China and she anticipated some opposition. This plan was short-lived because of her director's disapproval.

She also told Father Blowick that she had travelled over on the boat and by train to London with the Mother General of the Poor Servants of the Mother of God and her Assistant, and that she was able to elicit much useful information from them. She admired their 'beautiful spirit of all-embracing charity'.

While in London she had two experiences of God's nearness.

Kneeling at the altar rails for Holy Communion at the Oratory she heard distinctly pronounced in her ear the word, 'Visitation'. From this she understood that the Sisters of the yet unborn Congregation would gain the hearts of the Chinese women to Christ by visiting them under the same circumstances in which the most pure Mother of God visited her holy cousin, St Elizabeth.[25]

This experience influenced her so profoundly that later, when the congregation was founded, the feast of the Visitation of Mary was honoured as a special day. Moreover, until their habit was modernised following Vatican II, the Sisters' side-beads carried a bronze medal, commemorating the Visitation on one side and St Columban on the other.

Frances's second experience of God's nearness was her encounter with a young soldier whom she met on a crowded London street. He was a convert, but was not practising his religion. For some reason he was drawn to confide in her. She helped him to make his peace with God, and she saw him off when he left for the front that evening.

She returned to Dublin where she resumed her work with the Society of St Vincent de Paul in the parish of Our Lady of Lourdes, which comprised Sean McDermott Street and the adjoining area. On 17 August she wrote to Father Blowick telling him of a proposal made by a new convert friend that both of them set up a hostel in a depressed area on the north side of the city, for social workers, and possibly medical students. They had seen a suitable house in North Great George's Street. Frances wondered if they would need to get

the Archbishop's permission, though in her next letter to Father
Blowick she conjectured that 'it would take little short of a miracle
to obtain any sanction from the Archbishop.' Frances and her
friend knew that Dr Margaret Lamont had recommended the
establishment of hostels for medical students in Dublin and Cork,
and they based their plans on hers. Between them they hoped to be
able to finance the running of a hostel in which the students would
be charged only for food. They hoped to run this hostel on semi-
religious lines, with some prayers in common and times of silence,
'but with a cheerful atmosphere as that of a happy family'.

The idea ran into difficulties when Frances's friend talked to her
spiritual director, and he could not see why they should want to run
a 'lodging house'. Frances then 'decided to take the bull by the
horns' by going to meet this 'venerable Dominican'. In her diary
she recorded her first meeting with Father Finbarr Ryan OP on 19
August 1918 as a red-letter day in her life. He listened sympathetically as she told him in confidence about what she believed was
God's call, and he gave her every encouragement. Evidently he too
was deeply interested in the idea of medical missions, and had even
been in correspondence with Dr Margaret Lamont.

> It seemed probable that he would gladly have taken up the cause,
> as the Dominicans had fostered the new American Missionary
> Sisterhood of Maryknoll. But although this course presented
> many advantages it did not seem advisable at this juncture to
> start the Sisterhood under any other auspices but those of the
> priests of the Chinese Mission.[26]

Some years later the Prioress of Eccles Street wrote to Frances,
'Father Finbarr Ryan has been enquiring for you. He still believes
in you and in your mission, which many others do not.' Although
circumstances meant that they could not meet often, they remained
life-long friends, and Archbishop Finbarr Ryan did visit her many
years later in Cahiracon.

The idea of a hostel was short-lived. On 9 September Frances
wrote to Father Blowick telling him that her friend had decided not
to go ahead with the plan for the hostel. She herself would be

willing to undertake the project on her own, she had just about enough money for that, but her director was opposed to her running any financial risk. 'In fact, if anything could have shaken my vocation, his counsel of late would be more than sufficient to make me reconsider my decision.'[27]

Speaking of herself in the third person, she put on record how she felt at this time:

> To Frances it seemed that no motive of worldly prudence, if such it were, should stand in the way of God's work. Money would be well lost in such a cause and if necessary income and not capital could be expended. Social position counted for nothing with her, for it would not lessen any influence with the poor of Christ. Finally, in the event of failure, there would always remain some corner of the world in which to work for God.[28]

Her director was unyielding, but patient. In the face of her persistence he proposed that she consult another Jesuit, noted for his spirituality as well as for his business acumen. However, he was out of town. On the feast of Our Lady's Nativity, Frances prayed long and earnestly before the statue of Our Lady of Dublin, in Whitefriar Street church, asking for light and guidance. Suddenly she remembered that Father Blowick had gone to Father Fegan SJ when he was in doubt about his own vocation, and she decided to do likewise. At the end of a long interview, Father Fegan said: 'What will you say if I tell you that you should remain in the world?' His words, she said, fell like a blow, but after a moment's thought she replied: 'I should not feel bound to act on your decision, so certain am I of God's holy will for me.' He had been testing her, and now came the time for reassurance. 'If you were a man,' he said, 'I should tell you to go straight to Tullabeg!'[29]

But it was to Galway that she went, to talk again to her friend Bishop O'Dea. In her diary she referred to that meeting on the feast of the Exaltation of the Holy Cross. 'Dr O'Dea exhibited his usual fatherly solicitude, spoke of the deep constituent principle which was necessary in a solid spiritual foundation and thought it was time that some outline of a plan should be drawn up.'

The day after her meeting with Bishop O'Dea she drove to Shrule to meet Father Blowick and his council. Her love of nature, and of nature's God, shines through her description of that drive in an open car through vast tracts of bogland.

> The country was wrapped in mist, but the foreground speckled here and there with fluffy wads of bog cotton, and enlivened by its variegated pattern of wild flowers, seemed emblematical of a strange new life. The bogs themselves impressed one with thoughts of the greatness of eternity ... The car bumped and jolted as it splashed through the water and more than once, going over an invisible rut, threatened to throw out its occupants. With it all, the knowledge of God's Presence filled the soul with exhilaration at the prospect of difficulties to be encountered and overcome in His service.[30]

It was her first time to meet Father Blowick's council, and she knew that she was under scrutiny. It must have been a daunting occasion. Yet she spoke 'from the fullness of her heart' of her missionary call. Later she gathered from a friend that she had created a bad impression and she commented humbly, quoting *The Imitation of Christ*. 'We are so much as we are in the sight of God and no more.' Her own impression of the first priests of the Maynooth Mission to China was one of 'Christlike charity, old-fashioned courtesy and that spirit of hospitality which has come down from the Saints of Ireland.' In one of the lighter moments of the visit someone wondered aloud what the previous occupants of Dalgan Park, the de Clifford family, would think of the present little group and their plans for China. 'They would think us all mad, was the unanimous conclusion – yes, madmen and fools for Christ.'

During her visit Frances was given a long letter from Dr Margaret Lamont to study. Both Father Blowick and Father E.J. McCarthy, from America, had been writing to Dr Lamont and they had told her about the proposed foundation of a women's missionary movement in connection with the Maynooth Mission to China. In response to some queries from Father McCarthy, she had sent from Shanghai a long letter of information and advice. Frances appreciated Dr Lamont's commonsensical approach regarding women missionaries' way of living, including their dress.

> No starched collar or cuffs to add fresh irritation when anxious, tiring work, temperature and people's tempers, mosquitoes and prickly heat were already about equal to half a dozen hair-shirts and scourges! ... My great idea is to reduce drain on physical strength to a minimum and let them find their mortification in the unavoidably hard conditions, real hard professional work, etc. For the same reason they should be decently fed and get an occasional change.[31]

But, as has been noted earlier, Dr Lamont had some strange ideas about religious life, and Frances found herself rejecting instinctively her suggestions about organising the new missionary group according to professional qualifications.

One practical outcome of this visit to Dalgan Park was the suggestion that Frances should form a committee of about five candidates, somewhat as the first members of the Maynooth Mission to China had done. When Frances asked Father Blowick if he had any people in mind for the proposed committee, he replied that the only person he knew of was Miss Agnes Ryan of Monkstown, a friend of Father Ronayne's. And here Father Tommy Ronayne enters the story.

Although circumstances prevented him from joining the Maynooth Mission to China, Father Tommy Ronayne played an integral role in its beginnings. Ordained in Maynooth in 1913 for the archdiocese of Dublin, he was a classmate and friend of Father Blowick's. As students both of them had been deeply moved by Father Fraser, the Canadian missionary, who had spoken to them about China in 1911. In the years following his ordination, Father Ronayne began to correspond with Father Edward Galvin in China. When Edward Galvin arrived in Ireland in August 1916 hoping to do something towards establishing an Irish mission to China, the first person he contacted was Father Ronayne who offered himself for the new mission, provided that Archbishop Walsh would release him.

It was Tommy Ronayne who told Father Galvin that his friend John Blowick had also been considering the China mission, but for family reasons had postponed making a final decision. A brilliant student, working towards a doctorate in divinity, John Blowick had been appointed professor of dogmatic theology in Maynooth a year after his ordination. After hearing what Tommy Ronayne had to say about his friend, Father Galvin realised that here was the person he had been praying for, someone who would have the ability to take charge of the future Irish mission to China. He asked Father Ronayne to write to John Blowick to know if he could meet him. In that letter Tommy Ronayne told his friend that he himself was 'in it now, for good or ill, come what may.'[32]

It was on the doorstep of Father Ronayne's home, 16 Longford Terrace, Monkstown, that Father Galvin and Father Blowick met for the first time on 4 September 1916. They talked into the early hours of the morning, with Father Galvin pleading with Father Blowick not to postpone his decision but to join him in this new venture. John Blowick promised to give his answer after the Maynooth retreat, and once he had made his decision to throw in his lot with Edward Galvin things began to move quickly. Little more than a month later, the Irish Bishops at their general meeting gave their approval to the Maynooth Mission to China, and in October of the following year Father Blowick made his appeal for women missionaries to work alongside the priests of the Chinese Mission.

Frances was familiar with many of the details of those early days of the Maynooth Mission to China. Now she was to meet Father Ronayne, one of the key figures, no longer part of the group because his archbishop would not release him, but still enthusiastic and still hopeful that eventually he might be free to become a member.

When Frances got Father Blowick's letter telling her about Agnes Ryan she was staying with relatives in Monkstown. That evening she walked through the rain to the church and met Father Ronayne in the confessional. It was Saturday evening. She told him what Father Blowick had said, and he asked her to wait for him until he had finished hearing confessions. They then walked back to the presbytery through the pouring rain.

When Frances wrote her story of the events leading up to the founding of the congregation she spoke feelingly about her indebtedness to Father Ronayne. Speaking again in the third person she said:

> Believing in her missionary vocation, Father Ronayne was good enough to give her a large measure of confidence ... His intimate association with the pioneers and knowledge of all the circumstances, and above all, the influence of his deep personal spirituality, increased her faith in the enterprise. Later on, through many dark days, his sympathy sustained her faltering courage. At times he acted the part of the candid friend, when nothing remained to her but to cling on to the bare rock of confidence in the One Unfailing Friend.[33]

The following morning, Father Ronayne introduced her to Agnes Ryan and sent the two of them off to walk along the pier in Dun Laoghaire. Frances recorded the occasion in her diary: 'Introduced by Father Ronayne to Miss Agnes Ryan – in medical training for China.' As Agnes Ryan's confessor, Father Ronayne knew of her desire to give her life to God and he had talked to her about moves afoot to start a new congregation of women missionaries for China. As a result, she had started to study medicine, while continuing at the same time to support herself by teaching. That evening Frances wrote to Father Blowick, to tell him about her meeting with Agnes Ryan: 'This meeting was a real joy, for I found in her a kindred spirit, and I am confident that we shall be of mutual help and support in the great undertaking before us.'[34]

Frances was coping with a certain amount of stress at this time. She had to decide who would replace her in the work she had undertaken for various committees and charities when the time should come to leave it all behind. She was also anticipating much family opposition to her plans. But the biggest anxiety was uncertainty about the future, and her own sense of inadequacy. At the end of her letter to Father Blowick about her meeting with Agnes Ryan, in which she also asked his opinion about her writing about the proposed medical mission to her acquaintances in Rome, Cardinal Van Rossum and Cardinal di Belmonte, she said: 'I realise how little qualification either spiritual or intellectual I have for such great work, but am hoping all the time that if I am used to do some of the spade-work that the dear Master will send the right one to direct the work when the moment comes.'[35]

Father Blowick answered by return, reassuring her as to her place in the new venture, and trying to allay all her misgivings:

> I have no doubt at all that God has chosen you to lead this new enterprise and you must simply take the reins; you know I was just as bad myself, but the thing was thrust on me and I had to sink the personal point of view. We shall help all we can, but with the ladies you must take the initiative in many things. Everything depends on initiative and prudence to a certain point, but not too much – too much prudence will keep us from doing anything. The whole thing is quite novel in Ireland, nobody has ever heard of such a thing and the ground is virgin soil but the women and girls of the country will rally round you I will guarantee you that – and the Far East and all our organisation, which is strong among the best womanhood of the country, will be placed at your disposal ... Have no doubts on the matter. You see the work is God's, not yours nor mine. We happen to be instruments – weak, unworthy, if you like, but even the best is very little good and a person with ten times your qualifications or mine would be but a puny thing and quite unable to face such a herculean task. No, God is behind the whole thing and He will see it through. There is one saying of Our Lord's which has been a great support to us all along – it is that the sparrows and all these little things are watched over by God and surely He will care for us ... The watchword now is – FORWARD! Full steam ahead![36]

Father Blowick ended his letter by assuring Frances that she was not to worry about bothering him with letters, 'the more the better'. He would be seeing Dr O'Dea soon in Galway to see if this 'saintly, priestly and apostolic bishop, who lives and thinks and acts only for

God', had any more suggestions.

> That must be our motto: Love for souls, nothing else. It must be burned into the girls' minds, so that they can never lose sight of it; they must be taught to have an absorbing love of God, of our Master in the Holy Sacrament, of our Holy and Immaculate Mother, who must be their guiding star all through the hardships of the preparation and of missionary life afterwards.

Frances replied by return, thanking him for his consoling words, saying that she must not have less confidence in God than her brothers of the Chinese Mission, and trusting that because of her helplessness God will have to do everything. She agreed with Father Blowick about the spirit he would like to see animate the future sisterhood. This is what she longed for, for all of them. 'It is only through this burning love of God that we can hope to do anything for Him and for souls.'

Early in October Frances's director withdrew his opposition to her undertaking nursing training sometime in the future, but he still felt that the time had not yet come for her to consider religious life. She wrote to Father Blowick to tell him. She also told him that the annual general meeting of the Catholic Truth Society was coming up, and that she had been asked to host the meeting. It transpired that as a member of the executive committee she was called on to stand in for someone who had been assigned to speak on child welfare. After she had addressed the topic, she spoke about the need for lady doctors on the mission-field. Father Blowick's historic appeal at the Catholic Truth Society annual meeting of the previous year had brought her to where she now stood. As the first woman to throw in her lot with the Maynooth Mission to China, she now tried to make others aware of the need for women with medical and nursing expertise on the missions. At this time she was trying to withdraw gradually from public life. 'I feel the need of more time for prayer and thought, with such a Herculean task in front of us,' she wrote to Father Blowick. 'Conscious of my own weakness and inability, it is only confidence in God that keeps me up.'[37]

Father McConville, a Salesian working in India, home in Ireland

on holidays, had visited Father Blowick in Shrule and had told him
about a group of women he had worked with in India. The
Catechists of Mary Immaculate, with a single private vow of
chastity, were more like a secular institute than a religious order;
therefore they could engage in medical work and midwifery. 'To
my mind, it is the very thing for us,' Father Blowick wrote to
Frances, adding that he had asked Father McConville to call on her.
She invited Agnes Ryan along to her flat to meet Father McConville,
who spent an evening telling them what they could expect as
missionary religious, because they remained committed to this.
'He prophesied untold labours and trials, trials that would discourage the faint-hearted, but to those who really love God, a means of
advancing in the mystical life.'[38]

That same month of October marked the arrival of a third
member of Frances's committee, Margaret Gibbons, recommended
by Father John Heneghan, one of the original five who formed the
Maynooth Mission to China. He was editor of *The Far East*, which
had started publication in January 1918, and Margaret Gibbons
who wrote under the name 'Eithne' was contributing articles and
verses regularly. She wrote to Frances, telling her that her whole
heart was in the mission, and asking if she could be of any help.
When they met, Frances was immediately captivated. 'Eithne', she
said was the kind of person 'who could find her way to a person's
heart at once. Brilliantly gifted ... generous to a fault ... she was at
that time ready to make any sacrifice for the love of God and souls.'
Frances was taken aback when she discovered that Eithne had tried
her vocation twice already, but she reassured herself with the
thought that other holy people had a similar experience.

Very soon another candidate arrived, Teresa McCollam, who
was to play a vital role in those early days. She was closer in age to
Frances than either Eithne or Agnes Ryan, having worked for
twenty years in the Post Office. Frances recognised a kindred spirit.
Writing some years later she could say:

> Teresa McCollam was a grand natural character, with a freedom
> of spirit which recalled the Glens of Antrim of which she was a

native; she diffused an atmosphere of fresh air around her. An invincible faith and piety were guarded as the 'secret of the King.' She was intolerant above all of anything that savoured of formalism, straightforward to the verge of bluntness, full of common sense and with business capacity that would be a useful asset for organisation.[39]

Frances was in admiration at the sacrifice she was ready to make at her age, giving up her responsible position and the security of a pension for a venture which could result in failure and the loss of everything.

Like Margaret Gibbons, Teresa McCollam had been working for the Chinese Mission right from the beginning. She had contributed to the travel fund and was one of those who saw the first priests off to America. She was associated with *The Far East* from its first issue. She it was who started the page for Little Missioners, under the name 'Colum', the name that the magazine has retained to this day. It was as 'Colum' that Frances knew her. She struggled a long time with her vocation, feeling drawn to China but not to the religious life. Finally, Father Blowick urged her to talk to Frances: 'Go to that lady. She needs your help and sympathy, for her own people are against her going to China.' The introduction he gave her 'clinched a friendship which survived all differences of temperament, point of view and ultimate divergence of paths'.[40]

Frances now had three companions, each of them introduced and approved by the priests of the Maynooth Mission to China. While making a recollection day at the Sacred Heart Convent in Leeson Street on 24 October she again appealed to her director, telling him that she believed the time had come when God wanted her to undertake this work. 'Is it just,' she asked him, 'to keep others in uncertainty and to hold up the work of the Mission?' He prayed a while, and then gave his consent to her going ahead and training with her companions. 'In God's name, you may go,' he said, 'I believe that God is guiding you in this.'

Shortly afterwards Father Ronayne sent Frances another candidate, Marie Martin.[41] The second eldest of a wealthy Dublin shipping and timber-importing family, she was born in 1892. Now twenty-six years of age, she was praying to know what God wanted her to do with her life. She told her director, Father Ronayne, that if ever there should be a missionary congregation dedicated to medical work she would be interested. He told her about Lady Moloney, and suggested that they meet. They met at the presbytery in Monkstown, because for family reasons it seemed wisest that Marie's plans would not be made public for the present. All that the other members of the committee were told was that another candidate was hoping to join them. It is clear that from the beginning Marie felt part of the group. She wrote to Frances Moloney on 10 November, saying, 'It will be splendid to know exactly what you think best for each of us to do & prepare for this grand work ... You have a hard but grand fight before you.'[42] Frances recognised from the first the special calibre of this youngest member of the group. She found her 'a soul of heroic stamp, who in future years showed by a life of total self-sacrifice, a depth of spirituality rarely to be found.'[43]

The Maynooth Mission to China had started with a committee of five committed priests, and Father Blowick had suggested that Frances have a committee of five candidates before a start be made. She now had her group of five members: they were ready to start.

EIGHT

Growing Pains

On 16 November 1918 Frances met with Margaret Gibbons, Teresa McCollam and Agnes Ryan in her flat at 119 St Stephen's Green. They had come together to decide how best to prepare for their future mission to China. Marie Martin, who had decided to join the group, was not present.

The focus at that time being on medical or nursing training, Frances and her companions opted for short-term courses. In that way their spiritual formation would not be too long delayed, nor their eventual going to China. They decided on a six-month course in midwifery as a beginning. Agnes Ryan would continue her study of medicine. Their hope was that qualified doctors and nurses would join them later. This, the first formal meeting of the women's group, and all their future meetings, began and ended with prayer. The project was entrusted to Mary the Mother of God their chosen patron.

Both Father Blowick and Frances believed that Dublin would seem the ideal place to begin, but it looked unlikely that Archbishop Walsh would ever give his consent. He was old, in poor health, and not easily won over to new ventures such as the Maynooth Mission to China. Archdeacon Keown of the diocese of Clogher, Margaret Gibbons's spiritual director and a friend of Frances's family from the time they lived in Co. Monaghan, suggested that the women form a committee of prominent Catholic doctors, who would present their case to the Archbishop in the context of a medical mission to China. Father Blowick approved.

Consequently, Frances approached Sir Andrew Horne, Master of Holles Street Hospital, who had already shown an interest in the project. She also enlisted the support of other well-known Dublin doctors.[1] Sir Andrew agreed to chair the committee and asked Frances to draw up a statement of the purpose and objective of the women's group. Writing to Father Blowick she requested him to

send her another copy of Dr Margaret Lamont's book, *Twenty
Years in Medical Work in Mission Countries*,[2] which she would
like to quote in her report to the doctors, and asked somewhat
naively, 'Do you think that if we have all the Catholic doctors on
our side, it would be impossible for the Archbishop to ignore us?'[3]
Father Blowick was more realistic. He doubted if the Archbishop
would ever give them canonical approval, but he advised them to
go ahead with their training: 'It seems to me that the best thing is
for each of the ladies under your direction to begin training in her
respective department with the intention of coming to work in
China. That needs no sanction, as you cannot yet enter a novitiate
or anything of the kind.'[4]

At the same time, the doctors enlisted by Frances hoped to get
the Archbishop of Dublin interested in her idea of a Catholic
medical mission to China. In the statement she put before them she
said:

Those who are best qualified to form an opinion have decided
that a body of lady doctors and nurses would be a necessary
adjunct to the great Irish Missionary Movement of the present
day.

In order to meet this want, a number of Irish women of mature
age and experience, after taking due spiritual advice volunteered for such work, with the firm conviction that such is God's
will for them.

Of these, one has already advanced in her studies for the
Medical Profession – Agnes Ryan; the others have hospital
experience, and three are starting immediately on the maternity
course at Holles St. Hospital. If the suggestion meets with no
disapproval, it is proposed at the end of six months that a house
should be opened for students where a simple rule would be
followed and the candidates prepared as Catechists.

It is obvious that in view of the dangers, difficulties and
temptations of what may be an isolated life among the pagans,
that it would be essential to lay a strong foundation and to ensure
every safeguard to virtue and perseverance.

Provided therefore no objection be raised by Ecclesiastical Authority, the pioneers are desirous of either entering the Novitiate of some Religious Order, or of seeking the services of some experienced religious who would give them the necessary training.

The Medical Mission, when established, would in obedience to the Bishop of the Diocese, work in co-operation and under the direction of the Maynooth Mission to China, in so far as Canon Law will admit. Their labours will be extended to whatever country the Irish Missionaries are sent in obedience to the Holy See.

In addition to caring for the sick, the Association of Women Missionaries would not refuse any work which might promote the conversion of pagans to the true faith. They hope to have among their members some qualified to undertake the higher and other grades of education. A fund sufficiently large to make a beginning is available for the present. When the work and its needs become known, the Pioneers are confident that inspired by the old missionary tradition which has been Ireland's greatest glory, the labourers will come forward and the means will not be lacking.[5]

The doctors studied Frances's statement and at their meeting on 4 January 1919 Dr Denis Coffey, President of the National University of Ireland, made the following proposal: 'That the formation of an Irish Catholic Medical Mission to China is desirable, and that steps be now taken to gain the approval of the Ecclesiastical Authorities for the formation of such.' The motion, seconded by Surgeon Alex Blayney, was adopted unanimously.[6] Sir Andrew Horne agreed to put the matter before the Archbishop, but the latter, pleading pressure of work, excused himself from meeting with the doctors' representative. Nor would he have time to look over their proposal. 'New undertakings,' he said, 'must wait for some more favourable time.'[7]

Father Blowick was proved right: the women's group of the Maynooth Mission to China now knew that they could expect little encouragement from the Archbishop. But there was nothing to prevent them from proceeding with their professional training. At this stage, for practical purposes the pioneer group consisted of Frances, Margaret Gibbons and Teresa McCollam; Agnes Ryan and Marie Martin, who had indicated their intention of joining the group, had other full-time commitments.

Though Frances and her companions had agreed on how they would go about their immediate technical preparation for China, nothing had been decided about their religious formation. One of the problems Frances came up against here was that Teresa McCollam, while eager to go to China as a missionary, did not feel drawn to the religious life. Frances believed that if her friend became acquainted with some dedicated religious she might change. So they did the rounds of some of the Dublin convents. They visited Sister Spinola of the Irish Sisters of Charity, who had encouraged so many others to serve God in the religious life. Later they went to Mount Anville to meet one of Frances's former teachers who had been the first to know about her vocation. Everywhere they visited they were received warmly, but Teresa was not won over.

Yet Frances was convinced that it would be as religious that she and her companions would go to China, and from time to time she reminded Father Blowick of this. On 28 November 1918 he wrote to her saying that any bishop could sanction a new congregation in his diocese, and suggested that she talk to Dr O'Dea, the Bishop of Galway. If he was willing to accept them into his diocese, then they could start working on constitutions.[8] Frances called her companions together to discuss Father Blowick's suggestion, and they decided that she and Teresa McCollam should go to Galway to talk to Dr O'Dea about the possibility of establishing a novitiate.

They went by train to Galway on 7 December, and were welcomed by the bishop with his customary courtesy and kindness. In Frances's estimation he was 'a man of deep spirituality, gifted moreover with keen intelligence and sound practical judgement.' He advised them strongly to get a written undertaking from the priests of the Maynooth Mission to China that their services would be availed of after they had completed their training. 'You must not set out without your charter.'[9]

The next day Frances and Teresa arrived on Father Blowick's doorstep, rather anxious as to how they could broach the topic of a 'charter' without seeming to show a lack of trust in the priests of the Maynooth Mission to China. Fortunately, Father Blowick and his council sensed their dilemma and generously agreed to draw up a statement, binding to the extent that Canon Law would allow. Frances was exuberant. She was convinced that Our Lady was on their side. 'Is it not true to say that the future congregation was born on the feast of the Immaculate Conception, on the 8th of December 1918?'

Father Blowick asked if Frances would be willing to give the candidates their religious training; she demurred saying that she could not give what she herself did not have, but she did share with him some of her hopes for the future congregation. Her ideal was a congregation such as Christ would have founded among the holy women of his time. She felt unworthy to be involved in so holy a work, yet she had definite ideas as to what a religious congregation should be and what it should not be. It pained her to hear religious say, 'Our Holy Rule does not allow this.' This was an attitude she had come up against when engaged in works of charity in Rome and elsewhere. It was with sadness that she saw the priest and the levite passing by.

> Would it not be possible to follow so closely in Christ's footsteps that no act of charity asked in His name should ever be refused? That the sick, the sinful and the sorrowful should never look in vain to a missionary sister, or the cry of the mother and her helpless babe go unheeded? 'And Mary, rising up in those days, went into the hill country with haste.'1 Lk 39. Should not the missionary sister in company with Mary fly to the assistance of Elizabeth in her hour of need?[10]

After this crucial meeting with Father Blowick, Frances and Teresa again called on Bishop O'Dea, who was happy to hear what transpired in Dalgan, and who gave them some fatherly advice about planting deep so that the spirit would be lasting.

Two days after her return to Dublin, a letter from Father Blowick left Frances in no doubt as to where she and her companions stood in relation to the Maynooth Mission to China. This letter of 10 December 1918 stressing Frances's role, warrants lengthy quotation:

> With reference to our conversation on last Sunday, the Feast of the Immaculate Conception, I am happy to be able to say that:
>
> 1. The Council of our Society has formally declared that the work you contemplate entering on, the forming of a body of ladies for the purpose of nursing, teaching and medical work in our districts in China, is most necessary for the success of our work in China.
>
> 2. That the Council will formally guarantee, in so far as it is possible in the eyes of Canon Law, to accept the services of these ladies when they are qualified and trained, technically and religiously.
>
> This is about all that can be done formally so far, but you may rely on us to do everything that is in our power to assist you in every single way that is possible, no matter what the trouble may be. Let me say once and for all – and please keep it in mind whenever you have anything to ask us to do – that your work is in a very true sense ours too. Remember that we were looking around for some lady to begin such a work when you were sent here by God; there is no other way to put it.[11]

Deeply moved Frances replied that she and her companions hoped to be worthy of his trust, and to live up to the spirit of zeal and self-sacrifice of the priests of the Maynooth Mission to China.

> We still have much to learn, but no doubt the novitiate will do its work. Together with the gift of piety, I hope we shall get the fruit of the Holy Ghost: the spirit of joy, to enable us to remain cheerful in spite of difficulties and trials, in times of desolation and possibly isolation. I trust that the novice mistress will realise that we want this wide and happy spirit, straight as a die, but not tending to crush the individuality of any one, or to turn out all our

members in one pattern or mould. Rather would one have their souls expand in the sunshine of God's love and service.[12]

She added that it should be possible to get the basis of their religious formation in almost any order, and then to work out rules and constitutions to meet their own particular needs as missionaries. She believed that their constitutions should be characterised by 'a great love for souls, together with an absorbing love of our Divine Master in the Blessed Sacrament and of His Immaculate Mother.'

She could see some advantages in applying for admittance into the diocese of Galway. Apart from being near the priests of the Maynooth Mission, there was also the practical consideration that her brother-in-law had a vacant house and farm at Oranmore in Co. Galway, which might do for a beginning. Perhaps Father Blowick might be able to inspect it with her during the Christmas holidays and, should it prove suitable, she might be able to get it rent-free. When she and the other members of the group would meet next day, 14 December, they would study some estimates they had got for 'simple furnishing', so that she could send him a statement of what they would need when they, and hopefully some future candidates, would live together as a group.

Frances, Margaret and Teresa came to the meeting armed with lists of estimates from furniture, hardware and china shops. Their statement for Father Blowick amounted to £320, inclusive of bedding, bed linen and other necessities. They budgeted for what they later decided were luxuries: a couch and basket chairs for the community room. On the whole, the furniture list was spartan in its simplicity. For the refectory they asked for a plain deal table and kitchen chairs.

Frances had begun to sign her letters, 'Xavier', or 'F.X.', partly because of her devotion to the great missionary St Francis Xavier and also because she felt that her own name 'rather savoured of the world'; she preferred something simpler. She became 'Xavier' to her companions and from 20 December 1918 for several months, Father Blowick was writing to her as 'Sister Xavier', a practice he

later discontinued, possibly to avoid confusion regarding her
canonical status.

In his letter of 20 December Father Blowick announced that he
had just had a communication from Rome to the effect that the
Maynooth Mission to China would be going to Hankow, 'and soon
too. That will make your work perfectly necessary, and I have no
doubt that it will be strongly approved when the time comes.' He
told her that the January issue of *The Far East* would carry an article
he had written about them, that Father Heneghan would follow up
with an editorial in the February issue, and that they would be given
prominence month by month. Father Blowick's article in the
January 1919 issue of *The Far East* included an appeal for financial
help and asked that all enquiries about the women's branch of the
Maynooth Mission to China, and all donations, be addressed to
'XAVIER', c/o St Columban's College, Dalgan Park, Galway. He
was putting everything in Frances's hands.

As 1918 came to an end, the pioneers, Frances, Margaret
Gibbons and Teresa McCollam, were each of them coming to grips
with painful decisions. 'The boats were burning,' Frances wrote,
'and serviceable nets which had drawn souls to God must be left
behind.' She organised a sale of work so that the Catholic Business
Girls' Club, of which she was president, would be free of debt by
the time she left, and she attended one last meeting of the Belgian
Refugee Committee.

On 13 January 1919, Father Blowick submitted for Frances's
approval a form he had drafted to send to women who wished to
become part of the new venture. In it he told them, 'Lady Moloney,
32 Upper Mount Street, Dublin, is in charge of this part of the work
and I shall ask you to write to her immediately.' The form, of which
Frances approved, asked each applicant to state whether she felt her
vocation lay 'in the direction of nursing, teaching, medical work,
or in the general duties of a Sister in care of the poor'.

Even though the concentration at this time was on nursing and
medical training, Frances knew that from the beginning Father
Blowick had envisioned women with other qualifications joining
the Chinese Mission. He had stated in his Mansion House appeal

on 11 October 1917 that a body of teaching religious would also be needed in China, teaching nuns and brothers; he had even spoken of a branch for higher education.[13] Some days before he sent Frances the draft application form, he had asked a promising candidate to call on her. 'She may be able to take her diploma in teaching,' he wrote, 'and form the beginning of a teaching section in your body'.[14]

The house in Upper Mount Street was not yet ready for occupation when the first candidates presented themselves for interview. Consequently, Frances and Teresa met them in the old Gresham Hotel. Two of those interviewed seemed ideally suited. One of them took a temporary job to help her prepare for the Chinese Mission, but in the course of her training she changed her mind and went off to South Africa with a group of missionary Sisters who had been visiting Ireland looking for candidates. When Frances and Teresa interviewed their other candidate for a second time, they discovered a serious mental health problem which made her totally unsuited for missionary or religious life. However, their next candidate more than made up for this initial disappointment.

Father Blowick approved of Frances's sugggestion that they put their case to Cardinal Logue; consequently Frances and Teresa travelled to Armagh to meet him. They stayed at the Sacred Heart Convent, 'an oasis of refreshment and rest after the fatigues and trials of the past weeks'. The Cardinal received them cordially and spoke enthusiastically about the proposed mission to China. He was pleased to hear of the possibility of religious who would be part of that mission, and he wanted to hear all their plans. He kindly promised to recommend their proposal to the bishops of Ireland, and suggested that they themselves lay it before the Bishops' Standing Committee. When the interview drew to a close, he sent them away in his own carriage.

It was a hurried visit because Frances was due to begin her midwifery training in Holles Street Hospital the following morning, 16 January 1919. At lunchtime on her first day in the hospital she had an unexpected visit from Father John Heneghan who had come up from Dalgan. She noted that he was not ashamed to walk across Merrion Square with a nurse 'cloaked in blue with the funniest little old-fashioned bonnet tied with blue ribbon under the chin!' As he accompanied her across the Square he told her that he had said Mass for her that morning. 'We are all mad,' he said, 'in this sanest of possible sane worlds. A fool salutes a fool!'

During dinner break on the next two days Frances drafted a statement for presentation to the Bishops' Standing Committee, as the Cardinal had advised. As far as can be ascertained, it was similar to that submitted to the doctors, which Father Blowick had earlier endorsed. She and Teresa signed the covering letter, dated 19 January 1919, which was sent with their statement to each of the Bishops.

> My Lord Bishop,
> We venture to send you the enclosed statement relating to the proposed formation of an Irish Catholic Medical Mission to China.
>
> Being anxious to obtain the necessary ecclesiastical approval before putting the project on foot, the matter will be brought to the consideration of their Lordships at the next meeting of the Bishops' Committee.
>
> Trusting that we may obtain the blessing of the Church on our humble efforts to assist in Ireland's apostolic work,
> We are,
>   And on behalf of five others,
>   Your Lordship's humble servants,
>   (Signed) Frances Moloney
>   Teresa McCollam

Bishop Gaughran of Meath, the first to reply, said that he believed that the finger of God was in their project; within a few days encouraging letters arrived from the Bishops of Limerick, Down and Connor, and Galway. Bishop Kelly of Ross, Secretary to the Standing Committee, wrote that having studied their enclosures relating to a medical mission for China, the Bishops of the Episcopal Standing Committee instructed him to say that 'this fresh manifestation of active faith and missionary zeal among the women of Ireland has given them great satisfaction and they thank God for it.' He pointed out that their project would have to be approved by a general meeting of the bishops, and he asked them to submit as detailed a plan as possible for the next meeting in June.[15]

It was encouraging to have several bishops approving their project, already sanctioned by the Cardinal. There had been great jubilation about the Cardinal's endorsement of their dream. Frances had written to Father Blowick before leaving Armagh, and he replied by return expressing his delight. Agnes Ryan also wrote a long letter. 'It is a case of three cheers for the Cardinal!' she began, 'How perfectly splendid of him to offer to bring the matter before the bishops!'

It was in the midst of the flu epidemic which struck the country at the end of February 1919 that Frances drew up the first draft of what she proposed to present to the bishops at their June meeting. Her sister had written from Killyan to say that the entire household was down with the flu, and asking for her help. She responded immediately and undertook night duty for a week, until her patients were out of danger. At quiet times during the night she prayed, and it was in this context that she drafted an outline of the plan she proposed to present to the bishops at their June meeting.

Her first concern was the kind of spirit that should inform the future congregation, and she made note of the following:

Zeal for the conquest of souls; self-sacrifice; a burning love of Jesus in the Blessed Sacrament; devotion to Mary: her spirit in the Visitation; the interior spirit, without which outward activity has nothing to give; simplicity in one's dealings with others; hospitality according to the traditions of the old Irish Saints; intense cultivation of the family spirit, to foster fraternal charity and relieve the strain of missionary life; humility in work, all taking their share of household duties as far as the exigencies of professional work would admit; no lay sisters; an all-embracing charity – no act of charity ever to be refused; a happy relationship to exist between the members of the congregation and the

Maynooth Mission to China – as brothers and co-workers. No preference to be shown for any sister or priest; the spirit of criticism, either of superiors, equals or others to be avoided: any member showing such spirit could not be retained in the congregation.[16]

Before she returned to Holles Street Hospital, Frances showed her tentative plan to her friend the Bishop of Galway who, though still convalescing from the flu, read her plan with interest and explained some points of Canon Law. She would have found it convenient to have gone to Dalgan at this time to meet Father Edward Galvin, home from China, but he had gone to Cork to visit his mother.

In Dalgan several of the students had fallen victim to the flu epidemic, also the housekeeper and servants; Father Jim O'Connell's condition was critical. Teresa McCollam, waiting to get into Holles Street Hospital, hurried down to help. She proved so useful that Father Galvin suggested that she stay on to help in the college. Her companions were trying to cope with their disappointment when word came that Father Galvin would like Frances to go to Dalgan to meet him.

She described her first meeting with this strong personality who would later be her bishop in China. She and Teresa were going up the stairs when they were met by 'a tall commanding figure', who greeted them simply with the words, 'I am Father Galvin.' 'He seemed a towering individual,' she recalled, 'as of heroes and martyrs', but it was only after they had eaten and were sitting around the fire together that Frances felt at ease. Teresa slipped away to do a household chore and Frances had a chance to ask Father Galvin some questions, and to reply to his. He told her that in order to enter China she and her companions would need to be religious, and hardy women too: 'women who would be ready at a moment's notice to jump on a horse and ride any distance to a sick call, not afraid to turn up their sleeves and do a hard day's work.'

He would not have known of the ordeals Frances had survived in the West Indies almost twenty years earlier, or the demanding relief work she had organised at times of crisis. Long rides on horseback were not new to her, or turning up her sleeves to do an act of charity. Now, all these years later, she agreed in principle with Father Galvin, though she was less in agreement when he added that it was girls like the little maids in Dalgan that were needed for China. In her heart she knew that physical strength was not everything, that spirit and courage were even more powerful, and that an ardent love of God and enthusiasm for the spread of God's Kingdom could overcome many physical shortcomings; moreover, she was convinced that professionally trained women would be an asset in any mission field. She knew that Father Blowick would have thought likewise; he had even spoken of accepting women who could set up institutes of higher education in China.

Reassured by this meeting with Father Galvin, Frances and her companion returned to Dublin. The Dalgan priests had decided against asking Teresa to stay on as housekeeper, so she was now free to begin her maternity training and she joined Frances and Margaret Gibbons in the flat in Merrion Street. Over and above the long hours on duty in Holles Street Hospital, the three women had been living community life in so far as this was possible, with some religious exercises in common, including spiritual reading and the rosary in Irish. In this attempt at living community life, Frances was probably influenced by Margaret, who had tried her vocation twice already. Sadly, Teresa was not attracted to community life, nor to shared spiritual exercises. She felt differently about Mass and Holy Communion, where the three of them were united together at the beginning of each day.

That they managed to do all they did is incredible. Fortunately the matron allowed the three of them to do their night duty simultaneously; that meant that they could relieve one another when called out on a case. They were on duty from 9.00 p.m. to 9.00 a.m., after which they often had to visit homes where mothers had given birth during the night. Sometimes they did not get home until 2.00 p.m. Margaret, never robust, and subject to occasional bouts of discouragement, might have given up but for the way her companions stood in for her and took care of her.

During these months in Holles Street there was little correspondence with Dalgan, though Teresa was still in charge of the
Little Missionaries section of *The Far East*. Their free time was
limited because the course was so concentrated. Father Galvin
arrived unexpectedly one day towards the end of their training and
insisted on taking the three of them out for a half day in the Dublin
mountains. Next day, 7 July 1919, Frances wrote to Father Blowick,
congratulating him on being elected Superior General of the
Maynooth Mission to China, and she told him about their outing:

> We spent a heavenly afternoon on the Dublin mountains yester-
> day with Father Galvin and Father Heneghan. It was worth
> doing six months hard work in Holles Street to enjoy a mouthful
> of fresh air so much. We ended up with Benediction at Orlagh
> Monastery and made a tremendous inroad into the monastic
> supplies. Miss O'Flaherty [Teresa's close friend] and Miss
> Kenny were with us. The latter treated Father Galvin to her
> views as to how the mission (both sides of it) should be run![17]

Another happy interlude occurred when Father Jim O'Connell,
who had almost died from the flu during Frances's last visit to
Dalgan, arrived with two friends to invite her and her companions
to an evening's entertainment. One of the three declined because of
'conscientious objections'. Frances remarked wryly: 'Was it St
Teresa who said that some people imagine they must be always
serious lest their piety fly away!'

For some months a promising candidate, Elizabeth Brannigan,
had been in touch with the group and was a frequent visitor to their
flat. She had worked in the GPO with Teresa McCollam, and
Frances also knew her from her work among the poor of Dublin.
She seemed an ideal candidate. However, for financial reasons she
was advised to wait and not do anything precipitate, but to keep in
touch with Frances and her companions. As a future member of the
group, Eilís – as she was called – was introduced to Agnes Ryan and
went out to Stillorgan to visit her.

Finding the waiting tiresome, however, Eilís sent in her resignation from the civil service and Frances felt obliged to consult Father Blowick who had not been in touch with them for several months. He replied rather apologetically: 'For some time past I have had the guilty feeling that I was neglecting your community, but the fact is I am up to my eyes in work which cannot wait.' He told her to do what she thought best about Eilís Brannigan, and he promised to come to Dublin soon to talk over plans.[18] He was still unsure as to how the women's group would get their religious training, and their course in Holles Street was drawing to an end. In a month's time, Frances and Margaret would have finished their training, and Teresa would complete hers two months later.

Once again they celebrated the feast of the Visitation which, before the revision of the Roman Missal, was held on 2 July. In 1919 it had more meaning than ever before for the three pioneers, ministering as they were to mothers in childbirth. They decided to make the day a real celebration. In the morning they prayed together in the little hospital chapel, asking Mary to inspire their future apostolate to the women of China. When they finished work at nine o'clock in the evening they honoured the occasion with a special tea party followed by a ride on top of the Donnybrook tram, which was as much as they could afford. Donnybrook church was about to close for the night when Monsignor Dunne saw the three women in nurses uniform. Recognising them, he welcomed them hospitably into his presbytery and, entering into the spirit of their celebration, he foretold that Mary's Visitation would always be one of their days of special devotion.

Later that month, Father Charles Plater SJ, Rector of Campion Hall, Oxford, asked Father Blowick for information about the medical mission sisterhood being founded for China; someone had sent him a newspaper cutting. A man ahead of his time, Father Plater had been campaigning for the education of the working classes, the training of lay leaders and the setting up of interdenominational bodies.[19] With his breadth of vision he was deeply interested in the idea of a congregation of women medical missionaries. He knew several people who had been hoping for something like this for a long time, and he assured Father Blowick that they would give him all the help they could.

Father Blowick's reply was that the venture was not yet clearly defined, but that four women were in training for such a sisterhood, three of them as nurses and the fourth studying medicine. Many others were interested, he said, but until the group was canonically erected, he was not encouraging them. 'The lady who began the work is Lady Moloney, 32 Upper Merrion St, Dublin, and I would suggest that you write to her.'[20]

Lady Moloney, meanwhile, was preparing for her final examination in midwifery scheduled for 26 July. The day after the examination the results were announced, and she and Margaret Gibbons were rewarded by having their names head the list. Later that day, one of their companions, Bridie Flood, who had also passed the examination with distinction, found Frances on her knees in the garden, rocking a sick baby to sleep. She told her that from the day they had begun their course together she had wanted to belong to the group preparing for China, but that she had decided not to say anything until she was sure of her examination. She now wondered if there was any hope. Given Father Blowick's attitude about not accepting further candidates for the present, all Frances could do was to encourage her to hope and to wait. From now on this happy, outgoing young woman, though not yet formally accepted, was regarded as one of the group.

Father Blowick wrote to congratulate Frances and Margaret on their success. He also told them that he would not be able to get to Dublin for the present because of the pressure of other work, so on the first weekend of August the three mission nurses went on pilgrimage to Lough Derg. There they met Father Tierney from Dalgan, like them doing the rounds in his bare feet.

Afterwards, Frances went to Armagh to make a retreat with the Sacred Heart nuns. Mother Lavery, the Superior, was more than generous in answering all Frances's queries about the religious life as lived by the Society of the Sacred Heart. For Frances this retreat was 'a time of renovation and enlightenment. In His own sanctuary and home I implored of the Sacred Heart to make the future congregation like His own Heart, all embracing in its love and insatiable for the salvation of souls.'[21] During this retreat she reflected on the different forms religious life had taken down through the centuries. She admired the spirit of St Francis de Sales and St Vincent de Paul, but now, it seemed to her, God was looking for something different: 'It was in Mary's own way of the visitation they must win the women of China to the Sacred Heart.'[22]

She set about drawing up constitutions for the future congregation, and only realised later that the word was a misnomer; in her ignorance of canon law what she had drafted could be no more than a tentative and incomplete plan. But she had dipped into a handbook on canon law, and wrote to Father Blowick, sending him some relevant points. Among other things she had been thinking about suitable attire for the members of the new congregation.

> For the dress, I would suggest a thin white Irish serge, made simply with scapular and belt, to be varied in tropical parts by the same design in Irish linen. Aprons would be worn in hospital and a head-dress like the French Red Cross, but covering the hair. A veil to be worn out of doors, also a sun helmet when necessary.[23]

At the end of this long letter, Frances expressed some motherly concern for the health of the young priests preparing to go to China:

> May I suggest they should get the right sort of clothing. So many of the young priests died in Trinidad, seemingly for want of proper precautions. Thin woollen underclothing is the safest; the Jaeger are the best, and can be had at Poyntz in Grafton St. They should also wear cholera belts at night, and always carry pocket cases containing quinine and other medicines to take at the first sign of fever or dysentery.

She returned to Dublin from Armagh, hoping to go to Dalgan shortly to ask Father Blowick to look over the 'constitutions', but this plan had to be postponed because the Matron in Holles Street Hospital asked her to substitute for some weeks for the Assistant Matron. She was glad of the further experience. Meanwhile, the letters she received from Father Blowick at this time were not very encouraging; he seemed preoccupied with other affairs. However, she was willing to wait and to hold on in faith. Long afterwards she heard that it was Father Galvin who had advised Father Blowick to go slow with the women's branch. Father Heneghan wrote sympathetically, explaining that Father Blowick's health was largely responsible for the delay; when he recovered, he would cope with their situation.

> As for us here, we are all helped and strengthened by the thought of what you are all doing – and it seems low-down and mean and just not good enough that we have those fine old walks and trees and the silence, and you have the sick wards and pain. However, there is really an end to the six months.[24]

When he eventually wrote, Father Blowick seemed anxious about their financial status: 'I do not see how we can satisfy any Bishop that you will be able to begin with a sufficient sum of money, especially as the ladies do not seem inclined to take in dowries.' Frances replied, with her usual common sense, that they were not likely to get people with dowries until they were officially founded. For the present she was satisfied that with her money and Marie Martin's there should be enough to launch a group of seven or eight women. Her brother had handed over her fortune and, besides what had been already invested, she expected to have £2,500 after she had paid all her debts. Availability or non-availability of funds did not deter her; and in this respect she witnessed, as had other founders, to a deep reliance on the Providence of God. 'All the orders which have done good work for God and His Church,' she said, 'started in Holy Poverty'.[25]

She outlined for Father Blowick their immediate plans for the future: while waiting for the novitiate to materialise, she, Teresa McCollam and Margaret Gibbons hoped to get some training in general nursing. Meanwhile, Eilís Brannigan and Marie Martin expected to begin their midwifery course soon in Holles Street. She asked Father Blowick to excuse her writing: 'I have one hand on a baby's cradle, and he is just waking up and wants minding!'

Father Blowick, seeing how important it was that he and Frances meet soon, decided to postpone his holidays and invited her to visit

him in Dalgan. She and Margaret Gibbons travelled by train to
Tuam in the last week of September 1919, sharing a carriage with
Monsignor Joseph Shanahan, then Prefect Apostolic of Southern
Nigeria, and his secretary. Frances had heard about this dynamic
missionary, one of the outstanding figures in the Irish missionary
movement of the early twentieth century. A member of the Holy
Ghost Congregation, he had gone to Nigeria as a missionary in
1902 and largely by means of education he had established a
vibrant local Church. He was on a visit to Ireland looking for
recruits to expand his work. Frances was reaffirmed in her missionary vocation as she heard him talk about his African experiences;
she was also reaffirmed in her conviction that God was calling her
to China and nowhere else.

This was obvious too to Father Blowick, who welcomed her and
her companion with his usual warm hospitality. He read the
constitutions she had drafted, adding a note here and there, and
advised her to show them to the Bishop of Galway. But, as he was
away, Frances returned to Dublin on the evening train, and was
back on duty in Holles Street Hospital the following morning.

Here it may be opportune to look at Frances's various attempts
to draw up what she sometimes called a 'provisional rule', and at
other times, 'constitutions'. Five separate drafts exist, one of them
little more than a summary and another consisting of extracts. The
three longer versions, similar in content, carry an opening dedication in Irish: *Do chum glóire Dé agus Onóra na hÉireann* (For the
glory of God and the honour of Ireland.) The name of the proposed
congregation varies from draft to draft: two of them refer to
'Columban Missionaries of Mary Immaculate', a third gives the
name as 'Columban Missionaries of the Visitation', while another
has 'Missionary Sisters of St. Columbanus'. A final version has
arrived at the name by which the congregation is known today:
'Missionary Sisters of St. Columban', usually abridged to Columban
Sisters.

It is significant that these drafts still survive, together with a
much-faded page in a covering envelope with Frances's handwrit-
ing: 'Rough notes made when movement to begin the Congrega-

tion first started.' Here on this single page we find an outline of the spirit which she hoped would animate the rule of the future congregation and, as such, it is important to quote it in its entirety.

Since the earliest days the thought uppermost in my mind has been that God wanted a congregation such as He Himself would have founded amongst the Holy Women who followed His footsteps in Galilee. It would not have been the well regarded charity that will only see the poor at certain times. There would have been no wearying multiplicity of practices of Holy Poverty concerning buttons and pins, but real poverty – plain bare wooden tables with great order and cleanliness, but no waste of time and strength in polishing floors.

There would be fixed hours for spiritual exercises, school, dispensary, recreation, etc. but should a sick call come even at night the Sisters would be free to go, due precaution being taken for the safety of young Sisters. Even spiritual exercises would give place to urgent charity, remembering that when Our Lord called His disciples to come apart and rest awhile that they had to feed the 5,000 first.

Superiors would cultivate a great respect for their subjects, remembering that they were free instruments given them by God, not merely staves to be thrown down or taken up. Faults must be corrected but no nagging, and a proper proportion kept. Subjects would see Our Lord in the Superior, the latter should not make it difficult for them to see this resemblance. Where there is a great multiplicity of small regulations and Sisters have to account for every moment of their time and not move hand or foot without permission it is very easy for petty tyranny to creep in.[26]

The shortest draft, dated 8 December 1918, written partly in ink, partly in pencil, has been folded so often that it is in danger of coming apart. It begins by invoking the Holy Spirit and Mary Immaculate, 'Patroness of the Congregation', and consists of five concisely worded points:

I. The name of the Congregation shall be The Missionary Sisters of St. Columbanus.

II. The Congregation shall work in co-operation with the Maynooth Mission to China and, as far as Canon Law will allow, under their direction and in due submission to the Bishop of the diocese.

III. The Congregation will undertake any work which will promote the conversion of souls to the true Faith, the principal means to attain this object being care of the sick and education.

IV. The spirit of the Congregation will be that of all-embracing charity and no effort should be spared to meet various demands which may arise.

V. Members of the Congregation will include fully trained doctors, nurses and midwives as well as those qualified to undertake the higher and other grades of education.

Subsequent drafts add more detail. For example, she laid down that all members of the congregation including doctors and nurses would be trained as catechists; that they must be ready to take on any work, no matter how humble, to save souls; a happy family spirit should be fostered and there should be no criticism of others, in particular of superiors; the congregation will try to cultivate the individual talents and resources of each member, 'allowing freedom of action as far as is consistent with discipline and the religious spirit'; a happy relationship should exist between the members of the congregation and the Maynooth Mission to China, 'who must be treated with all the respect due as Spiritual Fathers as well as brothers and co-workers'; they propose to work with and under the direction of the Maynooth Mission to China, as far as canon law will permit, always subject to the local bishop, however 'this will not preclude their expanding to other countries where their services may be needed, but the Irish Mission [i.e. the Maynooth Mission to China] must always have the first claim on their services.'

What preoccupied her most was the spiritual life of the future members of the congregation. Much of what she wrote came from her own reflections and from her experience of the Sisters she had known over the years; some of it came from her reading of the constitutions of other religious, in particular the Sacred Heart nuns.

The Sisters must avail themselves of every means of cultivating their inner spiritual life, it being their mission to impart spiritual knowledge to others; let them drink into their souls from the source of all love and wisdom, pleading to the Sacred Heart for the meekness and humility which alone can draw down blessings on their apostolate. They must be characterised by a burning love for souls and for Jesus in the Blessed Sacrament, have a constant charity and mutual affection for one another and a great spirit of loyalty, first to the Holy Father and the Catholic Church, and to the Mission and to one another. May their spirit be a cheerful one as of members of a large happy family. Each religious house shall be modelled on a happy home with the spirit of the House of Nazareth as its ideal.

Concrete details entered into her planning: hospitality 'according to the tradition of the Irish Saints'; the religious habit already referred to in a letter to Father Blowick; a recommendation that Sisters engaged in active ministries should have space each day for rest and fresh air, and that good nourishing food should be provided in so far as the resources of the group would permit. In keeping with her devotion to the Blesssed Eucharist she proposed that daily Exposition be held in large communities. However, Father Blowick pointed out that this would be impractical. It was he who eventually wrote the Constitutions of the Columban Sisters in the summer of 1924, in time for the first profession ceremony on 29 September 1924.[27] Frances was ill at the time and, for medical reasons, had to interrupt her novitiate.

During her short visit to Dalgan in September 1919 she had a letter from her friend Anneence Fitzgerald-Kenny conveying the disheartening news that Mother Kevin of Uganda had to withdraw from Holles Street Hospital. She had come to Ireland, encouraged by her bishop, Bishop Biermans, to observe new trends in maternity nursing. Though already engaged in this ministry to women in Uganda, where she had saved the lives of many mothers and infants, Mother Kevin realised her need for further training. She had come to Holles Street Hospital early in September, while Frances was still substituting for the Assistant Matron and Teresa McCollam was drawing near the end of her course. Both were impressed by this intrepid Irishwoman, a religious of St Mary's Abbey, Mill Hill, London, who would later found the Franciscan Missionaries for Africa, as well as a congregation of African Sisters. 'Mother Kevin burned with an ardent zeal for souls,' Frances was to write later, adding that 'she had a graciousness and a charm about her that made religion attractive.'[28] Her reaching out to the little group of missionary nurses in affection and interest went far towards reconciling Teresa McCollam to the idea of religious life. She and Frances for their part showed Mother Kevin all they could, feeling intuitively that she might not be there for long.

Miss Fitzgerald-Kenny happened to be in the hall of Holles Street Hospital when Mother Kevin's stay of a few weeks came to an abrupt end. Archbishop Walsh, taking literally the injunction against religious engaging in midwifery, had sent along one of his Vicars General to tell her that she was to leave Holles Street Hospital immediately; it seemed immaterial that Mother Kevin's own bishop in view of mission needs had given his permission. She had nowhere to go, so Miss Fitzgerald-Kenny had taken her to the mission flat in Merrion Street.

She was there when Frances arrived back from her visit to Dalgan. Frances was moved by the charitable way in which she had accepted the Archbishop's humiliating action; her only recourse now was to go to Rome. Dr Margaret Lamont, who was working against great odds in India, would be there at the same time also trying to have the ban lifted on religious practising medicine and midwifery. Mother Kevin, who was supportive of Frances's plans and of the constitutions she had drafted, suggested that she go to Rome with her: that a joint appeal on behalf of the women of India, Africa and China would surely be effective.[29]

Father Blowick saw things differently. He had been talking to Father Shanahan and had concluded that the only way to get approval for a medical mission was to have the various missionary bodies throughout the world unite in putting the case to Rome. One individual, or three, would carry little weight. Nor was he in favour of Frances going to Rome. 'About the religious formation,' he added, 'my opinion is that it must of necessity come before you can be effective in China, but it is too soon yet to attempt the formation of a religious body for many reasons.'[30]

Frances wondered what reasons influenced Father Blowick. At the same time she was coming to terms with a problem which had arisen within the group, who up to now, in spite of different backgrounds and different attitudes to religious life, had related together amicably. The seeds of trouble, according to Frances, were sown by a well-intentioned but somewhat imprudent friend who, unaware of the damage caused, made a remark about money which offended Margaret Gibbons: at that time, Frances was paying all the expenses of the group. It was the same forthright friend who relayed some criticisms of Margaret's attire: she loved to wear bright colours that suited her vivid, some might say, gypsy colouring, and there were those who felt that this was inconsistent with her call to missionary life. Taken aback by the unexpected criticism, she humbly accepted to wear a black suit. Frances, who had loved clothes herself, sympathised with her, quoting Cardinal Newman:

> Ladies, well I deem, delight
>   In comely tire to move
> Soft, and delicate, and bright,
>   Are the robes they love ...
> 'Tis not waste, nor sinful pride,
>   – Name them not, nor fault beside -
> But her very cheerfulness
>   Prompts and weaves the curious dress.[31]

Margaret's newly aroused sensitivity about money matters had impelled her to speak privately to Father Blowick about her personal expenses, when she accompanied Frances to Dalgan at the end of September 1919. Later she went there on her own and arranged with him that her expenses and the cost of any further training would be met by the Maynooth Mission to China. With her attractive personality she made many friends among the priests in Dalgan, and agreed to take on the Little Missionary section of *The Far East*. This had been started by Teresa McCollam, the original 'Colum', who had carried on the work even while under the pressure of training in Holles Street Hospital. Objectively, Margaret Gibbons, with her teaching experience, may have been a better qualified editor of a children's page, yet Teresa was deeply hurt at having to relinquish something into which she had put so much effort.

On this visit to Dalgan, Margaret Gibbons got Father Blowick's permission to do her training in general nursing at the Mater Hospital, even though she knew that Frances had been offered a place for her in Jervis Street Hospital; this would have been a better option financially. Evidently, at this stage of the story, Margaret was causing hurt and some measure of confusion to both of her companions.

From the time that they had come together as a group, Frances had been carrying all the living and training expenses. When Margaret Gibbons wrote to her to convey rather bluntly Father Blowick's new arrangement regarding their financial affairs, Frances, aware of a potential source of trouble, sought advice from a Jesuit friend. She then wrote to Father Blowick giving her opinion that the bond between the three women could suffer if each of them chose to plan her own life without reference to the others, and was free to apply to the Maynooth Mission to China for whatever money she felt she needed. She suggested instead a monthly stipend, such as members of religious orders were given to cover minor expenses, recommending that this would be paid through whoever happened to be in charge of the group.

In reply, Father Blowick cautioned Frances that her companions were not yet religious: 'For the present they are ladies of the world and it is inadvisable to do anything which would interfere with their reasonable liberty and freedom, without their consent.' He advised her to reserve her own money till a later date, when things would be better organised, even though he appreciated her generosity in spending it on others. In words stronger than usual he said:

> As Superior of this Society and Mission, I have a good number of obligations to those ladies who are coming to work with our priests in China, both as regards their personal maintenance and as regards the kind of training they should receive, and it is my duty to have all these things carried out.[32]

In the light of their previous communication and the trust Father Blowick had always placed in her, Frances understandably felt hurt; but she did not overreact. Recalling the incident later, she said, 'After a little time of prayer and reflection I realised that "getting the worst of it" does not matter at all, so long as God is there at the back somewhere. He may leave us alone to stumble in our weakness, then He steps in and holds us up and bids us follow Him all the way.' Her reply to Father Blowick was humble, yet dignified. She gladly accepted his ruling, which relieved her of all responsibility for the maintenance and training of her companions; nevertheless, she pointed out that he had referred to only two members of the group, Margaret Gibbons and Teresa McCollam. 'I hope that you include Miss Ryan, Miss Martin and Miss Brannigan as belonging to our band.'

In his letter of 15 July 1919 to Father Plater SJ, Father Blowick had included Agnes Ryan as one of the group in training for the future missionary congregation. Moreover, Agnes was in frequent contact with Frances and her companions. Father Blowick also knew that Marie Martin had completed six months training in a Red Cross Hospital in England, with a view to joining the group. And he had already told Frances to use her judgement about accepting Eilís Brannigan, and arranging for her training. But, at this stage, he seemed anxious to build up the core group and he was not encouraging further candidates, though many were anxious to join. He told Father Plater that his immediate concern was to have the group canonically established as a congregation. Prudence suggested that the group be kept small. Financially the Maynooth Mission to China was limited in its resources: the expenses entailed in preparing priest missionaries for China, and guaranteeing their support while there, meant that any other expenditure had to be carefully assessed. Frances appreciated this fact, and consequently had been ready to use her own money to support the group.

Following another visit to Dalgan, Margaret Gibbons wrote to her again, to explain why she had appealed to Father Blowick for financial support:

> I appreciate most gratefully the generosity with which you have always treated me but I always felt uncomfortable that I was being financed from your private purse, not from the resources of the Mission – the thing wasn't square somehow; it wasn't businesslike. If I am working for the Maynooth Mission, the Maynooth Mission ought to maintain me.[33]

In retrospect, Frances could better understand Margaret's reluctance to have all her arrangements made and financed by another, when as yet there was no formal bond uniting the group.

In the letter quoted above, Margaret also informed Frances that Father Blowick had decided that the three of them should go into the Mater Hospital for general training, as soon as possible. This was not as easy as Father Blowick had presumed. The Superior was willing to take Frances, but her policy was to have only one extern nursing student at a time, and she would have no vacancy for intern students for another year. Some ecclesiastical strings had to be pulled: Monsignor Dunne, Parish Priest of Donnybrook, whose encouragement and hospitality had so cheered them a few months earlier, persuaded the Superior to take the three of them as extern students.

It was then that Margaret, despite her assertion of independence, wrote to Frances to make arrangements to get her into the Mater Hospital and wondered if she could stay with her again if Frances decided to take a flat: 'I would much prefer to continue living with you now that the financial difficulty has disappeared.' But Frances and Teresa McCollam had decided against renting another flat. The latter had been invited to stay with an old friend whose home in Glasnevin was conveniently near the Mater, and Frances had accepted the hospitality of the Dominican Sisters in Eccles Street. However, the Sisters could not accommodate Margaret, but she did eventually get lodgings nearby in Eccles Street.

Frances started her general nursing training in the Mater Hospital on 3 November 1919, and Margaret two weeks later. Teresa joined them early in January 1920. Margaret, never robust, found the work too taxing physically and resigned after some weeks. She remained a member of the group, and continued to be in touch with Dalgan through her work for *The Far East*.

Early in December 1919, Father Blowick and Father Galvin had gone to Rome, and had returned with the good news that the district of Hanyang had been assigned to the Maynooth Mission to China. Frances wrote immediately to congratulate Father Blowick, who replied that sixteen priests would soon go to China and that he himself would accompany them. On his return he would be better able to tell her what she and her companions could do in China. In the meantime, he said, the training they were undergoing was the best possible preparation for their future work. 'Please remember me to all the "Sisters",' he added, 'and tell them that I have not a spare moment all day for the present.' His use of the word 'Sisters' struck a welcome note of encouragement, especially because at this time Father Ronayne seemed to discourage Frances's efforts to bring the scattered group together for an occasional free afternoon.

Heartening news came from Australia. Archbishop Mannix had written to Father Blowick, suggesting that he ask permission from the Australian and New Zealand bishops to preach about the Chinese Mission in their dioceses, and to raise funds for the new mission. Dr Edward Maguire, who had resigned his chair of theology in All Hallows College, Dublin, to join the Maynooth Mission to China, was chosen for this mission, together with a younger companion Father James Galvin (not related to Father Edward Galvin). Before leaving for Australia on 10 December 1919, Dr Maguire visited Frances and her companions. 'He came in such a genial happy way,' she said, 'and partook of the frugal hospitality of the flat for an hour or two with so much simplicity as made the "Sisters" feel that in him they had gained a real brother.'[34]

He kept them in mind during his crowded early days in Australia, and when young women showed an interest in the Chinese Mission he told them about the little band of women at the other end of the world. Mary Scanlan, who had felt drawn to China for some time, was his first recruit. To prepare for missionary life she trained as a teacher with the Loreto nuns in Melbourne. Ellen Mapleback, a secretary in Melbourne, offered herself for the Chinese Mission after listening to a talk by Father James Galvin. Several other women evinced an interest, but these two remained constant. They did not meet until two years later, shortly before they left for the novitiate in Ireland. These two years were eventful for them, but much more so for their future companions at the other end of the world.

NINE

Nearing the Goal

Back in Dublin the political situation had worsened. Ambushes and killings were the order of the day, especially after the government called in the Black and Tans and the Auxiliaries. Nurses on duty in accident and emergency wards of the big Dublin hospitals had to cope with many gruesome situations. After spending the first three months of 1920 on such duty, Frances concluded that nothing could ever shock her again.

One dark winter's afternoon hurrying up O'Connell Street she walked into Father Galvin, who called to see her that evening at the Dominican Convent, Eccles Street,where she was staying. 'He spoke long and earnestly on the philosophy of suffering and of the grey martyrdom by which she could serve and glorify God for the salvation of souls.'[1]

Apart from that meeting, there had been little communication with Dalgan for some months, although Margaret Gibbons was still sending regular contributions to *The Far East*. It came then as a surprise when Frances had a letter from her friend Miss Fitzgerald-Kenny on 24 March, telling her that the first group of priests leaving for China were at the Central Hotel in Exchequer Street and would probably cross from the North Wall to Liverpool the following morning. She mentioned that Margaret Gibbons was at the Central Hotel with the priests, looking after Father Edward Galvin who had been ill, and added in her forthright way, 'It certainly seems strange to me that she should be there and you and Teresa absent.'

It is understandable that Margaret Gibbons, with plenty of free time on her hands, now that she had resigned from the Mater programme, should have been called on to help. What is surprising is her failure to find out if her companions knew about the imminent departure of the priests. Did she presume that they knew?

In his letter of 8 January 1920, Father Blowick had thanked Frances for her note of congratulations on the Maynooth Mission being given the district of Hanyang in China, and said that they hoped to send sixteen priests to China in the near future. Frances and Teresa had already heard that the ordinations had been brought forward to have four more priests ready for China. They had also heard the rumour that had been going around that the missionaries for China might leave on St Patrick's Day. Now at last Frances and Teresa knew, from the ever-faithful Miss Fitzgerald-Kenny, that the day of departure had arrived.

Within hours of hearing the news they had a visit from two of the older members of the group about to leave for China, Father Tierney and Father O'Doherty. As soon as they came off duty that evening they went to the Central Hotel where they spent the evening with the young priests and Father Joe O'Leary whose experience of China was a support and inspiration to the younger men. All were facing into the unknown, both the priests and the mission nurses, and some of them were only too well aware of their lack of experience. There was loneliness too, but it helped that others were there to share it. Frances and Teresa McCollam were moved by the generosity of these young men and returned to the hospital 'renewed and strengthened in heart and spirit.'[2] Father Blowick was staying with his friends the Ronayne family in Monkstown, so neither he nor Father Galvin were there when Frances and Teresa visited. Nor was Margaret Gibbons.

Next day Frances and Teresa asked for time off to see the priests leave from the North Wall. Miss Fitzgerald-Kenny met them at the gangway, telling them that Father Blowick wanted to see them. It was a short meeting. They were trying to come to terms with his remark that he might be away for two years when they were told that all visitors had to go ashore: some political prisoners were expected on board. As soon as the ship began to move Teresa hurried back on duty, but Miss Fitzgerald-Kenny, Frances and Eilis Brannigan, who had got up from her sick bed to join them, jumped into a waiting taxi and drove to the end of the pier. From there they ran to the edge of the breakwater, waving until the ship was a mere speck on the horizon.

On 28 March a postcard arrived from Father Galvin, posted in

Liverpool before they set sail. It ended with the words: 'Goodbye, will meet in China.' Some weeks later, he wrote to Frances from Omaha, Nebraska: 'With God's help you will soon be with us out there to do your part in bringing God's name to those benighted millions.'[3] He told her that he and his companions had done much to make the Maynooth Mission to China known in the United States, and that at the departure ceremony in Omaha more than two thousand people had crowded the cathedral, among them many Protestants. 'God will not forsake you,' he said in conclusion, 'and in a little while the way will be clear.' Father Galvin's encouragement meant much to Frances at this time, when the future of the women's mission seemed so vague and she had to cope with the prospect of Father Blowick being away for two years.

Father Ronayne was among those who had come to see the sixteen missionaries off on the first stage of their journey to China. It was literally a parting of the ways as he saw his friends depart for a mission still closed to him because of Archbishop Walsh's refusal to allow him to join the Maynooth Mission to China. His decision to consider some mission field other than China possibly dates from that day. Some months later he introduced Marie Martin to Monsignor Shanahan, telling him that she might be willing to go to Nigeria as a lay missionary. It is of interest that they met in Father Ronayne's presbytery, where more than three years earlier Father Blowick and Father Galvin had first met, and where Frances had her first meeting with Agnes Ryan and later with Marie herself.

As recently as Christmas 1919, Marie had written to Frances: 'It is great news to hear that Father Blowick will be starting so soon. I feel sure that once they are settled our little Mission will soon be wanted.'[4] It is not clear why, in a matter of months, Marie was looking towards Africa rather than China. Possibly Father Ronayne's new interest in Nigeria may have helped to change the direction of Marie's life, and like many another she was obviously influenced by Monsignor Shanahan's charismatic personality.

It was around this time that Father Ronayne, who had been spiritual director to Agnes Ryan as well as to Marie Martin, arranged that Agnes too would meet Monsignor Shanahan. The outcome of this meeting was that she also decided to go to Nigeria. Saying that it cost her much to do so, she went to the Mater Hospital to break the news to Frances and Teresa. 'The way of the Medical Mission was punctured by the cross,' Frances recalled. Naturally, she was greatly disappointed, yet she could understand the decision. 'It was all God's work,' she said, 'and the prospects for China [were] still so indefinite.'[5] She respected the choice made by Marie and Agnes and throughout her life regarded them as friends.

Because the future was so uncertain, Frances felt that in fairness she should suggest to Eilis Brannigan, their most recent candidate, that there were other mission possibilities apart from China. Eilis replied: 'Do you not feel bound to the Maynooth Mission? Truly there are many missionfields waiting for workers and everywhere we work for God – here as well as yonder. But, like you, unless clear direction to another sphere be given China must be my goal.'[6]

Inducements were not wanting to draw Frances and her companions away from their commitment to China. Frances spoke of an over-zealous missionary who tried to divert them to his mission, pointing out that 'a bird in the hand is worth two in the bush.' She did not name him, but it is likely from the context that it was the indomitable Monsignor Shanahan. Mother Kevin invited them warmly to Uganda, and a Jesuit missionary in China had also been in touch. Within the next few years others, including Father Ronayne himself, were equally unsuccessful in diverting Frances and her few companions from the road they felt called to travel.

Meanwhile, on 6 June 1920 Monsignor Shanahan was consecrated in Maynooth as Bishop of Southern Nigeria. He spoke to the assembled bishops and got permission to appeal to the priests of Ireland, as well as to the students in Maynooth, to give five years to the Nigerian mission. Father Ronayne was among the first to volunteer. Before he left for Nigeria at the end of 1920, he wrote to Frances from St Senan's College, Cahiracon, Co. Clare, recently acquired for the Maynooth Mission to China: 'If Father Blowick cannot give you any definite promise when he returns, it would be as well for you face our way and you will get a real welcome. This is only if Father Blowick cannot promise, or if his scheme will

entail a long delay.'[7] Frances and her companions were prepared to
wait.

At the end of July 1920, Frances, Teresa and Eilis Brannigan
went on a much-needed vacation. Eilis had finished her midwifery
course and was preparing to begin her general nursing in Jervis
Street Hospital. Frances and Teresa had survived some months of
intensive training, looking after hunger-strikers who had been
released in a near-dying condition from Mountjoy Jail. They had
many occasions to help these severely debilitated men, many of
whom were spiritually as well as physically ill, and they saw some
real miracles of grace. 'It was these little touches of Divine
Providence,' Frances recalled, 'which lightened an otherwise dark
road, giving them [Frances and Teresa] confidence to trust themselves entirely to the marvellous goodness of God.'[8]

Before going on vacation, Frances asked the Matron of the
Mater Hospital for three months leave of absence, so that she could
get some experience of tropical medicine in London. Teresa got
permission to do a course in fever nursing in Cork. In the Hospital
for Tropical Diseases in London, Frances met people of Chinese
nationality for the first time. Most of them were there as patients,
but among her fellow students she discovered two young Chinese
doctors. When they learned of her hope to work for their people,
they gave her every help they could.

While she was in London, Terence McSwiney, Lord Mayor of
Cork, died in Brixton Jail, having been on hunger strike for
seventy-four days. She attended the funeral, thereby incurring
some criticism from her fellow nurses. Some days later, Teresa was
present at the obsequies in Cork. She wrote to Frances on 3
November:

Everyone is feeling very tense here over Terence McSwiney.
What length of agony, what a will and spirit! ... The funeral was
wonderful and the military regulations were, as they usually are,
circumvented. Archbishops and bishops, including poor old Dr
Walshe, walked in their robes, and chanted over the grave. The
indignation at the forcible removal of the body at Holyhead was

just too great for any expression in words.[9]

Exaggerated reports had reached Frances when Patrick Street was burnt down, and she wired immediately to know if her friend was safe. Teresa replied:

Yes, I am perfectly safe, only very sick at heart to see so much of this beautiful city in utter ruins, and knowing the misery that must surely follow such wholesale and wanton destruction. A good deal of destruction had been going on last week during the night when by curfew law the city is in sole possession of the Forces of the Crown. Well it culminated on Saturday night ... At 9.45 a blaze lit up the city. It is said that petrol was distributed over the attached houses by a hose before fire was put to them. All through the night the flames lit up the sky and in the morning they were burning fiercely. There were bombs exploding, many rifle shots, and often the crash of falling buildings. At 5.00 in the morning the gas was cut off, and as that is the way this place is lit, the night staff had to work with the few candles available. On Sunday I went as near as was possible to have a look at the sad scene. Besides the damage in the Main Street, two other beautiful buildings were destroyed, that is the City Hall and the Public Library. Today we have the further news of the shooting of Canon Magner a well-known priest here. Someone was held up and about to be shot on the road and he came along and interfered, with the consequence that after much insult and rough usage he also was shot. We too had a visit from the forces of the Crown, just as Shandon rang out at midnight. They were hammering and battering the gate and shouting: 'Open the ... door or we'll blow it in about your ... ears!' Those of us who were in bed got up and put our money in our sleeves, for you know, of course, that in these raids and hold-ups the most shameful robbery of money and valuables goes on. Well, no one opened to them, and after a time they went on their way, probably having found out what sort of a place it was.[10]

Shortly after receiving this letter, Frances had a visit from Bishop Shanahan, who was passing through London; he gave her

news of the Nigerian Mission. Early in December Dr Margaret
Lamont came to visit, bringing good news: she had received a letter
of approval for her work from the Sacred College of Propaganda.
She invited Frances to a meeting she had organised in the Jesuit
Fathers' hall in Mount Street, London. Cardinal Bourne presided,
and he and others spoke to the large gathering about the work being
done by medical missions throughout the world. Regretably it
would take another sixteen years before religious would be free to
engage in the kind of work Dr Lamont was doing. Father Ronayne
came to say goodbye to Frances before leaving for Nigeria. He
brought her to Hammersmith to meet Archbishop Mannix, 'who
spoke in the warmest terms of the Chinese Mission'.[11]

As 1920 drew to an end, the members of the group were all
working in different places: Frances, back from London, was
continuing with her nursing training in the Mater Hospital; Teresa
was still in the Cork Fever Hospital; Eilis Brannigan was training
in Jervis Street Hospital; Bridie Fallon was nursing in a hospital
near Shrewsbury and still in touch. Margaret Gibbons had withdrawn from the group temporarily: she was to make a brief
reappearance later. They heard that she had organised a small
group in Galway to help the Chinese Mission, but Frances's letters
and Christmas greetings remained unanswered.

It had been a troubled year in many ways, yet it also held seeds
of hope. Invitations to other missions reaffirmed the women in their
belief that what they were doing was worthwhile, and they held
firm to the prospect of China. One of their more recent invitations
was to Hong Kong, off the coast of mainland China. Lieut. Col.
Bowen, an officer in the St Vincent de Paul Society, Hong Kong,
wrote at the request of the bishop, asking the women's group to
make a beginning in Hong Kong. He had heard from Dr Lamont
about the proposed new order for China, and he believed that they
were an answer to prayer. They might start a hostel for medical
students, or a small hospital and house of studies. A fund would be
organised to support them. Frances forwarded the letter to Dalgan,
where Dr Cleary was deputing for Father Blowick in his absence.
He decided against their accepting the offer: the women associated

with the Maynooth Mission to China, he said, should concentrate all their energies on China.

Almost thirty years later, in January 1949, the Columban Sisters eventually did make a foundation in Hong Kong in response to an appeal from the Hong Kong Anti-Tuberculosis Association. They agreed to staff a hospital which would attempt to cope with the ravages of this disease, rampant among the poor, especially among refugees from mainland China. Over the years the mission of the congregation in Hong Kong has expanded to include many kinds of missionary service: educational, pastoral, and ministries to those marginalised by physical or mental disabilities.

Returning back to work one cold evening in January 1921, Frances was getting off a tram at Eccles Street when she passed Father Heneghan about to board the same tram. 'Where is Father Blowick?' she asked abruptly. 'He arrived today!' was the answer, as the tram carried him off into the darkness. It was like 'ships that pass in the night – only a signal shown.'[12] A week later, on 23 January, a letter came from Father Blowick with the news they had been awaiting so eagerly for the past few years:

> I shall have to see you all as soon as possible. There is good news. The authorities in Rome have taken kindly to the work you have in hand and they have authorised the foundation of a sisterhood for our missions in China ... It will take a good deal of planning but at least we can now begin definitely.[13]

That day Frances happened to be on duty in the operating theatre where an urgent operation was scheduled. She barely had time to hurry over to Jervis Street Hospital during her dinner break to tell Eilis the good news, before returning on duty at 2.00 p.m. Her dinner that day was a cup of coffee, but she said, 'Wasn't it worth it all and a great deal more besides!' She sent Father Blowick's letter to Teresa, still somewhat apprehensive about her suitability for religious life, and therefore less excited by the news than either Frances or Eilis, though happy for their sakes. However, she returned to Dublin after her busy but fulfilling six months in Cork, and rejoined Frances in the Mater. Both of them had lost seniority by their absence, and technically they were again probationers, facing all the drudgery which this entailed. They had five more months to complete before sitting their examination.

Sickness among the nurses meant that the hospital was under-staffed. It was one prolonged emergency situation because victims of ambushes and raids were continually being carried in. There were no days off. Frances recalled that time off merged into time on, but that nobody complained. 'A look over to Mountjoy Prison, where the flower of Ireland's youth were ending their days, or a glance round the wards at the fine specimens of manhood mutilated or dying for Ireland's sake prevented any thought of self or ease.'[14]

In the third week of May 1921, Agnes Ryan went to the Mater again, this time to bid farewell to her friends. She had decided to postpone her final medical year so as to go to Nigeria with Marie Martin, both of them as lay missionaries. When they boarded the ship that was to take them to Calabar, they found awaiting them a telegram of good wishes from Frances. Marie replied on 25 May from the RMS *Elmina* of the African Steamship Company: 'I was sorry I was not able to get up to see you but having to spend my last week in bed left me very rushed the last few days – I would have loved to have seen you.'[15]

Some weeks later Frances and Teresa, together with other student nurses, sat the Mater exams which lasted a fortnight. When the results were published they found to their surprise that their names headed the list of successful candidates. They saw that they were listed as 'Passed with marked distinction'. Frances attributed their success to the prayers of a poor old lady, living in one room in Gloucester Street, who had got a campaign of prayer going for the two mission nurses. Father Blowick wrote to congratulate them and invited them to Dalgan to discuss the future.

By 2 July they had finished all the duties connected with the annual closure of wards, and were free to say goodbye to the Sisters and nurses with whom they had worked. Teresa went home for a rest and Frances went to Waterford to make a retreat under Father Nolan SJ, with whom she had worked on the Belgian Refugees Committee some years earlier. It was held in the Ursuline Convent,

Waterford, where three years previously she had wrestled with her vocation. This retreat was different; Frances too was different. The whole tenor of this retreat was peace and confidence, and it resonated with a Frances who now knew without a shadow of doubt the direction in which God was calling her. When the retreat ended, she and Teresa decided that the time had come to accept Father Blowick's invitation to go to Dalgan to discuss the future.

They arrived somewhat dishevelled. A fellow passenger, who thought that they had left the train when they had merely gone to the dining carriage, had put all their luggage on the platform at Moate, including their coats and hats. They decided to go ahead as planned so as not to cause confusion at the other end. By the time they reached Dalgan neither of them looked exactly presentable, though Teresa with her fine head of hair in total disarray looked the worst. 'Don't mind Teresa,' Frances whispered audibly to Father Heneghan who met them at the door, 'The strain had been too much for her!' For a moment he took her seriously, until Father Joe Mullen, standing nearby, broke into hearty laughter. 'The incident,' Frances said, 'served to melt away a thin coating of ice which had been gathering for some months.' Subsequent events confirmed her intuition.

Evidently Father Blowick wanted the two women to have a good rest after their busy year in the Mater, because the days passed and nothing was said about planning for the future. Finally, after five days, Teresa, unable to stand any further suspense, asked for an interview with Father Blowick. Only then did they learn that the Mother General of the Irish Sisters of Charity, Mother Agnes Gertrude, had agreed to send Sisters to set up the novitiate which they hoped to open in September or October at Cahiracon, Co. Clare.

Father Blowick's news about the novitiate was totally unexpected and somewhat disconcerting. The letter that brought Frances and Teresa to Dalgan had given them to understand that they were going there to plan the future with Father Blowick. Now they found that all the arrangements had been made without their being consulted.

Several times in the past few years Frances had spoken to Father Blowick about the novitiate, and had suggested that he ask either the Sacred Heart nuns or the Sisters of Charity to train the first novices. She had shared with him all her ideas and plans and he had treated her as the leader of the women preparing for China. Teresa McCollam and Margaret Gibbons, her close associates, were also regarded as the pioneers of the future congregation. Now everything had been taken out of their hands and decided for them.

It was not that they had any objection to Father Blowick's plans, which were the culmination of what they had been hoping for over the last few years. The problem was that they had not been involved in the decision. 'It was sprung upon them as it were, without any preliminaries,' Frances was to write later. Consequently, 'the sweetness and savour they might have experienced was almost totally lacking.'[16] 'It was all cut and dried,' she wrote to Father Michael Browne SJ, her spiritual director. The only consolation he offered her was that this was what the following of Christ was all about. 'But it took time,' she said, 'for these pioneers to realise that their call was to be rank and file men, not captains in God's army, and that they must aim at becoming not consciously great, but strong and supple instruments. In this way only, could God's work be accomplished.'[17]

Teresa was upset because, while convinced of her call to work with the Chinese Mission, she was still undecided about her call to the religious life. Frances went to Father Blowick to ask if there was any possibility of lay helpers being accepted for China: to put Teresa into a convent, she said, was like caging an eagle. He listened sympathetically, but told her that it could only be as religious that women missionaries would work alongside the Maynooth Mission to China. (Had Teresa been born some decades later, no doubt she might have been one of the leaders of the Columban Lay Missionaries.)

Frances wrote to convey the news to Eilis Brannigan, who replied in exuberant terms to say how happy she was to be one of the twenty chosen; she had heard that there were two hundred applicants. Sympathising with Frances's remark that she felt 'as dry as an old chip', she assured her that deep down she was very far from that.

Teresa, feeling the need to distance herself from the situation for a while, went with a friend for a month's holiday to the Isle of Man. Frances stayed nearer home with her sister's family in Galway. While there she visited Margaret Gibbons, still living in Galway. After many months of silence she had been in touch with Frances again. 'I feel wonderfully well and happy,' she wrote to her, 'but of course if tomorrow it were said to me, "We are ready; come!" Oh, wouldn't I come with never a look back again.'[18] In another letter she wrote: 'Who has had harder knocks than yourself, surely no one; as for me, well if I don't make meat I'll make mustard and there's still the barest chance that I'll make the meat.' Father Blowick, who still regarded Margaret as one of the founding members, drove over to see her. Like Frances, he appreciated her qualities and the gifts she would bring to the new foundation. It was not to be: for health reasons Margaret finally decided to withdraw from the group, warning them that they too should take into account the heavy physical demands of the novitiate:

> I do think that a man before he begin to build should see if he have wherewith to finish lest he be forced to leave his tower roofless. Girls especially should realise what a hard thing a religious noviceship is, for all it seems so calm and placid to the outside world. I tell you this because I know and you do not know; you have not experienced the weakening effects of a daily strain such as a religious noviceship is; great physical strength is more than half the battle.[19]

Undeterred, Frances and Teresa went on pilgrimage together to Lough Derg for the last time and afterwards enjoyed what Frances described as 'a happy bohemian holiday' in Donegal. At Glencolumcille they found a letter awaiting them from Father Blowick. Kindly and with much sensitivity he poured oil on the troubled waters, telling the two women how much he sympathised with their points of view. 'I feel the same in your case,' he said, 'as I would if a priest or student were to take me into his confidence and tell me his troubles and ask me to help. I would die to help and my only trouble could come from inability to do so or from doubt as to the right course.'[20] Much reassured, they replied telling him not to worry about them, that it was to be expected that women with their experience of life should find it harder to accept everything without question. 'One intends with God's help to make a complete self-surrender, but don't be surprised if there is occasionally a little inconsistency. We must do our best not to over-try the patience of the Sisters of Charity. It is so wonderfully good of them to undertake the task.'[21]

Frances was pleased to discover that Mother Mary Camillus Dalton would be in charge of the future novitiate, and she went to visit her. They had often spoken over the phone in the years when Frances was looking for help for needy invalids whom she had come across in the course of her work for the Society of St Vincent de Paul; she had never been refused. Mother Camillus now came straight from the kitchen to meet her; she had been standing in for one of the lay Sisters who was ill. 'Could any finer model or example be found for the training of missionary Sisters?' Frances asked herself.

Her meeting with Mother Camillus reassured her. And she was happy to hear that Father McArdle SJ had been able to allay some of Teresa's fears about the religious life. He told her that there was no danger of their being treated as schoolgirls and that they would find the discipline and rule meaningful. Because of his encouragement she felt more at peace. With each passing day she was adjusting better to the idea. 'Please God,' she wrote, 'when the time comes, my mind and heart will go with my body more completely than they have done till now.'

It transpired that Father Blowick's hope that the novitiate could start in Cahiracon in September or October was over-optimistic. Much work still needed to be done on Clifton House, the old farmhouse, which was being made ready for the novitiate and which Father Blowick himself described as more like a ruin than a residence.

Frances utilised the time of waiting to take further courses which might prove useful in China. She began a six weeks course at the Skin and Cancer Hospital in Hume Street. In October Teresa joined her and together they attended the clinic at the Skin and Cancer Hospital, and got some further experience at the Lock Hospital, Townsend Street. During the months of November and December they attended courses at the Eye and Ear Hospital, and took lessons from a pharmacist on compounding prescriptions. Happily for them they had been able to procure again the flat they had lived in earlier in Upper Merrion Street.

At the end of October Father Joe Mullen had written to tell them that Father Blowick would leave for Rome the following week. Teresa wrote inviting him to visit them in Merrion Street before leaving. He was happy to accept and came along accompanied by Father John Heneghan and Father Michael Boyle. It is of interest that it was Teresa who sent the invitation, and that it was to Teresa that Father Blowick had written some weeks earlier asking her suggestions for a habit for the future congregation. Back in August 1919, Frances had already sent him her suggestions.

In Father Blowick's absence, Father Joe O'Leary looked after all the business relating to the novitiate, and the selecting of candidates. Because of his experience in China, where he had been chaplain to some missionary Sisters, Frances and Teresa valued his advice. It was not necessarily the person with the highest qualifications, he said, who would make the best missionary, but the one best grounded in humility and discipline.[22] This was something that both of them took to heart.

At the end of November, Mother Agnes Gertrude wrote making an appointment to see Frances and Teresa on 1 December. She gave them the outfit list, explaining the different items where necessary. Teresa baulked at the required red flannel petticoat, but Mother Agnes Gertrude was adamant. Later they found Mother Camillus more sympathetic.

At the other end of the world news had reached Melbourne that the novitiate was about to be started. Mary Scanlan phoned Father Hayes and was invited to tea at Mentone, the headquarters of the Australian branch of the Maynooth Mission to China. Nellie

Mapleback was also invited, and that was how the first two Australian members of the new sisterhood met one another at last. It was early December. Dr Ned Maguire asked the two women if they could be ready in a week's time. Frances recalled the generosity with which they were ready to sacrifice a last Christmas with their families, and was happy for their sakes that their departure was postponed until the last day of the year.

The day that their future companions set sail from Sydney, Frances and Teresa were in Dalgan on a farewell visit. However, as the new year opened there was still no definite date for the opening of the novitiate. With Father Blowick's consent, Frances set about organising a Mission Guild among members of the St Vincent de Paul Society in Dublin. The idea spread quickly and Frances was confident that Dr Byrne, who had succeeded Dr Walsh as Archbishop of Dublin, would give his approval.

Then on 22 January, just one year after they had heard of Rome's approval of the foundation of the sisterhood, a letter came from Father Blowick. The date, 21 January 1922, was typed in red letters, and it was truly a red-letter day when this brief business-like note reached Frances and Teresa.

> At long last the day has been fixed and, if the skies fall this time I will not change it for anyone. It is the 7th February and if you travel to Ennis by the train which reaches there at 3.45 p.m. you will be met at the station. There is nothing new here. God be with you.[23]

The long wait was over. The two women decided to spend their last weeks in Dublin making final contacts with possible future members of the Mission Guild and finishing the programme they had begun at the Eye and Ear Hospital. They felt that no experience which might help in China should be lightly left aside, even at a time like this. Frances recalled how they took to themselves literally the words addressed by Christ to the seventy-two disciples: 'Heal the sick and say to them, "The kingdom of God has come near to you."' (Lk 10: 9) Frances also made time to visit some friends in Co. Monaghan. The annals of the St Louis Convent,

Carrickmacross refer to her visiting the convent while she was staying with the local parish priest for a few days shortly before leaving for Cahiracon.

At the last minute their friend Bridie Flood, who had been associated with the group for three years, changed her mind. Bridie had been like a ray of sunshine and they knew how much they would miss her. On the eve of their departure from Dublin several people came to bid them farewell, among them the Jesuit Provincial and several priest friends. Monsignor Dunne drew Frances aside. Regretfully he passed on a message from the Archbishop to say that he could not sanction the Mission Guild. Once again Frances's hopes were dashed. Throughout her life the Cross had marked many significant moments. This was no exception.

On 1 February 1922, the day that the Sisters of Charity were to arrive in Cahiracon, Frances and Teresa said their last goodbyes and left for the Sacred Heart Convent, Roscrea, where they had arranged to spend some quiet days preparing for the life ahead of them. Mother Rice and the community welcomed them cordially. The wheel had come full circle: the Sacred Heart nuns, who had played such a vital role in Frances's earlier life were there also at this crucial stage.

On 7 February what Frances described as 'the last remnant of the Medical Mission' arrived in Cahiracon. Summing it up later, she said: 'God's will had been manifested regarding the foundation of the new order, and putting aside their former hopes and plans they yielded up their personality to God in the hands of their new superiors.' With those words Frances concluded her account of the events leading up to the founding of the congregation. From now on her destiny was to be in the hands of others. The 'remnant' of the Medical Mission which arrived in Cahiracon on 7 February 1922 consisted of herself and Teresa McCollam. Six weeks later Eilis Brannigan joined them. Within a year both Teresa and Eilis withdrew from the novitiate and Frances was the sole survivor of the group she had organised and worked with so selflessly throughout four strenuous years.

The Irish Sisters of Charity had decided that instead of all the

prospective candidates arriving together, six of them would come
on 7 February and the rest later. Those who entered the novitiate
with Frances and Teresa were Elizabeth McKey, Elizabeth Walsh,
Elizabeth Dalton and Kathleen Brennan. The following young
women came next day: Nora Collins, Catherine McSwiney,
Margaret M. McDonnell and Mary Veronica Lees. On 16 February
the two Australian candidates, Mary Elizabeth Scanlan and Ellen
M. Mapleback, joined the group and on 22 March Elizabeth
Brannigan arrived.

How Cahiracon became the centre for the novitiate, and how the
Irish Sisters of Charity came to be in charge of the fledgling
congregation is worth recalling. The Maynooth Mission to China
had acquired the Cahiracon estate in early 1920 when they found
that their seminary in Dalgan Park, Galway, was becoming crowded.
At St Senan's College, Cahiracon, the seminarians could do their
preliminary studies in philosphy before moving on to Dalgan Park
for theology. Besides the main building given over to the seminary,
there were other houses on the extensive property. One of them,
Clifton House, within two miles walk from St Senan's, was more
spacious than the others and suggested possible future use as a
convent. The prospect of founding a congregation of Sisters for the
Chinese Mission now looked brighter.

Before Father John Blowick left for China in March 1920, with
the first group of priests of the Maynooth Mission, he instructed Dr
Patrick Cleary to contact the Bishop of Killaloe, Dr Michael
Fogarty, to know if he would be willing to admit into his diocese
'a congregation of women established for work on the China
Mission in connection with the Maynooth Mission to China.' In the
same letter he spoke of establishing 'a congregation of our own –
a congregation for which we might draft a set of constitutions best
calculated for the formation of good missionaries.'[24]

The following July Bishop Fogarty wrote to the Sacred Congregation for Religious. After giving a summary of the work already
achieved by the Maynooth Mission to China, he continued:

Inspired by the success of the said Society, Irish women also wish to co-operate in the conversion of the Chinese. There are many Sisters and many young women who wish to dedicate themselves to this splendid task. Among the Sisters are many whose zeal and talents are of such a high order as to fit them particularly well for the foundation of a new congregation. They are looking at various congregations, and there is no doubt that, in order to avoid any ill-feeling, it would be better to found a new congregation. A suitably large house with fifty English acres of land is available and will be given completely free to a new congregation of this kind. There will be no shortage of young women, nor will there be any lack of means for their support, and I am certain that the new congregation will be of great benefit in the work of spreading the Faith. On the other hand, it cannot be expected that any of the religious congregations already existing in Ireland would be able to carry out this work so well. For these reasons, I would like to found a new diocesan religious congregation with its own constitutions, which congregation would have as its particular object the conversion of the Chinese.[25]

On 29 December 1920 the Sacred Congregation for Religious replied, giving Bishop Fogarty permission to found 'a new institute of Sisters to offer their assistance to missionaries working to spread the faith, and especially in China'. Bishop Fogarty wrote to the Congregation for the Propagation of the Faith on 30 December specifying that what he requested was a canonical licence to found a new religious congregation, in conjunction with the Society of the Maynooth Mission to China, 'and with the special purpose of assisting and furthering the work of the Society in the evangelization of the Chinese'.

By mid-January 1921 Father Blowick, who had gone to Rome at the end of December, came home with all the required permissions. He was now faced with the challenge of how the future congregation was to be formed. He wrote to Mother Agnes Gertrude Chamberlaine, Mother General of the Irish Sisters of Charity, asking her advice:

There are many professed nuns, chiefly of the Mercy order, who have volunteered for China with the consent of their Superiors and their Bishops. Now I understand that such nuns, if they are to enter our new order as founders and trainers of the girls, must get a dispensation from Rome and also go through the novitiate again. This means that we have either to send them to some convent which would accept them for their novitiate or get a few Sisters from some other order on loan to act as Superior and Mistress of Novices in our own house. This again will delay the profession in our order for at least eighteen months and the fact is that we are badly in need of about twelve Sisters in China next September.

In these circumstances could you offer me any advice as to the best method of proceeding with the new order?[26]

Amused by his optimism in expecting Sisters to be ready in such a short span of time, Mother Agnes Gertrude replied immediately, pointing out some problems. Sisters leaving one order for another would have to get a dispensation from the Pope. Furthermore, 'if you mix up two or three sets of Sisters, who have been trained in various orders according to their respective rules and customs, is it likely that they will agree together? Or will each think (as well she might) that her own training was the best and ought to be followed by all the others?'[27] She reminded Father Blowick that as several Sisters of Mercy had applied to be part of the Maynooth Mission to China, his best plan might be to gather some of them under a good superior and prepare them for the work ahead by learning Chinese and anything else needed. Because their rule was already approved, presumably they would not need any dispensations. 'Of course a congregation of your own would be a very good thing,' she added, 'but would certainly take time.'

Father Blowick's next move was to consult Dr Kinane in Maynooth – a canon lawyer. The tenor of his letter makes it clear that he was definitely thinking of a totally new congregation rather than one comprising Sisters of other orders. Ten days later he wrote again to Mother Agnes Gertrude asking her if she would be willing to send some Sisters of Charity to China after the middle of August;

evidently Father Galvin was insisting that he needed twelve Sisters there by autumn. Referring again to the dire need for Sisters in China he added:

> You will think, if we are going to have our own Sisters why seek others? The answer is this: it will take some years to have the first of our own in the field. Secondly, there is scope in our district in China for as many Sisters as there are in Ireland ... Thirdly, when our own Sisters go to China they will be badly needed for up-country work while your Sisters would be more profitably employed in the large cities where the hospital work will be greatest and the need for girls' schools is dreadful.[28]

Mother Agnes Gertrude was attracted to the idea but finally refused the request, chiefly on the grounds that it would involve a change in her congregation's constitutions.

Meanwhile, Father Blowick had come up with another proposal:

> In order to assist us in making the new foundation of missionary Sisters, which Rome desired us to make, would you be prepared to admit a number of selected ladies to your postulancy and novitiate for your usual term of postulancy and novitiate, to prepare them to be the nucleus of the new congregation? ... I have the greatest desire that our first Sisters would be trained by the Sisters of Charity.[29]

He reminded her that Mother Mary Aikenhead had proceeded in a similar way when starting her own congregation. Mother Agnes Gertrude informed him that they could take no more than two postulants and that, since he was in a hurry, such a plan would not be feasible. She then reminded him of the fact already noted by Dr Cleary in his letter to Bishop Fogarty a year earlier:

> As well as I remember, you told us there was a house or houses on your estate at Cahiracon besides that used by the students. What would you think of fitting up one of these for a novitiate and, when making your request or petition to Rome re same, of asking permission for some nuns of an approved order, prefer-

ably the Sisters of Charity, to go there and train your postulants and novices in the usual way according to our constitutions and rules? In this way they would be all your own and have their future duties put before them well. You would require a Novice Mistress, an assistant and another to look after temporal affairs.[30]

Things were now clearer for Father Blowick. He consulted some canonist friends and was assured by them that, even if the candidates were trained according to the constitutions of the Irish Sisters of Charity, the new congregation could have its own rules and constitutions. He then submitted a formal request to the Irish Sisters of Charity, asking that a small number of Sisters be sent to Cahiracon to train the novices up to the time of their profession.

Mother Agnes Gertrude, having consulted her council, replied on 8 June, acceding to Father Blowick's request and asking him to send her a statement which she could present to the Archbishop of Dublin, Dr Byrne. The document sent in response to this request concluded with the words: 'The period during which the services of such Sisters are requested will be the ordinary period required for the postulancy and novitiate of the first band of girls who enter. The Sisters will have completed their work as soon as this band is professed.'[31] (In the event the Irish Sisters of Charity guided the new congregation from 1922 to 1930).

It was also necessary to get Bishop Fogarty's written permission for the Irish Sisters of Charity to undertake the training of a sisterhood in his diocese. He sent his 'fullest approval,' adding that 'The moulding of our new sisterhood could not be entrusted to more capable hands.'[32]

During the following months letters went back and forth between Mother Agnes Gertrude and Father Blowick. There was frequent correspondence too with Father O'Leary, who was looking after arrangements at the Cahiracon end. Towards the end of October Mother Agnes Gertrude went to Cahiracon with a companion to see the future novitiate and to decide what furniture would be needed.

Meanwhile, Father Blowick had drawn up some guidelines to help the Irish Sisters of Charity in their task of forming the new congregation. The Maynooth Mission to China, he said, would be responsible for the current expenses of the house: the Rectress would have at her disposal sufficient money to cover all their needs. Vegetables would be supplied by St Senan's College, Cahiracon, and the Sisters would have at their disposal some milch cows and all the necessary dairy apparatus. They could avail of the college's farm labourers as needed. The Maynooth Mission to China reserved the right of selecting candidates for the novitiate, because of the information already at their disposal. However, the Novice Mistress, upon further acquaintance with the young women, would judge whether or not they were suitable for the congregation. She would also have the power to dismiss postulants and novices if necessary. The Irish Sisters of Charity agreed the guidelines and added an amendment to the effect that the Mistress of Novices would submit periodic reports on the novices to the Superior of the Maynooth Mission to China.

By December, Clifton House was almost ready, except for some furniture which T. & C. Martin could not send until after Christmas. Father Blowick wrote to Mother Agnes Gertrude to know if the candidates could wear the same postulant's dress as the Irish Sisters of Charity, and he asked her to draw up a list of the candidates' outfit. In her reply, she told him that when Lady Moloney and Teresa McCollam visited Milltown the previous week, between them they had made out a list of what would be required. Incidentally, that was the occasion when Frances and Teresa were introduced to the disturbing possibility of having to wear a red flannel petticoat. Frances, who had been something of a fashion plate in her earlier years, accepted the idea with better grace than Teresa.

By the end of the year, Mother Agnes Gertrude finalised her appointment of three Sisters to the Cahiracon novitiate: Mother Mary Camillus Dalton, Sister Mary Alphonsus Harnett and a Lay Sister, Sister Mary Bartholomew McHugh. It was arranged that they should arrive in Cahiracon on 1 February 1922, the Feast of St Brigid. Clifton House consequently changed its name to St Brigid's,

and awaited the arrival a week later of the twelve young women
who would form the nucleus of a new missionary congregation. In
anticipation of their arrival, Bishop Fogarty wrote to Mother Agnes
Gertrude on 22 January:

> We are anxiously looking forward to the opening of the mission-
> ary sisterhood in Cahiracon next month, and we are fully
> sensible and deeply grateful for the favour you have done us in
> lending some of your nuns to train the postulants whom I hope
> they will imbue successfully and permanently with the excellent
> spirit of your own order. I have to leave home just now for some
> weeks, but on my return I will come at once to see the young
> community at Cahiracon. May the Holy Spirit enter the humble
> home with them and fill the inmates with the fire of Pentecost.[33]

TEN

Religious Life at Last

On 4 February 1922 Sister Mary Alphonsus Harnett, one of the three Irish Sisters of Charity assigned to train the new missionary congregation, wrote to her Superior General, Mother Agnes Gertrude Chamberlaine, describing their arrival in Cahiracon. On the afternoon of 1 February, the feast of St Brigid, Father Jim O'Connell met the Dublin to Ennis train and drove Mother Mary Camillus Dalton, Sister Mary Bartholomew McHugh and herself to Cahiracon in the college car. A horse and cart took their luggage: trunks and carpetbags and an assortment of boxes of various sizes and shapes.

The Sisters were first brought to the college, where they were given a warm welcome. After dinner, while waiting to be driven to their future home, a message came to say that the horse and cart with all the luggage had met with a mishap. Evidently, the horse had turned in at the entrance gate to the college in spite of all the efforts of the driver to keep the animal on the main road leading to Clifton House, their future convent. Horse and cart were now upturned in the ditch, blocking the entrance to the avenue. Eventually the matter was sorted out, but because of the delay it was after eight o'clock by the time the Sisters arrived at their new home which, in honour of the day, they christened 'St Brigid's'. It was a cold, bleak evening, but they found fires lighting in all the rooms and the Blessed Sacrament installed to welcome them. It was after midnight by the time they got to bed.[1]

Early the following morning they surveyed their surroundings, hidden from them by the darkness of the previous evening. The Annals of the Columban Sisters describe what they would have seen:

> An old farmhouse of moderate size, with sloping roof and dwarfed windows had been decked out in a coat of fresh whitewash. At this date there was no hint of a garden, rank grass and weeds grew almost to the door. A rough path covered with

loose unbroken stones led up to it. A mass of grey rock framed the back of the house rising to a slope covered with some weather-beaten stunted and gnarled trees. The scene was surely uninviting as the three Sisters of Charity entered the house to prepare it for the novitiate.[2]

But the Sisters were undaunted. Sister Mary Alphonsus wrote enthusiastically to her superior in Milltown about the preparations that had been made, and told her how transformed the place was since Mother Mary Camillus had last seen it: the whole house painted, shutters on the windows, useful built-in presses, and the items forwarded from Dublin shops had arrived and were unpacked. Father Blowick had arranged for the baker, butcher, and grocer to call for orders, and they were to be given a cow, to be tended by the man who looked after their pump, also some poultry. The students from the college were coming that day to make a path around the garden, which would be ready in time for the postulants' retreat. 'A great deal of spade work had been accomplished by the labour of brotherly hands, but the wilderness had not yet flowered!'[3]

On 7 February, a week after the Irish Sisters of Charity arrived, St Brigid's welcomed the first six postulants of the new congregation. Betty Walsh stole a march on the others by crossing the Shannon by boat. That afternoon three of her future companions arrived in Ennis by train: Frances Moloney, Teresa McCollam and Elizabeth McKey. They were met at the station and driven directly to St Brigid's. Elizabeth Dalton and Kathleen Brennan arrived that evening. The bleakness of the place must have struck these young women too, though what they remembered most was the warm welcome they received from those they regarded as 'the Mothers of our Congregation.'[4]

The following afternoon Margaret McDonnell and Mary Veronica Lees arrived in Ennis by train and reached St Brigid's in due course. No word had come from Nora Collins or Catherine McSwiney, but around midnight there was a loud knocking on the door: they had arrived. Miss Collins had left Skibbereen the

previous day and her companion had come from Macroom. Because of the troubled times they had been unable to make the
necessary train connections. The community annals relate that they
'had covered different sections of the route by motor, outside car
or other conveyance'.

Next morning the newcomers met their eight companions. The
strangeness of it all, coupled with weariness, was probably the
reason why one of the postulants noted in her diary: 'Sister Collins'
tears filled her egg at breakfast.' Loneliness is contagious, but
before it had time to spread Mother Mary Camillus announced that
the group had been invited to spend the afternoon at St Senan's
College. They set off after an early dinner, 'wearing their secular
clothes for the last time'. [5] The college staff and students welcomed
them cordially and they were shown over the house and grounds
and given a boat ride on the Shannon. After tea the students put on
a concert, in which the priests and the visitors also participated.
Frances, as the senior postulant, was conscious of Mother Mary
Camillus's injunction that they return before dark, but speeches
had yet to be made and she was reassured when the priests promised
to return with them and explain the delay.

Next day, 10 February, they donned the postulant's dress, but
not the bonnets which they received a day later. Their entrance
retreat, given by Father Halpin SJ, began on 14 February. They
were two days into the retreat when their two Australian companions arrived, Mary Elizabeth Scanlan and Ellen Mapleback. Mother
M. Camillus allowed the retreatants to interrupt the silence to give
the newcomers a warm welcome. The group was now complete.
Then unexpectedly, on 22 March, as a happy afterthought, Elizabeth Brannigan, one of Frances Moloney's first companions,
arrived to join the group.

In the early 1920s all novitiates had much in common. Stress
was placed on training the candidates to be men and women of
prayer and humility. On the whole, less emphasis was put on their
theological or academic preparation: that came later. Weekly
conferences were given on prayer, and commentaries on the rules
and constitutions helped to imbue novices with the spirit of their

congregation.

Cahiracon was no exception. Even before the candidates had
come together, Father Blowick had asked the Sisters of Charity to
make their own conferences available to the new congregation.
That meant that they were trained in Ignatian spirituality, adapted
to the use of active women religious. From the beginning they were
initiated into the spirit of charity that characterised Mother Mary
Aikenhead's congregation: the spirit incorporated into their motto:
'Caritas Christi urget nos' (2 Cor 5:14). 'Part of Mary Aikenhead's
greatness was that she saw the problems of her time and sought to
offer realistic solutions to them in the ways her Sisters served the
people.'[6] It was this spirit of practical charity, expressed in their
vow of service to the poor, which had drawn Father Blowick and
later Frances Moloney to hope that the training of the future
members of the new congregation should be in such hands.[7]

In one respect the novitiate in Cahiracon differed from that of the
Sisters of Charity: right from the beginning the emphasis was on
preparation for China. St Senan's College was within walking
distance, so there was daily contact with the priests of the Maynooth
Mission to China. They came to say Mass, hear Confessions, and
very often just to visit. The early annals refer frequently to talks
given by returned Chinese missionaries. One of them, Father
O'Connell, was on the staff of the college and he began classes in
Chinese with the postulants within some weeks of their entering.
Later, when Father Blowick had drafted constitutions for the new
congregation, he came from Dalgan Park, Co Galway, on various
occasions to explain them and to share with the novices his own
commentary on the constitutions. They found his enthusiasm
contagious.[8] Other members of the Maynooth Mission to China
also came to teach dogma, scripture and theology, among them
Father O'Dwyer, Father Harris and Father Heneghan.

Manual work took up a large part of each day. There were to be
no lay Sisters in the new congregation; therefore each of the
novices had to learn basic housekeeping skills. Apart from its
obvious practical value in facilitating the smooth running of a
house, it was held at the time that manual work helped to keep a

person humble. Those unaccustomed to such toil found it wearing. Sister Moloney, as Frances was now called, was often in trouble. As well as being sacristan and looking after the chapel, she was also given charge of the petrol lamps and the stoves. It took her some time to cope with the vagaries of the chapel stove. 'With an almost human-like contrariness', the Annals note, 'the chapel stove, so carefully banked and slacked at nightfall would be found cold and black in the morning. The poor Sister's attempt to coax it into flame frequently resulted only in filling the chapel and the throats of the congregation with smoke.'

Towards the end of May, Frances's health necessitated some days' stay in St Vincent's Hospital, Dublin, for treatment. She returned on 6 June with Mother Mary Camillus, and again involved herself in the novitiate routine, which was considerably easier on her in the summer months when she had no fires and fewer lamps to care for. At this stage she and her companions were looking forward to receiving the habit in a few months time.

Even before the first candidates had come together in Cahiracon, there had been much discussion about the dress of the new congregation. Frances had made her suggestions to Father Blowick on 12 August 1919, in a letter already noted.[9]

It was to Teresa McCollam that Father Blowick turned later. He wrote to her on 18 August 1921, asking if she could give him some help in designing the dress. 'As you say, I think the nurses costume would, with a few modifications, be suitable. For China there is wanted a dress that is compact and tidy to allow walking freely and all the heavy head-dress and such is altogether out of place.'[10]

A year later his views had changed considerably. On 9 August 1922 he wrote to the postulants through Mother M. Camillus replying to queries about the constitutions and rules. He ended his long letter with some remarks about the habit:

There seems to be a good deal of anxiety about one matter which should not cause any trouble to any Sister who is in earnest about the work which under God they have chosen to do. I refer to the question of the habit, or garb of the congregation. One thing only

I wish to say, namely, that the dress must be strictly religious in every detail. From some of the remarks which I have heard made on my last visit, I fear very much that some of the Sisters have very little idea of the circumstances of the country into which they are going. There is an idea prevalent that a garb should be designed which allows freedom for work, etc. If this can be done in such a way to leave the dress still religious very well; if not, then it must be religious, no matter what becomes of the other point.[11]

Earlier, on 13 May, Father Blowick had sent the Superior General of the Irish Sisters of Charity a long letter he had received from Father Galvin in Hanyang. This detailed document was written in reply to questions Father Blowick had sent about the training of the new congregation. He answered a query about the habit by saying that it could be based on that of the Irish Sisters of Charity, but with a cap like that worn by the Infant Jesus Sisters, 'very like the cap worn by elderly Irish women in some parts of the country, but black'.[12] However, the twelve women in the novitiate had different ideas. They sent their suggestions to Father Blowick under the heading: 'Proposed Habit for Irish Missionary Sisters':

Material: For winter wear – Woollen material of Irish manu-
             facture.
             For summer – Irish linen or Chinese silk.
Colour: Grey.
Shape: A plain tunic of walking length.
Neck: A white kerchief.
Sleeves: Of medium width with white nainsook under-
             sleeves, fastened to camisole and detachable.
Waist: A leather belt.
Additions: A full length scapular to be worn in full dress and
             detachable for working.
Ornaments: A silver Celtic Crucifix. Rosary Beads of bog oak
             or Irish Horn.
             When taking Vows a silver Celtic ring.
Head-dress: A grey veil, fastened on with a white or grey band

encircling the head, on which is embroidered the motto – 'Peregrinare pro Christo' ['To be a wanderer for Christ'] – in Chinese. Novices will wear white veils and plain band.[13]

Father Blowick sent the above proposals together with his own comments to the Superior General of the Sisters of Charity. Objecting to the head-dress, he queried whether the veil and the v-shaped neckline were too 'worldly'. The idea of a scapular to be removed indoors did not meet with his approval and he referred to Father Galvin's suggestion of a short cape, though he himself would not favour this because it was worn by another missionary congregation. Mother Agnes Gertrude replied, sending her comments on each item of the proposed habit. She felt that it would be unwise to stipulate Irish linen which might be difficult to procure outside Ireland, and she pointed out that silk was not allowed by canon law. A cape (or guimpe) would seem preferable to a scapular. If the Sisters he referred to had theirs fastened in front, then the new congregation could have theirs fastened at the back, or vice versa. She was in favour of a cap with a veil attached rather than a band, which would make the Sisters look like nurses.

In such a manner did the habit of the Columban Sisters evolve! Early photographs show the first novices dressed like the Sisters of Charity, except with a different kind of collar and a very simple soft cap to which a veil was attached. Later, while the first Sisters were still novices, the head-dress was adapted to afford more protection against the sun, and the design chosen remained substantially unchanged until habits in general were simplified after Vatican II.

It was late August 1922 before the design of the dress to be worn by the future novices was finally decided. That left little time to make habits for the twelve women due to be admitted into the congregation. (The thirteenth, Kathleen Brennan, had left in August because of bad health.) Patterns of grey material were requested from the Foxford Woollen Mills, and one was chosen. However, when a roll of striped material arrived instead of what had been ordered, there was some consternation. Mother M.

Camillus and Sister Moloney set off for Limerick by car. Because of the Civil War which had begun a few months previously, part of the road was almost impassable but they got to Limerick and purchased what was needed. Time was moving on, so dressmakers from McBirneys in Dublin were employed to make the first habits. They stayed at St Brigid's for a week.

On 6 September Father Blowick gave a talk to the twelve postulants. He spoke for fifty minutes and told them 'many hard truths'. So too did Father Connolly, who gave the retreat preparatory to reception of the habit from 25 September to 4 October. His focus was on vocation and he encouraged anyone who felt she did not have a missionary vocation to leave the novitiate. 'Hats off to such a one!' he said. Three of those listening to him were so disturbed by his words that they decided to withdraw. Vera Lees left to follow her obvious attraction to the contemplative life. This did not surprise her companions who were saddened however to learn that Teresa McCollam and Margaret McDonnell had also decided that they did not have the necessary vocation to be missionary religious.

Teresa McCollam had been Frances Moloney's staunchest friend and support in the years leading up to the founding of the congregation. Both of them strong personalities, they were nevertheless able to forge strong bonds of friendship based on their mutual interest in the Maynooth Mission to China. Even when others left the little group, temporarily or permanently, Teresa had remained constant at Frances's side, involved in her concerns and often acting in her name. She lived in Frances's flat and underwent nursing training with her; they went to Lough Derg together and spent holidays and free time with one another. Frances was to say later that the introduction Teresa brought her from Father Blowick 'clinched a friendship which survived all differences of temperament, point of view and ultimate divergence of paths.'[14] Frances was aware of her friend's reservations about becoming a religious, and she must have witnessed her struggle to adjust to the demands of novitiate life. 'Long accustomed to act on her own initiative she found difficulty in giving up her own judgement, and bending it to all the small exigencies of religious life.'[15] Teresa's decision to leave would not have surprised Frances but it would have grieved her deeply. In the Annals where Teresa's departure is noted, the writer adds: 'Our Mothers in Christ have told us that her name should not be forgotten, because she largely contributed by her exertions to bring about the founding of the Congregation.' Now of the original group only Frances and Elizabeth Brannigan remained.

The first nine novices received the habit on 4 October 1922. The Bishop of Killaloe, Dr Michael Fogarty, officiated and gave the novices the religious habit and their new names. Frances Moloney became Sister Mary Patrick of the Holy Cross. (The first Columban Sisters adopted the Sisters of Charity custom of adding to their religious name the devotion that appealed most to them, a practice that was dropped within two years.) Devotion to Christ's passion was a constant in Frances's life from early childhood, from the time when she used to cover the crucifix over her bed with cotton wool to keep Jesus warm. In the intervening years the harsh reality of suffering, both physical and emotional, had drawn her ever closer to Christ Crucified. And if she could have seen into the future on her reception day, she would have learned that in years to come her devotion to the Cross would be her chief mainstay through the many trials and disappointments she would be called on to face.

Bishop Fogarty was an eloquent speaker and he spoke with feeling to the nine young women who were making history as the foundation-stones of a new missionary venture. He concluded his address with these words:

> The future history of the new congregation is still Heaven's secret. May the religious habit you are the first to wear become famous for its conquests in religious history. It descends upon you with the blessings of Saint Columban. May his virtue adorn your lives and make glorious the habit you wear, until Christ calls you home to receive the virgin's or the martyr's crown.[16]

After the ceremony the visiting priests and students gave an impromptu concert in honour of the occasion. Father Blowick, happy to see the congregation he had striven to establish take shape, gave the closing remarks. He spoke movingly, stressing his hope that charity would be the hallmark of the congregation, whose two great devotions would be a personal love of Our Lord in the Blessed Sacrament and of his Blessed Mother. He had written the very same words to Frances Moloney four years earlier, when she was beginning to gather around her a little group of like-minded women: 'Love for souls, nothing else. It must be burned into the girls' minds ... they must be taught to have an absorbing love of God, of Our Master in the Holy Sacrament, of our Holy and Immaculate Mother who must be their guiding star all through the hardships of the preparation and of the missionary life afterwards.'[17]

Signing herself Sister Mary Patrick of the Holy Cross, Frances wrote to Mrs Martin, Marie's mother, thanking her for her letter of congratulations: 'It was all very touching and impressive,' she wrote, 'and the happiness of it all was almost too great to bear – the culmination of all one's hopes and prayers for years.'

Shortly after the Reception ceremony, four American postulants arrived. First came a car with their luggage, the likes of which had not been seen before in those parts. A few minutes later four ladies stepped out of the second car, 'all enveloped in travelling coats and cloaks, their features almost hidden by large tortoiseshell goggles.'[18] It became obvious that more accommodation was needed urgently. Plans were drawn up to build a large wooden hut that would contain a chapel, a dormitory for fifteen novices and a novitiate room. Meanwhile, in January 1923 a second group came from Australia: Sisters Pryer, Griffin and Nicholson. 'They brought youth and piety and an overflow of good spirits along with them, and did delightfully outrageous things in the eyes of all their elders, with the greatest possible innocence.'[19]

Only one of the four American postulants, Sister Mary Magdalen O'Grady, survived the novitiate. She left two years later before profession, and joined the Good Shepherd Sisters in the United States. Ronnie Nicholson, one of the recently arrived Australians, also left and early in 1924 Sister Emmanuel Dalton, one of the first group to receive the habit, had to withdraw because of ill health.

Meanwhile Frances Moloney's health was causing some concern. On 19 February 1924, she was again admitted to St Vincent's Hospital, Dublin.

During her two weeks stay in St Vincent's Nursing Home awaiting surgery, Sister Mary Patrick – as she was now called – wrote to Cahiracon almost daily, acknowledging the many letters she received, asking necessary permissions and passing on her doctor's reports. She had the luxury of a private room, she wrote, 'with electric light and all the comforts of modern civilisation'. A far cry from the smoking fires and petrol lamps of Cahiracon! She felt out of place, though she admitted that the solitude gave her time to read and pray. Friends came to visit, among them Father Blowick who came to see her within a few days of her being admitted. He advised her to go ahead with any treatment or surgery indicated: it was important to get well before going to China, where it would be less easy to attend to medical problems. She told him of Mother Mary Camillus's wish that the events that led up to the founding of the congregation should be written up, and he said that this was exactly what he wished; he could fill in any gaps in the correspondence, also letters from other missionary organisations with whom he had been in touch. They could never publish anything in their own lifetime, but it would be invaluable for the records of the congregation.[20] Later generations of Columban Sisters have reason to be grateful to Mother Mary Camillus and Father John Blowick for being aware of history-in-the-making and for preserving that history.

On 26 February, Sister Mary Patrick had a visit from Father Ronayne and Marie Martin, back from Africa and preparing to enter the Holy Rosary Sisters' novitiate in Killeshandra. Teresa McCollam called twice, and Margaret Gibbons, another member of the first group, came another day. Her sister Freddie asked if she could come up to be with her, but was advised to postpone her visit until after the operation. By that time her husband and eldest daughter who had the flu would be better. Sister Mary Patrick consulted Mother Mary Camillus about making her will. Not that there was a vast sum left after the expenses of the years of preparation in Dublin, but she was still due £1,000. (Her brother later informed her of an additional small legacy, which would be forthcoming.) The day before the operation she drew up her will. 'It took three interviews to finish the matter, and legal verbiage enough to dispose of a kingdom.'[21]

Sister Mary Patrick's letters from hospital reveal qualities that might have escaped attention otherwise. Having placed her life totally in God's hands she now welcomed his will expressed by those placed over her, yet with such a spirit of freedom that she had no problem in dialoguing with her superior or respectfully putting her own suggestions. The ease with which she communicated her doctor's opinions and her own reactions to these were the marks of a mature woman not diminished in any way by the training she was receiving in the novitiate. As concerned as ever for her friends and for those in need, she asked permission to see in her hospital room her former housekeeper, Fannie O'Connor, who was going through a hard patch at the time and needing spiritual help. Fannie's clothes were in poor shape and Sister Mary Patrick asked permission to give her a new golf jumper she had never worn. She wrote with concern about a few of the novices who were ill, and each letter contained an up-to-the-minute bulletin about Father Thomas Doyle, a priest of the Maynooth Mission to China, who was a patient in a nearby room. She would have been aware that a few of her companions had to leave the novitiate because of health problems. Yet so deep was her conviction that God had called her to the Chinese Mission that she never seems to have entertained the thought that her own health might prove an obstacle.

Her recovery was slower than initially expected. She had hoped to be back in Cahiracon for Easter, but it was 7 May before she was well enough to travel. Meanwhile she spent the first weeks of her convalescence in St Vincent's Nursing Home until there was a vacancy in Linden Convalescent Home. While waiting she wrote to Mother Mary Camillus asking for the loan of a copy of the French edition of Père Olivier's book on the Passion, a version she was long familiar with. She also asked for a Latin grammar so that she could puzzle out some queries she had about the Latin of the Mass.

The Sister in charge of the nursing home, Sister Mary Ignatius, suggesting that she lay Rodriguez aside for the present, gave her the Life of Father Bernard Vaughan to read. This would have brought back memories of her sojourn in Wales, nearly twenty years earlier, when the Vaughan family lived nearby. Father McArdle SJ, an old friend, visited her from time to time and encouraged her to read the life of St Francis de Sales, his favourite saint. On one such visit 'he even arranged the pillows and made me more comfortable, which shows that the hospital training of the SJ novitiate is to some purpose.'[22]

As soon as she was well enough, she saw her visitors in the parlour. She made little of the exertion this called for or of her general post-operative discomfort, but writing to Mother Mary Camillus on 7 April she let slip the following: 'The last few days I seem incapable of the slightest mental or physical effort beyond the exertion of going downstairs, and my wretched nerves are all on edge. Please God it is only a phase of the convalescence and that a week or so at Linden will complete the cure. I am longing to return to Cahiracon.' Singleminded, she was looking forward to completing her novitiate, and then hopefully leaving for China. She ended this letter of 7 April by telling Mother Mary Camillus about 'a lovely little dream' she had on her feastday, St Patrick's Day:

It came during a short doze in the morning – I saw myself as a little ship in mid-ocean. Behind me all was grey, and waves were breaking on the shore. But the little ship just sailed into a glorious line of sunshine, with all its sails set towards the bright horizon. It gave me extraordinary comfort and I am trying to work it into my life.

Because of her slow recovery her stay in Linden was longer than planned. Her stay of three weeks there did, however, give her a chance to meet some old friends. Frank Duff, founder of the Legion of Mary, called to see her with the president of the St Vincent de Paul Society, Mr Lalor. Her old friend Father Turley also came. Father Ronayne paid another flying visit. She enjoyed a dance concert organised by the Sisters in Linden, where she met two old

friends, a Miss Willman who had been a member of the Business
Girls' Club when Frances was President, and a Mr Field who had
been a Member of Parliament at the same time as her father. She
was shown a beautiful embroidered vestment, and intended to trace
the pattern which could be useful for Father Galvin's embroidery
school in Hanyang. Her back was still giving her trouble and her
doctor cautioned her before she left Dublin not to do too much
manual work for three months. But optimistic by nature, she
returned to the novitiate early in May, hopeful that before long she
would be able for as much as her considerably younger companions.

That was not to be. Instead of becoming stronger after her return
home, she began to show symptoms of other health problems: there
was a recurrence of the empyema that had almost caused her death
as a schoolgirl, and a hint of possible tuberculosis. The writer of the
early annals notes that Sister Mary Patrick was called to bear the
full weight of the Cross to which she was so devoted. 'From month
to month on her return her health failed, and at last she was obliged
to seek a last remedy in the warmer clime of France – just when the
great day of her Profession was at hand.'

Meanwhile, in the weeks following her return from hospital she
had met Father Galvin again. Home from China, he visited St
Brigid's and made a few further adaptations to the habit: he would
prefer black to grey because the Buddhist nuns in China wore grey,
and he suggested changing the head-dress to better suit the tropical
summer. At this time Sister Mary Patrick's friend of earlier days,
Sister Joseph Conception Vavasour, was assigned to Cahiracon.
Frances was delighted: in the years when she worked for the St
Vincent de Paul Society in Dublin Sister Joseph Conception had
generously facilitated her whenever she was at a loss to find
someone to host an outing for poor children from the back streets
of Dublin. Another significant event in those weeks between
Frances's return from hospital and the temporary interruption of
her novitiate was Dr Michael O'Dwyer's election as Superior
General of the Maynooth Mission to China. Father Blowick's
health was giving cause for concern. Consequently the Chapter

members decided to relieve him of the heavy burden of office, though he did stay on as Dr O'Dwyer's Vicar General. One of the new Superior General's first acts was to write to Frances. She replied on 15 July, thanking him for his 'Christlike compassion', and for offering Mass for her:

> May the sublime prayer you offer obtain for me the grace to become meek and humble of heart. Perhaps it was to teach me this lesson that Our Lord sent me in His Mercy my illness, which shows me my own impotence and absolute dependence on Him. I am not worrying D.G. but have moments of dereliction. Mother Camillus is my Angel of Consolation, helping me in soul and body. My poor prayers, such as they are, are for you and the Mission. If I can do no more, the first round of the rosary is yours each day.[23]

But the most providential event of those difficult weeks was the community retreat, given that year by her friend and spiritual director Father Michael Browne SJ. This retreat brought her immeasurable consolation. It strengthened her in her vocation, which would survive despite long months of ill health and absence from the novitiate. Meanwhile, her family had heard of her condition and of the doctor's suggestion of a change of climate. Her sister wrote to Mother Mary Camillus expressing her concern, and suggesting that Sister Mary Patrick join her and her family at Wimereux in the north of France, where they were spending the summer. It was a healthy place, she said, high on a hill and with good sea air. Her sister would remember the place, which was near Boulogne where she had spent many happy holidays as a child. Freddie could book a room for her in a small hotel near theirs and she could join them for meals, if she felt well enough and provided it would pose no danger to the children: her husband was anxious about that. Two weeks later, reassured by Mother Mary Camillus's reply, she wrote again suggesting that her sister see a specialist in London to verify the diagnosis of the local doctor. 'I feel so much for her, poor thing, this breakdown is indeed a sore trial for her and for the infant Mission – but God will, I hope, restore her to health

– to fulfil her desire to work for Him – as she has always done all her life.'[24] Freddie had come to realise by this time that nothing but China could bring happiness to her sister.

Mother Mary Camillus accepted the family's suggestion and arrangements were made for Sister Mary Patrick to travel to London, with an Irish nurse also making the same journey. She stayed overnight in Dublin at 97 Leeson Street and wrote to Dr O'Dwyer from there, thanking him for 'the magnanimous decision' that he and his council had made regarding her profession: they had agreed that she could make her vows as soon as she recovered her health.

> When I so crudely asked you not to consider my years of membership in the Mission, it was more than my life which I placed at your feet, but I felt bound in justice to make this great renunciation. Even when your generous offer came I still hesitated, perhaps it was a last temptation of the devil. During the retreat I was given light and direction to see clearly that your decision as my Superior was God's decision and I humbly bow my head and say with Our Lady, 'Fiat mihi secundum verbum tuum.' Now I am completely happy and at peace, and can never be grateful enough to God and to you.[25]

When she arrived in London, she first went to stay with her brother's family. From there she wrote to Mother Mary Camillus, thanking her for procuring berths for herself and her companion on the boat and for all her care. Her brother, she said, had already made an appointment for her to see Dr Maurice Wilkinson, a specialist with consulting rooms in Wimpole Street, and he was also looking after her passport which she would need for France. She referred with amusement to a visit from her father's old butler, Barker, who recalled that when she was a little girl 'she always did things with a hop, skip and jump,' but now, he advised her in a fatherly way, she should take things easier.

She wrote again on 4 August after seeing the specialist. He had found the weak spot but could not yet make a definite diagnosis. If she did have tuberculosis, he was confident that it could be cured in a few months and that it would not come against her going to China. He would arrange for further tests.

Meanwhile, her brother and his wife were going to Scotland, and she asked if she could stay in the Sisters of Charity nursing home in Hackney or anywhere where she could get Holy Communion. 'I know the dear Lord is with me anywhere, but I hunger for His Bodily Presence.'[26]

Her next letter on 7 August came from St Joseph's Private Nursing Home in Hackney. She had seen her doctor again and he was of the opinion that her recurrent temperature did indicate tuberculosis. He put her on tablets and spoke about injections. A few days later, she wrote to say how happy she was in her new surroundings. The place was 'was like a railway station with trains leaving all day for Heaven – some are express and go direct, others – just a few, stop at the Junction of Purgatory – and the Angels are so busy. You can positively feel them around, waiting to carry off the departing souls, and simply fussing round those who are at all obdurate.'[27]

Her doctor started the injections. That involved going to see him at his consulting rooms. She sometimes used the occasion to go to Farm Street for Confession. On one of her trips she bought painting materials and a book on perspective and water colours: Mother Mary Camillus had commissioned her to paint a special spiritual bouquet card, for a special anniversary of Father O'Connell's.

She heard from Cahiracon about the constitutions Father Blowick had drawn up for the congregation and regretted not being there when he read them to her companions.

> I know you understand how deeply I feel being far away while the momentous reading is taking place, but for that also I can thank Our Lord for it keeps me little and nearer to Him. The continual uncertainty as regards myself leaves me so entirely in God's Hands that I feel like a little atom resting there.[28]

Her arm was swollen from injections, and the recurrent temperature left her with constant feelings of fatigue. Yet she struggled to write the occasional letter, regretting that she could not be in more frequent contact with her Sisters in Cahiracon and with her friends. Fighting against the lassitude caused by her illness, she wrote a letter of congratulations to Killeshandra, hoping that it would be in time for the reception of the first novices of the new missionary congregation for Africa. At the same time she wrote to Cahiracon asking the novices to pray for their sister novices in Co. Cavan.

On 22 August her reaction to the serum injections showed beyond doubt that she did have tuberculosis. She was relieved that her condition was finally diagnosed: treatment could now begin. Dr Wilkinson assured her that she would be cured in four months or, at most, five. He was insistent that she should not return to the novitiate until completely cured; otherwise she 'would be a drag on the community for the rest of her life'. He agreed to her going to stay with her sister at Wimereux and promised to show her how to give herself the necessary injections. He would post her the medication as needed. Her anxiety about the expense her illness was putting on the young congregation comes through in her letters, also her determination to entrust the matter to God's Providence.

Once the decision was made that she should go to France, she had to consider the problem of attire. She had been advised to wear secular dress: anti-clericalism was rampant in a country governed at that time by parties of the left. She wrote to Mother Mary Camillus asking what she should do about her habit. Her sister, she said, had sent her a coat and skirt and her sister-in-law had bought her a black frock coat. 'If I have to change,' she asked sadly, 'may I wear a widow's bonnet and veil?' Seventy years later her niece Aylish Fane-Saunders recalled how heartbroken she was when she had to lay aside her habit and change back into secular dress. She also had to leave aside her religious name: once again she became Madame Moloney.

She crossed over to France with her brother-in-law, John Chevers, on 4 September, and wrote to Mother Mary Camillus from Wimereux five days later, thanking her for the big bundle of letters that had arrived just before she left Hackney. She still had a temperature but had begun to feel better. 'I have suffered great desolation in trying to settle down to secular life,' she said. Before she left London, Dr Wilkinson had told her that once she was cured she could take on any kind of work, and she felt hopeful. 'The weakness and depression nearly overpower me sometimes but, in Father de Caussade's words, faith answers: "Keep firm, go on and fear nothing." '[29]

Her letter did not make that day's post, so she was able to add a postscript thanking her fellow novices for another batch of letters. She asked permission to move to a small private hotel in the town of Wimereux: she was staying right beside a noisy hotel where loud music and dancing continued into the small hours. As a result she was finding it hard to sleep, and her sister insisted that this was holding her back. Moreover, if she moved into a hotel in the town she would be closer to the church, and could have Holy Communion brought to her more easily.

A week later she wrote from Hotel Pension Bouvier in the town of Wimereux. She was now quite happy with her accommodation, which was 'quiet and homely and close to the church'. It had been arranged that the Curé would bring her Communion. Her sister and family stayed on in Le Bungalow and were in and out daily to visit her. An unexpected companion now arrived in the person of Miss Margaret Furlong, an old friend of hers and of Anneence Fitzgerald-Kenny. She had been travelling around France when she heard about her friend Frances from Miss Fitzgerald-Kenny. She now appointed herself unofficial companion to her friend of earlier days. It was a mixed blessing: she was old and partially blind, which put a certain measure of responsibility on Sister Mary Patrick, much as she welcomed the companionship. Some weeks later her much loved stepmother Louise Owen Lewis also came to stay at the Hotel Bouvier.

But despite the closeness of family and friends Frances's heart was in Cahiracon. On 22 September she wrote to congratulate the seven novices preparing for profession on 29 September, the feast of St Michael. Hoping that it would be a day of 'supreme joy' for each of them, she asked that there would be no sorrow or regret that her own joy had been deferred. 'The dear Lord knows what is best for each of us. May His Holy Will be praised.' She, without whom the little congregation would not have come into being, could not be with her companions when it would be formally established. She hid her disappointment bravely:

> Now Sisters dear, let me join you in heartfelt thanks to God for the accomplishment of the Foundation of the little Sisterhood. And after Him in gratitude to the priests of the Mission, to Mother General, and most especially to our dear Mother Camillus and Sister M. Alphonsus who have borne the heat and burden of the day in training us. I am making the Novena to St Michael for your intentions, and will be united with you at Holy Communion, which the Curé will bring me on the 29th.[30]

The day after the first profession ceremonies of the new congregation, Father Blowick gave a talk to the newly professsed Sisters and to the novices. 'Yesterday,' he said, 'took place what we have been looking forward to and hoping for during the past six years.' Looking ahead into the distant future, he asked what the spirit of the members of the congregation would be in fifty years time. 'It will be what those seven Sisters who made their vows yesterday, what you and those who immediately follow after you make it. It will depend on your spirit of charity and obedience.' He concluded his talk by referring to the absent person who was uppermost in many people's thoughts:

> Another thing I would like to speak of is something that is very near all our hearts I'm sure, that is, the absence of Sister Mary Patrick. We don't know why God did it, but we do know for certain, whatever His reasons, it was certainly for her good and for your good. You are praying for her, I'm sure, for it must have been a tremendous sacrifice for her. She must have been looking forward to yesterday with extraordinary zeal, but I am sure and know that she is taking it in the right spirit, for I must say that I have never met so far a more generous soul, a more Christlike soul, or a more humble soul.[31]

A few hours after the first seven Columban Sisters were professed, Bishop Fogarty formally erected the congregation, naming Sister Mary Finbarr Collins as the first Superior General, Sister Mary Teresa Brannigan Vicar General and Secretary General, and Sister Francis Xavier Mapleback and Sister Mary Joseph McKey First and Second Councillors respectively. The Bishop asked Mother Mary Camillus to continue as Novice Mistress with Sister Mary Alphonsus as her assistant.

Sister Mary Finbarr's appointment came as an unpleasant shock to her: she had just returned from hospital the previous evening and within twenty-four hours had been professed and then appointed Superior General. She protested her total inability for the task, but the Bishop was adamant. Sister Mary Patrick wrote to her as soon as she heard the news, to tell her how happy she was to tender her 'most loving allegiance'. 'I can never forget your unselfish devotion in my illness,' she wrote, 'when suffering yourself without a word to anyone, and I have always felt that I owed my life very much to your good nursing.' She had good news to report: her doctor was now allowing her to go to the church for Holy Communion.

In a letter to Mother Mary Camillus written on 13 October 1924 she mentioned that she had written to Father Blowick 'a few lines of congratulation on the birth of the little congregation which he founded.' In the same letter she asked Mother Camillus for permission to use the discipline: her health was much improved and she was obeying her doctor in eating well, so she felt the need of some form of penance. (She was given the permission she requested.) She referred to the fact that she was re-reading the life of Blessed Philippine Duchesne who, like her, had to wait many years before reaching the mission field and who, like her, had experienced a long novitiate. She reminded Mother Camillus that she was still one of her brood; though not yet hatched out, she was still able to chirp.[32]

The day after the profession of her companions, Father Blowick had spoken of Sister Mary Patrick's deep humility. Nowhere did it express itself more nobly than in the letter to Father Blowick referred to above:

Ever since the glorious news of the Birth of the little Congregation reached me I have had it in my heart to write to you, but a
stupid kind of shyness held me back. I am confident however
that you will not take it amiss to receive the heartfelt congratulations of one of your oldest recruits, though still a novice. On
the 29th as I tried to follow in spirit the great events in Cahiracon
I thought how happy you must be to see the first Profession in
the Sisterhood which you founded. Heretofore, I have been
nothing but a useless member of the mission and a trouble to
yourself, but with God's grace, I hope with renewed health, to
make a fresh start in some humble corner of the vineyard,
wherever I may be placed. [33]

However, her recovery was slower than anyone could have
foreseen and her doctor would not hear of her returning to Ireland
before the following summer. He advised her to go south with the
birds, which she eventually did, after meeting with Dr Wilkinson
when he passed through Paris on his way to the south of France
himself. Like so many of the English gentry of the time he was
going to winter in Pau, a popular resort in the southwest of France,
near the foothills of the Pyrennes. He suggested that this too would
be a suitable place for Frances to build up her strength. If she went
to Pau he could give her the injections she needed and monitor the
progress of her treatment. She wrote all this to Mother Camillus,
telling her too that her confessor in Boulogne was upset that she
was still in Wimereux despite the changed weather. Besides, the
Hotel Bouvier was closing down for the winter months and all
guests had to leave. Consequently she and her two companions had
left for Paris on 10 November. Miss Furlong's sight had disimproved
still further and Mrs Owen Lewis was quite lame, so it was a case
of the invalid helping the helpers. They were in Paris for the
Armistice Day celebrations, and the bustle and noise cured Sister
Mary Patrick of any wish to be there again. 'Sometimes in the
novitiate,' she wrote to Mother Camillus, 'I used to long to see Paris
again, but now it seems full of husks, and I long for the solid food
of religious life with its unpurchaseable peace.'[34]

In Paris they met a sister of Mother Camillus, who very kindly offered to take care of Mrs Owen Lewis for a while. This at best could only be a temporary arrangement, so Sister Mary Patrick spent the rest of her time in Paris looking for a quiet hotel or a convent where her stepmother could be accommodated. On her last day in Paris she found a suitable place. 'It made my heart ache,' she wrote, 'to leave the poor old lady amongst strangers. She is seventy but does not look it. There is something very sweet and childlike about her, but sometimes it is the spoilt child!' She was happy to leave her stepmother in good hands.

Meanwhile, she and Miss Furlong had proceeded to Tours while waiting to get accommodation in Pau. From there she wrote to Mother Camillus saying that she felt so much stronger that she would like permission to work among the sick poor in Pau: the Daughters of Charity might allow her to visit a few of the sick people in their care. She asked if there was any other useful way to occupy herself. Some lace-making material she had asked for had not arrived, not would her eyesight be equal to much of that, but she could do some embroidery. She also asked for a copy of the Chinese textbook they were using in the novitiate, and the first volume of Nouet's Meditations: Advent was approaching.

Dr Wilkinson, however, did not approve of some of these exertions. He visited Sister Mary Patrick as soon as she arrived in Pau and was delighted to see her looking 'years younger'. He found her so much improved that he gave her a certificate of being non-contagious: some guest-houses required this. He also told her that it was no longer necessary to have her own special cup and cutlery. He offered to come himself to give her the inoculations, and he generously invited her to drive to Lourdes with his family, on condition that there would be no plunging into cold baths. However, she was unable to go to Lourdes just then.

She continued to recuperate slowly, getting her injections regularly and taking exercise as much as the lassitude associated with her illness allowed. She took up organ lessons and, at Mother Camillus's request, began to compile suitable prayers for a congregational prayer manual. Drawing on her writing skills she wrote a detailed account of her travels for the novices in Cahircon, calling them 'Pilgrim Notes' because of all the holy places she and Miss Furlong had visited, not only in Paris but also in Tours and Marmoutiers. They were in Tours for festivities in honour of St Martin, celebrated with great pomp and pageantry. Traditionally St Patrick is said to have spent some time there as a disciple of St Martin, and it was said that St Columban had also gone there on pilgrimage. 'The spirit of St Columban was with me,' she wrote, 'as I knelt where he had knelt in loving homage, and I thanked him for having led me amidst the waters of tribulation to this meeting tryst of God's holy servants.'[35]

News of the death of one of the Dalgan students impelled her to send her condolences to Dr Michael O'Dwyer, the Superior General. She concluded her letter by referring again to his promise to allow her to go forward for profession whenever she recovered her health:

I was very glad to receive a copy of the Constitutions which Father Blowick kindly sent, and hope to make them my earnest study in view of Profession, whenever, and in what manner it may be God's will to admit me. To you, dear Father, I owe undying gratitude for that assurance which forms my chief incentive to live.[36]

Her stepmother kept asking to join her in Pau and she eventually agreed, even though it would demand more effort than she was yet able for. There was question of Mrs Owen Lewis bringing a companion with her, a Swedish friend. That would help, Sister Mary Patrick remarked, leaving her more time for the silence and solitude which she felt she needed at this time which she called, 'the winter of my discontent'. Even though the doctor was satisfied with her progress, she found the treatment enervating. She wrote to Cahiracon saying that she was due to finish the injections by the end of February and would then go elsewhere to build up, possibly to St Jean de Luz, a fishing town on the Atlantic, close to the border with Spain, and still a popular holiday resort noted for its seaweed baths. In Pau she and her companions were obliged to stay in a guest-house because they were unable to get more than a few days accommodation in a convent. One of the attractions of St Jean de Luz was that they could now stay in a convent.

Before leaving for St Jean de Luz, she and Miss Furlong fitted in a visit to Lourdes, where they arrived in time to celebrate the feast of Our Lady of Lourdes on 11 February. Afterwards she sent another instalment of her Pilgrim Notes to the novices in Cahiracon, telling them that she had prayed for each of them by name at the grotto, on the feast of Our Lady of Lourdes. She prayed, she said, that each Sister in the congregation would be given 'an intense devotion to Our Blessed Lady, which was earnestly impressed upon us by Father Blowick and Dr O'Dwyer. No missionary could be successful without this great love and confidence for all things in the dear Mother of God.'[37]

After their few days in Lourdes they left for St Jean de Luz where at the end of February Sister Mary Patrick suffered another setback and had to spend a week in bed. The doctor now ordered her not to leave St Jean de Luz for another month. He suggested that she then spend two weeks in Wimereux, where he would see her again before she left for home. He believed that she would eventually be strong enough to go to China, but he could not guarantee lasting good health.

As soon as she felt well enough she attended some Home Economics classes, which she felt might help her in China. She wrote home to Cahiracon with a touch of humour that she would soon be fully prepared to teach the Chinese how to make cream buns and macaroni! She also told the Sisters that on her feast-day, 17 March, her sister-in-law Kathleen Moloney brought her to visit a convent of Trappistine nuns near Biarritz. Many of them were living the eremetical life in great austerity: she was happy to get the promise of their prayers for the fledgling congregation.

Sister Mary Alphonsus, acting for Mother Mary Camillus who was ill, wrote to tell Sister Mary Patrick that she and the local doctor, Dr Garry, would prefer if she did not return until mid-May. That was a disappointment: she had hoped to be back by 3 May, a day she always celebrated as the anniversary of her vocation. At the

same time she realised that she still needed to build up her health
and she accepted the decision as coming from God. Her spiritual
nourishment at the time was de Caussade's *Abandonment to Divine
Providence*. 'No other reading satisfies my spiritual needs,' she
wrote, 'as does Père Caussade's doctrine, which makes God's Holy
Will so dear under all circumstances. Life would be very hard at
times were it not for the knowledge and experience of God's loving
Providence. His dear Love makes all things acceptable.'[38]

Yet she was still human and she felt it deeply when she had to
say goodbye to her stepmother and to her sister-in-law Kathleen
who had brought along the eighty-year old Father Berard, who had
been the Moloney's chaplain many years earlier in Cefntilla.

> Now my heart is very heavy, leaving the dear ones who came all
> the way to St Jean de Luz to be near me. The renewing and
> rebreaking of the old ties is like tearing the bandage off a fresh
> wound. How Our dear Lord suffered when His garments were
> torn off, and how little one's own poor sufferings are in compari-
> son. Fiat to everything.[39]

From Boulogne she sent the novices the final instalment of her
Pilgrim Notes, giving a detailed account of her visit to the
Trappistines, also of a pilgrimage to Poitiers and an aborted one to
Loyola. She described her excitement at finding so many relics of
early China missionaries in the museum of the Vincentian Fathers
in Paris. Longing to be back in Cahiracon once more, she told the
novices that it was only 'the Great White Presence at Exposition
each day' that kept her patient.

She also wrote from Boulogne to Mother Mary Alphonsus,
asking permission to visit her old friend Lady Greville when she
would stop off in London to meet her family. She also mentioned
the possibility of visiting an art needlework centre: she was still
searching for ideas for Father Galvin's embroidery school in
Hanyang. This letter reveals the tranquil spirit in which she faced
back to insert herself once again into religious life.

> I wrote to Mother M. Finbarr to tell her that I was a half broken
> reed in order that all might be fair and square and the Congrega-

tion could still reject me if necessary. At the same time I hope and trust that the dear Lord who has led me by the hand these last seven years will allow me to carry out my vocation to the end. The doctor, who alternately raises and depresses one's hopes told my sister that I would have as good a chance as anyone in China. It will be as God wills.[40]

After a few days in London she crossed over to Dublin, spent the night with the Sisters of Charity and arrived back in Cahiracon on 11 May 1925 to a heartwarming welcome. On the 23 May she wrote to Dr O'Dwyer, thanking him for allowing her to go forward for profession. In this short but moving letter she told him how she felt:

The long years of waiting and suffering have taken any exuberance of happiness, but God has given me instead the gentle peace of one who is entering the harbour after a long journey. The unspeakable privilege of belonging irrevocably to God is well worth any amount of striving, and a lifetime is too short to prepare for it.[41]

She was home at last.

ELEVEN

China: the Dream and the Reality

On 7 June 1925, a few weeks after Sister Mary Patrick returned to the novitiate, the Sisters were told that Mother Mary Camillus who had guided them through the critical early years of their training was being recalled because of ill health. She was replaced by her assistant Sister Mary Alphonsus, who now became Superior and Mistress of Novices. The news brought sadness; the annalist of the time recorded for future generations how the Sisters felt about losing Mother Mary Camillus: 'Her figure will always stand out in our memory as one of the most Christlike we have ever known ... showing us Our Lord in every detail of her daily life, yet never standing in the line of our vision ... Gentleness marked all her dealings ... She understood the psychology of the modern girl better than most.'[1]

Facing up to their loss, the members of the young congregation gave their allegiance to Mother Mary Alphonsus who would guide them through the next five years. A much revered figure, she was very different in personality from Mother Mary Camillus, with less openness and flexibility, a person who perhaps at times took responsibility too seriously. It was she who now attended to Sister Mary Patrick's religious formation in the weeks leading up to her long-deferred profession.

The immediate preparation for this was the annual eight-day community retreat. It was an unusual kind of retreat: the director announced in his first talk that the whole retreat would consist of 'a series of talks on the fundamental truths of our holy Religion', because he believed that there was no better foundation for the religious life. Eight days of dogmatic theology could have been heavy going, even if occasionally relieved by other topics, yet Sister Mary Patrick evidently felt nourished by the experience. To the end of her life she kept her notes from this particular retreat in three notebooks; the two which survive have the appearance of being well thumbed. Twelve years later (1937), in one of her first conferences as Superior General, she quoted almost verbatim words spoken by her retreat director in July 1925 about the virtue of simplicity. It appears that she wrote down almost every word of those retreat lectures; later retreat-notes surviving from her years in China tend to be summaries.

On 29 July 1925, the day after the retreat ended, Dr Michael O'Dwyer, Superior General of the Maynooth Mission to China, received her vows in a beautiful ceremony which – according to the community annalist – Sister Mary Patrick herself had helped draw up. Several of the Columban Fathers were present as well as her old friend Father G. Turley with whom she had worked among the poor of Dublin, and Father Tommy Ronayne who came specially from Killeshandra for the occasion. One dearly loved person, Mother Mary Camillus, was absent, but the flowers she sent decorated the altar. *Veni Sponsa Christi* (Come, spouse of Christ), the motet that was to be part of so many profession ceremonies down through the years, was sung for the first time. Another of Frances's favourites, *Sancti Venite* (Come, you holy ones), was sung to an old Irish chant, the music of which arrived just in time for the ceremony. 'The Little Flower had her fall of snow on her clothing day, Sister Mary Patrick the old Irish music she loved.'[2]

She enjoyed Irish music again on 25 September, Mother Finbarr's feast, when the priests from the college came to visit and provided a concert. But, on the whole, the days were too busy for music. On 1 October she and her companions began a series of lectures on the constitutions, given by Father Blowick. The three-hour long sessions were enlivened by the speaker's humour and did not seem overlong because of his clarity of thought and expression. There were also lectures about China, and time was apportioned to studying Mandarin. Father Peter Blowick, Father John's brother, came to give classes on apologetics, and the Sisters had occasional talks on spirituality and theology from Dr O'Dwyer and Father Carr. Sister Joseph Conception, who had been sent to be Mother Mary Alphonsus's companion, enlisted the Sisters' help for the embroidery classes she organised to give occupation to the young women of the neighbourhood, and the sick poor of the area were visited in their own homes.

China seemed a distant dream until, towards the end of March 1926, a letter came from Father Blowick to say that he had decided to book shipping accommodation for a group of Sisters to travel to China the following autumn. Accordingly, a letter was sent to Propaganda Fide asking permission to establish a foundation of missionary Sisters in China. Those who would form the first group were named: Sisters Mary Theophane Fortune, Agnes Griffin, Philomena Woods, Lelia Creedon and Patrick Moloney. All of them except Sister Mary Patrick were under thirty years of age; she was fifty-three. Sister Mary Theophane, one of the youngest, was appointed superior of the group.

There was question of two Sisters of Charity accompanying the pioneers but their superiors finally decided otherwise; it seemed more fitting that Mother Mary Finbarr, Superior General of the young congregation, should travel with the group and help them make the first foundation in China. Meanwhile preparations went ahead to get ready for the eventual departure of the Sisters, who had to bring with them everything necessary for setting up a new foundation. Father Blowick came from Dalgan Park to give them further lectures on the constitutions. Afterwards they made their annual retreat and had time for a short holiday before leaving Cahiracon for China on 11 September.

In spite of poor health, Mother Mary Camillus travelled from Dublin on 8 September to bid the five pioneers farewell. That brought joy to them and to those they were leaving behind. 'It was fitting,' Sister Mary Patrick wrote later, 'that she and Mother M. Alphonsus should be reunited for the launching of the little craft they had built together. Its guidance through the seething waters of China now fell on Mother General M. Finbarr and the young Superior, Mother M. Theophane.'[3]

There was the inevitable loneliness as they parted from their companions to face into the totally unknown. In those years missionaries to the Far East could not presume on ever seeing home or family or friends again. Yet before leaving St Brigid's they joined in singing the *Te Deum* and felt strengthened as the mission hymn resounded: 'Go ye afar, go teach all nations ... and I with you shall be, until the end of time.' Those were the last words they heard, sung by breaking voices, as the cars drove away from St Brigid's. As they passed the college gates the assembled students cheered them on, and in Kildysart the townsfolk sent them on their way with blessings. At Ennis station Father Blowick and Father Harris were waiting to lead the Sisters on the next stage of their journey. They said a painful goodbye to Mother Mary Camillus and Mother Mary Alphonsus, who returned to St Brigid's to console those left behind.

It was dark by the time they reached Cork and there on the platform to meet them was the ubiquitous Miss Fitzgerald-Kenny, who insisted on driving three of them to Cobh. The others followed by train. In Cobh the travellers were given a warm welcome by the Mercy Sisters, whose generous hospitality they availed of for the next two days. At 3.00 a.m. on the morning of 13 September they got ready to leave for the tender. Frances remembered it vividly:

> Out into the cold and rain they went forth with Fathers Blowick and Harris. No moon or stars lit the road as they found their way to the tender. It was a foretaste of the realities of missionary life. Without was utter blackness – light and peace and joy within.[4]

At the quayside they met the young Columban priests who were to travel with them to China: Fathers John Loftus, Charles Donnelly, Joseph Hogan, Michael Fallon, James Linehan and Alphonsus Ferguson. A two-hour journey on the tender brought them before dawn to the SS *Bremen*, which would carry them on the first stage of the journey. There were further goodbyes to those returning on the tender, among them Father Harris who had been their devoted spiritual director, and Miss Fitzgerald-Kenny whose normally exuberant good spirits forsook her as she parted from her friend of a lifetime.

It was still dark as the Sisters watched the tender leave on its return journey to Cobh; their last link with Ireland was severed, and they must have wondered when, if ever, they would see that country again. But someone pointed to the dim horizon where there was a slowly expanding rim of light. Did Sister Mary Patrick remember the dream she had more than two years previously when she saw herself as a little ship in mid-ocean, everything around her grey. 'But the little ship had just sailed into a glorious line of sunshine, with all its sails set toward the bright horizon. It gave me extraordinary comfort.'[5] As the oldest and most experienced of the travellers her presence would have strengthened her companions.

After two days at sea they reached Bremen, the first stop on their long journey. Three days later they travelled by train to Hamburg, where they boarded a larger steamship, SS *Coblenz*. This would bring them all the way to Shanghai, a journey of approximately thirteen thousand miles. At Genoa they were joined by twenty-two Sisters belonging to the Italian Canossian congregation and twelve Italian priests, all destined for China. Other passengers also came aboard, mostly families returning to Hong Kong or Shanghai. There were several small children of various nationalities who immediately gravitated to Sister Mary Patrick and her companions.

The various ports of call broke the monotony of the long sea-voyage. At Port Said the travellers got their first taste of the Orient. The weather became intensely hot in the Red Sea and they were relieved when they arrived in the Indian Ocean to experience a gentle breeze. Most of the group went ashore at Colombo though Sister Mary Patrick, who was hoping to meet her nephew Norman Chevers, stayed on board. Norman, who had been invalided out of the British Army, had gone to Ceylon to study tea planting but for health reasons had decided to give it up and go to Australia. His Aunt Frances was disappointed to discover that he had already left. As her first nephew, Norman was special and in the years before she entered she had supported him in many ways. He died in Australia in 1935, so they were destined not to meet again.

Father Blowick's plan was to accompany the Sisters part of the way only. He finally bade them farewell in Colombo. 'He seemed as loath to go as the Sisters were to part with him who under God was responsible for their foundation. Twice he bade them farewell, then with a final blessing he ran quickly down the gangway.'[6] They watched until they could no longer see him. Then slowly climbing the stairs they found their usual corner of the open deck and prayed beneath the stars. 'Then all vain regrets were stilled,' wrote Sister Mary Patrick. 'They [the Sisters] found rest in Him who is the completion of whatever transcends our mortal vision.'[7]

Singapore was their next port of call, and here the missionaries experienced the warm hospitality of the Sisters of the Infant Jesus, many of whom were Irish. The SS *Coblenz* reached Hong Kong on 3 November, and some passengers disembarked. The Sisters also went ashore and visited the Maryknoll Convent, where they met Sisters who had to flee from their mission in mainland China because of the unsettled political situation there. They were waiting anxiously, hoping to return when circumstances should improve.

Letters from the Maynooth Mission priests in China had to some extent prepared the pioneer Sisters for a country going through the throes of intermittent localised warfare. Father Blowick had referred to this when he preached at Benediction in Cobh Cathedral the evening before the group set sail: many would blame the Superiors of the Maynooth Mission for sending out priests and Sisters at such a time, he said, but 'the folly of man was the wisdom of God.'[8]

China in 1926 was in a state of flux. The Boxer Rebellion of 1900 had ushered in a century in which all the old traditions would be uprooted, and in which the China that we know emerged. Basically rebelling against western influences in China, the Boxers, members of a secret society called 'The Righteous Harmonious Fist', swept through the northern provinces of China and eventually marched on Peking, where they were supported by the army of the Empress Dowager in their attack on the foreign concessions.

In quick retaliation, countries with diplomatic personnel in China organised a punitive expedition that captured and looted Peking. A year later the Empress Dowager, who had gone into hiding, returned. During the uprising she had ordered the extermination of foreigners, but she later realised that a policy of limited accommodation was the only way in which the Manchu dynasty could survive. It was already obvious that the days of imperial rule were numbered.

While the western powers continued to encroach on China, the Manchu dynasty still hoped to ensure its survival by supporting a programme of reforms such as an anti-opium campaign launched by the Empress Dowager in 1906. However, the pressure for more radical change was too great. In 1911 the Manchu dynasty was overthrown by those who favoured a republican form of government. Rebellion quickly swept the country and Dr Sun Yatsen was elected provisional President of the Republic of China. He was soon ousted by a powerful warlord, Yuan Shikai, who died however in 1916, shortly after taking the retrograde step of declaring himself emperor. His obvious rejection of the principles of constitutional government dealt irreparable damage to the idea of a republic, and left a vacuum which was soon filled by a succession of warlords who controlled China until 1928 and, in certain areas, even longer. These militarists, often little more than bandit chiefs, had their own private armies; they levied taxes on the people, often issuing their own currency, and they exercised considerable political and civil power. Meanwhile Sun Yatsen was still a force to be reckoned with. From his base in Canton he led the Nationalist Party (Kuo-min-tang, KMT for short) from its inception in 1911 until his death in 1925, when he was succeeded by a young general, Chiang Kai-shek.

Chiang had received his military training in Japan and was head of the KMT Military Academy in Canton. As a young man he had become a Christian in order to marry into a wealthy Christian Chinese family. The fact that his wife was the younger sister of Sun's wife meant that he was close to Sun and the likely person to succeed him. In the Canton coup of 1926, when Chiang seized power in the KMT, he ordered the arrest of all Communist and pro-Communist members of the organisation. The Chinese Communist Party had been founded in 1921. In its early years it adhered to the policy of the Soviet Union that a bourgeois nationalist revolution was essential before a socialist revolution could take place; therefore Chinese Communists were expected to support the KMT. Marxist policy, introduced by the Soviet Union, also insisted that a revolutionary force had to be led by workers in the towns, not by peasants. This played into Chiang Kai-shek's hands: it was relatively easy for him to control Communist uprisings in the cities. In fact, the history of China might have developed differently if a Communist leader called Mao Zedong had not emerged. Rejecting Moscow's advice, he took to the countryside and, as the later history of China shows, he succeeded.

Mao, born into a comfortable peasant family in 1893, trained as a teacher. Radicalised early on by the injustices inflicted by the landlords on the peasants, he found sustenance in *The New Youth* magazine, which had helped to introduce Marxism to Chinese intellectuals. He was one of the delegates to the first congress of the Chinese Communist Party in 1921. After Chiang Kai-shek expelled the Communists from the KMT in 1926, the party was driven underground. Mao went to the countryside, where he began to organise the peasants, though it took him some years to convince other members of the Communist Party that the peasants were capable of being a revolutionary force. Meanwhile, hoping to reunify China, Chiang led his army northwards in 1926, in a move against the warlords. He established the Nationalist headquarters in Nanking, and was responsible for crushing an abortive attempt by the Communists to take over Shanghai. What was called the Northern Expedition brought the Nationalist army into the Yangtze valley and heightened the possibility of an extended war.

Wuhan, the triple city on the Yangtze, comprising Hankow, Hanyang and Wuchang, where the 1911 revolution had started, was now to host another revolution and another army. It was here that the Columban Fathers had their mission territory and it was here that Frances and her companions would establish the first foundation of the Columban Sisters in China.

The newly arrived Sisters had a theoretical knowledge of recent Chinese history; soon they would be caught up in the actual events of the time, which hitherto they had only heard of at second-hand from letters sent home by China missionaries. With Hong Kong behind them, they could now look forward to reaching their destination in a matter of days. They arrived in Shanghai on 7 November. After disembarking, they were brought to the convent of the Daughters of Charity, where they joined the community for supper, and were afterwards shown to their 'little white beds draped with mosquito nets'. The following day Father John O'Leary, superior of the Columban Fathers in Hanyang, arrived to welcome them. He told them that everything was ready for them in Hanyang except that the house was in one place and the furniture in another, so he advised them to stay on in Shanghai for a few more days.

They eventually left Shanghai for Hanyang on the evening of 11 November, on the river boat, the *Luen Ho*. Sister Mary Patrick remarked that all the Irish in Shanghai seemed to have gathered to see them off. It was Armistice Day and the foreign concessions in Shanghai were in a festive mood. It reminded her of a St Patrick's Day celebration in Dublin – in reality it was an eve of Waterloo scenario, though that was not yet evident. Some of those who came to see the Sisters off expressed concern for their safety: there had been sporadic fighting along the banks of the Yangtse and some boats had come under fire. But the Sisters felt confident that God who had brought them thus far would bring them safely the rest of the way.

The vast expanse of the Yangtze, was around them. Ten miles wide for approximately forty miles, then narrowing to five miles and later to one, the Yangtze, 6380 km long, is the third longest river in the world and irrigates a vast and fertile countryside. For the first part of the journey upriver all that could be seen were rice paddies stretching as far as the eye could see. The river itself was like a busy thoroughfare with weather-beaten junks plying in both directions, carrying all sorts of cargo, chiefly human: these junks were the only homes that some people ever knew. As the *Luen Ho* continued upriver the scenery changed, revealing green hills backed by the craggy picturesque mountains which are so much a feature of Chinese art, and on the river banks they could see villages where people were industriously going about their business.

In the middle of the night of the 14 November the Sisters were awoken by loud noise and by light shining through their portholes. Their immediate reaction was one of alarm, fearing that the boat had been fired on, as on earlier trips; it was small comfort to know that the upper deck had been coated with iron on both sides to protect the passengers. Actually, the reason for the commotion was that the boat had cast anchor in the midst of some foreign battle-ships so that two Chinese generals could come on board. Later that day they stopped at Kiukiang and noticed American and British warships patrolling the area. Near the mouth of the harbour they saw the wreck of a steamer which had been blown up a month earlier with 1500 Chinese on board. Two boat-loads of wounded Chinese soldiers were carried on board the *Luen Ho*; they were put on the lower deck, exposed to the elements.

The Sisters finally reached Hankow at noon on 15 November 1926. After a short delay they were brought by launch to Hanyang. Their journey of thirteen thousand miles was at an end. Mother Mary Finbarr was the first to step ashore. It was raining and the mud was thick underfoot, but all hearts were full of joy. The Sisters were conducted up slippery steps and through a dark tunnel of an archway. They soon found themselves in rickshaws being carried down the long main street of Hanyang. Sister Mary Patrick left on record how she felt:

> The road and the open fronted shops and houses were teeming with men, women and children. These were the people to whom the missionaries were to bring the Great Message. How would it be delivered and how received? This reverie was cut short with a bump! The party led by Father Quinlan, Vicar General and Pastor of Hanyang, were in the cathedral compound. Loud detonations struck the ear. Firecrackers were exploding all round. The Chinese Catholics were welcoming the new arrivals … The church door was wide open … And kneeling before the tabernacle the Columban Sisters received the grandest welcome of all.[9]

Another rickshaw ride in teeming rain eventually brought them to their temporary home beside the Christian Brothers school, near

a graveyard on the outskirts of the city. The priests, brothers and the
American Loretto Sisters had been busy preparing the house: the
new arrivals found beds made, the table set and a well-stocked
storeroom.

Father O'Leary said Mass for them the following morning – a
Mass in honour of Our Lady, Help of Christians and Queen of
Peace – but sounds of war rather than peace came through the
windows of the makeshift chapel: military manoeuvres were being
conducted in the nearby football field. Later one of the priests
described the situation faced by the pioneer Sisters:

> All day long could be heard the drums of war. For beside them
> was the Bai-yai-tai field where troops drilled and marched, and
> banner-waving, flag-carrying crowds listened to the oratory of
> Communistic speakers. And as night came down, one heard the
> shouted slogans, the fruit of this oratory: 'Death to the foreigner'
> and 'Death to the Church'. But daily they went about their tasks,
> those Sisters, learning the language of those men and preparing
> to combat the gospel of hate with that of love.[10]

Monsignor Galvin, who was up-country on visitation when the
Sisters arrived, wrote to them apologising for his inability to
welcome them 'with joy bells'. He would not return to Hanyang
before February. From time to time they heard news of him, often
from places close to the firing line, and his courage strengthened
theirs. They went ahead with their language study, absorbing what
they could of the culture around them and making their house more
habitable. Much work had to be done on the chapel but their efforts
were eventually rewarded. Those who had acquired a few words of
Mandarin accompanied one of the Loretto Sisters on her visits to
the sick and the dying.

By mid-December they were ready to celebrate their first
Christmas away from home, but because of the curfew they could
not plan for Midnight Mass. Still, on Christmas Eve they kept vigil
till midnight and then sang the *Adeste*. Frances recorded how she
felt:

The great Middle Kingdom with its teeming millions recked little of that tiny group of religious in their midst just as the great pagan Empire of Rome had recked little of the Birth of the Child God at Bethlehem. Yet the earth was that Child's Footstool and it was in His honour the glad tidings of peace and good will rang out on the frosty air echoing the Angels' song of 2,000 years ago.[11]

Christmastide did not bring peace to the little band of missionaries in Hanyang. Early on the morning of St Stephen's Day they saw a big platform being erected at the end of the nearby football field, and crowds gathering in hundreds and thousands. Communist agitators mounted the platform and their fulminations resounded throughout the whole area. At one stage the listening throng turned and looked towards the convent, and the Sisters knew that they were the target of some of the recriminations. Later they discovered that insulting posters had been affixed to the convent door. Not far away the Loretto Sisters were subjected to the same treatment, and Christian Brothers returning from Wuchang to Hanyang met with abusive language from the crowds of demonstrators in the streets.

The Columban Fathers' superiors were in constant touch with the Chinese Minister for Foreign Affairs in Hankow, a certain Mr Chen, a Chinese Catholic born in Trinidad. His sympathies were with the missionaries, but he was powerless in the face of so much anti-foreign feeling. On 6 January 1927 a mob of coolies attacked the British Concession in Hankow. After putting up a stout defence the British were forced to concede. The immediate result of this was that all British shops, factories and business houses were closed down, and women and children evacuated to Shanghai. Elsewhere in China the entire British population, including Protestant missionaries, made a sudden departure.

Meanwhile the priests continued as best they could in their up-country mission stations. On 2 February a messenger arrived post-haste to report that Fathers Pat O'Connell and Frank McDonald had been captured by bandits in Ko-Ja-Dzae. Fortunately it was possible to negotiate their release some days later. The two young priests arrived in Hanyang, still bearing the marks of their assault, but anxious to return as soon a possible to their mission. Unexpectedly, the Sisters' neighbours, the Christian Brothers, left Hanyang without any prior warning, on 22 February. The new education laws together with all the anti-foreign agitation made it almost impossible to run a Catholic college. That same day the Columban Fathers decided that it was no longer safe for the Sisters to stay on in what had now become an isolated and dangerous situation. They gave them a few hours to pack up everything and leave for the relative safety of the cathedral compound within the city of Hanyang. Here soldiers came in and out of the compound all day. Very soon the military made a move to take over the Sisters' temporary convent, but they were diplomatically forestalled by Father Quinlan, Monsignor Galvin's Vicar General.

The situation in Central China was deteriorating fast. The Japanese concession in Hankow came under attack, and foreigners were leaving on all available boats. In Nanking several Europeans were massacred, including some missionaries. The burning question among the Columban Fathers was whether the Sisters should remain in Hanyang or not. The British and Australian consuls wanted them out[12] but Mr Chen, in charge of Foreign Affairs in Hankow, wanted them to stay, assuring them that they would be as safe in Hanyang as anywhere else. Finally, the American consul insisted on the Loretto Sisters leaving and as the situation was worsening by the hour the Columban Sisters were also forced to depart for Shanghai on 5 April 1927, less than five months after their arrival in Hanyang. In a letter of 7 April, written on the river-boat carrying them to Shanghai, Sister Mary Patrick described how she felt:

How sad it was to ride down the main street of Hanyang in our rickshaws, to see the busy teeming population all intent on their business: the old banker with his nanny-goat beard and silver scales to weigh the silver ounces, the quack doctor with his Materia Medica, the tea houses with those quaint figures sitting at little polished lacquer tables sipping their bowls of tea or arguing over their games of Chinese chess. So many quaint houses and quaint scenes, down to the coffin house with gaily covered sarcophagi and the busy carver decorating these coveted caskets. The fish lay in baskets and boxes by the side of the road, men sat in chairs being shaved, women washing their babies; such a medley of people, in and out, jostling one another on the road. It was just the same as the day we came, and now we were going away. Would any single soul be the better for our coming? Not a word was said as we passed down, no one interested as to whether we came or went.[13]

A hostile crowd had gathered at the landing stage, shouting at the boatmen not to allow the foreigners on board. Eventually however the Sisters, accompanied by Father Fallon, were able to procure a sampan which ferried them to the river-steamer, *Kungwo*. There were 270 refugees on board and cabin accommodation for only twenty-four. Consequently the captain refused to take any more passengers. It looked for a while as if the Sisters might be turned back, but eventually space was found in an area near the kitchen. The *Kungwo* stopped at Nanking and from there on had a convoy of two gunboats, British and American.

On arrival in Shanghai on 10 April, Palm Sunday, the Sisters found accommodation in the Franciscan Missionaries of Mary hospital at Yiangtse-poo, four miles from the city. With characteristic magnanimity, the superior gave shelter not only to them but also to the Loretto Sisters from Hanyang, although she was already providing accommodation for three other refugee communities.

War appeared to be inevitable. A large number of warships of different nationalities was anchored in the harbour at Shanghai and some had gone up-river to Hankow. Military planes were much in evidence. The refugee Sisters in Yiangtse-poo undertook as one of their ministries to keep up continuous prayer for peace before the Blessed Sacrament. They also helped as much as they could with the household tasks, and gave some time each day to language study. In mid-June a cable came from Ireland asking Mother Mary

Finbarr, the Superior General, to return home. She had shepherded the first group to Hanyang and had stayed with them through all the difficult early days as they set about establishing the first Columban Sisters community on Chinese soil. Congregational business now awaited her in the motherhouse. Moreover, the date of her final profession was drawing near. By the time she reached Cahiracon again she had been absent for eleven months.

Shortly after she set sail for home, the Sisters in Yiangtse-poo heard of Monsignor Galvin's elevation to the episcopacy. It was the last piece of good news they were to hear for some time. Throughout the long hot summer they succumbed one by one to illness. At the end of July Mother Mary Theophane and Sister Mary Agnes were rushed to hospital, both of them with dangerously high temperatures. Sister Mary Agnes was diagnosed as having typhoid. Death seemed imminent yet she survived, though it was several weeks before she was out of danger; altogether she had to spend five months in hospital. Sister Mary Philomena was laid up for some weeks with an injured foot, and then got what was called Shanghai fever. Sister Mary Patrick herself ran a fever and was in bed for a week, nursed by one of the Loretto Sisters, because the only Columban Sister on her feet was Sister Mary Lelia.

While the Sisters were trying to cope with all this illness, word came in the middle of August that Father John O'Leary had died suddenly at Sung Ho at the age of thirty-five. As Superior of the Columban Fathers in China, he had been the Sisters' friend and adviser from the time of their arrival in China. They were shattered by the news.

They heard of the preparations being made for Monsignor Galvin's consecration as bishop on 6 November, and applied to the British Consul for permission to return to Hanyang for the occasion. The permission, when it did come, was too late. However, before they left Shanghai, the Sisters had the joy of seeing Sister Mary Agnes recovering satisfactorily, though they knew that she would be unable to travel for at least another month.

Once again they boarded a Yangtze river-boat. It was dark night and all the ship's lights were blacked out. They were told that it was plated with steel for protection but were relieved that it was not put to the test on this occasion. The most exciting feature of this journey up-river was that on the fourth and last day the ship passed Nationalist troops on the march to Hankow. Together with their mules and baggage carts they stretched in single file along the river bank and the Sisters could almost distinguish the umbrellas and teapots carried by the individual soldiers. It was exciting to be part of history in-the-making, travelling alongside an invading army. They soon discovered that it was like so many 'invasions' in the China of the time: the occupying army retreated and Hankow fell into the hands of the incoming troops without a shot being fired.

The Sisters arrived back to a quieter Hanyang: the Communist troops had left and with them the agitators with their anti-foreign slogans. There were fewer people around: an army had just marched through the city. As the Sisters returned to the little convent near the cathedral they noted that it was exactly a year to the day when they had first arrived in Hanyang on 15 November 1926, the feast of St Gertrude. For over seven months of that year they had been refugees. The priests had guarded the convent well in their absence and the Loretto Sisters who had returned in Hanyang a few weeks previously had everything ready for them when they arrived.

That afternoon, Bishop Galvin paid the Columban Sisters a visit. He had been up-country when they arrived the previous year, so this was his first time meeting them. He invited them and the Loretto Sisters to the Columban Fathers' house in Hanyang, where he entertained them and organised group photographs. Afterwards he accompanied the Columban Sisters on their way home. Sympathising with their feeling that they had accomplished very little in their first year in China, he reminded them that they were not there to convert the Chinese but to be at God's disposal. Sister Mary Patrick was impressed by his 'deferential courtesy, revealing humility ... but not derogating from his dignity'.[14]

It looked as if peace had come at last. The Sisters resumed their visitation of the sick and the dying. It was now wintertime as they picked their precarious way through the slush and mud of the narrow side streets of Hanyang, hoping that the medicine bottles they were carrying would not come to grief. This was work that Sister Mary Patrick felt privileged to do. Her grasp of Chinese was minimal, but she soon found that the people went more than half-way to meet her, especially when they saw how much she loved the children. All the skills so painstakingly acquired in earlier years in Dublin hospitals were now put to use. Furthermore, she had to devise other skills to suit situations never envisioned back home. Opium poisoning was a case in point: her simple remedies were usually successful. Bound feet were another unforeseen problem: in the harsh Hanyang winter they were liable to ulceration from poor circulation. Her heart bled for the women forced to endure such senseless pain. She too suffered from her feet, and arthritis had already begun to disfigure her hands. As she trudged home wearily through the muddy streets of Hanyang did she sometimes wonder where was the Lady Moloney of yesteryear?

She was a devoted missionary, much loved by the poor of Hanyang. A Sister who lived in the same community remembers how the coolies had no better friend. Despite her limited grasp of the language, she would joke with them and when it was she who needed a rickshaw there was always a scramble as to who should have the privilege. The same Sister recalls Sister Mary Patrick's cheerfulness in community, in spite of the tiredness and inner pain that seems to have marked much of her first years in China. She had expected to suffer. In one of her early spiritual notebooks, on a scrap of paper there is a rough draft of an offering of her life for China, a radical development of her prayer, 'Let us two be together now and always.' It is undated but because of the reference to Ireland one might guess that it was written some time in the politically disturbed years betweenn 1918 and 1922, long before she set foot in China.

O Sacred Heart of Jesus, united to my intense desire for the salvation of souls, O beseech Thee through the love of Thy Blessed Mother to grant that I may not be unworthy of shedding my blood for the conversion of China. Fearing all things from my weakness I trust in Thy tender pity to sustain me throughout my agony. I implore Thee to bestow this grace on all who suffer for the Faith, and shed Thy blessings on Ireland and on all who are dear to Thee and me.

Shortly before Christmas 1927, Chiang Kai-shek began a major offensive against the Communists whom he had begun to expel from the KMT the previous year. Now he weeded them out of the army and broke diplomatic relations with Russia. The Communist Party was driven underground, not only in Hankow, Hanyang and Wuchang, but throughout central China.

While peace prevailed again in Hanyang it was otherwise in the countryside, where the Communists had fled and were now joining forces with groups of bandits. Usually looking for ransom money, they tracked down foreigners, especially Christian missionaries. Christmas 1927 was a particularly harrowing time for the Columbans up-country. Father Luke Mullaney and his servant were captured by three well-dressed and well-groomed bandits who demanded a large ransom. Fortunately they were released unharmed after a few days. Others were not so fortunate. Father Frank McDonald and Father Pat O'Connell were badly beaten by a hostile crowd and held captive for a month before Bishop Galvin was able to have soldiers sent to rescue them. At the end of April 1928, Father Lalor was captured by bandits and left for dead. Against all the odds he survived. These and similar incidents did not deter the priests from staying with their people throughout this turbulent time.

Had everything gone according to plan, Sister Mary Patrick would have made her final profession on 29 July 1928. Sadly, on 3 May of that year a letter came from her Superior General, Mother Mary Finbarr, to say that she had not been accepted for final profession in the congregation but that she could renew her vows for another three year term. It was a painful coincidence that the letter relaying this decision should reach her on 3 May, feast of the Finding of the Holy Cross, a day sacred to her because she always associated her vocation to China with that date in 1918.[15] Ten years later, to the day, the fateful letter arrived which postponed her final profession for a further three years.

Writing to Father Blowick in 1931 she recalled the painful occasion:

> This year I hope to become an accepted member of the Congregation after 13 long years of trial and repeated crosses. I did not expect to live to see that day when on the 10th anniversary of my call to China I was notified of my rejection for final vows. It was the feast of the Finding of the Holy Cross, and it is only the remembrance of Our Lord's Passion and Cross that has kept me alive.[16]

Because of its impact on Sister Mary Patrick's life and spirituality it is necessary to look for a while at this painful episode in her story. How did it happen that she, without whom the congregation could not have come into existence, was obliged to postpone her final vows in the same congregation? Undoubtedly, there were elements that militated against her, posing problems right from the beginning, both for her and for her companions. While it would have been fitting that she, who for such a long period of time had given herself wholeheartedly to the cause of the Chinese Mission, should lead the pioneers – after all, was she not 'The Pioneer of the Congregation'[17]– yet she was not given this role but was called on to give her allegiance to a young woman half her age and her junior by profession. When the group left Ireland for China Sister Mary Patrick was fifty-three years of age, more than a generation older than any of her companions, all of whom were in the twenties: she could have been their mother. Both she and they would have been conscious of the age difference. They also knew that she was their senior by profession and that in those years precedence in religious orders was determined by such factors. Yet they saw that she who was the only one among them with any experience of life in a mission country was not given authority of any kind.

They would also have been conscious of the fact that of all the members of the first group she was the only one with the kind of professional expertise needed in the China of the time. Her familiarity with different types of nursing and her initiation into tropical medicine and pharmacology were invaluable skills. Moreover, at different periods of her life and in different countries she had visited and cared for the sick poor. When a person with such practical experience is put in a situation where she has to obey the directives of someone younger and less experienced than herself, conflicts of opinion are virtually inevitable.

Obedience had posed few problems for her in the novitiate, where she was able to relate in an adult way to superiors who took account of her maturity and age. But now she was obliged to obey a young woman, undoubtedly of considerable competence, who may have felt threatened by someone so much older and with so much more experience of life. Outspoken and frank, Sister Mary Patrick would not have been slow at proffering suggestions and advice. At a time when the ideal was the practice of 'blind' obedience her common sense led her to question certain decisions, decades before such dialogue became the accepted norm. Consequently she was occasionally regarded as lacking the true spirit of religious obedience, as it was understood in those years.

Another complicating factor at this time was her health and its implications for community living. Although she was certified as being free of tuberculosis when she returned to the novitiate after her year in France, later events were to prove otherwise: the disease was merely quiescent and would flare up again two years after her arrival in China. She carried the bacilli with her and the accompanying symptoms, physical and psychological. She may have attributed the fatigue and lassitude to climate and age; the psychological symptoms would have been more difficult to cope with.

Experts on the disease speak of the danger not only of becoming a victim of pulmonary tuberculosis but also of an associated anxiety neurosis. 'Even in well-balanced personalities some degree of anxiety and depression will be present ... it is very often suppressed.'[18] Remembering her previous illness, Sister Mary Patrick may have recognised some of the symptoms. On the other hand, the members of her community with no medical expertise would have been less aware. Consequently they did not always understand when she was out of sorts, nor could they empathise with her in what they believed was over-concern for her health.

This was actually a feature of the depression associated with her illness. Victims of such depression find it notoriously difficult to describe. Someone who battled with it for many years attempted to do so: 'It is a positive and active anguish, a sort of psychical neuralgia wholly unknown to normal life.'[19] Although those words were merely an attempt to describe an extreme form of depression, they still hint at what Sister Mary Patrick was enduring at that time.

Another concern which seems to have weighed heavily on her in her first few years in Hanyang was that she felt held back from working with the poor to the extent that she desired. Circumstances were against her. Understandably, at her age she found it hard to learn such a complicated language as the version of Mandarin spoken in Hanyang though, through dint of perseverance, she acquired enough to cope with her daily ministry. It added to her problems that the Rule, at that time, required a Sister to have another Sister as companion whenever she went out on a work of charity. This was not always practical. The biggest block, however, was that Bishop Galvin was slow about building the dispensary in which she had expected to work; he knew that if he built at that particular time there was danger that the military might take over the building for their own purposes, as they had already done with any well-built houses in the city. Eventually, when the situation became more stable, he did make provision for a proper dispensary. Meanwhile Sister Mary Patrick had to be content with makeshift quarters in the convent.

A combination of some or all of the above factors would appear to have been behind the postponement of Sister Mary Patrick's final profession. Those living close to her could see how shattered she felt, but she was determined not to allow her personal disappointment to cast a cloud over others. Her letters to Cahiracon were, as ever, full of appreciation for all that the missionaries were doing in China, and of concern for all at home – not a word crossed her lips about her own disappointment or pain. Instead what came through was her compassion for others enduring hard times or coping with family problems. She was particularly conscious of the novices in Cahiracon and throughout her three years of waiting and uncertainty she continued to send them newsy, witty letters as if there were nothing in her heart but joy. In all her letters, including those written between 1928 and 1931, the recipients would have noted her vivid powers of observation, her sense of beauty, a warm humanity and, at times, a gentle, playful sense of humour.

It is only in the correspondence with her spiritual director, Father Michael Browne SJ, that the real anguish of this phase of her life comes through. These letters also reveal that even before Sister Mary Patrick's superiors made their decision about her profession, she herself had a question-mark. On 27 December 1927, five months before she received Mother Mary Finbarr's painful decision, Father Browne had sent her eight closely-written pages in reply to a letter of hers as to whether or not she should take final vows. He suggested that she put before her superiors in Ireland a statement regarding her position in China, and he drew up a rough draft of the points she would need to present: her vocation which was to work for the poor in China; her training for that; the fact that she was at that time cut off from working directly for the poor. (As explained above, at that point Sister Mary Patrick was not able to visit the sick poor as often as in her earlier months in Hanyang, when she sometimes had one of the Loretto Sisters as her companion.) Father Browne, listing the points that Sister Mary Patrick should present to her superiors, concluded with the following: 'I have no external work of any kind to do, and my life, as a religious, is more contemplative than active, yet all my training has been for the active life. I am not specially drawn to the contemplative life.'[20]

He advised her to wait for a reply from her superiors before proceeding further. If they approved of her making final profession, then she herself would still need to discern whether or not she should go ahead. On the other hand, if her superiors advised against her making final profession it would be unwise on her part to think about forming a new religious order; it would seem more feasible to join an already established congregation or a lay institute. He advised her, however, not to think along those lines but to wait in patience for the reply of her superiors. 'The great source of your trials and sufferings,' he wrote, 'is the want of sympathetic direction. Loneliness and discouragement through want of a human voice to cheer you on has crushed you.'

Whether or not Father Browne read more into Sister Mary Patrick's cry for help than she intended is not clear. From her letters of that period it is obvious that she felt friendship and affection for the members of her community, though the age gap and different life experiences would have been a barrier to intimacy. She also had some good friends among the Columban Fathers, in particular Father Cornelius Tierney. She felt deeply his assignment to the new mission in Kiangsi and his subsequent death as a captive of the Red Army. Bishop Galvin, from the time when he first met her on the stairs in Dalgan Park, appreciated her calibre and her generosity. He understood what she was going through and he stood by her at this difficult time.

She had not yet sent the statement suggested by Father Browne, nor is there any evidence that she ever did, when he wrote to her again on 26 March 1928, giving his reasons why she should stay in the congregation: '(1) You deliberately made choice of this life after a long and trying novitiate. (2) There is no clear call to anything better or higher. (3) Leaving these Sisters would mean abandoning religious life.'[21]

Presumably she acted on Father Browne's advice and asked to be admitted to final profession. However, her superiors back in Ireland, aware of some of her misgivings, were also coming to a painful decision. Mother Mary Finbarr had arrived back in Ireland the previous August. She and Sister Mary Patrick had been part of the original founding group of the Columban Sisters; they were also good friends. In the months she spent in Hanyang and Shanghai, Mother Mary Finbarr would have recognised that Sister Mary Patrick was going through a vocation crisis: indeed the matter may well have been discussed between them. After her return to Ireland she would have been in communication with Frances's superior in Hanyang and with Frances herself. However, any major decision would not be taken independently of Mother Mary Alphonsus, who in large measure guided the destiny of the congregation at this time. As mentioned earlier, she did not have the breadth of vision of her predecessor, Mother Mary Camillus: on the contrary, a certain rigidity and formality characterised her dealings with the young congregation. It would be impossible as well as unfair to conjecture how far that influenced the decision to postpone Sister Mary Patrick's final profession.

All that we can be certain of is that during Dr O'Dwyer's visit to Cahiracon at Christmas 1927, Mother Mary Finbarr told him that there was question of not allowing Sister Mary Patrick to make her perpetual vows. On 31 March 1928, she wrote to him about some items of congregational business. In her last paragraph she referred again to the matter of not accepting Sister Mary Patrick for final profession: 'We have now decided that this is the best course to take under the circumstances, and we intend to communicate our decision to her next week, of course she can renew her temporary vows for another period of three years. I do hope it will not upset her too much.'[22]

How upset she was is clear from her letter to Father Blowick, quoted earlier. Although three years had passed, time had not softened the pain. The coincidence of the news arriving on the anniversary of the day she always associated with her vocation to China made it all the more shattering. With great kindness and understanding her friend and spiritual director Father Browne, who had helped her through other crises in the past, now supported her and helped her to put her suffering in the context of the Passion of Christ. He assured her that there was no surer road to Heaven than the road of suffering and humiliation, which she was following.[23] He helped her to face the future with courage, trusting in God's providence, which he saw had guided her life since she had first talked to him about the idea of a religious congregation for China. 'I could not see then any way through all the difficulties that seemed to beset the project. Yet God's loving care has brought you through the ordeal and will bring you at last to that crown of justice in His Kingdom which He wills you to win.'[24]

Few, apart from her spiritual director, realised Sister Mary Patrick's inner suffering at this time. She must have gone through a veritable crucifixion of the spirit. Father Browne had referred to the loneliness she had endured through the absence of 'sympathetic direction'. Her letters took at least six weeks to reach him and a further six weeks before she had a reply. Her friend Father Tierney was superior of the new Columban mission in Kiangsi. He was a faithful correspondent but letters did little to supply for his actual presence. The members of her community, fine and dedicated women all of them, could not intrude in the sacred place where she fought out her lonely battle, nor were they invited to. Many years later she told a young Sister that in those difficult years in Hanyang her only solace was her crucifix, which she clasped close to her in bed at night, joining her anguish with that of Christ on the Cross.

On 30 July 1928, the day after she renewed her vows in a quiet ceremony in the convent chapel in Hanyang, Sister Mary Patrick wrote to her Mother General. She began by describing the journey down the mountain from Kuling and the breath-taking scenery along the way.

> I think it was all providentially arranged by the dear Sacred Heart to soften the trial, for I have been through Gethsemani the last few weeks … I was rather unnerved after a bad night, but was given strength to renew my vows without a breakdown. When our dear Lord came, my soul was filled with peace, and I felt glad to have this little holocaust to offer Him Who all through my life has been so good to me.Needless to say no one was forgotten at the moment of renewal in colloquy with our Divine Spouse, and most of all I prayed with all my heart for your intentions, dear Mother General, and for the Congregation.[25]

Gradually she lifted the veil a little to a few close friends in Cahiracon, writing to one of them:

> Our dear Lord has allowed everything to happen as it did, and His grace has sustained and strengthened His poor servant through every trial. However hard and bitter the suffering, it is a great favour to share in the Cross of Christ, for in losing all earthly joy and consolation one turns more to God and receives a greater share of His love.[26]

A few months later, in the course of a letter to another Sister in Cahiracon, she said: 'One does not always realise the value of suffering when it comes, but with God's grace one becomes accustomed to have sorrow as one's companion, and to understand its Heaven-sent significance and vitality.'[27] She sent Christmas greetings as usual to her Mother General and referred to a letter of affection and sympathy from her former novitiate companions:

It comforted me much, and I should like her and the others to know how much I appreciate their true kindness, but it would not be right to look for sympathy. God means some of us to sow in tears what others shall reap in joy, and clearly it is by suffering we have to pay the price for souls we are seeking to save. I know how unworthy I am to become the Spouse of Christ or to do the least little thing for Him, hence this long wait.[28]

While she waited in patience for God's time, externally her life continued as before. With the other members of her community she took her turn in supervising the housekeeping in the Columban Fathers' central house in Suan, work which she found congenial. She also had the task of compiling the community annals, which she did with her usual dedication and competence: her early experience of writing for society journals had given her a happy facility for such work.

Physical illness was also part of those years of enforced waiting. Soon after she renewed her vows in July 1928, her health began to deteriorate. By the end of the year her lungs were once again affected, and she also needed treatment for high blood pressure. A severe cold in April 1929 seems to have activated her latent tuberculosis. Her condition worsened rapidly and she became so gravely ill that she was anointed on 27 May. Two days later, the superior of the International Hospital in Hankow wrote to Mother Mary Theophane giving the doctor's report. He was of the opinion that her recovery would be slow, because of her serious condition; he had already started her on the tuberculin treatment.[29]

A letter came from Father Browne expressing his sympathy. He quoted Psalm 27:4: 'One thing have I asked of the Lord, that will

I seek after; that I may dwell in the house of the Lord all the days of my life.' Ever since he first knew her, he said, that had been her desire. She herself wrote from the International Hospital to Mother Mary Alphonsus, thanking her for her letter and prayers and telling her about her slow progress in fighting against the tuberculosis, which had left her so weak that she was unable to join the rest of the community who had gone up the mountain to Kuling to escape the oppressive heat of Hanyang in summertime. They needed that, she said, after nursing her through the most critical stage of her illness: one night all of them stayed up with her. In spite of all her pleading, she added, they wore themselves out in looking after her, and she prayed that God would reward them. She connected her physical breakdown with what she had gone through the previous year:

> I know that the mental anguish of the past year has told on me. At the time I did not expect to pull through the three appointed years. But Our dear Lord and His Blessed Mother have helped me over some of the worst moments, and I know that He has allowed it all for my own sanctification and that of other souls. And now I lie like a little child in His arms enjoying complete peace with him, apart and alone.[30]

By the end of July she was able to join the other members of her community in Kuling, where it was hoped that the cooler mountain air would help her convalescence. There she submitted to the prescribed regime of rest and good food, gradually recovering her strength. By September she was considerably better, though tests showed that she still carried some tubercle bacilli. It would be a long time before she would be in good health again.

TWELVE

Alarms and Excursions

On 2 February 1929 Sister Mary Patrick's four companions made final profession in the convent chapel in Hanyang. She now became the only member of her group not yet finally professed. As a result, her status in the community changed: from being the senior of the group by profession she now became the junior. In the ordinary day-to-day life of the community this made little difference, but it did become significant the following year when the Sisters prepared for the first General Chapter of the congregation. According to the constitutions, only a Sister who had made final profession was eligible to be elected delegate. Nor could a Sister not yet finally professed be voted into any office of leadership in the congregation. In effect, Sister Mary Patrick was precluded from playing any part in the first General Chapter of the congregation she had helped to found, whereas her young companions were eligible to be not only delegates but also to be elected to the congregation's administration.

She would have realised the significance of her changed status in the community. Yet when her Mother General wrote to ask if she had any reservations about any of her companions being admitted to final profession, she replied that after reflecting on the matter and praying about it she had nothing to say by way of objection. In words that convey some of the poignancy of her own situation she added:

> If there were anything very serious, I suppose that even situated as I am, it would be my duty to report it; but I am thankful not to be in a position that would oblige me to report the failings of others. In considering one's own shortcomings one becomes more tolerant of others ... I would be very sorry indeed if any of the four were held back from final profession.[1]

In the same letter, she referred to her own attitude to her missionary vocation. Although she was always happy when at prayer, she did not believe that she had a contemplative vocation. Rather, she could always find God best in his suffering members. 'In China, the work is often physically repulsive, but what matters when one considers the soul. With the blessing of the Cross on the work, it may be God's Will to make it fruitful for souls. I am terribly afraid of my unworthiness standing in the way.'

Her unworthiness was voiced again two days after the final profession ceremony of her companions when she wrote to Sister Joseph Conception in Cahiracon, telling her of the joy she felt in the happiness of her Sisters, the first Columban Sisters to make final profession in China. They, on their part, marvelled at how caring she was for all of them that day, showing no sign of her own disappointment. Still, in her letter to Sister Joseph Conception, her closing words gave a hint of how she felt. She did not dare to write to the novices, she said, 'for what must they think of their first and eldest Sister who was not good enough to make her final vows, but I know that you will pity and not condemn. And pray for me that Our dear Master may give me a sight of Thabor, if it be His Holy Will.'[2]

Sister Mary Patrick herself gave a detailed account of the occasion in the Hanyang community annals. The tiny chapel was scarcely big enough, she said, for the Sisters to prostrate, and only those priests who formed the choir could be squeezed in; the others stayed outside with the neighbours and helpers whose hands were itching to let off the customary firecrackers. Bishop Galvin had come down from up-country through snow and ice to preside at the ceremony. In moving words he told the Sisters that soon they would be working among the suffering poor of Christ in the country districts he had envisioned for them. The previous day, he had taken over one of the closing sessions of their retreat to talk about their missionary life. He would like to see them at work in country parishes, 'going down among the people, seeking them in their own wretched homes. They must be prepared to rough it, sharing the hardships of the priests'. [3] He put St Columban before them as their model and spoke with such eloquence and enthusiasm that he deepened the devotion of his listeners to their patron saint. Sister

Mary Patrick's lifelong dedication to St Columban found nourishment in his words.

Another saint who became her friend at this time was St Gertrude. Mother Mary Alphonsus had sent her a copy of the life of this great saint and she wrote to thank her, telling her what comfort she was finding in the story of this holy woman who in spite of continual poor health lived in constant awareness of God.

> It was her simplicity and confidence that made her so pleasing to the Sacred Heart. I like her way better even than the Little Flower's. It seems a pity that devotion to this beloved friend of Our Lord should have fallen into abeyance. He said He had chosen her to be the light of nations and through her He wished to enlighten a great number of souls. St Gertrude must be interested in us as she brought us two years running to Hanyang on her feast![4]

The Sisters needed all the spiritual help they could get, because in the spring of 1929 hostilities had broken out again between the opposing factions in China. The Wuhan cities, including Hanyang, were being terrorised by bands of Communists. Even the servants were afraid to go into the city. But once again General Chiang Kai-shek came to the rescue: with the backing of the Chinese fleet he entered Hankow without a shot being fired. The Nationalist flag once more flew over the whole of Hanyang, including the convent. Some of the retreating Communist forces passed through the city on their way north. Fearful for their safety, some family-members of the Sisters' helpers sought refuge in the convent. It was a busy time in the dispensary, especially when an epidemic of flu broke out. Just when the Sisters were stretched to the utmost Sister Mary Patrick became gravely ill again.

Fortunately, reinforcements were on the horizon: on 27 November 1929 a second group of Columban Sisters arrived in Hanyang: Sisters Dolores Callan, Colmcille McCormack, Columban Kennedy, Basil McBrearty, Michael Mongey and Ignatius O'Keeffe. They faced into the severest winter Central China had experienced for seventy years. The Chinese claimed that there must be a new God of the cold: the old one had never been so cruel. Hundreds died of cold and hunger. Rickshaw coolies in Hankow froze to death in their chairs. Little children came to the dispensary suffering from chilblains and frostbite and were treated with the best the Sisters had to offer: an ointment devised by a Franciscan Brother from melted candle ends and Chinese oil. Actually it worked. In whatever time was available the Sisters visited the destitute in their homes, bringing what relief they could.

The fact that there were now eleven Columban Sisters in Hanyang was an incentive to forming a second community. It looked as if Bishop Galvin's hope of having Sisters in country areas could now become a reality. Even before the new group arrived he had made up his mind to build a convent in Father Walsh's parish, Yuin Lung Ho, but because the place was being constantly raided by bandits, it was difficult to keep workmen, who fled whenever there was a rumour of bandits in the neighbourhood. But the Bishop was convinced that this was where the Sisters should go. Consequently work continued on the convent. The wall surrounding the compound had just been finished when, on 21 November, a large force of bandits invaded the town and burnt every house within sight.

Obviously a town in ruins could not be the centre for a women's catechumenate; subsequently the Bishop chose Sientaochen for the new community. This town, with a population of 30,000 people, was situated 150 miles northwest of Hanyang on the river Han. It had never been attacked by bandits and was considered safer than most other towns in the vicariate. It had a thriving Catholic community, including at least a thousand old Catholics whose families could trace their faith back for more than two hundred years. There was a fine church, catechumenates for both men and women, and a school. Two zealous young priests were in charge of the parish: Father Patrick Laffan and Father James Linehan. They sent word to the Sisters that they would be happy to vacate their house for them until a convent could be built. It was only later that the Sisters discovered that when the priests handed over their house to them, they themselves moved into the boys' former catechumenate, little better than a barn, where their make-shift accommodation consisted of boards on wooden trestles.

Sister Mary Patrick was pleased to find herself numbered among those who were to form the new community, with Sisters Mary Lelia, Dolores, Columban and Michael. Sister Mary Lelia was appointed Superior. Before dawn on the morning of 15 April 1930, Tuesday of Holy Week, they left Hanyang by river-boat and arrived in Sientaochen the following day, causing some consternation when they walked into the church just as Father Walsh was reading the gospel for Spy Wednesday. The congregation had never before seen nuns and it took some explaining by the catechist before Mass could resume quietly. Afterwards the old Christians gathered around and gave the newcomers a heartening welcome.

They settled in quickly and happily. Immediately they began to prepare the Altar of Repose for the following day, Holy Thursday. The altar boys conferred together and decided that the Sisters must sing the Mass on Easter Sunday. One of them succeeded in borrowing a small harmonium; it was old with no stops, but by pedalling vigorously Sister Mary Patrick was able to produce music. In the process, she very nearly provoked a riot: the people who had packed into the church from all corners of the vast parish had never seen or heard the likes before. The priest had to leave the confessional to restore order.

On Easter Monday, Sister Mary Columban wrote a cheerful letter back to the Hanyang community. 'Grace seems to be falling from the trees here,' she said. And Sister Mary Michael wrote to say that it was all joys, no sorrows. It looked as if Sister Mary Patrick would thrive in this atmosphere. A dispensary was set up for her in a separate building near the Sisters' house and patients began to come. 'I feel as if I had reached China at last!' she wrote back to Hanyang. On Holy Saturday there had been two baptisms. 'This affected me like last year and I wept for joy. There is nothing makes one realise so much how worthwhile is the Mission.'[5] Sister Mary Dolores and Sister Mary Columban got the catechumenate under way, and the other two members of the group were busy putting the convent in order.

Then on Friday of Easter Week, 25 April, the storm which shattered all their hopes broke. The previous night the Sixth Communist Army had surrounded the town secretly, waiting for dawn. As soon as daylight came they charged through the streets from four points, shooting to right and left while they shouted the fearsome word, 'kill!' These were something other than the ragtag bands that sporadically terrorised the towns in the northern section of the province. There were thousands of them and all of them carried firearms. The militia, whose business it was to protect the people, were taken completely off-guard and there was little resistance.

Bishop Galvin, who had come on Monday to welcome the Sisters, had planned to leave on Wednesday, but business prevented him and he decided to leave instead early on Friday morning. Consequently, he was saying Mass with Father Walsh at 5.30 a.m. that morning when they heard rifle fire. Two of the Sisters were in the church and the other three hurried there as soon as they realised what was happening. The Bishop who had just finished Mass came to meet them, saying, 'The Communists have come.' Father Linehan was on the altar consuming the Blessed Sacrament, and Father Laffan and Father O'Collins were collecting the sacred vessels, which they then buried outside. (Father O'Collins who had come to help with the Holy Week ceremonies had not yet left for his up-country parish.) Very soon the Communists forced their way into the compound, a red flag was erected outside the gate and sentries were posted at each entrance.

Meanwhile the priests and Sisters had found temporary security in the sacristy, but before long the Communists found their way into the church and it seemed wiser to go to the Sisters' convent. The Bishop suggested a cup of coffee, which Sister Mary Patrick hurried off to make. By this stage the whole place was overrun by soldiers, and the Bishop advised the Sisters to go to the adjoining catechumenate, where they would be less visible to the marauding gang. Looking back on the event later, everyone remarked on how magnificent the Bishop was. 'Not a trace of anger or confusion, but cool and equal to anything. Every few minutes he was wanted at the house, or he was moving around the compound to see if there was any chance of escape for us, and through it all he was just himself, thinking of everyone and never of his own danger.'[6] He brought in the officer in charge who told them that they had nothing to fear, that they were doing good work just as they the Communists were, and that they were under the same flag!

By this time a group of soldiers had entered the catechumenate where they were milling about. The Sisters sensibly decided to return to their house and get some breakfast before matters might change for the worse. They collected the Bishop and priests and they all had something to eat in the Sisters' refectory, watched by a group of violent-looking men. Before they had finished eating, other armed men burst into the room. The Bishop got up and prevailed on the intruders to follow him outside. Father O'Collins and the Sisters stayed where they were. They could hear the sound of objects crashing in the nearby church. The soldiers were smashing up everything they could lay their hands on, and looting what they believed they could use or sell: vestments, altar linen, the sanctuary lamp. They broke up the tabernacle and destroyed all the statues.

The Sisters were still in the refectory with Father O'Collins when Father Laffan came in, put his pipe on the sideboard, and said to Father O'Collins, 'Give me absolution. I have to go.' As he left the room he asked the Sisters to pray for him. 'I shall always see that picture,' wrote one of them, three weeks later. 'Then came the Bishop, his face twitching, and trying hard to control his voice he said, "Paddy is gone".' He told the Sisters that he had been around the compound several times and that there was absolutely no hope of escape: every exit was guarded.

Earlier they had discussed the possibility of getting away and the Bishop had asked Mother Mary Lelia if they would take a chance of escaping if it arose, or if they would prefer to stay. Speaking for the five of them, she answered, 'If you say we should go, we'll go, and if you say, stay, we'll stay!' They had unreserved confidence in their Bishop. 'Our Lord seemed nearer than ever before,' wrote one of the Sisters some weeks later. 'In that refectory He was almost visible, and the Bishop was just taking His place and looking after us, and what was there to worry about ... It is hard to explain how we could feel so much at peace with all the danger ... God made everything so easy and the thought of the next world brought us no fear either.'[7]

They left the refectory, moving to the convent office which they felt would be more private. When tidying the place the previous day the Sisters had come across an old gun; they had barely time to hide it behind a heavy chest before the soldiers burst in. There were medicines in the room too which the Sisters had brought with them from Hanyang for the sick poor. As soon as the soldiers saw the medicine press they stripped it bare. The Sisters then retreated to an upstairs room where they found all their clothes thrown on the floor, and saw that the Communists had taken their blankets, rugs and umbrellas: every Chinese soldier in those days carried an umbrella strapped to his back. Meanwhile the Bishop had come to tell them that Father Linehan had also been taken, and that probably they would take all the priests in turn. 'When I go,' he said, 'you are all coming with me.' To this they agreed. Nobody would relish being left to the mercy of these men.

He brought them some books he had rescued from downstairs, together with a loaf of bread and a tin of jam. Someone hid the food in a cupboard, but the men who had glared so menacingly at them in the refectory came in, found it and threw it out the window. They tossed the Sisters' clothes around, made a show of loading their guns, playing with the triggers and pointing them at the Sisters. They were in this situation for over two hours, tension building up all the time. Something was bound to happen soon. What did happen was not at all what they were expecting.

Sometime after noon, Bishop Galvin stood in the doorway and said, 'Sisters, follow me!' He had discovered that the sentry at the back gate had gone away momentarily, and he decided to risk an escape. How he got the Sisters out of the room and past the sentry at the front gate nobody could ever explain. The sentry obviously believed that the back gate was still under guard. The little procession passed from the Sisters' compound into that of the women's catechumenate, then into the priests' compound and out the back gate. The Bishop told Father Walsh and Father O'Collins to wait until they were safely away, and then to follow.

They walked cross-country for about five hours, expecting every moment to be followed, or to be confronted by local Communist sympathisers. Shortly after they began their long walk they stopped so that the Sisters could remove the conspicuous white caps which held their veils in place. They had just resumed walking when a bandit came riding towards them down the road. He was within fifteen yards, yet he did not see them, just as the sentry at the front gate of the compound had seemingly not seen them either. One of the Sisters wrote later that the people of Sientaochen insisted that the bandits were blinded while they passed, just as had happened when St Peter had miraculously escaped from the hands of his captors in the early days of the Church (see Acts 12:10). These fugitives of a later age kept to the fields, at times retracing their steps when they suspected danger ahead, once lying flat in a field of wheat, some of them hiding under bean frames. At another time they were hidden from sight by some graves while six armed Communist soldiers passed within a hundred yards.

After that narrow escape they rested briefly in a clump of trees, hoping to get far enough away from Sientaochen to be able to cross the Han River safely, while there was still light. It was at this stage that Sister Mary Michael produced from the folds of her cloak a bottle of brandy salvaged before the Communists had raided the medicine press in the convent office. Bishop Galvin wrote later that every priest and Sister had a welcome sip as the bottle passed from hand to hand, and that it gave them new life and courage.[8]

They resumed walking, with occasional short rests, till at about 5.00 p.m. they reached the river. They had walked twelve miles since they had slipped out the back gate of the compound around noon. Some time later Bishop Galvin was to write: 'I was glad that the Sisters who followed me were young Irish girls to whom brisk walking presented little difficulty.' He had forgotten momentarily that one of the group, Sister Mary Patrick, was fifty-seven years of age and still recuperating from her illness of the previous year. It says much for her stamina and will-power that she could stay the course with the best of them.

They crossed the river in a sampan, and then had to walk another few miles to get the two boats that would take them to Hanyang. They were not yet out of danger, though they felt considerably safer as they sat on the bottom of the boats moving down river, eating bread and hard-boiled eggs. Nor were they fussy about the condition of the food or the boats. The Bishop accompanied them for a short distance. He then entrusted them to the Father O'Collins and Father Walsh and returned to the vicinity of Sientaochen, where he would be better able to work for the release of Father Laffan and Father Linehan.

When darkness fell, the boatmen informed the group that they could not travel by night, so they cast anchor. That was a night of suspense – they were not yet far enough away for comfort from the Communist Sixth Army – yet some members of the group did manage to sleep on the bare boards on the bottom of the boats; it was the sleep of exhaustion at the end of a nerve-racking day. At dawn they weighed anchor and resumed their journey, hoping to get as far as the Columban parish of Whan-ja-san by mid-day. This parish was some distance inland. They disembarked at the most convenient point, then walked a few miles and crossed a lake before reaching the priests' house. Fathers Pigott, Maguire and Devlin had not heard about the attack on Sientaochen and were shocked to see the muddy, bedraggled, travel-weary group that landed on their doorstep. After a good meal and a short rest the travellers set off again and arrived at the Sisters' convent in Hanyang at 9.30 p.m., 26 April, a day and a half after their extraordinary escape. The Hanyang community had been celebrating the feast of Our Lady of Good Counsel, the titular feast of the convent, when news came about the attack on Sientaochen. They now welcomed the weary travellers with great joy and relief, thanking God for what was truly a miraculous escape. What was uppermost in everyone's thoughts now was the safety of Father Laffan and Father Linehan.

Bishop Galvin wrote to Mother Mary Lelia on 28 April from one of the mission stations near Sientaochen, saying that it was a miracle that they had escaped. 'We had gone only a short time when they rushed to the back to find us. They followed us but didn't know in what direction we had gone. The Catholics say God blinded their eyes.' He told her that as soon as he had heard that the Communist forces had withdrawn from Sientaochen, he had returned, only to find the whole place looted. He had sent Ma, a trusted helper, to try to contact Father Laffan and Father Linehan. People knew where they and their captors were, but he himself could not proceed any further without risking capture, and that would help nobody. He ended with the words: 'In the midst of all the ruck I want to say how grand you and the Sisters were.'[9] Later, after he had time to assimilate the experience, he wrote:

> No words of mine can convey the glorious spirit of comradeship which bound together that little fugitive band and the fortitude and courage which the Sisters displayed during that terrible day. They were simply wonderful. The awful agony which they went through can never be put into words. Nor can any of us ever cease thanking God, for it was He who led them out to safety.[10]

But the Sisters knew that they owed their safety under God to the Bishop. They now shared his anxiety about Father Laffan and Father Linehan. Every day they had Exposition of the Blessed Sacrament during which they stormed heaven for the priests' release. The Bishop accompanied by Father Pigott stayed up-country, as close as he could to the Sixth Army and the captive priests. The soldiers were constantly on the move, going in the direction of their stronghold, the Red Lake. Two of the Sientaochen Catholics had offered to follow the army, hoping to be able to contact the priests. They discovered that what the Reds wanted was a ransom, in the form of guns, not money. Other Communist troops were also on the march, also going in the direction of the Red Lake. Consequently, it was no longer safe for the Bishop and Father Pigott to continue to presume on the hospitality of the Catholic family who had been sheltering them; they might put these people in jeopardy.

They returned to Hanyang. Awaiting them there was a formal

letter from the two captured priests, asking for guns or money. Father Laffan had once told the Bishop that if he was captured he wanted him to ignore any request for a ransom. In this letter he hinted that Father Linehan agreed with him. But the Bishop realised that there was little hope of release for the priests if he did not make some gesture of compliance with the request. He arranged a meeting with the leader of the Communists in Hankow, and got him to agree to go to the Red Lake to negotiate a settlement. It was a long slow process, not made easier by the news that the two priests were seriously ill.

Chiang Kai-shek was once again in the ascendant and rumours were rife that if he moved against the Communists at the Red Lake they would probably kill off all their prisoners. Consequently, when another ransom note came there was no gainsaying the gravity of the implications if it were not paid. The dramatic attempt to get the required ransom paid in time is worthy of a place among the most sensational of thrillers. If Admiral McLean of the British Navy had not provided the gunboat *Mantis* for a record-breaking dash up the Yangtse, it is doubtful if the two priests could have been saved. However, after more than seven months in captivity, they eventually arrived back in Hanyang on 2 December 1930 in good spirits, though gaunt and scarred after their traumatic experience.

Meanwhile, on 20 July, Mother Mary Theophane and Sister Mary Lelia had left for Ireland to attend the first General Chapter of the Congregation. Mother Mary Theophane was an *ex officio* member; Sister Mary Lelia was elected by the group. Although Sister Mary Patrick was not eligible to attend this crucial Chapter in the history of the congregation, she sent the two delegates on their way with cordial good wishes. At one of the ports of call on their way home they had a letter from her, in which she brought them up to date on all the community news, telling them too how much they were missed. In a more personal vein she gave a brief glimpse into what was nourishing her spiritual life at this time. Once again it was St Gertrude.

I have discovered a lovely book for spiritual reading. It is 'The

Love of the Sacred Heart,' illustrated by St Gertrude. It is quite orthodox and historically accurate. There is a lovely Preface by Archbishop Goodier. He says that St Gertrude may be said to have brought nearer together Heaven and earth than any other mystic. And the note that rings through all her writings is the love of Jesus Christ for the individual soul ... the way He solves the mystery of human suffering, the reward He provides even in this life for anyone who will give Him love for love.[11]

Sister Mary Patrick was blessed in having this peaceful oasis within herself, because externally things were about as bad as they could be. Several of the towns in the vicariate had fallen to the Communists and it seemed as if it was only a matter of time before Hanyang itself would come under attack. Finally, on 31 July, word came that the Communist forces were within ten miles of the city, that they had the place surrounded and were preparing to attack. Immediately the Bishop instructed the Columban and Loretto Sisters to come to the priests' central house in Hanyang, where arrangements were made to get them to Hankow as speedily as possible. As foreign women, they were in obvious danger.

Hankow itself was not immune to the likelihood of attack, but, if it did come under fire, there were possibilities of escaping down-river to Shanghai. Moreover, foreign warships were anchored nearby. The Sisters found the city pervaded by an atmosphere of fear. People suspected of Communist allegiance were arrested on the slightest pretext and many were beheaded on the streets. Public executions took place regularly on Hankow's once fashionable racecourse. Barricades were erected around the cathedral and the Canossian Sisters'convent where the refugee Sisters were staying. When the situation in Hanyang deteriorated, arrangements were made for the girls in the catechumenate and those working in the Loretto Sisters' embroidery school to cross over to Hankow. The crisis passed when more foreign gunboats arrived, causing the Communist forces to withdrew. After three anxious weeks the Sisters and the girls in their care were able to return to Hanyang, though for months they kept their bags packed in case they might have to escape again at a moment's notice.

Back in Hanyang they involved themselves again in work that had been slowed down by the extremely hot summer: the unremitting heat had brought exhaustion and sickness to both priests and Sisters. The dispensary was nearing completion and they prepared for its opening. St Joseph's, the girls' catechumenate, needed to be repaired and extended. Classes had to be prepared, and the sick poor visited in their homes. Some women and children refugees, given shelter in the convent when their parish was taken over by the Communists, were able to go home at last, and three young Catholic women from Sientaochen who had been staying with the Sisters since the attack on that town also returned home.

Finally, on 3 October 1930, the long-awaited dispensary was opened. Word spread quickly and from early morning the Sisters were kept busy every day with patients queuing up for their ministrations. Sister Mary Ignatius and Sister Mary Michael looked after the dispensary and Sister Mary Patrick was in charge of the pharmacy. She was also given the special ministry of looking after any of the priests or seminarians who were ill. That meant that at times she was extremely busy. Over and above their work in the dispensary, the Sisters also visited the sick poor who were unable to come to them.

Meanwhile, word had come from Ireland that the first General Chapter of the congregation had elected Mother Mary Theophane, their Superior in Hanyang, as Mother General, and that Sister Mary Lelia had been elected to her council. Sister Mary Agnes became the new superior in Hanyang. Sister Mary Patrick wrote to Mother Mary Theophane, this time to congratulate her on being elected Mother General. She assured her of her own 'affectionate loyalty', saying that each day she prayed for her that she might be blessed with every necessary grace for herself and others. 'May you be the interpreter of Our Lord's own wishes for the Congregation and thus your reign will be one of justice and love.'[12] She was glad, she said, that Mother Mary Lelia with her experience of China was one of her councillors, though she would be missed in China. They had hoped for 'a renewal of those brief but happy days at Sientaochen', where

Mother Mary Lelia had been in charge.

Some weeks later she wrote again to her new Mother General, sending Christmas greetings. Sientaochen was peaceful at last, she said, and was being protected by a garrison of 6,000 soldiers. The parish priest was hopeful that if war did not erupt again the Sisters could return at Easter. Things were more stable at present in the Hanyang vicariate than in Kiangsi, where her friend Father Tierney was still in the hands of his captors. 'My heart is heavy, for Father Tierney was my first friend on the Mission and has remained so under all circumstances. But I know that whatever happens he will face it with the indomitable courage of his consistently holy life.' She asked for a new crucifix to replace her profession crucifix, apparently snatched from her neck. Even a small one would do. 'I am content however to bear the humiliation of being without one. It may help towards the conversion of some soul. It is in our hearts the dear Lord looks for His image.' Then, practical woman that she was, she suggested that it would help them greatly if they were sent a young Sister with some training in laboratory work. Correct diagnosis was such a problem.[13]

Back in Ireland the year 1930 was also highly significant for the Columban Sisters. Not only was it the year when they held their first General Chapter, but it was also marked by the departure of the Sisters of Charity. On 25 April they left Cahiracon to return to their own congregation. The annalist of the time recorded how the news of their going affected the members of the young congregation: 'The blow was swift and heavy … The letter from Milltown announcing the momentous decision reached us on 31 March. Next day, when mid-day recreation had ended, Mother General retained us in the Community Room and there with tears falling from her eyes and a voice broken with emotion, she told us that God had sent our little congregation its first heavy Cross.' She told them that she was writing to Bishop Fogarty, asking him to use his influence to have the decision rescinded. She and several of the Sisters also wrote in the same vein to Dr O'Dwyer, and to the Mother General of the Sisters of Charity, Mother de Ricci, asking that the Sisters be allowed to stay on until at least after the first General Chapter of the congregation, due the following September. But, despite all the appeals, the decision was adhered to.

With hindsight, it would seem that this was a logical time for the Sisters of Charity to withdraw. They had guided the young congregation through eight crucial years; now the time had come for the members to stand on their own feet and prepare for their first General Chapter. Yet, while they appreciated the logic of the situation, many of the Sisters in Cahiracon found the suddenness of the decision hard to accept. They had to be reassured that both congregations would still be bound together by bonds of friendship. Speaking on their behalf, Mother Mary Finbarr wrote a long letter to Dr O'Dwyer, subsequently published in *The Far East*, paying tribute to each of the Sisters of Charity who had given herself so devotedly to training the first members of the congregation. In concluding, she summed up how she and the little community in Cahiracon felt:

> ... And now they are gone. But I know that no vital separation has been effected. The truest mutual affection united us. Their joys and sorrows and all the interests of their Congregation will always be ours. May God keep us faithful to their magnificent spirit, and pay the debt of gratitude we owe them but could never hope ourselves to pay.[14]

It would be some weeks before the Sisters in China heard about the departure of the Sisters of Charity. When they did so, they could not but be struck by the coincidence that the Sisters of Charity had left Cahiracon on the very day that five of their own number had escaped with their lives from the hands of the Communists in Sientaochen. They would have wondered if there was a connection in God's mysterious providence between the pain experienced in Cahiracon that day and their own miraculous escape.

Their situation was still precarious. If 1930 was a difficult year, 1931 was in many ways more harrowing. From January on, the Sisters became accustomed to loud bangings on their gate during the night hours, as refugees from outlying villages harassed by bandits poured into the city. Many were given food and shelter in the convent compound. Consequently the number of people in the care of the Sisters was continually increasing. In the midst of all this there was an outbreak of smallpox and many of the catechumens were infected. The scare continued for weeks. As a precaution, a special fumigating room was added to the dispensary, and crowds were vaccinated. Those showing symptoms of infection were sent to hospital immediately. Despite all the care taken, a few young children in the catechumenate succumbed to the disease and died.

If the refugees were living in cramped quarters, so too were the Sisters. There were now nine of them living in a house built for five. Sientaochen had been an attempt to alleviate this situation, but it had failed. Then in February 1931 Bishop Galvin offered them some land beside the church to build a convent. Approval came quickly from Ireland and work began immediately. Early in April there was talk of another Communist uprising and the city prepared itself for attack. However, nothing happened. Life went on as usual in the dispensary and catechumenate, and work continued on the new convent.

On 15 April a cable came from Ireland to say that Sister Mary Patrick and Sister Mary Basil were to make their final profession on 2 June. Sister Mary Patrick's long wait was at an end. In a letter which she wrote to Father Blowick at this time she referred to the pain and uncertainty associated with the long drawn out years of waiting. 'After thirteen long years of trial and repeated crosses', she hoped to become 'an accepted member of the congregation'. She remarked again on the painful coincidence of receiving the news of not being admitted to final profession on the tenth anniversary of her call to China. 'It is only the remembrance of Our Lord's Passion and Cross that has kept me alive.'[15]

There is no surviving record as to how she felt on the actual day of her final profession, apart from references in the Hanyang Annals to the joy of both Sister Mary Basil and herself on that occasion. The annalist recorded the ceremony in some detail: Bishop Galvin received the Sisters' vows and gave the homily; the altar looked beautiful with lilies sent by the Canossian Sisters and asparagus fern and begonias from the Columban Fathers' garden;

fourteen priests were entertained to lunch. Three of the Canossian Sisters came from Hankow that afternoon and some of the Loretto Sisters came the following day to congratulate the two Sisters. The annalist noted how joyful everyone was 'because of the Sisters' joy'.

Soon afterwards the oppressive summer heat swept down on them once again, harder to endure because the convent was now uncomfortably crowded: the new convent was not yet ready. To alleviate the situation, the superior decided to send four of the community for a holiday to the mountain resort of Kuling. Sister Mary Patrick was one of the four. It was providential that she and her companions had this chance to renew themselves physically and spiritually in view of what they were to face immediately afterwards.

Even as they left for Kuling, on 16 July 1931, the Yangtze River was rising daily, though nobody could have guessed what the outcome would be or the calamity that was building up. Flood control has been a perennial problem throughout Chinese history. At different periods down through the centuries the summer rains, on top of melting glaciers from China's western mountains, have brought extensive flooding to the areas surrounding the lower reaches of China's three great rivers, the Yangtze Kiang, Huang He and Si Kiang. Rich alluvial deltas able to support vast numbers of people have been formed by these rivers, but these same rivers have at times also brought disaster. Shi Huang Di, leader of the Qin dynasty which wrested power from the warring states comprising ancient China in 221 BC, not only built the Great Wall and left us his terra-cotta army, excavated in our time, but also devised a huge irrigation system to control flooding. However, in spite of his attempts and those of his successors down through the centuries, floods can still cause havoc in Central China. This will no longer be the case when the Chinese Government has completed the Three Gorges Dam, scheduled for inauguration in 2009.

On 28 July 1931 the Yangtse burst through a vital dyke protecting the city of Hankow, and caused one of the worst natural disasters in history: the Central China Flood of 1931. Thousands

were drowned and many more left homeless. The Hanyang area
was one of the places worse affected. The water rose to fifteen feet
high in the Columban Fathers' central house in Suan. The priests
and seminarians, after trying to salvage what they could, sought
temporary refuge in the Sisters' convent which, because of its
situation, had escaped flooding. When Bishop Galvin returned
from Shanghai on 29 July he found not only Suan and its environs
but most of his vicariate inundated by water. In many places only
the roofs of houses could be seen. Dead bodies of people and cattle
floated on the vast expanse of water, and crops due for harvesting
were totally destroyed. Simon Winchester, in his book, *The River
at the Centre of the World*, refers to the devastation wrought by the
flood of 1931.

> The consequences of what the history books now record as the
> Central China Flood were staggering, the figures numbing and
> barely credible. More than 140,000 people drowned. Twenty-
> eight million people were affected – forty million by some
> estimates. Seventy thousand square miles of central China were
> submerged. Twelve million people had to migrate or leave their
> ruined homes.[16]

Bishop Galvin wrote home saying that in all his years in China
he had never seen such a terrible sight. 'From the hill at the rear of
the Mission the whole country as far as the eye can reach, is one vast
sea of water.'[17] What really broke his heart was the number of
homeless and starving people who day by day poured into the city,
looking for food and shelter. Every available building was given
over. Very soon the Sisters' catechumenate was filled to overflowing. The refugees kept coming and by 18 August the Sisters' new
convent, in which they had not yet lived, was accommodating more
than three hundred refugee women, ranging in age from grand-
mothers to infants in arms. It was a handsome three-storey house
fronted by wide verandas, never intended for the purpose to which
it was now put, and it took some measure of ingenuity to pack in
three hundred people and then feed them. At a later stage the
building housed over four hundred. Altogether the Columbans

sheltered and fed about eight hundred people, from early August 1931 until the floods began to abate in mid-October.

Financial aid came from abroad, from such diverse sources as the Holy Father and the Emperor of Japan. Public concern became more widespread after Charles Lindbergh's aerial photos of the flood-stricken areas were published. But foreign aid, even though it helped, could only touch the surface of such a calamity, because diseases of the most virulent kind came in the wake of the floods. Cholera broke out among the refugees in the new convent, and Sister Mary Patrick and Sister Mary Dolores spent most of each day looking after them. Refugees in other parts of the city also fell victims to cholera, typhoid and dysentery. The Sisters were on constant call; those without medical expertise had received a condensed course in tropical medicine from Columban Father Francis McDonald, a qualified doctor, and from Sister Mary Patrick and Sister Mary Ignatius, both of them trained nurses. Sister Mary Patrick's intensive course at the School of Tropical Medicine in London now stood her in good stead.

Many refugees had settled at a place called the Black Hill, outside the city confines. Daily two Sisters went there accompanied by two boys who carried their heavy medicine baskets. Later the boys were replaced by seminarians. Twenty-five medicine baskets were prepared each day, because the priests were also engaged in this ministry to the sick and dying refugees, both on the Black Hill and in the other refugee camps around Hanyang. The Loretto Sisters, who gave shelter to two hundred girls, also worked tirelessly among the refugees. Each evening when they returned from the different camps the priests and Sisters handed in their medicine baskets to be restocked before they set out the following day.

Getting to the Black Hill was an achievement in itself. It entailed a walk of twenty minutes before boarding a boat to get to the other side of the flood lake, then some further walking before crossing another stretch of water by a makeshift bridge consisting of a single plank – not for the faint-hearted. Sister Mary Patrick, who suffered much from her feet, found the journey particularly difficult, though she tried to make light of it. Finally the Sisters arrived at their beat: a hill, a road and a riverbank, then another hill, all swarming with refugees. To protect themselves from the elements, many of these had built crude shacks, usually no more than straw mats supported on bamboo poles. The sick were lying on the ground and often the Sisters had to crawl over various obstacles to get to them. Most of them were suffering from dysentery, but many had cholera and the Sisters also treated cases of smallpox, scarlet-fever, beri-beri and influenza.

En route to the Black Hill, crossing the flood lake by boat, the Sisters sometimes diagnosed and treated sick people whose families rowed them out from the riverbank. Often they were hailed from passing junks by boat-people anxious about sick family members. That meant climbing aboard the junk on a plank, or getting there by transferring from their own boat to a sampan. 'Then we crawl through tiny hatchways and do tightrope walking along the riggings till we reach the heart of the "mystery-ship".'[18]

The missionaries had been coping with the situation as best they could for some weeks when the Hanyang National Relief Company was set up. Father Maguire was immediately appointed to administer the Health and Sanitation Department and Father Murphy to look after food supplies. That left the Sisters free to give all their time to the sick and dying. Opportunely a Chinese doctor arrived on the scene in time to cope with a serious outbreak of cholera. Together with the priests and Sisters he began a series of anti-cholera injections. They sometimes inoculated as many as 900 people a day against cholera, typhoid and paratyphoid. The project was successful and as the floods abated so too did the cholera epidemic. It was in a spirit of gratitude that Bishop Galvin wrote home on 25 November:

> It is almost miraculous how effectively the Lord has preserved us from serious illness during all this time. When we think that the priests and Sisters, whom I mentioned, are working in the Black Hill all day with nothing but a few sandwiches to eat until their evening meal – when we think that, with one exception, all

have escaped the diseases that are rampant, we feel very grateful to God.[19]

The one exception mentioned by the Bishop was Sister Mary Ignatius, who contracted a severe case of cholera. It was Sister Mary Patrick who diagnosed her illness and insisted on getting her to hospital. Writing home a few weeks later, she said she would never forget that journey down the Yangtze. The patient had to be carried on an improvised stretcher on a narrow Chinese boat which at times looked as if it was about to capsize. They had a problem when they reached Hankow, because none of the boatmen, fearing infection, would allow them to board the barge that was essential to get them to the hospital. When they eventually reached the security of the hospital Sister Mary Patrick burst into tears: the strain was over and her much-loved Sister would recover. But Sister Mary Ignatius's long convalescence depleted by fifty per cent the nursing personnel in the community and placed an added burden on Sister Mary Patrick. A month later she too had to be hospitalised. There was nothing seriously wrong: nothing but sheer exhaustion. Smallpox had broken out again among the refugees in the catechumenate and the new convent, and she was once again involved in an intensive vaccination programme. Fortunately the epidemic was short-lived.

Meanwhile, though the floods had abated, there were still many refugees both in the city and at the Black Hill. Earlier the Bishop had purchased land for a future extension to the Sisters' catechumenate. He now decided to give it over to refugee Christian families whom the mission would house and feed. Anxious about the many people on the Black Hill, still trying to survive in spite of the weather, he also rented a house to accommodate the most destitute. Sheltering hundreds of refugees in the Sisters' new convent was intended as a temporary emergency measure only. It was now time for them to leave but, realising how difficult it would be for them to return to their own villages, many of which were now under Communist control, the Sisters decided to allow the refugees to stay on in the convent until the end of winter. This would entail further congestion in the old convent because three new Sisters were due to arrive in January.

Things began to settle down gradually. It took time and energy to cope with the aftermath of the floods. Hanyang was still sheltering many of those made homeless, and people continued to live in shacks on the Black Hill. The Sisters went out there regularly to help the sick.

The apparent peace was shattered once again when, on the evening of 30 January 1932, the Bishop came to tell the Sisters that Communist forces were approaching and that Hanyang was in danger. He slept in the convent that night, on a mattress on the floor of the chapel. The night passed peacefully, but by the following evening the situation had deteriorated so much that the Bishop sent over two of the priests to guard the convent while he and another priest kept watch from the roof of the Loretto Convent. It was another uneventful night, but the danger was increasing hourly. Once again the Columban and Loretto Sisters and the Hanyang priests had to pack up and leave for Hankow at short notice. The Canossian Sisters once more came to the rescue and allowed the Sisters to stay in some of their unused classrooms.

After a week it was obvious that Hanyang would not be attacked this time and that it was relatively safe for the missionaries to return. The Bishop and priests left for Hanyang on 6 February and four days later it was considered safe for the Sisters to return. At this stage the Bishop decided that the time had come to encourage the refugees to leave. On 20 February they began to move out of the catechumenate and over the following days they quietly left the new convent, thanking the priests and Sisters for the help that saved their lives. Some young homeless widows were allowed to stay on in the centre adjacent to the catechumenate. There they would be given food and shelter.

After the Sisters' new convent was vacated the Bishop set about getting it ready for them. He sent over one of the priests to supervise the cleaning and disinfecting needed after it had housed so many refugees for almost six months. Because illness had been rampant throughout that time it was decided to fumigate the entire building.

It would take months before the final touches would be complete and the Sisters could move in.

Meanwhile there was another outbreak of cholera. This time the Sisters were better able to cope. They now had their own equipment for giving saline intravenously. Consequently, there was no further need to send cholera patients to hospital in Hankow, which was also badly affected by the epidemic. Seven of the Hankow Canossian Sisters contracted the disease and three of them died. In Hanyang the seminarians and others who had not been inoculated previously were now inoculated.

It was a busy time: it took six Sisters to respond to all the sick calls. Cholera continued into the summer, which was exceptionally hot with the thermometer rising to 108F some days. Sister Mary Patrick was kept busy going from one case to the next, while Sister Mary Michael worked single-handed in the dispensary. At the height of the epidemic Mother Mary Agnes decided to build a shed near the dispensary where patients could be brought for treatment. That would make things easier for Sister Mary Patrick. When the Bishop heard about this plan he provided bricks so as to make a more solid building. But the cholera epidemic was on the wane by the time it was built. The following year what was known as the Cholera House became a classroom to cater for an overflow from the catechumenate.

Sister Mary Patrick wrote to Mother Mary Theophane, who was preparing to come out on visitation, asking her to bring her old crocodile leather case, if it was still in Cahiracon:

> It was fitted with a washable lining to hold medicines and would be very useful these times when two or three sets of Sisters are out in different directions … Just one more request, dear Mother, of a more spiritual nature. Would you be able to get that life of St Gertrude published by the Benedictines of Stanbrook – edited by Father Dolan, OSB. It would be such a treat for Sister Mary Gertrude – who is well worthy of her name!'[20]

Mother Mary Theophane arrived on 2 December 1932, presumably carrying with her the crocodile leather bag and the life of St

Gertrude. She was pleased to see how the Sisters' work had developed over the previous two years, despite warfare, floods, epidemics and illness. Together with Bishop Galvin she drew up plans for the new catechumenate, and listened to the Sisters' hopes for the future expansion of the mission. Dr O'Dwyer, Superior General of the Columban Fathers, had also come to China on visitation at this time and, after he and Mother Mary Theophane had finished their canonical business, they sailed for Manila on the first stage of their journey home.

The following years were a time of consolidation. Sister Mary Patrick's health seemed considerably better and she was able to carry a heavy workload. Care for the sick Sisters and priests was always her priority. 'She was in her element nursing them,' a Sister remarked. The shape of her life at this time was formed by the many sick calls that marked each day. No matter how severe the weather was, or how she was feeling, she never failed to respond to an appeal for help, no matter what its source. We hear of her visiting the destitute in their miserable huts, seeking out sick beggars, professional and otherwise, going to a Buddhist temple in the hope of weaning a Buddhist nun off opium, working on people who had taken overdoses, or swallowed hairpins or mercury to spite inconsiderate husbands. She treated all sorts of ailments: the daily quota of burns, ulcers, opium poisoning, and tuberculosis, and the fortunately rarer cases of dysentery, typhoid, cholera and smallpox. In June 1935 reference is made in the Hanyang convent diary to the fact that she had treated over twenty cases before noon, going from one house to another. Sometimes she spent the whole afternoon as well as the morning ministering to the sick. One of her constant worries at this time was how to get food to the destitute people she met on her daily sick calls. But her chief concern always was that the sick and dying would be brought the message of God's love so that they would be prepared to meet Him. She and her companions baptised countless babies and adults during those years.

The pattern of her days was once more broken when, in July 1935, the Han River and consequently the Yangtze again burst their banks and it looked as if there would be a repetition of the calamity of 1931. Fortunately the flood waters began to subside after ten days, and the strong summer sun helped to dry up the place. Even though the local papers estimated that approximately ten thousand lives had been lost in the Hanyang area, the devastation was less serious than in 1931. This time there were no refugees in Hanyang, and no places of misery and pain comparable to the Black Hill, four years earlier.

The year 1936 opened on a note of hope. The new catechumenate was finished and already had its complement of young women, sent down by priests up-country, to be trained as catechists. Three new Sisters had arrived to replace those sent to make the first foundation in Kiangsi in 1935. That in itself was cause for hope: the Columban Sisters were by now so well established that they could extend their presence in China to another mission area, Bishop Cleary's diocese of Nancheng. This was where Sister Mary Patrick's friend Father Tierney had been superior until his capture and death in Communist hands. She had set her heart on being one of the pioneers there, but God had other plans in store.

According to the Sisters' constitutions, another General Chapter of the congregation was due in September 1936. This time Sister Mary Patrick was eligible to be a delegate. However, she was not elected by her community, so together with them she submitted suggestions to the Chapter and waited eagerly to hear about the decisions made. As September drew to an end there was an air of excitement and expectancy while they watched out for the cable that would announce the names of those elected to guide the congregation through the next six years. 'I wonder who the new Mother General is!' said Sister Mary Patrick excitedly as the Superior arrived in with the cable in her hand. 'Well, you don't have to worry anyway!' was the retort of a Sister standing beside her. When the cable was read to them they learned that three members of Hanyang community had been elected to office in the congregation's administration: Sister Mary Philomena and Sister Francis Xavier were elected councillors and Sister Mary Patrick had been chosen as the new Superior General.

THIRTEEN

At the Helm

Sister Mary Patrick accepted her election to the onerous office of Superior General as God's will for her and for the congregation; there was never any question of refusing to carry this new burden. The elections had taken place on 30 September 1936, immediately after the formal opening of the General Chapter. In accordance with the constitutions Bishop Fogarty presided, assisted by Dr Michael O'Dwyer, Superior General of the Columban Fathers. The following day the Bishop wrote to Mother Mary Theophane the outgoing Superior General, authorising the Chapter to proceed with its business 'as it would be highly inconvenient to wait until confirmation of the newly elected Superior General is obtained.'[1]

Two days later, on 3 October, a cable arrived from Hanyang: 'Accept election seek ordinary's confirmation. Patrick, Xavier, Philomena.' However, the Chapter did not wait for their arrival but continued with its agenda. The major decision made was that the new Superior General, with the consent of her council, should take steps to prepare the constitutions for approval by the Holy See. In addition, several points of observance and good order were agreed upon, some of them relating to the prayer life of the Sisters and others to their daily living. Into the midst of this another cable arrived on 10 October: 'Kindly postpone final meeting anxious to discuss native sisterhood. Patrick'.

The Chapter honoured this request and adjourned until further notice. Meanwhile, Mother Mary Patrick and her two companions, Sister Francis Xavier and Sister Mary Philomena, left Shanghai on 18 November on the first stage of their long journey home. 'Sr Mary Philomena and I were terribly sad at leaving China,' she wrote to a friend. 'Sr Francis Xavier had hardly been there long enough to form attachments.' Their ship put in at Manila where Father John Heneghan, Superior of the Columban Fathers, met them and brought them to visit the Fathers' parish in Malate. It was

22 November, the feast of Our Lady of Remedies, the parish fiesta, and a carnival spirit pervaded the entire place. If they had tried to time their visit for such a joyful occasion they could not have fared better.

Evidently letters of congratulation caught up with the travellers at different ports of call, because Mother Mary Patrick wrote from Marseilles on 12 December to Mother Mary Brendan and the Silver Creek community, thanking them for 'the very kind way in which you have accepted me as your Mother. May God grant I may not be too unworthy of the confidence reposed in me. The Congregation is His, and I lean all my weakness on Him Who can do all things, knowing how He loves us.' She referred to the telegram she had sent to the Chapter asking the delegates to postpone the final session until her arrival. She explained why: soon after she had received the news of her election she had visited the Sisters' new mission in Kiangsi province, where she had met a group of dedicated young Chinese women who she believed could become associated with the congregation. In Hanyang there were also some fine young women teaching in the catechumenate who would like to become Columban Sisters. 'I am anxious to find out what the majority of our Sisters think about the matter,' she wrote. 'If we took Chinese postulants I do not think it would be advisable to send them home for the Novitiate. They can be tested just as well in China.'[2]

Eventually, on 21 December, the three travellers reached Cahiracon. They had called on Bishop Fogarty on their way through Ennis and he had confirmed Mother Mary Patrick's election as Superior General. The final meeting of the Chapter which had been postponed until her arrival, took place two days later on 23 December 1936. At this session the new Mother General put before the Chapter members a proposal to found a native Chinese sisterhood, which would be affiliated in an external way to the congregation. They agreed unanimously. Although some expressed reservations about the practical working out of the proposal, the majority were happy to leave the implementation of the matter to the Superior General and her council. The matter of an American novitiate, which had also come up at the previous Chapter, was aired again. The majority agreed to have a postulancy in the United States, but not a novitiate: American candidates would join the Irish novitiate. (Four years later this decision was to have unforeseen consequences.)

After the session of 23 December 1936, the Chapter was dissolved. The first item on the personal agenda of the new Mother General was to give some unexpected joy to the delegates who had come from a distance. Although it was almost unheard of in those days that Sisters should visit and stay with their families, she made sure that each of them had a chance to do so. She herself travelled to Foxford with Sister Mary Philomena and Sister Mary Agnes to visit Mother Mary Alphonsus, of whom the annalist of the time stated: 'Her affection for and interest in the little Congregation will never diminish I am sure – neither here nor hereafter.'[3]

In mid January 1937 Father Blowick, reponding to Mother Mary Patrick's request, came to Cahiracon to give the Sisters a triduum. This consisted of four lectures each day. 'The closing lecture was truly very touching for he gave us, with obvious emotion, a summary of the beginnings of the Society and told us that our Congregation was contemplated almost from the first – that it really originated on a certain day when he received a letter signed, Frances Moloney.' 'And,' he added, 'she is now here as your Mother General.'[4] Once again the Columban Fathers who had played an active role in the formation of the first Sisters returned to Cahiracon as spiritual directors; Father Tim Harris came regularly as well as Father Ronan McGrath.

As Mother General, Mother Mary Patrick saw that one of her priorities must be to make the congregation better known in Ireland, and she was indefatigable in her pursuit of this goal. Within weeks of her election she herself engaged in promotion work in the archdiocese of Dublin. The congregational annals record the kindness and interest with which she and her companion, Sister Frances de Sales, were received in the different schools and university halls of the archdiocese. 'But nowhere was Mother General so heartily welcomed as in her old Alma Mater, the Mater Misericordiae

Hospital where she and the little group that had gathered around her before the founding of the congregation ... were received and trained as nurses.'[5]

She addressed a convocation of women students in University College Galway, again with Sister Francis de Sales, and then went to Ballinasloe to meet a group of nurses before travelling north to visit the St Louis convents in Monaghan and Carrickmacross. Afterwards she proceeded to Belfast, in spite of heavy snow, and spoke to the nurses in the Mater Hospital. She then visited her friends in the Sacred Heart convent in Armagh before returning to Cahiracon. Up to the time when she left for the United States in May 1937 she was engaged in trying to interest people, especially young women, in the Chinese Mission. The very morning of her departure from Cobh, she made time to address the students in University College Cork and before she left Ireland she arranged that others would carry on the work in her absence.

Her purpose in going to the United States was first of all to visit the community in Silver Creek, New York where since 1930 the Sisters had been in charge of the domestic arrangements of the Columban Fathers' minor seminary. She also wanted to investigate requests for other foundations in the United States, one of which was to establish a sanatorium in San Diego, a project initially favoured but eventually not pursued. In Chicago she had an interview with the Cardinal, in the course of which she suggested that if a Chinese parish were to be formed in the archdiocese the congregation could send some Sisters. In this she was years ahead of her time. However, the Cardinal decided that the moment was not opportune. During her few months in the United States, Mother Mary Patrick made many friends who became generous benefactors to the congregation. Their help was timely because when she met Father Waldron, director of the American region of the Maynooth Mission to China, he informed her that the Society could not afford to pay the Sisters in Silver Creek for their services. If Sisters were sent to work for him in the offices in Omaha, they would be paid. Mother Mary Patrick declined that offer because of numbers.

She arrived back in Ireland in July 1937, after attending an international nurses' congress in London on the way home. In her absence a request had come for the Columban Sisters to take over a school in Shanghai for the children of White Russians in exile. The Cardinal Prefect of Propaganda Fide had written to her about the matter, saying how much the Holy Father had the work at heart, and how he hoped that any Sisters assigned to that work would eventually adopt the Slav-Byzantine rite, so as to be better able to work towards the reunion of the Churches. Mother Mary Patrick and her council found the proposition attractive, especially when it had come as a direct request from the Holy See. They were informed that a school was already in existence and that the proprietor, Miss Brennan, an Irishwoman, was anxious to hand it over. There would be no problem about staffing such a school because at this stage there were some highly qualified teachers in the congregation. Another factor which would have been consid- ered was the benefit which would accrue to the Sisters in China from having a house in Shanghai. Having weighed all aspects of the proposal, Mother Mary Patrick decided to accede to the request, and Sister Francis de Sales and Sister Catherine Labouré were assigned to the new mission. Sisters from Hanyang and Kiangsi would join them.

The Shanghai foundation was made in 1938 and the school, called Sancta Sophia, carried on a highly successful ministry until 1949 when the majority of White Russian exiles fled from the rapidly advancing Red Army. The Sisters teaching in Sancta Sophia adopted the Slav-Byzantine rite followed by the students and their parents. Shanghai with its many foreign concessions was a very beautiful city in those years when the Sancta Sophia School flourished; it was regarded as 'the Paris of China', 'the Queen of the Orient'.[6] Moreover, because of its international character, it was a relatively safe place where the Sisters from Hanyang and Nancheng could stay in times of political upheaval, or when they needed a well-earned rest.

On 20 June 1938, writing to Mother Mary Dolores in Hanyang, Mother Mary Patrick spoke about the need to extend the scope of the constitutions, as Dr O'Dwyer the Superior General of the Maynooth Mission to China had recommended. She quoted from him:

> Now I know the value and the worth of your Congregation, I know also the necessity of an outlet if the congregation is to flourish. I do not see that our missions can supply that outlet. I think therefore that your Congregation should seek an outlet, preferably in other pagan missions and, if this is not possible, on work like that proposed in the San Diego project. In that case your Congregation should get its Constitutions extended.[7]

At the time pressure was being put on Mother Mary Patrick to provide Sisters to staff a school in San Diego, chiefly for Mexicans 'from across the border'. Dr O'Dwyer pointed out that this would not be in accordance with the Sisters' constitutions which specified that the Sisters would work in conjunction with the priests of the Maynooth Mission to China, in their mission areas. This was why he advised widening the scope of their constitutions, as Mother Mary Patrick had herself suggested years earlier in the first drafts of her provisional rule. In her letter to Mother Mary Dolores, Mother Mary Patrick asked her to explain the situation to the Sisters.

> In telling the Sisters about this, be sure to make it clear that our being authorised to accept work on other missions, which may be a matter of absolute necessity if our numbers grow as they seem to be at present, does not mean our putting the Society in a secondary place. It must always be our first care and allegiance to meet all the wishes and requirements of the Fathers of St Columban and to co-operate with them as we have hitherto done to the very best of our ability. The priests seem to think it will be better for our Congregation to be more responsible for its own finances than it has been ... I can quite see that once we have made a good beginning in that way, we should be able to raise funds somewhat on the same lines as other congregations have done.[8]

However, the next foundation Mother Mary Patrick was involved in was in the Columban Fathers' well-established mission in the Philippines. Bishop Madriaga of the diocese of Lingayen had invited the Sisters to his diocese and on 8 December 1938 she and her council decided to accept the invitation. The Bishop already had Columban Fathers working in his diocese and he had heard of the Sisters through them.

Meanwhile, Bishop Fogarty had given his approval for the opening of a secondary school in Cahiracon for boarders and day-pupils. This was a providential decision made shortly before the outbreak of war when it would become impossible for Sisters to travel to the East and when even local travel would become problematic. The school in Cahiracon proved to be a blessing to many parents over a wide radius, by providing a good education which did not involve distant travel. It also gave scope and further training to Sisters with teaching qualifications whom the war situation held back from the missions.

The school in Cahiracon was particularly welcome to the people of Kildysart and the neighbouring area. From the earliest days of the congregation when Sister Joseph Conception used to bring the young Sisters with her to visit the neighbours, especially those sick or in trouble of any kind, a warm relationship existed between the Sisters and the people of the locality. It was taken for granted also that those who worked in the convent or on the farm were all part of the extended family. Thus when Michael Malone the gardener noticed that his foster-child John Haugh was showing some artistic talent, he spoke about him to Mother Mary Patrick and told her about the statue of the Sacred Heart which John was carving from a piece of driftwood a neighbour had picked up on the beach. Using a small saw, pen-knives and some used safety razors which he had collected from the neighbours, John whittled away on the wood until the statue took shape. When it was finished he showed it to Mother Mary Patrick. Her own earlier training in art helped her to recognise how gifted the young boy was. She asked him to leave the statue with her for a few days. In due course he discovered that she had brought the carving to a meeting of the County Council in

Ennis, asking that the boy be given an opportunity to study wood-carving. A fortnight later, Clare County Council awarded him a scholarship to the Benedictine School of Arts and Crafts at Glenstal Abbey. The scholarship was for five years and included cabinet-making, design, wood-carving and general education.

This happened in 1937 when County Council scholarships were exceedingly rare, especially scholarships to study art. In 1946, after John had completed his studies in Glenstal, the Abbot and Benedictine community awarded him a further two-year scholarship to the École des Métiers d'Art in their abbey in Maredsous, Belgium. After completing the course, he returned to Ireland where he was commissioned to carve the Stations of the Cross for the chapel in Dublin Castle. In the years since then he has carved many other sets of stations and many beautiful statues; work of his may be seen in several churches and colleges, here in Ireland and further afield in England, Australia, Africa and the United States. Although over the years he has accepted other commissions, he has focussed almost exclusively on religious art. Work of his has been shown regularly at the annual exhibition of the Royal Irish Academy. It is now sixty years since Mother Mary Patrick recognised that remarkable talent, and John Haugh often recalls his indebtedness to her and to the Columban Sisters in the Cahiracon of his day. 'She was a great person, who has given me the greatest chance of my life. She recognised the artistic possibility of my effort, and with great kindness, gained for me the means to achieve and develop that craft.'[9]

War broke out in Europe on 3 September 1939. One of its consequences was that it became practically impossible to communicate with the Sisters in China and the Philippines. Because of her anxiety for their safety and health, Mother Mary Patrick decided to travel to the East even though Bishop Fogarty had some misgivings. She left Ireland on 29 October 1939 and spent Christmas in the Philippines before proceeding to China. Happy at the progress she could see in the three mission areas, she began her return journey from Manila on 22 June 1940. Accompanying her was Sister Mary Vianney, who for medical reasons was re-assigned to the United States where Mother Mary Patrick planned to spend a few months before returning to Ireland.

She visited some of the big cities in the United States, in the hope of raising much-needed funds for the congregation. 'It is uphill work,' she wrote to a friend, 'and I would sooner be going round the lanes of Hanyang with the medicine bag. But that is not God's will.' Her hectic schedule took its toll, and in October 1940 she had to spend five days in hospital because of high blood pressure. The war situation in Europe was worsening and she realised that it was important to get back to the motherhouse as soon as possible. But by this stage it was almost impossible to book a passage back to Europe: most of the ships on the north Atlantic route had been commandeered to carry armaments for the war zone. Finally, at short notice, through a family contact in the British Admiralty, she was able to procure accommodation on the *Western Prince*, a large (10,926-ton) British liner bound for England.

It happened that Ellen Muldoon, a young Irishwoman who had completed her postulancy in the Silver Creek community, was waiting to come to Ireland to do her novitiate; at that time, the only novitiate in the congregation was in Ireland. Mother Mary Patrick warned her of the dangers of the journey, telling her that seventeen ships had been sunk in the Atlantic the previous week, but Ellen replied that she had decided to face the danger rather than wait indefinitely. Moreover, her mother had given her whole-hearted consent. Mother Mary Patrick's face lit up; she had spent the previous night in prayer, asking God to guide Ellen according to his will. She now felt at peace.

They left New York on 6 December 1940 on what Mother Mary Patrick called the most beautiful ship she had ever travelled on, and she had known several. It catered for only one class of passenger: first-class. The saloon was furnished like an English stately home, and she was delighted to see over the mantelpiece a large reproduction of Fra Angelico's fresco of two Dominicans welcoming Christ in the person of a guest; she had often admired the original in St Mark's in Florence.

Among the Sisters' fellow-passengers were some English families returning home, a British vice-admiral, an eminent constitutional lawyer, and a well-known correspondent of *The Manchester Guardian*. Also on board was George Catlin, husband of Vera Brittain, of *The Testament of War* fame and father of the present-day British politician Shirley Williams. An economist, he had been lecturing at Kansas City University as had been his practice for some time for part of every year; he had also been lobbying on behalf of the British government for destroyers to help the war effort. (How his wife, Vera Brittain, a dedicated pacifist, accepted this we do not know.) George Catlin recalled many years later in his published memoirs that the decks of the *Western Prince* were covered with planes, intended for the British forces.[10] A high-powered delegation of Canadian officials, on business connected with the supply of munitions, was also on board. The leader was the Hon. C.D. Howe, Canadian Minister of Munitions and Supplies. With him were the Canadian Director-General of Munitions Production and other officials of that department.

The *Western Prince* had air surveillance as far as mid-Atlantic and everything seemed to be going smoothly for both passengers and crew. Mother Mary Patrick and her companion settled down to enjoy the journey as best they could. They prayed community prayers together as if they were at home in their own convent, and they talked much. Mother Mary Patrick was trying to set Ellen's mind at rest and she shared with her many stories about her own novitiate, telling her what she had found hardest. Years later Ellen said that even then, as a young woman, she was deeply impressed by Mother Mary Patrick's faith. She was struck by the conviction with which she said: 'God never makes a fool of anybody!' and 'All our happiness lies in the interior life.' 'It struck me then that she knew God in a way I did not, she seemed to be at ease with Him.'[11]

Ellen, Mother Mary Patrick's junior by more than forty years, also felt at ease with her. She enjoyed her older companion's sense of the ridiculous, which could break out in unexpected ways. As the only young person on board, and the only unattached female, Ellen attracted plenty of male attention. One of the ship's stewards, in particular, started to pay her considerable notice, which Ellen found embarrassing: she had turned her face to a different kind of life and moreover the man seemed old and was decidedly not handsome. One day he met her on the deck alone and invited her to go dancing with him that evening. Not taking no for an answer, he came along during dinner that night to ask if he could take 'the young damsel' dancing. Mother Mary Patrick, seeing Ellen's discomfiture, froze him in his tracks. Looking severely at him, she said in her best *grande dame* accent: 'Sisters don't dance!' The unlucky man left in some bewilderment and she laughed heartily, telling Ellen that she would not be bothered by him again. Neither of them could have foreseen that they would soon meet the same gentleman again, under very different circumstances.

On 13 December when they were about two hundred miles off the coast of Iceland, and four hundred miles west of Scotland, a special gala dinner followed by a dance marked the beginning of the Christmas festivities. The two Sisters retired earlier than the others. Mother Mary Patrick had been talking to the captain that evening and he had spoken about the ever-present danger of submarines. Consequently she decided that it would be wiser for Ellen and herself to sleep partially dressed. To be ready for an emergency, which they hoped would not happen, they packed two small linen bags with a change of clothing; that would be as much as they would be allowed in a lifeboat. In one of the bags Mother Mary Patrick put a small flask of brandy and in the other a heavy-duty torch which she had already used in the London blackout the previous year. For the first time they left the light on in their tiny bathroom. Then, having said their prayers, they fell asleep.[12]

At 5.45 a.m. they were thrown out of their bunks by the force of a violent impact: the ship had been torpedoed. Mother Mary Patrick told Ellen not to be afraid, that God and his Blessed Mother were with them. They hurried into their habits and veils, and seized their cloaks and shawls and the two little linen bags they had prepared the previous night for just such an emergency. Pulling on their life-belts they hurried to the lifeboat station on deck. When nothing seemed to be happening, Ellen ran back to the cabin for her watch and holy-water bottle. When she returned, her anxious companion

was about to scold her when there was a call for the passengers of
No 5 lifeboat. The two Sisters were picked up bodily and thrown
in. Just before the boat was lowered, Ellen's would-be admirer
jumped into the boat, and then hurried out again, returning with a
blanket for Ellen who was shivering with cold and shock. 'He
risked his life for his lady love!' commented Mother Mary Patrick
dryly.

The six lifeboats were lowered into a heavy sea. Only one of
them had a motor; the others were dependent on what seemed
rather flimsy oars. It was not yet dawn. Looking up, Mother Mary
Patrick saw the morning star and was reminded of Mary, the
Mother of God. This verse ran through her head: 'The hour before
the dawning/ The darkest of the night/ One star in all its beauty/
Floods with its golden light/ ... When o'er life's treacherous ocean/
Fierce storm winds swept at night/ Never pilot sought the Pole Star/
as we thy guiding light.' She felt the Mother of God near to her as
never before.

It was bitterly cold and the water was washing over us, and the
little Sister was shivering with cramp. The sailors tried to keep
their hearts up by swearing and joking. Then after a time, I
ventured to suggest it would be well to say a prayer, for only God
could save us. I started the Our Father and many of them joined
in. Afterwards some of the men came and said what a comfort
it had been to them. We then sang hymns to Our Lady, the Ave
Maris Stella and Hail Queen of Heaven.[13]

Forty-five minutes after the first explosion the German submarine fired a second torpedo. On the bridge of the *Western Prince* the
captain blew three blasts of farewell as the ship sank slowly before
their eyes. Meanwhile Ellen had seen German helmets when the
submarine surfaced briefly, and her concern now was that the
survivors would be shot. Mother Mary Patrick assured her that this
would not happen, that, in a sense, they were prisoners of war. The
submarine, like the ship, vanished. 'And then, nothing in view but
the gloomy dawn horizon and the little boats with their crowded
cargo, the waves, with a cold wind. And it began to sleet.'[14]

High waves on the horizon sometimes raised false hopes of ships coming their way. However, they knew that a speedy rescue was unlikely: merchant ships had their orders to steer clear of waters where submarines had been sighted, and only some of the lifeboats were equipped to send out SOS signals. It was these weak radio signals that were eventually picked up by a small Scottish collier, travelling with its cargo from Glasgow to New York. When the lifeboat crews realised that it really was a ship on the horizon, not a wave, and that it seemed to be moving away from them, they rowed as fast as they could and two hours later reached the rescue ship. To their relief they discovered that it was British. Mother Mary Patrick used to laugh in later years at the alacrity with which she and her fellow-passengers all claimed to be British, although in the passenger manifesto she had listed herself as being from Co. Monaghan!

The only way to get aboard the rescue ship was by means of a rope ladder. As the youngest person there, Ellen Muldoon was urged to be the first to climb. Scared of the high waves, she refused at first but finally agreed to have a rope tied around her and to be hoisted out over the choppy sea. Mother Mary Patrick was hauled up in a coal basket. Her fellow-passengers teased her afterwards, saying that nothing could be seen of the Mother Superior but two little feet dangling over the edge.

Welcome hot drinks awaited them as soon as they got on deck, but with so many extra people on board what was a small boat, space was at a premium. They had to take turns lying down. The ship carried sufficient food for its own crew, but not enough to cope adequately with 152 extra people, cold and hungry after nine frightening hours in open boats. The galley contained only two saucepans. Yet, nobody complained: merely to be alive and safe was enough. They knew that one of the six lifeboats had sunk at the point of being rescued. It was the best equipped of the boats, the only one with a motor, a cabin and a radio; at the lifeboat station many of the passengers had cast envious eyes on those allocated to it. But just as it approached the collier it was overturned by a high wave and a rush of water from the scuppers. Some of the passengers were able to swim to safety but those in the cabin were lost, including a prominent Canadian official, C.D. Howe's financial adviser and friend, the Hon. Gordon W. Scott. Altogether it was estimated that eighteen people lost their lives in the incident, including a young honeymoon couple who had gone back to their cabin to salvage some of their wedding presents. Because of censorship restrictions the number of those lost may have been played down in the reports released to the media.

Some of the rescued were suffering from shock and a few had to be treated for injuries. One man had to have his leg amputated. After a day on the rescue boat, Mother Mary Patrick became seriously ill and Ellen was afraid that she was about to die. However, after a day she rallied. Then they had another scare: they were warned that an enemy submarine was in the vicinity. Accordingly, on a bitterly cold December evening the captain ordered all the passengers on deck and informed them that if the ship was hit by a torpedo they were to jump into the sea. There they would be picked up by the convoy which had hurried to their aid on orders of the British Admiralty; before the captain of the *Western Prince* had gone down with his ship, he had radioed England for help. It was of vital importance to the war effort to ensure the safety of the important Canadian and British officials on board.

Ellen Muldoon remembers that for a second time they felt a frightening impact. On this occasion, however, it was not from a torpedo but from the reverberation when a nearby British destroyer sent a depth charge into the submarine before it could attack. The impact was so great that Ellen wondered why some of the passengers had not jumped into the sea! Once again she marvelled at Mother Mary Patrick's fortitude. 'One virtue I would say she had to a very high degree and that was fortitude and confidence in God. Those were her two really strong points: confidence in God and fortitude. That she could endure and that she helped me to endure.'[15]

Eventually, after three and a half days, they sighted the Hebrides in the distance and before long they were into the Clyde. The British vice-admiral and the Canadian officials with George Catlin disembarked at Gourock. The rest of the passengers got off at Glasgow. Mother Mary Patrick believed that it augured well that they landed on 18 December, feast of Our Lady's Expectation, Our Lady of Good Hope. She and her companion managed to avoid the reporters and photographers waiting to interview the survivors, also the banquet prepared for them. Their one concern now was to get home in time for Christmas. It was C.D. Howe who provided the information sought by the journalists, and who was quoted in the Irish newspapers over the following days. Strict censorship control meant that the British papers carried less extensive coverage.

The Sisters spent their first day on dry land getting passports and travel documents, and the following day took the boat to Belfast. On the way to the boat Mother Mary Patrick decided to go to confession – as if being through a shipwreck was not penance enough, remarked Ellen. After some searching they succeeded in finding a Catholic church and a priest who initially looked with much suspicion on these two strange women, one of them dressed in a colourful Chinese robe and the other in a well-worn sea captain's coat. In no way did they resemble the Columban Sisters whose pictures he had seen in *The Far East*. After hearing their confessions he believed them, and could not do enough to help.

They finally arrived in Dublin, 'like two bedraggled sea birds', and on Friday evening 20 December they reached Cahiracon. All the Sisters were assembled at the hall door to welcome them home. Four days later Mother Mary Patrick wrote a letter to all the houses of the congregation. 'It is an indescribable joy to find myself once more in this peaceful abode,' she wrote. 'It is like a beautiful dream come true and I cannot thank God enough for having spared me yet a while longer to work for Him. Pray for me, dear Sisters, that the remainder of my life, however short it may be, will be filled with God's love and His work.'[16]

Sir George Catlin in his autobiography, *For God's Sake, Go!*, written over thirty years later, described the whole incident in detail. In view of the fact that his 'prized diary' was the only object apart from his passport which he seized as he left his cabin on the ill-fated *Western Prince*, we can expect that his memoirs were based on diary records and that they are authentic. He wrote that, as a result of seeing a highly competent captain go down with his ship, he sent a petition to the Admiralty, requesting that captains be instructed to leave sinking ships rather than go down with them. Later, in the early 1970s, his opinion was reinforced when he succeeded in tracing the captain of the submarine responsible for the sinking of the *Western Prince*. For years he had wanted to express his appreciation of the submarine captain's humanity in waiting for three-quarters of an hour to fire the second torpedo which sank the doomed ship. Such a delay was contrary to orders and involved some risk to him and his crew, but it meant that the survivors escaped with their lives. The submarine captain replied to his letter, saying: 'I remember exactly the *Western Prince*. I observed the lifeboats lowered and separating in the twilight.' He was happy to know that so many of the passengers and crew were saved and he too regretted the captain's death.[17]

On her return to Cahiracon after the ordeal of the shipwreck, Mother Mary Patrick was happy to see some new faces in the novitiate which now numbered seventeen novices and seven postulants. However, the ongoing war caused her some practical problems. There were shortages of basic foods: tea, coffee and white flour were almost unobtainable, although having their own farm produce meant that nobody need go hungry. The financial situation of the congregation was also an anxiety; the Sisters knew that they could always count on the generosity of the Society of St Columban, but they were aiming at becoming financially independent. Mother Mary Patrick had been successful in her efforts to collect money in the United States and was personally carrying some hundreds of dollars on her at the time of the shipwreck. The notes survived the high seas, wet but intact. The bulk of what she had collected had been placed in a fund in the United States. A thousand dollars were sent to the Philippines to acquire a school in Ozamis. Later, when the Japanese invasion was imminent, some further money was sent for the support of the Sisters in that mission.

Money could be transferred to the missions but not personnel, at least not until travel should become safer. Mother Mary Patrick accepted the enforced delay as an opportunity to have Sisters trained professionally for their future missions. On 18 June 1942 the congregation purchased 56 Merrion Square as a house for student Sisters. In October of that year, with a view to seeking papal approval for the congregation, Mother Mary Patrick asked the Columban Fathers to transfer legal ownership of Cahiracon House and estate to the congregation. (It had been given to them for their use in 1927.) The Society of St Columban was amenable to the request and Dr O'Dwyer applied to Rome to make the necessary transfer.

Earlier that year the Japanese had taken Manila and communication with the Philippines was cut off for almost three years, except for the very rare letters that were smuggled out by U.S. servicemen. One of Mother Mary Patrick's greatest anxieties in the years 1942 to 1945 was the safety of the Sisters in this mission. Finally, in the summer of 1945 the war in the East came to an end, and Bishop Fogarty fixed 29 September of the following year as the date for the opening of the next General Chapter – which had been postponed from 1942 because of the war.

On 27 September 1945, an interesting letter reached the motherhouse: a request from Cardinal Mooney of Detroit for one or two Sisters to direct the novitiate of a proposed new missionary congregation for Japan. After much discussion Mother Mary Patrick decided to accede to the request, and appointed Sister Mary Carmel Pryer, who had been released from internment camp in Shanghai, to supervise the new project. She had been one of the first novice directresses in the congregation. A much-loved person, she helped to form the new congregation, the Missionary Sisters of St Francis Xavier, until her premature death in 1952.

The Detroit project and a foundation in Burma were among Mother Mary Patrick's last major initiatives as Superior General. On 22 October 1945 she acceded to a request from Columban Monsignor Patrick Usher, Prefect Apostolic of the Prefecture of Bhamo in Upper Burma, that Sisters be sent to the Columban Fathers' mission there. The remaining months of her term of office were spent in preparing for the General Chapter. Much of her effort

went into the revision of the constitutions. On 10 July 1946 she
wrote to Mother Augustine of the Holy Rosary Sisters, asking if
she could borrow a copy of the Roman *Normae* relating to the
revision of constitutions. Her own copy given her by the late Father
Louis Nolan OP had gone down with the *Western Prince*, and she
was of the opinion that the Chapter members might like to refer to
this document. She asked the Holy Rosary Sisters' prayers for
God's blessing on the Chapter, adding, 'I am looking forward to
laying down my heavy charge and am confident that a new era of
progress for the Glory of God is before us.'

It had been a heavy burden for a woman no longer young, and
never robust. Those ten years as Superior General had been busy
ones, complicated by the fact of war and the congregation's limited
resources. Yet she carried the burden bravely. Her successor
Mother Mary Vianney always said that she had never met a more
heroic soul. It was this inner strength which had carried her through
those ten action-filled years. No matter how disturbing the situation she never lost her conviction that the work was God's and that
He would see it through. Back in December 1918, she had been so
impressed by Bishop O'Dea's advice that 'we must plant deep that
the spirit may be lasting,' that she had quoted his words to Father
Blowick. She herself planted deep. On the ill-fated *Western Prince*
she had told Ellen Muldoon that 'All our happiness lies in the
interior life.'

She tried to make that happiness a reality for the Sisters in every
possible way. For that reason she appointed as novice mistress a
truly contemplative soul, Sister Mary Philomena. She also ensured
that retreat masters and confessors, and solid spiritual reading,
were available to help the Sisters grow spiritually. Even in small
ways she tried to keep alive 'that longing for God which is at the
foundation of all religion'. One way was through celebration. She
loved to celebrate congregational feast-days, also Sisters' personal
feasts. Some Sisters still treasure cards she painted on the occasion
of their profession, or for some feast-day. At Christmas and Easter
and on the feast of St Thérèse, Patroness of the Missions, she
painted a card for each Sister in the community, each card with a

different inspirational quotation.

She kept in constant contact with the Sisters throughout the congregation through letters and occasional spiritual conferences. Shortly after she took office as Superior General she sent her first conference to the members of the congregation at home and abroad. It echoed some of the dreams she had for the Sisters, which she had expressed nineteen years earlier in her provisional rule: zeal for souls, love of the Church, devotion to Jesus in the Blessed Sacrament, and to Our Lady, hospitality in the spirit of the early Irish Saints. But above and before everything else came charity, especially towards one another. 'Fraternal charity is the distinguishing mark of the Mission [i.e. the Maynooth Mission to China], and I like to think that it is in our Little Congregation to a very marked degree.' Before sending out her first conference she showed it to Father Blowick for his opinion. He replied on 26 January 1937: 'I have read your conference notes carefully and every word of them is good. If the spirit of that address can be infused into the congregation it will do an immense amount of good.'[18]

In her conferences as Superior General she showed an great reverence for the vows of religious life, for their spirit as well as their practice. She instanced different ways in which the Sisters could practise poverty in their clothing, means of travel, furnishing of houses, but she told them not to stint on food because this could affect the Sisters' health. She added, 'Economy should not degenerate into meanness.' There was nothing to be improved on in their chapels or sacristies, but they could be a little more generous with flowers when they had them. 'It is but returning His own gifts to the Creator of all beauty.' She encouraged the Sisters to write to their relatives and friends and spoke of the family spirit she would like to see in every convent. It was in such an atmosphere that charity and obedience could blossom. Her appreciation of the sacredness of vowed chastity may have caused her, in the eyes of some, to be over-protective of the young Sisters. In this she was expressing the attitude of her generation, as well as her own upbringing and her experience of life in colonial society.

She often spoke of the cordial relationships that should exist also with Sisters of other congregations. 'Maybe we have something to learn from their charity and hospitality.' Both at home and on the missions, she wrote, they should be prepared for those times when life might seem bleak and desolate. Speaking out of her own past experience, she wrote:

> Feelings of weariness and disgust are apt to arise everywhere. We all suffer from it at times. It is not sinful, if we do not yield to it by giving way to discouragement and melancholy. The best remedy I have found is to cultivate a spirit of gratitude for our vocation, which is the highest privilege God could possibly confer on anyone. But we are not disembodied spirits, so we also need relaxation at times. I rely on Superiors to see to this.[19]

In her conferences to the Sisters, she often quoted from the works of Abbot Marmion whose Trinitarian vision was similar to that of Father Blowick. And she often referred to St Teresa. 'The great St Teresa said she had to exercise all her self-control not to be peevish with her Sisters at times.' There was the occasional flash of humour, as in remarks like the following: 'Bishop Ullathorne said that if there was any community where no one caused annoyance, the Reverend Mother should sell her best cow to purchase one!' However, there was one habit that she found hard to tolerate, and that was negative criticism of any kind. Both in her conferences and in her day-to-day dealings with Sisters she could come down heavily on this. Other failings she could overlook with compassion and understanding. She was too big a person to keep a tally of a person's faults – there was nothing small or petty about her – so, if she did correct someone, that was the end of it; it was immediately forgotten.

By the time the General Chapter of 1946 was convened, Mother Mary Patrick was in her seventies and not in good health; she would have surgery for cancer later that year. Yet she was elected on the first count to be Vicar General to the new Superior General, Mother Mary Vianney. She accompanied Mother Mary Vianney to Rome in April 1947 to seek approval for the new constitutions. In Rome her friendships of earlier years stood her in good stead. Cardinal Canali, who as a young priest had often visited Sir Alfred and Lady Moloney in their apartment in Rome, welcomed the Sisters graciously and helped to expedite their business. It was a great joy to Mother Mary Patrick to have the new constitutions finally approved by the Holy See.

Another joy of that period was a visit in 1950 to Luxeuil in France to honour St Columban, patron of the congregation as well as of the Society of St Columban. Even though she was in the late seventies at the time, she worked tirelessly to organise this pilgrimage of the European Friends of St Columban. Cahiracon became the centre for the secretariat and she looked after the extensive correspondence entailed. She and Sister Mary Annunciata were among the more than twenty thousand participants who attended the celebrations. Archbishop Angelo Roncalli, then Papal Nuncio to France (later Pope John XXIII) honoured the celebrations with his presence, as also did Taoiseach John A. Costello, Minister of External Affairs Seán McBride and Eamon de Valera, leader of the Opposition. Mother Mary Patrick brought home with her a small plaster reproduction of Claude Grange's dramatic statue of St Columban, sculpted specially for the occasion, together with a deeper desire than ever to see St Columban honoured in the general Roman calendar.

In her years as Vicar General, Mother Mary Patrick was responsible for one final initiative of vital importance to the congregation: a missionary magazine called *Star of the East*. Its purpose was to make the congregation better known and to encourage vocations and benefactors. She had honed her writing skills many years earlier as society columnist for *The Lady* and *The Gentlewoman*, and she evidently enjoyed being engaged in similar work again, this time recounting mission news rather than society functions. She designated recently professed Sister Carmel Mongey as her sub-editor, and Carmel helped to carry some of the burden involved in producing a magazine. Letters from Sisters in the different missions were their main source of material. Other input was commissioned. Knowing that many readers relish a story of romance, especially one carried forward from one issue to the next, Mother Mary Patrick got friends of hers to produce some for the magazine. She remembered too that the women's magazines to which she had contributed, so many years earlier, usually had household hints and recipes. Consequently, she incorporated similar material in the early issues of *Star of the East*. Not noted for her housekeeping skills, she occasionally took liberties with recipes, on one occasion lopping off some of the ingredients for a Christmas cake when she needed the space for something she considered more important! Over the years the magazine acquired its own devoted clientele and it continued its mission until 1972, when it became incorporated into *The Far East* magazine.

Mother Mary Patrick's years as Vicar General to Mother Mary Vianney came to an end at the General Chapter of July 1952. In October of 1953 she accompanied Mother Mary Dolorosa, one of the general councillors, to a conference of religious superiors in London. However, the real purpose of the visit was to see her nephew Michael Chevers who was gravely ill. She was staying with her niece Aylish when word came that he might not live till evening, and they hurried to Reigate to be at his side. Mother Mary Patrick was able to prevail on him to make his peace with God, reminding him of how she had held him in her arms when he was baptised. She arranged for a Jesuit to come by taxi from Farm Street, when he refused to see any of the local clergy, and Michael died in peace some weeks later. While visiting him she met her nieces Frieda and Bobbie, Michael's sisters, who had come to say goodbye. Her stepdaughter Gladys came up from Hampshire to meet her and together they spent the afternoon with her godchild, Sir John Tyrwhitt and his family.[20]

She returned home, at peace about her nephew and happy to have met so many of those dear to her. Henceforward she would not be able to visit them, but they would visit her and she could devote her time to enjoying the peace of Cahiracon, working on the magazine and welcoming the friends whose presence meant so much to her. Family members continued to visit her, bringing her great joy. Among them was her stepdaughter Gladys with her family, her niece Aylish, her much-loved grandnephews: Kevin and Terence Fane-Saunders, Seán Smith and, later, Max and Michael Chevers, on holidays from Clongowes. Meanwhile, her health had begun to deteriorate. In 1957, when the motherhouse was transferred from Cahiracon to Magheramore, she asked to stay on in Cahiracon, a place so full of memories for her, for what she knew could be at best a matter of a few more years. As an *ex officio* member she attended the General Chapter of 1958, held in Magheramore. The day it ended she returned again to Cahiracon, the cradle of the congregation.

FOURTEEN

Journey's End

Mother Mary Patrick's last public involvement in the affairs of the congregation was her presence at the General Chapter of 1958, the first Chapter to be held in the new motherhouse in Co. Wicklow. The very afternoon it ended she set forth on the return journey to her beloved Cahiracon, still a busy place even though the generalate and a flourishing novitiate had transferred to Magheramore. A small knitting industry which had been started some years earlier had been given a fresh impetus when new machines were donated. The purpose of this knitwear business was to give employment to local girls so that they would not be forced to emigrate. From a small beginning with two workers it now employed sixteen. Mother Mary Patrick was pleased to see this small industry flourishing: she appreciated the employment it gave locally while also realising that the more successful it became the less danger there would be of the congregation withdrawing from Cahiracon.[1]

The year 1958 to 1959 was a lonely year for her in some respects. After being the heart of the congregation down through the years since its beginning, the Cahiracon community now found itself on the fringe. Moreover, Mother Mary Patrick's increasing physical infirmities made travel difficult; she was now obliged to forego visits to Dublin to see her family and friends. However she kept in touch with them by letter. On 17 November 1958 she wrote to her much-loved niece Frieda, sharing her own experience of journalism and encouraging her to become similarly involved. She told her about the knitting industry and the problem faced by the community in maintaining the farm. 'But God never fails us and we can always trust in His Providence.' She had taken out her paintbrushes again. 'I am trying to catch the autumn tints in watercolour for the Sale of Work. I am hoping to go to Dublin for it, as it is a good opportunity to see Michael and Max [her grandnephews]. Father Rector very kindly lets them loose for the occasion.'

Even though her health was deteriorating, she managed to live a full life as long as she was physically able. She took her daily walk, weather permitting, in the grounds she had come to love so much: she had always been a believer in fresh air and exercise for herself and for others. She could be seen making her way along the tree-lined path to the shrine of Our Lady of the Woods, as straight-backed as ever though now carrying a stick, limping slightly as a result of a broken hip sustained some years earlier.

Several of those closest to her throughout her long life had died in recent years: her beloved sister, Freddie in 1950, and her nephew Michael in 1954. Her faithful friend over many years, Sister Joseph Conception, had gone to God in 1953. Bishop Fogarty, so closely associated with the beginnings of the congregation, died in 1955, and the following year Bishop Edward Galvin, her friend of Hanyang days. Two years later in October 1958 Monsignor Patrick Usher died; in her years as Superior General he had initiated the Sisters' foundation in Upper Burma. A few days earlier news had come of the death of Pope Pius XII who had approved the constitutions of the Columban Sisters back in 1947. She had many memories, happy and sad, to treasure on those solitary walks to the shrine of Our Lady of the Woods.

Gradually she had to depend on others to look after many of her personal needs. Sisters who looked after her room and saw to her fire recall how graciously she accepted even the smallest act of service. Gratitude had always been one of her outstanding characteristics. Out of a sense of poverty she sometimes demurred if she felt that her fire was banked too high.

In January 1959 she had an attack of shingles that lasted some weeks. She had barely recovered when on the evening of 20 February she suffered a serious stroke which left her paralysed on her left side. Her speech and vision were impaired, yet she could recognise people who stood close to her and make attempts to speak. She was given the Last Sacraments and seemed fully aware of what was happening. The doctor believed that she could last one or two days at most.

As death appeared imminent, Mother Mary Gemma Shelley,

elected Superior General the previous summer, went to Cahiracon
with her councillors. However, by 24 February, Mother Mary
Patrick had rallied so much that they returned to Magheramore.
Years earlier, as a schoolgirl in Brighton when her family had been
called to what was thought to be her deathbed she had announced
emphatically that she was not dying. So now, she was equally
insistent that God was not yet calling her home. One member of the
General Council, Sister Mary Dolorosa Ryan, stayed behind to
help the local Superior, Sister Mary Pauline. It was obvious that the
stroke had affected Mother Mary Patrick's already precarious
health and that from now on she was living on borrowed time.

It became a matter of some urgency to have the new cemetery
in Magheramore properly enclosed and blessed. This was done. A
new catafalque was purchased and all the requisites for a solemn
Requiem Mass. Before Mother Mary Patrick had become ill the
new Superior General, Mother Mary Gemma, had made plans to
visit the different missions of the congregation in the spring of
1959. It was important that she should fulfil this commitment.
Consequently she left Ireland on 10 March 1959. Shortly afterwards Mother Mary Patrick's condition deteriorated. She was
again anointed. From then on it was a case of many setbacks and
occasional slight improvements.

She co-operated as fully as she could with her doctors and
nurses, confident that she would soon be able to look after her own
personal needs again and do further work for God. 'We should try
to live as long as we can,' she used to say, 'because with every
breath we give praise to God.'[2] When she was being helped to
exercise her paralysed arm she endured the pain with great patience, offering it up for the intentions of Pope John XXIII and the
reunion of the Churches – a cause dear to Pope John and herself.[3]
One of those who nursed her at that time remembers how she often
apologised for being a burden on the young Sisters who looked
after her, and of how they assured her of how grateful they were to
be asked to help her who had done so much for the congregation.
This seemed to make her happy.

On 18 April, the day after her eighty-sixth birthday, the community annals recorded that she was again anointed although she herself did not feel gravely ill. However, she had become weaker and was sleeping very little. In the following weeks her condition stabilised. It was possible to bring her downstairs in a wheelchair, and sometimes she was well enough to be wheeled to the shore that was so conveniently close to the convent. This was a great joy to her. Throughout it all she retained her interest in everything that was happening, at home and on the missions, and for each individual Sister.

On 23 July 1959 she suffered another stroke. This was less severe than that of the previous February, but in some ways it was more upsetting because it left her with painful muscle spasms. Her speech was also affected, though this righted itself after some days. For the first time she began to speak of dying. All those who looked after her remarked on her great peace of mind as she accepted the fact that she would soon leave them. She asked for and received Holy Communion every day up to the day she died. From now on she was just waiting to go home.

The question of where she would be buried was a delicate matter. Everyone knew of her love for Cahiracon and no one would have wished to broach the idea of her being buried elsewhere. However, one day she asked the inevitable question: 'Where am I going to be buried?' Sister Mary Pauline hesitated a moment before answering tentatively, 'I think we are all to be buried in Magheramore, in the motherhouse.' Much to her relief, Mother Mary Patrick replied in a firm voice, 'That's as it should be!' She had now given everything.

Sometimes at night she would wake up feeling nervous and afraid. Then she and whichever of the young Sisters was doing night-duty would talk together and say the prayers that she loved: the *Memorare*, the triple invocation, 'Jesus, Mary and Joseph' and a prayer of resignation to the one who had been the focus of her lifelong devotion, the Sacred Heart of Jesus. Sometimes she asked her nurses to sing the hymn, 'To Jesus' Heart All Burning', and she herself, to their amusement, would try to sing along with them. The prayer that she had learnt from her father so many years ago and

which had been her joy and inspiration throughout her long life
now spoke to her with a new immediacy: 'Dearest Lord Jesus, if
Thou wilt have me, by the help of Thy grace, I will have thee, and
do thou have me. Let us two be together now and always.'

She spoke often about the early days of the congregation, and of
the Sisters who had been associated with her at that time.

> She loved to tell me about each one, and to know that I was
> interested. I could only admire how she trusted the young
> Sisters, and prayed for their wellbeing. She would often say, 'I
> will pray for each dear Sister when I go to heaven.' She was
> interested in and asked about the works of the Congregation to
> the very end ... Her wonderful spirit remained with her always.
> Each night she reminded me of the spirit of hospitality, which
> was so characteristic of the Congregation, and prayed that it
> would continue so. 'Is St Joseph's open?' 'Did the visitors get
> tea?' she would sometimes say.[4]

One of the young Sisters who nursed her was deeply impressed
by the fact that her patient never complained about not being able
to sleep, yet was so concerned that her nurse should rest a little. 'She
was always thinking of others.'[5] Her senses gradually became
impaired. Her greatest loss was the sense of sight, which meant that
she was unable to read or write. A few years earlier her hearing had
begun to cause her problems.

However, her sense of humour stayed with her to the end, and
she could laugh with her characteristic throaty laugh whenever
someone had a funny incident to relate. She sometimes recalled
humorous situations in which she had found herself long years ago.
She could laugh at herself when she remembered how as a novice
she had charge of lighting the fires in the laundry and sacristy. They
were forever going out on her, and she consequently came in for
some correction. 'In desperation she turned to St Joseph and all of
a sudden the fires began to burn brightly. Then one morning she met
Michael Moylan [the handyman around the convent] coming out
and he told her that he had been lighting fires "as usual".'[6] She
remembered an old man she had nursed in the Mater Hospital who

had given her the price of a bottle of stout.

She was praying for the canonisation of Edel Quinn and Pope Pius XII, and she listened intently while one of her nurses read their life-stories to her. She also prayed to Dom Marmion and Father John Sullivan SJ for cures for friends who had asked her prayers. She spoke with admiration of the Legion of Mary. Frank Duff was a personal friend of hers, as were Miss Plunkett and Miss Scratton who were his valiant helpers in attacking the prostitution problem in Dublin of the early twenties. It had been at her farewell party in February 1922, before she left for the novitiate in Cahiracon, that Frank Duff first met these two women who were to figure so prominently in the early history of the Legion of Mary.[7]

A Sister who nursed her at the time said later: 'She often spoke of the spirit of the congregation and talked of the qualities that she wished for in each Columban Sister: the spirit of charity, especially for each other, and the spirit of hospitality. She hoped that the bond of deep friendship that already existed between the Society and our Congregation would always be there.'[8]

She realised that the time for farewells had come. She began now to speak of all those whom she loved, her family first of all and then all those who had been her co-workers and friends throughout all the years from the very first days 'when someone mentioned the word "China".'[9]

> Her personal debt, and the Congregation's, of gratitude to Fr John Blowick was uppermost in her thoughts ... The Congregation's privilege of being associated with the Society of the Maynooth Mission to China; all the Fathers of the Society, living and dead, who had contributed to our temporal and spiritual founding; the Sisters of Charity; her own co-novices; in fact every group in our Congregation, down to the latest set of novices, were spoken of with the great and loving concern of the first volunteer – the eldest sister, in every sense of the word![10]

On 27 July she spoke about dictating some letters the following day but, fearing that there might not be a tomorrow Sister Mary Pauline decided to start on them immediately. The dictation flowed without hesitation and the messages in each letter were given 'with the clearness and decision of one who had something to say and said it'.[11] The first of her farewell letters was to Father John Blowick. Others followed, mostly to her family. The letter to Father Blowick followed him around for some days. Immediately he received it on 4 August he set out for Cahiracon and was at Mother Mary Patrick's bedside that afternoon.

The short letter that drew Father Blowick to hasten to the bedside of his friend of so many years ago was remarkable in its humility. She implicitly handed over to him her own role in the founding of the congregation, free enough now to go to God with empty hands, leaving it to others to remember the vital and irreplaceable part she herself had played. After all, what did it matter who got the glory? 'To God alone, glory, honour, power.'[12]

Dear Father Blowick,
As I am getting near the end of my existence, I feel impelled to express my very deep gratitude to you for the great privilege you conferred on me in admitting me into your Congregation of the Missionary Sisters of St. Columban, to whom I feel proud to belong.

It was a glorious thing that our Sisterhood was founded by, and associated to the Society of the Maynooth Missions which has done and is doing such wonderful work for God and souls.

Asking your prayers for my poor soul, I promise to remember you if God will admit my poor soul to Heaven!

Respectfully and gratefully in Christ,
Mother Mary Patrick[13]

In a covering letter Sister Mary Pauline told Father Blowick that Mother Mary Patrick had been talking much about the early days of the congregation and of her gratitude to the Maynooth Mission founders. She wished to acknowledge all of them, even though her greatest debt of gratitude was to Father Blowick.

Not many details remain of this meeting of Mother Mary Patrick and Father Blowick. It was certainly a historic and moving moment both for them and for the congregation. These two who, under God, had been responsible for the founding of the Columban Sisters, and had worked and suffered in that cause over so many years, were together again as one of them now stood on the threshold of eternity. We do not know all that transpired, except that it brought Mother Mary Patrick great happiness and that she said it was the crowning privilege of her long life. She gave Father Blowick one of her dearest treasures, a little black rosary beads, blessed and given to her by Pope Pius XII in 1947, and much prayed on.

Father Blowick had to leave again that evening but he returned on 6 August and stayed until 12 August when, to his regret, he had to leave. During his week in Cahiracon he had other meetings with Mother Mary Patrick. It meant much to him that she had sent for him and that in their last meetings together she had encouraged him to visit the Sisters more often. At the time he needed that invitation; it was given magnanimously. During that week in Cahiracon, at her request, he addressed the Sisters on the spirit of the congregation. 'We all felt that for her it was a time of great union of heart and mind with him, whom she fondly spoke of as "Our dear Father Founder".'[14] This visit brought about a noticeable change in the relationship of Father Blowick to the congregation: from then on he was happy to visit the Sisters more often than he had for years.

On 9 August Mother Mary Eucharia, Vicar General and friend of Mother Mary Patrick, travelled from Maghermore to visit her. Afterwards she described that visit:

> She told me she was dying very happy about everything, past, present and future ... When I asked that she would watch over us from Heaven, with a quick flash of her old spirit, she reminded me of Purgatory and asked the Sisters not to leave her long there, as she would then be close to us in Heaven. She reminded me of her love for the Russian Apostolate and asked that we would cherish it; spoke of the needs of South America and the coming Council, and when I knelt and asked her blessing her last words were of unity and love.[15]

One of the Sisters who nursed her at this time was much impressed by her frequent prayers for the young Sisters in the congregation. They were her special concern. 'She asked me at least ten times how many Chinese and Filipino Sisters we had now and also their religious names.'[16]

After Father Blowick's departure on 12 August Mother Mary Patrick slipped back again. On 13 August death seemed near. On this date forty-six years earlier her beloved husband, Alfred, had died. She may have wondered if the Lord would take her home on that same date. It was one day during her final illness that a Sister coming into her room heard her murmur, 'Alfred! Alfred!' Now it looked as if they would soon be reunited.

On the night of 13 August she seemed to be in anguish of spirit as well as great physical distress. It was a stormy night, windy and cold. At times she would cry out, 'Deliver us from evil, poor weak things of this world!' or repeat the intercessions of the prayer, *Anima Christi*. Feeling helpless, all her nurse could do was kneel at her side and pray with her. Towards morning peace came and Mother Mary Patrick slept a little. She awoke disappointed that she was not already in the presence of the Lord. It was evident that her last day had come. 'Her breathing was difficult, but she was never more alert, even remembering Mother Mary Carmel's anniversary. When it was said to her that God would come for her very soon and take her to Heaven for the Assumption, there was a joyful calm in her reply, "What a wonderful privilege!" '[17] She recognised everyone and asked all sorts of down-to-earth questions about the farm and the workmen, in particular Tom Murtagh, who had worked for the Sisters for so many years.

In the early afternoon her agony began again and the community gathered around her bed to say the Rosary. She seemed happy to see them there, smiling at each Sister as she came in. She asked that the Glorious Mysteries be recited and she tried to join in. Later she lapsed into a coma. Thinking that she would last for several hours the community retired at the usual time but Sister Mary Pauline and Sister Mary Nugent stayed on, saying the Rosary and reciting her favourite prayers and aspirations. Sometimes she moved her lips as if she was joining in, and she seemed happy and peaceful. At one stage Sister Mary Pauline asked if she would like a drop of water and her last word was a grateful 'please'. Soon afterwards at one o'clock on the morning of 15 August, feast of Our Lady's Assumption, her breathing grew slower and easier. She died five minutes later. What she had felt was almost too much to hope for had happened: she had gone home on Our Lady's feast.

The following day, Mother Mary Patrick's remains were brought from Cahiracon to Magheramore where she would be the first Columban Sister to be interred in the new cemetery. Accompanying the remains were Columban Bishop Patrick Cleary, Father John Blowick and the community chaplain, Father Donal O'Farrell. The Sisters who travelled with the cortege were Sisters Mary Veronica, Regis, Mary Nugent and Una Moane. Two Holy Rosary Sisters, who were on promotion work in the neighbourhood and were staying in Cahiracon, drove the Sisters to Magheramore. Just as the undertakers were about to lift the coffin into the hearse, Miss Fitzgerald-Kenny, Mother Mary Patrick's friend of a lifetime arrived, true to form. An old lady herself now, she had driven all the way from Claremorris and now accompanied the friend she had stood by for so many years on the first stage of her final journey. They had travelled many roads together: this would be the last.

The funeral took place on 17 August 1959. Archbishop John Charles McQuaid of Dublin presided at the Mass in the convent chapel and afterwards gave the Absolution. He spoke of how deeply he regretted not having heard of Mother Mary Patrick's illness: if he had, he would have gone to Cahiracon to visit her. With him in the sanctuary was Bishop Patrick Cleary of the diocese of Nancheng, China. Father John Blowick, with whom Mother Mary Patrick had been so closely associated in founding the congregation, celebrated her Requiem Mass and later officiated at the graveside. Dr Michael O'Dwyer. Superior General of the Society of St Columban and several of the Columban Fathers who had known Mother Mary Patrick in the early days were also in attendance, together with many of the local priests. The Missionary Sisters of the Holy Rosary were represented and the Medical Missionaries of Mary, among them Mother Mary Patrick's friend of a lifetime Mother Mary Martin. The wheel had come full circle:

those who were there at the beginning of her religious life were there again at the end. She had spoken affectionately of them as she waited for God to call her.

Mother Mary Patrick's niece, Aylish Fane-Saunders came from England. Her stepdaughter Gladys Stephenson was there, also Father Tom Moloney and his sister, relatives of Sir Alfred Moloney. The attendance included many of her friends both new and old, who came to bid her a last farewell.

After the funeral, tributes began arriving from all quarters of the globe. First to come were the telegrams and messages of sympathy from the Columban Sisters and priests in different mission fields. From Rome came a letter from Mother Anna Dengel, foundress of the American Medical Mission Sisters, saying, 'She was a strong and brave soul and a wonderful foundation stone for your community and a strength and inspiration far beyond it.' Referring to Mother Mary Patrick's support for Dr Agnes McLaren's pioneering work in the cause of Catholic medical missions, she added, 'It must have been balm to the soul of Dr McLaren to find understanding and encouragement.' She spoke of the impression Mother Mary Patrick made on her of utter simplicity and humility.[18]

From a French Benedictine Abbey came a letter from an old friend, Sister Columba Belinda Butler. 'I was really fond of her,' she wrote, 'we knew one another intimately and for so long – we were young together in the gay days of Dublin ... Fidelity in friendship was one of her many good qualities.'

Fidelity in friendship was re-echoed by many of those who wrote in the days immediately after Mother Mary Patrick's death. The mother of one of the young Sisters on the missions spoke for many others when she wrote saying, 'We feel as if we have lost a real and true friend.'

Cesira More O'Farrell, who knew her as a young girl in London, wrote recalling her wedding and remembered how she had invited along the many factory girls she had taught and befriended, and who loved her for it. 'When one looks back over the years, how few can say in truth, "I did my little bit!" Her friends must say it for her now.'

Letters came from many of the Columban Fathers who knew her in the early days, one of them, Father Paddy O'Connor, saying that 'she was already a heroine more than forty years ago in Dublin.' Her courage and heroism were referred to in several of the tributes paid her.

The Mother General of the Holy Rosary Sisters, Sister Mary Gabriel, wrote: 'Her great apostolic soul rejoiced when she heard of the growth of missionary work anywhere – it mattered not by whom that work was accomplished.' From the Franciscan Missionary Sisters for Africa came the tribute: 'She was one of those great missionary pioneers who have done so much for God and her country.' Sister Mary Bernadette wrote from the Galway Poor Clare Convent, referring to the fact that Columban Bishop Quinlan had said that Mother Mary Patrick should be canonised for the work she did for the plague-stricken in China.[19]

Another friend of bygone days, Mother Eveleen Coyle, wrote from the Sacred Heart Convent, Mount Anville, recalling her first meeting with Lady Moloney when they worked together on a committee for Belgian Refugees. 'I've yet never forgotten the profound impression made on me by the charity, kindness, humility and meekness of Lady Moloney, and from that time on I have always looked on her as a saint.'[20] She also remembered Lady Moloney's fidelity and heroism in visiting the cancer patients in the Union hospital, a foretaste of her later experiences in China.

The loss to her family was immense. After her sister's death in 1950 it was she who had kept the far-flung family together. Her loving care for all of them, especially for the younger members, was one of the guiding principles of her life. She became for them a kindly providence concerned for all their needs, especially those that were spiritual or educational. Her grandnephews, Michael and Max Chevers and Seán Smith are living testaments to her concern and care for the younger members of her immediate family. Her niece Aylish Fane-Saunders could truly say, 'I personally feel that a great pillar of strength has been removed from the family, but I'm sure we will all turn to her in heaven now as we did on earth and she will be able to guide us even better.' Nancy Chevers, her nephew

Michael's wife, wrote saying how relieved they were that her sufferings were over. 'We rejoice rather than feel sad, for we have always looked on her as a saint ... I shall always remember her with love and affection and gratitude, for I always felt that it was through her prayers that my husband, so happily, received the Last Rites of Holy Mother the Church.'

Father Aubrey Gwynn SJ, friend over many decades, whose mother had also been her friend, wrote: 'She was indeed a valiant woman and your congregation owes her an immense debt of gratitude.' Over the years the members of the congregation which she founded with Father John Blowick, have recalled that debt with love and appreciation and have tried to keep the memory green. Certain qualities are always remembered whenever and wherever she is mentioned: her deep faith noted by so many; her heroism; her enduring missionary spirit; her compassion for all those in need in any part of the world; her humanity; her understanding of the young Sisters and her vision for their future – the future of the congregation; her concern that charity would be the distinguishing mark of the congregation; her personal kindness; above all, her unwavering integrity. One of those who watched with her the night she died wrote later:

> From her we have received a shining example of great charity, self-sacrifice and zeal for souls – and always undaunted courage. Those of us who were privileged to be at her deathbed saw her die as she had lived, valiantly and full of faith, praying and conscious to the end, joyful and peaceful in her anticipation of the coming of her Lord.[21]

As a novice thirty-five years earlier she had a dream in which she saw herself as a little ship in mid ocean. 'Behind me all was grey, and waves were breaking on the shore. But the little ship had just sailed into a glorious line of sunshine, with all its sails set toward the bright horizon.'[22] Now, after much journeying and at times treacherous seas, the little ship of her life had reached a safe haven at last.

Notes

PROLOGUE   An Anglo-Irish Background

1. Mother Mary Patrick's unpublished memoirs, Columban Sisters' archives. These were written at the request of Mother Mary Vianney who succeeded Mother Mary Patrick as Superior General.
2. The beatification cause of David Henry Lewis was introduced by the decree of 4 December 1886, in which he was listed as 'David Lewis alias Charles Baker'.
3. This is the actual wording on the marriage certificate. The Church of Ireland was disestablished three years later, in 1869.
4. John Betjeman was Press Attaché at the British Embassy in Dublin, 1941- 43. He retained a lifelong interest in Monkstown Parish Church which was featured in the BBC documentary, *Betjeman's Dublin*.
5. John Bateman, *The Great Landowners of Gt Britain and Ireland* (fourth edition, London , 1883), p. 269.
6. U.H. Hussey de Burgh, *The Landowners of Ireland* (Dublin, 1878), p. 270.
7. Trimleston House was bought by developers in 1967, and demolished. The stone gate-lodge on Merrion Road is still inhabited.
8. Cardinal Cullen's papers, Dublin diocesan archives.
9. Alan O'Day, *Reactions to Irish Nationalism*, 1865-1914 (Dublin, 1987), p. 48.
10. Emmet Larkin, *The Roman Catholic Church and the Home Rule Movement in Ireland* (Dublin, 1990), p. 102.
11. Peadar Mac Suibhne, *Paul Cullen and His Contemporaries*, Vol.1, (Naas, 1961), p. 70.
12. F.H. O'Donnell, *A History of the Irish Parliamentary Party* (London, 1910), p. 118.
13. Gladstone papers, British Library MS. Dept.
14. *The Guardian*, in which the correspondence appeared, was not the newspaper of that name but a serious Church journal.
15. Gladstone papers. Also published in *The Guardian*, 26 July 1876, p. 990.
16. Mother Mary Patrick's Memoirs, Vol. 1, p. 19.
17. Stephen Gwynn, *Experiences of a Literary Man* (London, 1926), p. 11.

CHAPTER ONE   Early Years

1. Mother Mary Patrick's Memoirs, Vol. 1, p. 1.
2. Renowned as a spiritual director and guide, the saintly Père Olivaint was massacred by the Commune with four of his Jesuit companions on 26 May 1871. Their beatification process was introduced in Rome in 1937.
3. Memoirs, Vol.1, p. 2.
4. Cardinal Cullen papers, Dublin diocesan archives.
5. Ibid.
6. Ibid.

7. Memoirs, Vol. 1, p. 4.
8. King George V of Hanover (1819-1878) lost his throne in 1866 when Hanover was annexed to Prussia and lived in exile for the remainder of his life, mostly in England, where he is buried in St George's Chapel, Windsor. Related to the Hanoverian kings of England.
9. Cardinal Cullen papers, Dublin diocesan Archives.
10. Memoirs, Vol. 1, p. 6,
11. Ibid.
12. Ibid, p. 7.
13. Ibid.
14. Ibid., p. 12.
15. Ibid.
16. Ibid., p. 11.
17. Mark Bence-Jones, 'Rossmore Park, Monaghan, Co. Monaghan', in *Burke's Guide to Country Houses*, Vol. I, Ireland (London, 1978).
18. Lord Rossmore, *Things I Can Tell* (London, 1912).
19. Memoirs, Vol.1, p. 14.
20. Ibid.
21. Ibid., p. 15.
22. Ibid..
23. Ibid., p. 16.
24. Ibid., p. 18
25. Ibid.
26. Ibid., p. 19.
27. Ibid.
28. Ibid.
29. Ibid., p. 21.
30. Margaret M. Clutton, née Petre, 'Eight Years at Brighton', *The Chronicle*, 1934, p. 76.
31. Clutton, op. cit., p. 77.
32. Clutton, op. cit., p. 78.
33. Memoirs, Vol. 1, p. 25.
34. Ibid., p. 24.

CHAPTER TWO **Coming of Age**

1. Memoirs, Vol. 1, p. 32.
2. Ibid., p. 33.
3. Ibid., p. 34.
4. Julian Treuherz, *Victorian Painting* (London, 1993), p. 106.
5. Memoirs, Vol. 1, p. 36.
6. Ibid., p. 40.
7. Ibid., p. 41.
8. MS. letter of *circa* 1950, Columban Sisters' archives.
9. Memoirs, Vol. 1, p. 43.
10. Ibid., p. 44.
11. Ibid., p. 47.
12. Cardinal Cullen papers, Dublin diocesan archives.
13. Memoirs, Vol.1, p. 52.

14. Ibid, p. 53.
15. Ibid.
16. Ibid.
17. Ibid., p. 54.
18. Ibid.
19. Ibid.
20. 'Object of the Charity, as defined by its Charter', quoted in annual reports of the Governors and Guardians. In modern times the words 'without fee or reward' are omitted.
21. John P. Prendergast, *The Cromwellian Settlement of Ireland* (Dublin, third edition, 1922), p. 177.
22. Memoirs, Vol.1, p. 59.
23. Ibid., p. 60.
24. Ibid., p. 63.
25. Ibid.
26. Ibid., p. 64.
27. *The Lady*, 11 March 1897, p. 310. A sketch of 'Miss Owen Lewis's Wedding Dress' accompanied this report.
28. Memoirs, Vol. 1, p. 65.
29. Ibid.

CHAPTER THREE   **Life in the West Indies**

1. Thomas P. O'Neill, ' The Organization and Administration of Relief, 1845-52', Robert Dudley Edwards and T.D. Williams (eds.) *The Great Famine, Studies in Irish History, 1845-1852* (Dublin, 1994), p. 225.
2. Walford's *County Families of Great Britain and Ireland* (London, 1860).
3. Very Rev. P. White, *History of Clare and the Dalcassian Clans* (Dublin, 1893).
4. H. de Watteville, *The British Soldier* (London, 1954), p. 174.
5. Ibid, p. 177.
6. Letter in Public Record Office, London.
7. Since 1858, at the express wish of Queen Victoria, the men of the 1st West India Regiment wore uniforms modelled on the dress of the French Zouaves: a white jacket under a shorter red one laced with yellow braid, and loose blue knickerbockers. This was worn with a red fez wound about with a white turban.
8. Alfred Moloney, C.M.G., *Sketch of the Forestry of West Africa with particular reference to its present commercial products* (London, 1887). Copy in Rhodes House Library, Oxford.
9. Op. cit.
10. Letter in Kew Gardens library archives, London.
11. Report in Kew Gardens library archives.
12. Ray Desmond, *Dictionary of British and Irish Botanists and Horticulturists* (London, 1977).
13. Sir Alfred Moloney, 'Reminiscences of my Work and Wanderings in British Honduras' (Port-of-Spain, 1902). Rhodes House Library, Oxford, has a copy of this and other addresses and memoranda of Alfred Moloney.
14. Op. cit.

15. The same address had been given earlier to the British Association in Newcastle.
16. Moloney, 'Reminiscences of my Work and Wanderings in British Honduras', p. 7.
17. Memoirs, Vol. 1, p. 66.
18. Ibid., p. 69.
19. Ibid., p. 70.
20. Ibid., p. 71.
21. Ibid.
22. Ibid., p. 73.
23. The Sisters of St Joseph of Cluny had been in the Caribbean since 1822, when a foundation was made in French Guiana within the lifetime of the foundress, Ven. Anne Marie Javouhey. In 1835 she agreed to a foundation in Trinidad. It was from there that other foundations were made in the British West Indies.
24. Records of the Sisters of St Joseph of Cluny, West Indies, in the Motherhouse, Paris.
25. Memoirs, Vol. 1, p. 78.
26. Ibid.
27. Ibid., p. 79.
28. Andrew Boyle, *The Riddle of Erskine Childers* (London, 1977), p. 79.

CHAPTER FOUR **The Land of the Green Bay Tree**

1. Memoirs, Vol. 1, p. 82.
2. Ibid.
3. Ibid.
4. Ibid., p. 84.
5. Ibid., p. 87.
6. St Joseph of Cluny records, Motherhouse, Paris. Part of the five-yearly report submitted from the different missions.
7. Ibid.
8. Memoirs, Vol. 1, p. 91.
9. Ibid.
10. L. Keppel, *Happy Memories of a Saint* (London, 1944), p. 130 et passim.
11. Bridget Brereton, *A History of Modern Trinidad, 1783-1962*, (Kingston, 1985 rep.), pp. 148-150.
12. British Colonial Office papers, Public Record Office, London.
13. Memoirs, Vol. 1, pp 93-95.
14. Ibid.
15. British Colonial Office papers.
16. Ibid.
17. Brereton, p. 151.
18. British Colonial Office papers.
19. Ibid.
20. Ibid.
21. Ibid.
22. Letter in British Colonial Office papers.
23. Memoirs, Vol. 1, p. 95.
24. Ibid., p. 97.

CHAPTER FIVE **'Bobbie, find me a home!'**

1. Memoirs, Vol. 1, p. 100.
2. Mary Braddon, *Lady Audley's Secret* (London, 1862)
3. Memoirs, Vol. 1, p. 103.
4. Ibid., p. 109.
5. Letter of 17 November 1958, Columban Sisters' archives.
6. 'Notes and News', *The Planet*, 14 September 1907, p. 4.
7. 'Notes and News', *The Planet*, 27 July 1907. p. 5.
8. 'Notes and News', *The Planet*, 20 July 1907, p. 4.
9. Memoirs, Vol. 1, p. 112.
10. Memoirs, Vol. 3, p. 13.
11. *The Gentlewoman*, 12 October 1907, p. 512.
12. Memoirs, Vol. 1, p. 116.
13. Ibid., p. 117.
14. Ibid.
15. Mother Mary Patrick's Letters of Spiritual Direction, Columban Sisters' archives.
16. Ibid.
17. Memoirs, Vol. 3, p. 4.
18. Ibid., p. 10.
19. Ibid., p. 16.

CHAPTER SIX **The Roman Years**

1. Memoirs, Vol. 3, p. 29.
2. Ibid.
3. The Poor Servants of the Mother of God are a religious congregation of women, founded in 1808 in England by Mother Mary Magdalen Taylor, with the co-operation of Lady Georgiana Fullerton, initially to work among the poor of London. The congregation was approved by Leo XlII in 1885.
4. Memoirs, Vol. 3, p. 31.
5. Both letters are in the Columban Sisters' archives.
6. Memoirs, Vol.3, p. 37.
7. The Sisters of St Dorothy (also called Dorotheans) were founded by Paola Frassinetti in 1834, at Quinto, Italy. They have spread outside Italy to other countries. Their primary apostolate is the education of youth.
8. Memoirs, Vol. 3, p. 41.
9. Ibid.
10. Ibid, p. 46.
11. In Annotation 19 of *The Spiritual Exercises*, St Ignatius says that if a person has not the time or the resources to follow the full Exercises, 'that person should take an hour and a half daily,' following the same order as the Exercises. He does not stipulate the amount of time to be given to completing the Exercises.
12. Published by the Institute of Jesuit Sources, St Louis, 1978.
13. David L. Fleming SJ, *The Spiritual Exercises of St Ignatius, A Literal Translation and a Contemporary Reading*, p xvi.
14. Letter in the Columban Sisters' archives.
15. Memoirs, Vol. 3, p. 49.

16. Ibid., p. 50.
17. Ibid., p. 51.
18. Ibid, p. 53.
19. Ibid.
20. Letter in the Columban Sisters' archives.
21. Developers have since taken over the property, and only a remnant of the original house remains.
22. *A Layman's Retreats*, p vi.
23. Op. cit., p. vii.
24. Letter in Columban Sisters' archives..
25. Devotion to St Thérèse had begun immediately after her death in 1897, and was already widespread.
26. Hieronymo Dal-Gal, *Pius X, The Life-Story of a Beatus* (Dublin, 1953), p 230.
27. Frances Moloney's MS. spiritual notebooks, Columban Sisters' archives.

CHAPTER SEVEN **Call and Response**

1. Archbishop Walsh papers, Dublin diocesan archives.
2. Father Nolan's papers, Irish Jesuit Province archives.
3. Thomas Fallon was a member of the Society of St Vincent de Paul. Influenced by him, Frances later got involved in this work.
4. Sister Mary Patrick's Letters of Spiritual Direction, Columban Sisters' archives.
5. Ibid.
6. Roger Casement was born in Co. Dublin in 1864. As a member of the British consular service he highlighted human rights violations in Africa and South America. He joined the Irish Volunteers in 1913, and was executed on 3 August 1916.
7. Brian Inglis, *Roger Casement* (Belfast 1993 ed.cit.), 43 ,133
8. Memoirs, Vol. 4, p. 13.
9. From an interview with Wing Commander Patrick J.T. Stephenson, Frances Moloney's step-grandson, 3 October 1991.
10. 'Events previous to the founding of the Congregation', p. 9. (Written by Sister Mary Patrick at the request of her Superior, possibly between 1925 and 1926, though some sections may have been written earlier. This comprehensive MS. will be referred to here as 'Events'. Sister Mary Patrick uses the third person form in speaking of herself.
11. 'Events', Vol. 1, p. 3.
12. John Blowick, 'The Maynooth Mission to China', paper read at Catholic Truth Society Annual General Meeting, Dublin, October, 1917.
13. It was not until 1936, almost twenty years after John Blowick's appeal, that Rome lifted the prohibition against religious practising medicine and surgery.
14. In 1941, the Columban Fathers' seminary, Dalgan Park, keeping its original name, was transferred to Navan, Co. Meath.
15. Letter in the Columban Sisters' archives.
16. Archbishop Walsh papers, Dublin diocesan archives.
17. Katherine Burton, *According to the Pattern, The Story of Dr Agnes McLaren and the Society of Catholic Medical Missionaries* (New York, 1946).
18. Father Blowick never met Dr McLaren, but he was sufficiently impressed to

translate her life written in French. In August 1918 he promised to send Frances the original tattered copy as soon as he had finished the translation.
19. Letter in Columban Fathers' archives.
20. Letter of 15 June 1918 in Columban Sisters'archives.
21. Letter of 7 July 1918 in Columban Fathers' archives.
22. 'Events', Vol. 1, p. 8.
23. Ibid.
24. Ibid., p. 9.
25. Ibid.
26. Ibid, p. 11.
27. Letter in Columban Fathers' archives.
28. 'Events', Vol. 1, p. 12.
29. Ibid..
30. Ibid., p. 12-13.
31. Ibid., p. 14.
32. Bernard T. Smyth, *The Chinese Batch* (Dublin, 1994), p. 61.
33. 'Events', Vol. 1, p. 15.
34. Letter of 22 September 1918 in Columban Fathers' archives.
35. Ibid.
36. Letter of 24 September 1918 in Columban Sisters' archives.
37. Letter of 3 December 1918 in Columban Fathers'archives.
38. 'Events', Vol.1, p. 18.
39. 'Events', Vol.2, p. 1.
40. Ibid.
41. Cf. Mary Purcell, *To Africa With Love: The Biography of Mother Mary Martin* (Dublin, 1987).
42. Letter of 10 November 1918 in Columban Sisters'archives.
43. 'Events', Vol. 1, p. 3.

CHAPTER EIGHT **Growing Pains**

1. The Doctors' Committee for the Formation of an Irish Catholic Medical Mission to China consisted of: Sir Andrew Horne FRCPI; Sir Joseph Redmond MD; The Right Hon. M.F.Cox PC, MD; Dr Denis Coffey; Alex Blaney FRCSI; Joseph O'Carroll MD; Alfred J. Smith MD; Reginald J.White MD; Dr Alice Barry; Dr James Meenan MB; W.J. Dargan MD.
2. Dr Margaret Lamont, *Twenty Years in Medical Work in Mission Countries* (Shanghai, 1918).
3. Letter of 15 November 1918, Columban Sisters' archives.
4. Letter of 17 November 1918, Columban Fathers' archives.
5. Report of 4 Jan.1919 Meeting, Columban Sisters' archives.
6. Ibid.
7. Copy of letter of 7 January 1919, Columban Sisters' archives.
8. Letter of 28 November 1918, Columban Sisters' archives.
9. Letter of 11 December 1918, Columban Fathers' archives.
10. 'Events', Vol.2, p 10
11. Letter of 10 December, Columban Sisters' archives.
12. Letter of 13 December 1918, Columban Fathers' archives.
13. Columban Fathers'archives.

14. Letter of 8 January 1919, Columban Sisters' archives.
15. Letter of 24 January 1919, Columban Sisters' archives.
16. 'Events', Vol.2, p. 24.
17. Letter of 7 July 1919, Columban Fathers' archives. Orlagh belongs to the Augustinian Fathers.
18. Letter of 8 July 1919, Columban Sisters' archives.
19. Patricia Edge, 'A Workers' College', *The Tablet*, 18 February 1995, pp. 214-215.
20. Copy of letter of 15 July 1919, Columban Sisters' archives.
21. 'Events', Vol.2, p. 33.
22. Ibid.
23. Letter of 12 August 1919, Columban Fathers' archives.
24. Undated letter, written in late June 1919, Columban Sisters' archives.
25. Letter of 18 September 1919, Columban Fathers' archives.
26. Columban Sisters' archives.
27. Copy in Columban Sisters'archives.
28. 'Events', Vol.2, p. 38. Cf. Mother Kevin's biography by Sister M. Louis, *Love is the Answer* (Dublin 1964).
29. Letter of 25 September 1919.
30. Letter of 27 September 1919, Columban Sisters' archives.
31. J.H. Newman, 'My Lady Nature and Her Daughters,' in *Verses for Various Occasions* (London, 1890).
32. Letter of 16 October 1919, Columban Sisters' archives.
33. Undated letter of late October 1919, quoted in 'Events', Vol.2, p. 42.
34. 'Events', Vol. 2, p. 38.

CHAPTER NINE   **Nearing the Goal**

1. 'Events', Vol.3, p. 14.
2. Ibid., p. 15.
3. Ibid. p. 16.
4. Letter of 27 December 1919, Columban Sisters' archives.
5. 'Events', Vol.3, p. 17.
6. Ibid..
7. 'Events', Vol. 3, p. 24.
8. Ibid., p. 17.
9. 'Events', Vol. 3, p. 23.
10. Ibid.
11. 'Events', Vol. 3, p. 25.
12. Ibid.,26.
13. Ibid., pp. 26-27.
14. Ibid., p. 29.
15. Letter of 25 May 1921, Columban Sisters' archives.
16. 'Events', Vol. 3, p. 32.
17. Loc. cit.
18. 'Events', Vol.3, p. 33.
19. Ibid.
20. Ibid.
21. 'Events', Vol. 3, p. 34.

22. Ibid., p. 36.
23. Ibid., p. 38.
24. Letter of 10 May 1920, Columban Fathers' archives.
25. Original Latin document, Columban Fathers' archives.
26. Letter of 14 March 1921, Religious Sisters of Charity archives.
27. Letter of 16 March 1921, Columban Fathers' archives.
28. Letter of 26 April 1921, Religious Sisters of Charity archives.
29. Letter of 6 May 1921, Religious Sisters of Charity archives.
30. Letter of 9 May 1921, Columban Fathers' archives.
31. Document dated 21 June 1921, Columban Fathers' archives.
32. Letter of 30 September 1921, Religious Sisters of Charity archives.
33. Letter of 22 January, Religious Sisters of Charity archives.

CHAPTER TEN   **Religious Life at Last**

1. Archives of the Religious Sisters of Charity, Dublin.
2. Columban Sisters' Annals, 1922.
3. Ibid.
4. Ibid.
5. Ibid.
6. Katherine Butler RSC, *Mary Aikenhead, A Woman for all Seasons* (Strasbourg, 1984), p. 18.
7. Letters of Father Blowick and Lady Moloney in 'Early Documents', Vol. 2.
8. Edward Fischer, *Maybe a Second Spring* (New York, 1983), p. 21.
9. Cf. Chapter 9.
10. Columban Sisters' archives.
11. Columban Sisters' archives.
12. Archives of the Religious Sisters of Charity.
13. Columban Fathers' archives.
14. 'Events', Vol.2, p. 1.
15. Columban Sisters' Annals, 1922.
16. Columban Sisters' archives.
17. Letter of 24 September 1918, Columban Sisters' archives.
18. Columban Sisters' Annals, 1922.
19. Ibid.
20. Letter to Mother Mary Camillus, 3 March 1924, Columban Sisters' archives.
21. Letter of 5 March 1924, Columban Sisters' archives.
22. Letter of 25 March 1924, Columban Sisters' archives.
23. Columban Fathers' archives.
24. Columban Sisters' archives.
25. Columban Fathers' archives.
26. Letter of 4 August 1924, Columban Sisters' archives.
27. Letter of 9 August 1924, Columban Sisters' archives.
28. Letter of 18 August 1924, Columban Sisters' archives.
29. Père de Caussade's *Abandonment to Divine Providence* was one of Frances Moloney's constant spiritual supports.
30. Letter of 22 September 1924, Columban Sisters' archives.
31. Columban Sisters' archives.
32. Letter of 13 October 1924, Columban Sisters' archives.

33. Letter of 8 October 1924, Columban Fathers' archives.
34. Letter of 11 November 1924, Columban Sisters' archives.
35. Pilgrim Notes, dated Christmas 1924.
36. Letter of 3 December 1924, Columban Fathers' archives.
37. Letter of 12 February 1925, Columban Sisters' archives.
38. Letter of 29 March 1925, Columban Sisters' archives.
39. Written the day she left St Jean de Luz, Monday in Holy Week, 1925.
40. Letter of 22 April 1925, Columban Sisters' archives.
41. Columban Fathers' archives.

CHAPTER ELEVEN   **China: the Dream and the Reality**

1. Columban Sisters' Annals, 1922-1937.
2. Eilis Brannigan, 'An account of the early days: September 1924 to February 1926.' MS. notebook in Columban Sisters' archives.
3. Hanyang Annals, 1926 to 1930, recorded by Sister Mary Patrick. Columban Sisters' archives.
4. Ibid.
5. Letter of 7 April 1924, Columban Sisters' archives
6. Hanyang Annals.
7. Ibid.
8. Ibid.
9. Ibid.
10. Ibid.
11. Ibid.
12. The Irish Free State had as yet no diplomatic presence in China. Hence Irish citizens continued to come under the protection of the British Consul. Sister Mary Agnes, as an Australian citizen, was the concern of the Australian Consul.
13. Sister Mary Patrick's letters from China, Columban Sisters' archives.
14. Hanyang Annals.
15. Events, Vol. 1, p. 3.
16. Columban Fathers' archives.
17. 'Our Sisters,' *The Far East*, April 1926.
18. W. Pagel, F.A.H. Simmonds, N. Macdonald, *Pulmonary Tuberculosis* (London, 1953), p. 247.
19. William James in *The Varieties of Religious Experience*, cited by William Styron, *Darkness Visible* (London, 1992), p. 17.
20. Sister Mary Patrick's Letters of Spiritual Direction, Columban Sisters' archives.
21. Ibid.
22. Columban Fathers' archives.
23. Letters of Spiritual Direction, 4 June 1928.
24. Ibid. 2 August 1928.
25. Letters from China, Columban Sisters' archives.
26. Ibid.
27. Ibid.
28. Ibid.
29. Koch's discovery of the tubercle bacillus in 1882 affected the subsequent

treatment of tuberculosis. Nowadays tuberculin is used for diagnostic purposes only and chemotherapy has taken over in the management of pulmonary tuberculosis.
30. Letter of 27 June 1929.

CHAPTER TWELVE **Alarms and Excursions**

1. Sister Mary Patrick's letters from China, Columban Sisters' archives.
2. Ibid.
3. Hanyang Community Annals (1926 – 1930), Columban Sisters' archives.
4. Letters from China.
5. Ibid.
6. Letter from Sister Mary Dolores to Sister Mary Malachy in Cahiracon.
7. Ibid.
8. *The Far East*, August 1930, p. 186.
9. Columban Sisters' archives.
10. *The Far East*, loc.cit.
11. Letters from China.
12. Ibid.
13. Ibid.
14. *The Far East*, June 1930, pp 144-5.
15. Columban Fathers' archives.
16. Simon Winchester, *The River at the Centre of the World* (London, 1997), p. 153.
17. *The Far East*,, November 1931. p. 26.
18. *The Far East*,, January 1932, p. 4.
19. *The Far East*,, February 1932, p. 28.
20. Letters from China.

CHAPTER THIRTEEN **At the Helm**

1. Letter in Columban Sisters' archives, Magheramore.
2. Ibid.
3. Annals of the Congregation, 1920-1937.
4. Ibid.
5. Ibid.
6. Cf. Conor O'Clery, 'Shanghai', *The Irish Times*, 25 January 1997.
7. Columban Sisters' archives.
8. Ibid.
9. Letters to author accompanying his MS. 'Memories of Mother Patrick'.
10. Sir George Catlin, *For God's Sake, Go!* (London, 1972), p. 264.
11. Sister Ellen Muldoon, MS. 'My Memories of Mother Mary Patrick.'
12. Letter of Mother Mary Patrick to the congregation, 24 December1940.
13. Ibid.
14. Catlin, pp. 270 - 71.
15. Sister Ellen Muldoon, interview with writer.
16. Letter to the congregation.
17. Catlin, p. 273.
18. Copy of letter in Columban Sisters' archives.

19. Mother Mary Patrick's conferences, Columban Sisters' archives.
20. Details from Mother Mary Patrick's letter of 5 October 1952 to her friend, Maureen O'Kelly.

CHAPTER FOURTEEN   **Journey's End**

1. In 1962 the Columban Sisters sold Cahiracon to the Salesian Sisters. The knitting industry had already been phased out.
2. Sister Mary Nugent, letter to Mother General, 20 August 1959.
3. Ibid.
4. Ibid.
5. Ibid.
6. Sister Una Moane, letter to the congregation, August 1959.
7. Frank Duff, *Miracles on Tap* (Dublin, 1961, p. 3.
8. Sister Una Moane, letter August 1959.
9. 'Events', p. 3
10. Sister Pauline McAndrew, letter to the congregation, August 1959
11. Ibid.
12. Cf. Rev. 4:11.
13. Mother Mary Patrick's last letter to Father John Blowick was dictated on 27 July 1959. On 15 September 1959, Father Blowick, conscious of the historic value of this document, returned it together with Sister Pauline's covering letter, so that they could be preserved in the congregational archives.
14. Sister Una Moane, letter August 1959.
15. Sister Mary Eucharia McElligott, letter to the congregation.
16. Sister Una Moane, letter August 1959.
17. Sister Pauline McAndrew, letter August 1959.
18. Letter of 22 August 1959. This and other tributes to Mother Mary Patrick after her death are in the Columban Sisters' archives.
19. Francis Herlihy, *Now Welcome Summer* (Dublin, 1948), pp. 34-35.
20. Mother Eveleen Coyle RSCJ, 'Some memories of Mother Mary Patrick,' MS.
21. Sister Pauline McAndrew, 'The Breaking Dawn', *The Lanthorn*, Christmas 1959.
22. Sister Mary Patrick, letter of 7 April 1924.